MOTHERS UNDER FIRE
Mothering in Conflict Areas

MOTHERS UNDER FIRE
Mothering in Conflict Areas

EDITED BY
Tatjana Takševa and Arlene Sgoutas

DEMETER

DEMETER PRESS

Funded by the Government of Canada
Financé par la gouvernement du Canada

Demeter Press
140 Holland Street West
P. O. Box 13022
Bradford, ON L3Z 2Y5
Tel: (905) 775-9089
Email: info@demeterpress.org
Website: www.demeterpress.org

Demeter Press logo based on the sculpture "Demeter" by Maria-Luise Bodirsky <www.keramik-atelier.bodirsky.de>

Cover art: Kirsten Halffield

Printed and Bound in Canada

Library and Archives Canada Cataloguing in Publication

        Mothers under fire : mothering in conflict areas / editors, Tatjana Takševa and Arlene Sgoutas.

Includes bibliographical references.
ISBN 978-1-926452-17-3 (paperback)

        1. Mothers—Social conditions. 2. Mothers—Violence against. 3. Motherhood. 4. Social conflict. 5. Women and war. 6. Children and war. 7. Mother and child. I. Sgoutas, Arlene, 1966–, author, editor II. Takševa, Tatjana, 1970–, author, editor

HQ759.M97 2015   306.874'3   C2015-903975-4

For all women who mother in difficult times and circumstances, honouring their strength and resourcefulness.

Table of Contents

Acknowledgements

This book would not have been possible without Arlene Sgoutas' excellent idea to propose a collection on this topic; she graciously took me on board the project, and I am very grateful to be part of it. Thanks to all the authors who contributed to this book with the fruits of their labor, on paper and in their work with mothers and families in areas of conflict, and to the external readers for their constructive feedback—this book has greatly benefited from your perspective. Thanks to Andrea O'Reilly for her energy, encouragement, and patience in ensuring that all deadlines are observed. At home, as always, my family has sustained me throughout this work, and it is because of their sense of humour, tolerance, and affection that I face all challenges with some degree of equanimity: Steve, Nino, Sofia, and Mila, thank you for being you.

—Tatjana Takševa

A heartfelt thank you to Andrea O'Reilly for taking a chance on an idea and continuing to nurture motherhood scholarship. My deepest gratitude to Tatjana Takševa for taking the lead on many aspects of this project and making sure that we stayed on track with our deadlines. Without her kindness and patience, this book would not have come to fruition. Much appreciation to all the authors who have given voice to mothers and families in area of conflict. To my family, thank you for loving and supporting me.

—Arlene Sgoutas

Introduction

How Conflict Shapes Motherhood and Motherwork

TATJANA TAKŠEVA AND ARLENE SGOUTAS

IN 2000, THE ADOPTION OF Security Council Resolution (SCR) 1325 recognized the disproportionate and gender-specific impact of conflict on women and children. This landmark resolution on women, peace, and security expresses concern "that civilians, particularly women and children, account for the vast majority of those adversely affected by armed conflict" and calls for women's "equal participation and full involvement in all efforts for the maintenance and promotion of peace and security" (United Nations Security Council). Additionally, it reaffirmed the importance of adopting a gender-oriented perspective in peacekeeping operations and peace-building processes for all participants. The significance of SCR 1325 in directing international attention to the subject of women and conflict situations has made it increasingly difficult to ignore women's experiences and gender concerns in analyzing conflicts and in formulating effective preventive and corrective actions. According to this shifting perspective, women appear at the center of conflicts in unprecedented ways: as combatants, as peace advocates, as targets of physical and sexual violence, and as the group in society that is expected to sustain everyday life, even under catastrophic conditions. Yet, despite significant strides to improve the living conditions and well-being of women and children affected by conflict, the 2014 Save the Children *State of the World's Mothers* report lists unsettling vital statistics that testify to the reality that more work remains to be done: more than 250 million children under age five live in countries affected by armed conflict; fifty-six percent of maternal and child deaths

1

take place in fragile settings; worldwide, women and children are up to fourteen times more likely than men to die in a disaster; for every person killed directly by armed violence, between three and fifteen die indirectly from diseases, medical complications, and malnutrition; the average refugee situation lasts seventeen years. Clearly, more work is needed to propel greater systemic changes in terms of policy and the effective delivery of humanitarian aid to improve the wellbeing of mothers and children in conflict and post-conflict zones.

In her book *The Curious Feminist: Searching for Women in a New Age of Empire,* Cynthia Enloe critiques the forms of political and institutional power that seem to be set up to replicate existing hierarchies and challenges the presumption of the "busy cause-and-effect rationalist" discourse of conventional international relations that "margins stay marginal, the silent stay voiceless, and ladders are never turned upside down" (23-24). Mothers are often those who remain at the margins (those who lack public power and who are often the object of other people's power), and one's identity as a mother is habitually overlooked as a category of analysis. There-fore, adopting the premise that there are many diverse forms of power that inform the relationship between dominant ideologies about women and war and women's lived realities, this collection seeks to deepen the "women and conflict" agenda by privileging the voices of mothers as victims, survivors, and resisters, and to investigate the contexts of power in a variety of conflict situations, as well as their impact on those who mother. Our collection thus aims to provide a preliminary framework for investigating the impact that violence and conflict have on mothers and mothering. The chapters in the collection highlight not only the particular dif-ficulties mothers face in various geographic locations where conflict has been prevalent, but also the ways in which mothers display agency to challenge and negotiate the circumstances that oppress them. The chapters in this volume thus collectively challenge the discourse of victimhood that usually prevails in the representations of mothers and motherhood in areas of conflict by problematizing it. While there is no doubt that mothers and children are victims of violence in conflict zones as well as the victims of shortsighted and gender-biased post-conflict policies that exclude or marginalize their voices, as all of the chapters in this collection highlight, their victimization is often intertwined with aspects of individual and collective agency, resourcefulness, and remarkable adaptability in the face of tragedy and disaster that reframe their survivor subject positions in a more positive and agentive light. The perception that women in general and mothers in particular are especially vulnerable in times of conflict and displacement often lies in the fact that armed warfare today involves civilians, and women are often the ones left to provide for themselves and their families. The perception is also due to the fact that women and girls are far more likely to suffer sexual violence during conflict and displacement regardless of the perpetrators' motivation, and that some groups of women, such as pregnant women, nursing mothers, mothers of small children, and female heads of households are more likely to be adversely affected by the conditions produced by armed conflict (Lindsay 28-9). The particular nature of a mother's vulnerability, however, is not an easily determined category, but exists in accordance with the specific nature of each situation and circumstance. A more complex and nuanced representational perspective of mothers emerges from the chapters in this collection, making visible the dialectic of maternal identities often actively negotiated between the poles of victimhood and agency.

Within the field of international relations, there is a considerable body of feminist scholarship from the last few decades that explores women's experiences of conflict and the gendered nature of mainstream war and security paradigms (Cohn; Yuval-Davis; Cockburn; Enloe 1990; 2000; 2004; Afshar and Eade). Feminist scholars have effectively demonstrated the ways in which war, conflict, and the processes that surround them are deeply gendered and experienced differently by women and men (Enloe; Cockburn and Zarkov; Anderlini). A number of studies reveal the roles women play and should continue to play in peace-building activities and policies and in the aftermath of conflict in their local communities and beyond (Rubio-Martin; Meintjes, Thursen and Pillay; Bouta, Frerks and Bannon; Handrahan). Recent scholarship on women and conflict provides a more nuanced understanding of the roles women have during conflict, as well. Rather than seeing them only as spectators or victims, a number of studies highlight the reality that women in armed conflict become the head of their households and take on the active responsibility for obtaining resources and building networks of support within their communities, but that they also are, in some cases, active combatants (Moser and Clark; Bouta and Frerks; Kuehnast, de Jonge Oudraat and Hernes). While these studies deal with women and conflict, and at times with children and conflict, contributions to existing studies dealing with violence, conflict, and motherhood are few. One notable exception to the scarcity of studies that treat the subject from the specific perspective of mothers and motherhood is the 2010 issue of the *Journal of Motherhood Initiative for Research and Community Involvement*, devoted to mothering, violence, militarism, war, and social justice, and featuring essays on a broad range of perspectives related to mothering in conflict zones. Another is Julie Peteet's work on Palestinian activist mothering as a "paradoxical practice that is simultaneously agential and limiting but one that may present an analytical potential for identifying previously ambiguous forms of subjectivity and creative agency" (103).

The main objective of the book, which is targeted towards an interdisciplinary audience, is the investigation of mothering in the contexts of conflict. The chapters in this collection treat conflict in a broad sense, defined as the absence of peace. This perspective includes violent conflict with three common characteristics: 1. non-cooperative, destructive, widespread action; 2. violation or capture of property rights concerning assets, persons, or institutions; 3. instigation by some degree of group activity (Brück and Vothknecht). It also includes the post-conflict period, referring to the aftermath of war. While the aftermath of war may exclude direct structural violence, according to the nature of twenty-first-century warfare, it may still include elements of violence, or the threat of violence, as well as forms of ongoing cultural violence. Cultural violence refers to those aspects of culture, such as religion, ideology, and language, that are used to legitimize structural violence and that tend to linger in the aftermath of conflict, affecting the treatment and quality of life of affected populations (Galtung and Fischer). The post-conflict period is thus often identified as negative peace. In peace and conflict studies, the two terms—conflict and peace—are understood relationally. While one aspect of peace is represented by the absence of direct violence (negative peace), peace also refers to a "mental and spiritual condition marked by freedom from disquieting or oppressive thoughts and emotions," in the sense of "peace of mind" and "inner peace," as well as a "tranquil state of freedom from disturbances and harassment" (Barash and Webel 4). Thus while "post-conflict" refers to the aftermath of war, the period is often marked by low-intensity violence and other forms of insecurity that persist even when basic peace has been achieved, thereby preventing the achievement of "peace of mind." When mothering in these conditions, the lack of freedom from disquieting or oppressive thoughts and emotions has direct impact on how mothers see their social roles and often impedes their efforts to mother effectively. In this sense, we understand that violence and nonviolence are not mutually exclusive, but that they exist on a continuum, something that many of the chapters clearly demonstrate in their investigation of the extent to which this continuum affects those who mother and shapes their mothering practices.

Mothering is seldom easy and almost never straightforward, even in circumstances that can be considered ordinary, or at least free of armed conflict, violence, and its consequences. Whether trying to juggle multiple work obligations while mothering on an ongoing basis or having to deal with one's own health concerns or those of one's children, the loss of a spouse or child, or loss of precarious employment, for many motherwork presents significant daily challenges. Some of the more benign challenges may simply have to do with raising children whose physical and emotional needs may be at odds with the mother's own personality. As Sara Ruddick points out, "Mothering itself can be a training in attending to unsettling differences" (57). In addition, maternal subjectivity is often overlooked in describing and defining motherwork. Both philosophers and psychologists reveal that "thought-provoking ambivalence is a hallmark of mothering" (Ruddick 68), and that "being constantly attentive and attuned to the needs of someone else for whom one has total responsibility at all times is a daunting task" often resulting in "negative feelings of irritation or frustration" (Raphael-Leff 7). In most cases, the continuous tasks inherent in mother work and the ambivalence mothers feel are balanced and alleviated, even in impoverished and oppressed groups and even if in varying degrees, by the pleasures children bring in tolerably good times.

However, this volume is concerned with mothering that crosses the boundaries of what may be counted as ordinary and with motherwork unfolding in conditions that consistently fail to present "tolerably good times" for the mother as well as children. If we posit that effective mothering entails the daily care of children based on attending to their physical, psycho-social, and emotional needs, the present volume sheds light on the extent to which effective motherwork is affected, mediated, and compromised by conditions of conflict understood broadly, and the absence of peace in its extended definition. Everyday maternal tasks, both physical and emotional, become exponentially more difficult in times marked by social and political unrest and violence and their aftermath. It is these larger forces that hinder motherwork in its most essential forms and prevent mothers from meeting the demands of their children for growth and nurture.

Conflict, war, displacement, and the absence of peace bring poverty, ill health, disquiet, depression; they also disrupt family and community structures and thus set up a series of conditions that interfere daily with mothers' best efforts and limit their functionality as nurturers. Stress, anxiety, and depression take their toll not only on the mothers' wellbeing, but the children's as well, since the presence of these factors may affect "all aspects of child development and increase vulnerability to abuse and neglect" and may result in later detrimental effects on the children's cognitive functioning, increased likelihood of depression, and antisocial behaviour (Cox and Barton 218, 222). Thus conflict and the absence of peace have affective consequences for the mother-child relationship and complicate in significant ways the nature of care that mothers can provide for their children. Mothering during conflict means performing motherwork in conditions of physical, spatial, and economic difficulty, as well as [conditions of] psychic difficulty that move beyond the self-evident challenges of everyday life in times of peace. Young children especially depend on the caregivers in their environment for support, and when traumatic

6

events occur, it is crucial to support mothers so that they can perform motherwork effectively. Recent research on resilience and the development of successful coping mechanisms in children and adolescents living in areas of political violence and in high-stress situations shows that children's coping responses increased when their caregivers displayed positive emotional responses to the adverse conditions (Tol et al.). A multi-systemic approach to intervention is required to ameliorate the symptoms of trauma and improve the likelihood of positive outcomes for both mothers and children in terms of enabling their economic autonomy, as well as a "peace of mind." This perspective carries particular relevance to chapters in this volume dealing with mothering in post-conflict conditions, including refugeeism and displacement.

Mothering in conflict zones thus emerges as a daily practice we term "difficult mothering," attributable to the pervasiveness of conflict and/or the threat of violence permeating daily experiences. Difficult mothering refers to the difficulties mothers face in carrying out daily tasks related to childrearing and ensuring the basic health and safety of their children, but also to the difficult nature of relationships between mothers and children that occur due to situations of conflict. In that sense, difficult mothering is both a pragmatic concept and a philosophical one. It is pragmatic in that it relates to the everyday obstacles in the mothers' conflict-defined environment that may interfere with the mothers' own ideas about the optimal way to mother. Conditions of conflict and their pervasive consequences make difficult and problematic what may be considered the everyday and the routine. However, difficult mothering is also a philosophical concept in that it encompasses all the somatic, psychic, moral, and ethical difficulties mothers experience in conditions of conflict, both as subjects and in their relationships with their children, as they struggle with mothering tasks and survival dilemmas on a daily basis. Uncovering the critical humanitarian and development needs in war-torn communities around the world is necessary to identify the actions needed to support women who are raising children under some of the most difficult circumstances.

The 18 chapters in this volume are divided into three parts: *Part I: Violence, Conflict, and Mothering Re-constructed, Part II: Im-*

migration, Displacement, Refuge, and Part III: *Mothers as Fighters, Activists, Resisters*. Due to the general goal of the collection to investigate how conflict and its aftermath affect mothers and shape mothering practice, all chapters to some extent cut across the three sections thematically. The division is pragmatic, based on the dominant context in which each chapter engages with the issue of motherhood and conflict. All chapters implicitly treat the everyday experiences of mothers as situated sources of knowledge about motherwork in the context of intersecting differences and geo-historical conditions of conflict (see Olivieri and Leurs). Providing insight into these mothering practices contributes to producing new knowledge about the lived experiences of women and children in various geographic locations affected by unrest, displacement, and violence. Methodologically, the chapters reflect diverse disciplinary perspectives through which scholars and field practitioners reveal how various types of conflict and their aftermath shape mothering practices.

The chapters in the first two sections respond to the question: What global but also local space-time relations defined by violence or the threat of violence determine how mothers engage in motherwork? Reflecting the broad scope of motherhood studies in general and the present volume specifically, this section brings together both conceptual and empirical research based in sociology, anthropology, ethnography, and philosophy. Informed by an interdisciplinary and intersectional gender framework, the chapters shed light on mothers' everyday experiences and the wider impact of conflict–related circumstance, such as immigration, refugeeism, and displacement, on the daily experience of mothering.

The first section, *Violence, Conflict, and Mothering Re-Constructed*, examines how motherhood is constructed during and in the aftermath of conflict. The chapters in this section highlight the realities and experiences of mothering in locales such as Sri Lanka, the occupied West Bank, Afghanistan, post-demobilized Columbia, the United States, Rwanda, Bosnia, and Pakistan. Each chapter draws on the actual voices of mothers, either in interviews or personal narrative, to draw attention to both their susceptibilities and the ways in which, individually and collectively, they overcome adversity. Rebecca Walker's, "Negotiating

Risk: Exploring the Experiences of Mothers During the Conflict in Eastern Sri Lanka" uses ethnographic research in eastern Sri Lanka to explore the role that mothers have played in creating networks of trust and support amidst a context of continual loss and fear. Charting the experiences of mothers whose children have been abducted by the Tamil Eelam (LTTE), with their links to women's human rights group, this chapter considers how they have strategized and supported one another to find paths forward. This work demonstrates both the impact of conflict on women as well as the strategies of survival, which more often than not are made possible and sustained by mothers.

In "Holding Everything Together: Palestinian Mothers under Occupation," Bree Akesson draws on her conversations with eighteen families in the occupied West Bank and annexed East Jerusalem. The chapter explores the shifting role of mothers in raising their children during occupation and everyday violence in the occupied Palestinian territories. As a reaction to the prevailing conditions under this oppression, family systems have become stretched and tightened. The role of mothers in this stretched family system helps to understand how best to protect children and families, respond to their needs, and ameliorate the negative consequences of occupation and violence.

Carol Mann's chapter, "Giving Birth in War-Torn Afghanistan," is written primarily from the perspective of a passionate humanitarian practitioner and an advocate for the rights of women in war. The chapter describes the influence of conflict and its ramifications through economic and social issues on giving birth in Afghanistan in relation to two periods: the influential decades that three million Afghans spent in refugee camps; and the problems birthing mothers encounter in rural areas since the NATO intervention until today. In her discussion, Mann also reveals the significance of the under-reported link between the increase of child-brides and juvenile mothers with the mass cultivation of opium.

Lindsay Jones and Myriam Denov draw on interviews to examine the situation of female ex-combatants in Colombia's ongoing civil conflict in "Mothering in the Context of Isolation and Insecurity: Tracing the Experiences of Young Women Formerly Associated with Armed Groups in Colombia." The realities and experiences of these young women highlight their internal struggles with respect to negotiating an identity following demobilization, coping with trauma, and establishing good relationships with their children. Above all, this chapter sheds light on the resilience, courage, and strength of these inspiring young mothers who must reintegrate into communities within an ongoing context of war and few social supports.

In "Maternal Pedagogies in Swat Valley, Pakistan: On Faith, Jihad, and Peace," Lubna Chaudhry analyzes the role of mothers in guiding their children to understand the choices they make with respect to their ideological relationship with the Taliban, their alliances with other community members, and their stances on peacemaking. Drawing on ethnographic data, Chaudhry delineates how mothers expressed their views with the intent to teach and advise on a range of topics, such as faith, jihad, and peace. Even though the Swat Valley in Pakistan is a patriarchal society with quite rigid demarcations of duties, entitlements, and spaces, mothers are revered, and as they and their children grow older, mothers have a strong influence in molding their behaviours and options in life, including their careers.

Although not typically considered war, Liliana Rossman examines the experiences of gang-involved mothers in "Mother'hood: Mothering amidst Gang Warfare" by analyzing interviews with former gang members in San José, California. The term "mother'hood" reflects gang-involved Latina mothers and their experiences during pregnancy, birth, and mothering amidst gang warfare. This chapter thus examines the intersection between gang membership and motherhood, and how gang-involved mothers can envision a future beyond the gang. It demonstrates the workings of difficult mothering in the aftermath of the mothers' involvement in urban warfare, highlighting in particular the mothers' agency in reinventing their identity as women whose own moral code compels them to engage in what they see as effective motherwork.

The complex combination of pragmatic and philosophical factors that contribute to how motherhood is constructed during conflict is particularly evident in cases of mothering children born of war time rape. Chapters 7 and 8 in this section, Claudine Umulisa's, "We Are Also Mothers: Rwandan Women With Children Born of Genocide" and Tatjana Takševa's "Raising Children Born of Wartime Rape in Bosnia: A Maternal Philosophy Perspective," deal with mothering practices and maternal ambivalence as they pertain to mothers raising children who are perceived as "children of the enemy" by the mothers' communities, but who also by virtue of their identity trigger traumatic memories for the mothers themselves, thus problematizing their maternal work and making day-to-day maternal care exceptionally difficult.

Based on her interviews with ten women, Umulisa explores the impact of sexual violence and the resulting pregnancy and birth on the motherhood of rape victims in post-genocide Rwanda. Umulisa analyses the women's narrative concerning their mothering practice and their feelings toward their children. The women in the study speak of their experiences of mothering a "child of enemy" in complex ways, revealing that they all feel they are rejecting their children while being marginalized by their families and community due to their children's identity. Their testimonies underscore that the identities of the children (as being born of rape) are central to both mothers' and their children's marginalization. Umulisa's research shows that being subject to sexual violence has affected the mothers emotionally, physically, socially, and economically, all of which has profound and long-lasting impact on their children.

In the final chapter in this section, based on a small body of recorded personal narratives, Takševa highlights the experience of Bosniak women who have been raped and forcefully impregnated by Serbian militias during the recent Balkan war, and who decided to keep and raise their children. Takševa adopts a maternal philosophy perspective as a critical lens through which some aspects of the women's mothering practice can be contextualized and understood. The chapter sheds light on some of the factors that inform the maternal work of Bosnian wartime rape survivors and their relationship with their children and provides a new framework for understanding their experience. This framework stands in contrast to dominant media narratives that define Bosniak survivors of rape almost exclusively in terms of their victimhood, and medical and psychiatric discourse that tends to pathologize them and their relationship with their children, often implying a normative bias. Looking at the complexity of their maternal practice through a philosophically informed perspective offers the potential to humanize their experience, reframe them as survivors rather than victims, and situate their mothering within the context of a broad and varied spectrum of mothering practices. At the same time, what is equally evident in both this chapter and in Umulisa's, is that the experiences of mothers documented in both chapters constitute difficult mothering in both the pragmatic and philosophical sense.

The changing nature of civil wars over the last few decades and the increase of attacks on civilian populations has led to unprecedented numbers of displaced and refugee populations. According to the Internal Displacement Monitoring Centre in Norway, the global number of people internally displaced by armed conflict, generalized violence, or human rights violations stood at 26.4 million at the end of 2011 (IDMC 8). Women and children constitute the great majority—eighty percent—of refugees and internally displaced peoples in the world (*Status of Women Canada*). The chapters in *Part II: Immigration, Displacement, Refuge* highlight two realities concerning difficult mothering. First, they examine the constraints placed upon mothers and the challenges of providing adequate maternal care in circumstances marked by oppressive and unrefined immigration and humanitarian service-delivery policies that limit and disrupt maternal agency. Second, they highlight the circumstances in which ongoing conflict or the threat of violence, coupled with continued insecurity and the lack of physical, economic, and social infrastructure, present serious obstacles to effective mothering and force mothers to make difficult choices. Most chapters in this section provide policy recommendations informed by specific local contexts and aimed at improving the living conditions of mothers and children affected by conflict in a variety of ways.

In "Fractured Mothering: The Impact of U.S. and Arizona Immigration Policies on Spanish-Speaking Immigrant Mothers with U.S. Citizen and Non-U.S. Citizen Children," Sally Stevens and Rosi Andrade utilize interview data on Spanish-speaking Mexican immigrant mothers in the U.S. to explore the impact of current U.S. and Arizona immigration policies on mothers and their families. In particular, the chapter explores women's abilities to mother their children amidst policies and laws that are exceptionally restrictive and punitive. While the chapter points to how U.S. citizen children with immigrant mothers are affected by these laws, it also brings to light further constraints on immigrant mothers' ability to mother their non-U.S. citizen children. The result is fractured mothering sanctioned by current immigration policies, where, for example, a mother cannot secure equal access to healthcare and services for all her children.

The extent to which armed conflict and its aftermath disrupt family structures and contribute to difficult mothering on a daily basis is also evident from David Eichert's chapter, "When Tragedy is Not Enough: Female Syrian Refugees in a New Homeland." Eichert details the extensive and complex challenges Syrian refugee mothers face due to their gender and diminished social status as displaced persons. The chapter highlights the plight and survival techniques of Syrian refugee mothers who are confined by strict cultural norms and family commitments and are therefore more impoverished than their male counterparts, forcing some mothers to make difficult decisions. The lack of other employment opportunities for female refugees, coupled with health problems, childcare needs, and cultural stigmas against women working, sometimes force female refugees to sell sex for money, and force Syrian mothers to consent to marry off underage daughters to older men. The personal statements made by Syrian refugee mothers reveal their dissatisfaction and frustration with the lack of adequate support they receive from the international community.

Anwar Shaheen and Nasish Khan's chapter, "Motherhood Out of Home and Hearth: Experiences of Pakistani Mothers in Displaced Families" is based on a sample of twenty mothers in two conflict zones in Pakistan with different administrative status— FATA (Federally Administered Tribal Areas) and PATA (Provincially Administered Tribal Areas). The authors describe how a series of government-led military operations, implemented in response to local anti-government insurgents, effectively destroyed the lives of civilian populations, physical infrastructure, crops, and livelihood sources, leaving women and children among those most affected by the consequent displacement. The authors show that motherhood duties in these two regions in Pakistan are undergoing change because the concept and dynamics of the roles mothers play in various segments of Pakistani society are exposed to rapid change. These changes are geared by various political and economic factors, but also by the conditions of displacement, which in many cases dictate the level of independence and control over household matters that women are allowed to assume.

In "Refugee Mothering, Resettlement, and Mental Health," Jacqueline Ciccio Parsons, Rebekah Pender, and Larry Parsons focus on the narratives of refugee women relocated to Canada and the United States and the refugee mothers' negotiation of a new culture and homeland cultural traditions, her fear for personal safety, and other mental health challenges. Long after a mother from a nation affected by conflict settles in a new country, she may still experience the psychological impact of her past trauma. Mental health related issues, including fear, depression, anxiety, paranoia, psychosis, complicated grief, guilt, and Post Traumatic Stress Disorder, are often part of the refugee mother's reality, challenging her ability to mother effectively. Their chapter calls for developing respectful and culturally responsive models of counselling immigrant mothers as a way of helping them cope with past trauma and resettlement.

In their chapter, "Mothers' Decision Making Power: A New Vision for Working with Internally Displaced Persons," Tushabe Wa Tushabe and Brillian Besi Muhonja uncover mothers' experiences from two cases in East Africa to underscore the need for a new vision that redefines need assessment, services, and service delivery to internally displaced persons (IDPs). As agencies continue to base their definition of services, assessment, and service delivery to IDPs on the "traditional" family structure whereby men are treated as heads of their family, women who are mothers become further disadvantaged in their ability to make decisions about their lives and their reproductive health. The chapter explores collective motherhood as a site of empowerment for African women, and women's social structures such as money pools, ability to make food, and financial and health decisions as a way to use such structures to help improve need assessment and service delivery in IDP camps in East Africa.

The final section of this collection, *Part III: Mothers as Fighters, Activists, Resisters*, shifts the focus to how mothers display political agency and forms of resistance in times of conflict and how they challenge the circumstances that oppress them. The chapters in this section emphasize the reality of women who, alongside motherhood, chose to take active part in fighting out of belief in its moral and ethical justification, as well as those who politicized their role as mothers in their outspoken critique of a corrupt political regime and an unjust war. What becomes evident in the chapters is not only the diversity of relationships that exist between mothers, motherhood, and forms of conflict, but also that through those diverse relationships women as mothers or advocates of a matrocentric perspective challenge traditional patriarchal discourses of the "good mother," the "good citizen," and the "good soldier," as well as common national and masculinist justifications of war and military action. The chapters also reveal that by examining women's roles as participants in conflict we often find that women's reasons for participating in actual and political wars may be as varied as men's.

Lidiya Zubytska's "Mothers as Soliders: Beyond the Veil of Gendered War" analyses the intersections between parental and militant roles of women engaged in combat and the challenges of committing to militancy while leaving young children behind. Such mother soldiers do exist and they do not fit easily into the gendered understanding of the role of women in conflict since they neither comply with the "beautiful soul" image of women in war, nor do such examples conform to traditionally conceived "motherly" agency: acting to alleviate the fate of their children by providing specific kinds of care. Her case study of Ukrainian mothers who joined the Ukrainian Resistance forces in 1939-1954 show that as mothers engaged in violent partisan and other subversive activities, they relied on a civilian network of Ukrainian villages to sustain their military activities and take care of family members left behind the front lines.

Based on conversations with mothers in a Mayan women's group, Rachel O'Donnell focuses on a collective group of active opponents to the Guatemalan army in "'The Change Was Very Strong': Rural Mayan Motherhood and Activism during the Guatemalan Civil War." In this chapter, women's *testimonies* of experienced violence are used as significant political documents that are useful in constructing a collective feminist consciousness and history. The chapter focuses on the role of women as mothers and activists in the Mayan community through the particular and individual experiences of one Aipu mother.

In the next chapter, "Challenging the Official Story: Alicia Kozameh, Alicia Partnoy and Mother Activism during Argentina's Dirty Wars (1976-1983)," Benay Blend explores how both writers imprisoned during Argentina's Dirty Wars used political motherhood as a means to challenge authority. Blend's analysis reveals how Partnoy, an imprisoned member of the Mothers of the Plaza, considered that being part of a movement allowed her to translate concern for her child into communal struggle, recognizing no separation between motherhood and activism and illuminating a prison culture organized to defy the official story. Alicia Kozameh, on the other hand, writes a first-hand account about a cell in which women were allowed to keep their children for only three months, circumventing the ban on oral/written communication as part of a larger struggle against authority. Blend shows that by balancing personal and collective representations, Kozameh also gives voice to approximately four hundred children who were taken away by authorities, often placed in homes of those responsible for their torture. In the case of both authors and activists, Blend highlights the portrayals of angry, not idealized, mothers, capable of inventing a movement based on the politics of collective action.

Kristina Passman Nielson's chapter, "Lamentation in Classical Antiquity: Telling the Truth about Women, Children, and War" reveals the ideological and subversive nature of literary representations of female lamentation in two of Euripides' plays: *Iphigenia in Aulis* and *The Trojan Women*. She analyses the plays in the context of women's responses to tragedies and loss that are all too common in war. Her discussion reveals historical continuities in practice and perception regarding women's role in war not only as victims but as resisters as well. Passman Nielson points out that while the lamenting words of grief that speak to the experience of mothers, daughters, and families during war are gendered, and thus may seem irrelevant to the larger war enterprise, through their language of lament these dramas continue to subvert the hegemonic and patriarchal discourse of war, and serve to put a human face to war and provide an implacable reminder of the truth of what war actually costs. Here, maternal lament and publically articulated grief over the loss of loved ones in war acquires a collective function of resistance, embodied in the maternal characters who speak the grieving words.

The public relevance of maternal grief and its controversial political and activist potential is illustrated in the final chapter in this section, but in a contemporary context. Linda Pershing's "Blaming the Mother: The Politics of Gender in Cindy Sheehan's Protest of the Iraq War" is a critical analysis of the gendered representations of Cindy Sheehan and her peace activism from 2003-2007 that developed in response to her grief over losing her son in the U.S.-led war in Iraq. Pershing investigates the ways in which Sheehan's identities as a woman and mother became focal points for extensive and often derogatory cultural commentary about her, as she was seen to transgress the role assigned to her by the nationalist military and patriotic script: that of the grieving mother who quietly honours her son's ultimate sacrifice for his nation. From the perspective of a feminist scholar of folklore and popular culture, Pershing examines negative reactions to Sheehan, interpreting significant aspects of sexism and misogyny that shaped public discourse about Sheehan as a mother and an activist who dared to use her maternal grief as a basis for a comprehensive critique of the Bush administration's policy on the Iraq war.

Taken together, the chapters in the collection raise awareness of the attitudes and actions of mothers in times of conflict, as well as their needs in areas affected by military and/or political violence worldwide. As such, the collection provides a basis for developing multiple policy frameworks aimed at improving existing systems of support in local contexts. In 2015, fifteen years after the adoption of UNSCR 1325, the world continues to grapple with the challenge of ongoing violence. For every successful peace process that has resulted in negative peace, that is, the absence of direct warfare, new forms of violence, insecurity, criminality, and gender-based violence have emerged demanding that stakeholders draw upon all existing capacities in efforts to establish peace in a more meaningful, comprehensive way. The chapters in this collection draw attention to the particular needs of mothers in the new global context of violence and peace—building efforts, as displaced women, female heads of households, female combatants and ex-combatants, rape survivors, and women who challenge the ideological base of the patriarchal war machine. They collectively advance our understanding of how violence and insecurity affect the work of mothering.

WORKS CITED

Afshar, G. and D. Eade, eds. *Development, Women and War: Feminist Perspectives*. Bloomfield, CT: Kumarian Press, 2003. Print.

Anderlini, S. N. *Women Building Peace: What They Do, Why It Matters*. Boulder, CO: Lynne Reinner Publications, 2007. Print.

Barash, P. David and Charles P. Webel. *Peace and Conflict Studies*. New York: Sage, 2013. Print.

Bouta, Tsjeard and Georg Frerks. "Women's Roles in Conflict Prevention, Conflict Resolution, and Post-Conflict Reconstruction: Literature Review and Institutional Analysis." The Hague: Netherlands Institute of International Relations, 2002. Print.

Bouta, T., G. Frerks and I. Bannon. *Gender, Conflict and Development*. Washington: World Bank, 2005. Print.

Brück, Tilman and Marc Vothknecht. "Impact of Violent Conflicts on Women's Economic Opportunities." *Women and War: Power and Protection in the 21st Century*. Ed. Kathleen Kuehnast, Chantal de Jonge Oudraat, and Helga Hernes. Washington: United States Institute of Peace Press, 2011. 86-114. Print.

Cockburn, Cynthia. *From Where We Stand: War, Women's Activism and Feminist Analysis*. London: Zed Books, 2007. Print.

Cockburn, Cynthia, and Dubravka Zarkov, eds. *The Postwar Moment: Militaries, Masculinities, and International Peacekeeping*. London: Lawrence and Wishart, 2002. Print.

Cohn, Carol. "Sex and Death in the Rational World of Defense Intellectuals." *Signs* 12 (1987): 687-718. Print.

Cox, John and Joanne Barton. "Maternal Postnatal Mental Disorder: How Does It Affect the Young Child?" *Parenthood and Mental Health: A Bridge Between Infant and Adult Psychiatry*. Eds. Sam Tyano, Miri Keren, Helen Herrman and John Cox.

Hoboken: Wiley-Blackwell, 2010. 217-229. Print.

Enloe, Cynthia. *Bananas, Beaches and Bases: Making Feminist Sense of International Politics.* Berkeley: University of California Press, 1990. Print.

Enloe, Cynthia. *Maneuvers: The International Politics of Militarizing Women's Lives.* Berkeley: University of California Press, 2000. Print.

Enloe, Cynthia. *The Curious Feminist: Searching for Women in a New Age of Empire.* Berkeley: University of California Press, 2004. Print.

Galtung, Johan and Dietrich Fischer. *Johan Galtung: Pioneer of Peace Research.* Berlin: Springer, 2013. Print.

Handrahan, L. "Conflict, Gender, Ethnicity and Post-Conflict Reconstruction." *Security Dialogue* 35 (2004): 429-28. Print.

Internal Displacement Monitoring Centre (IDMC). *Global Overview 2011 People Internally Displaced by Conflict and Violence.* Geneva: Norwegian Refugee Council, 2012. Web. 15 April 2015.

Journal of the Motherhood Initiative for Research and Community Involvement. "Mothering, Violence, Militarism and Social Justice" 1.1 (2010). Print.

Kuehnast, Kathleen, Chantal de Jonge Oudraat, and Helga Hernes, eds. *Women and War: Power and Protection in the 21ˢᵗ Century.* Washington: United States Institute of Peace Press, 2011. Print.

Lindsey, Charlotte. *Women Facing War: ICRC Study on the Impact of Armed Conflict on Women.* Geneva, Switzerland: International Committee of the Red Cross, 2001. Print.

Meintjes, M., M. Thursen and A. Pillay, eds. *The Aftermath: Women in Post-Conflict Transformation.* London: Zed Books, 2001. Print.

Moser, Caroline and Fiona Clark, eds. *Victims, Perpetrators or Actors? Gender, Armed Conflict and Political Violence.* London: Zed Books, 2001. Print.

Olivieri, Domitilla and Keon Leurs, eds. "Introduction." *Everyday Feminist Research Praxis.* Newcastle: Cambridge Scholars Publishing, 2014. xxiv-xxxv. Print.

Peteet, Julie. "Icons and Militants: Mothering in the Danger Zone." *Signs* 23.1 (1997):103-129.

Raphael-Leff, Joan. "Healthy Maternal Ambivalence." *Studies in the Maternal* 2.1 (2009): 1-15. Print.

Rubio-Martin, R., ed. *What Happened to the Women? Gender and Reparations for Human Rights Violations.* New York: Social Science Research Council, 2006. Print.

Ruddick, Sara. *Maternal Thinking: Toward a Politics of Peace.* New York: Ballantine Books, 1989. Print.

State of the World's Mothers 2014: Saving Mothers and Children in HumanitarianCrises. Save the Children, 2014. Web. 5 December 2014.

Status of Women Canada. "Women and Armed Conflict." Government of Canada Publications. 2015. Web. 19 April 2015.

Tol, Weiste A., Mark J.D. Jordans, Brandon A. Kohrt, Theresa S. Betancourt, and Ivan H. Komproe. "Promoting Mental Health and Psychosocial Well-Being in Children Affected by Political Violence: Part I—Current Evidence for An Ecological Resilience Approach." *Handbook of Resilience in Children of War.* Ed. C. Fernando and M. Ferrari. New York: Springer, 2013. 11-27. Print.

United Nations Security Council. 4213th Meeting. *United Nations Security Council Resolution 1325.* 31 October 2000. Web. 27 January 2015.

Yuval-Davis, Nira. *Gender and Nation.* London: Sage, 1997. Print.

PART I:
VIOLENCE, CONFLICT, AND MOTHERING RE-CONSTRUCTED

1.
Negotiating Risk

Exploring the Experiences of Mothers During the Conflict in Eastern Sri Lanka

REBECCA WALKER

MOTHERHOOD IN PARTICULAR has claimed an important role in the framing of women's participation both in supporting and challenging the protracted conflict between the Government forces and Liberation Tigers of Tamil Eelam (LTTE) (Samuel; de Alwis, "Motherhood"). The war, which spanned three decades, ended in May 2009 after a bloody and brutal defeat of the LTTE by the Government forces.[1] According to Samuel, during the height of the conflict, women activists claimed that the use of the identity of motherhood was a "necessary form of 'protection' in a climate where state repression was at its height and opposition to military presence and military activity was fraught with danger" (185-203). This was particularly true in the north and east of the country, areas that have faced some of the worst devastation and disruption during the conflict, including the loss of thousands of lives with the death and "disappearance" of numerous Tamil-speaking men and women and the fracturing of communities and families.[2] The forcible recruitment of children by the LTTE, and after 2004 by the TMVP (Tamil Makhal Viduthalai Pulikal or Tamil People's Liberation Tigers; a militant group that broke away from the LTTE in 2004), was also a reality that few families could escape. While men often joined armed groups or were forced into hiding, women took on the challenge of survival. To care for their families, women had to find ways to provide for them financially and to deal with the daily realities of displacement, risk, and threat. These responsibilities were also taking place within a context where Tamil women were constricted by the ties of the gendered ethnic discourse of "the good Tamil woman" (Schrijvers 329).

However, while attention has been paid to the formation and apparent demise of women's organizations and activism in the face of escalating war, what has been less noted is the work of women and particularly mothers not simply in surviving the war but in challenging the everyday violence and pushing for change amidst increasing militarization of spaces and the silencing of oppositional voices (de Alwis, "Interrogating the 'Political'"). Drawing on ethnographic research in Batticaloa, eastern Sri Lanka, during the period of 2005-2007, this chapter explores the experiences of mothers and their attempts to challenge the violence around them with the support of an informal human rights group, the Valkai group. Alarmed by the escalating violence, the Valkai group brought mainly local citizens (mostly women but also a number of men) together to find ways in which they could try to reach out to those affected by the protracted conflict. One such strategy was to bring together the mothers of conscripted children to share their experiences and build on the networks of support they had already been forming as they fought to get their children back. Often meeting outside LTTE camps (where their children were being held) and in other spaces, mothers were extremely active in challenging those making claims on their everyday worlds and particularly their children. Thus I suggest that despite an assumed demise in the role of women actively engaging in opposition to militarism and war in Sri Lanka, that work *is* being done by women. This is work that is not always obvious and which weaves through and around their everyday experiences of violence and fear. Moreover, in comparison to the more overt and visible organization of women and mothers, the apparent invisibility and quietness are the very factors that enable the work of the mothers with the Valkai group to continue. This work therefore demonstrates both the impact of conflict on women as well as the strategies of survival, which more often than not are made possible and sustained by mothers. I begin this chapter by briefly describing the context of war in eastern Sri Lanka and how it has impacted women. I then consider the formation of the Valkai group and focus on the mothers' meetings as a way of highlighting the role of mothers in eastern Sri Lanka.

BATTICALOA AND EVERYDAY VIOLENCE

Framed on either side by the sea and the lagoon, the district of Batticaloa forms part of the northern and eastern regions of Sri Lanka that the militant group, the LTTE (drawn from the island's minority Tamil-speaking population), sought to secure and establish as a separate state, which they called Tamil Eelam. With Sinhala, Tamil, and Muslim populations having almost equal presence within areas of ethnic concentration, the diverse and distinctive ethnic demography of the east stands in contrast to the northern province, where Tamils are the dominant group (McGilvray and Raheem). Marked by occupation, Batticaloa is a town that has been under the control of different military groups: the Sri Lankan army (SLA), the Indian Peace Keeping Forces (IPKF), and the LTTE. The aforementioned split in the LTTE in 2004 also led to a TMVP challenge of the military rule of the Tigers. Despite being militarily much weaker, the TMVP who were unofficially supported by government forces, were successful in gaining control of Batticaloa and bordering eastern regions. The presence of so many military groups also meant that Batticaloa, like many other places of conflict, represented a mosaic of intricately woven lives and histories with allegiances and opinions sutured across critical boundaries and spaces, ultimately trapping people within their own contexts. The lack of space and overlapping lines of control meant that the LTTE (and later the TMVP) were able to ensure continued (and often enforced) support of their movement. This support included the collection of taxes from families and businesses already impoverished by the conflict, the distribution of propaganda in schools and temples, armed training for villagers (including the young and the elderly), and the conscription of children to fight on the front lines. Such tactics ensured that while not everyone was considered a cadre, every individual, family, and community were linked and connected to the LTTE in some way (HRW "Living in Fear").

At the time that I began research in Batticaloa in January 2005, communities across the east were just coming to terms with the enormity of the tragedy of the 2004 South Asian tsunami, which on the east coast alone had taken more than 3,000 lives, devastated homes and livelihoods, and left thousands more displaced. Against the backdrop of an unraveling ceasefire, failed peace talks, and a chaotic tsunami response, the political situation, which had experienced a temporary reprieve after the tsunami, was once again worsening day by day. It was through the network of families, knitted by the Valkai group and extending across the eastern border villages and towns where violence was often the most intense, that I was introduced to the multiple strategies and spaces that people used in their daily routines to cope with the violence that surrounded them. I met with mothers fighting to get their conscripted children back from the LTTE or TMVP, men under threat and hiding in the shadows of darkened homes, and grandparents mourning the loss of children who had survived detention and torture by the army, only to be taken by the waves of the tsunami. These experiences were not new or uncommon under the prevailing conditions of protracted war, yet as much as people had come to recognize suffering and pain, this did not mean that their everyday experiences were defined by violence. For these mothers, fathers, grandparents, and grandchildren, life was about learning to negotiate, to push at small cracks and spaces in the prevailing structures, and to work their lives around and beyond violence. This negotiation was reflected particularly in the experiences of mothers who sought to keep families together and keep their children safe while the violence around them wavered and waned, sometimes controlling every movement and action and at other times enabling "normal" life to carry on.

WOMEN AND VIOLENCE:
TRADITIONAL VS. "EMPOWERED" TAMIL WOMEN

Women have played an active part in the war in Sri Lanka in a number of different guises, including as armed combatants (in the Government forces and the LTTE), as primary income generators and heads of households, and also in resisting war both collectively and on an individual basis.[3] Subsequently, this participation has raised some interesting questions about gender identity in which gender constructions have been seen as strategic symbols in the struggle (Schrijvers).

The challenges faced by women during wartime has frequently been captured within the dichotomous "suffering" and "resilience" trope in which the struggle for Tamil-speaking women in particular is translated in terms of the "empowerment" of women's lives. This is contrasted with the traditional role of the Tamil woman in which she is seen as circumscribed by gendered norms rooted both in Tamil culture and in Sri Lankan society more broadly (Thiruchandran). This has been used most effectively by the LTTE through the incorporation of the language of women's liberation into the movement, claiming to "free" women from the constraints of traditional Tamil culture (de Mel).

Despite the presence of counter-discourses (encouraged by women's movements and globalization) and the fact that access to education and jobs in the public domain as doctors, lawyers, and teachers have been opened to women, the ties of the gendered ethnic discourse of "the good Tamil woman" have remained tightly bound in many communities and areas. Consequently, women have remained largely defined through their relationship with men (Schrijvers). Based on research with Tamil women in refugee camps during the 1990s, Schrijvers notes that between the two extreme images of the Tamil woman as soldier and suicide bomber, on the one hand, and the poverty-stricken, dependent refuge, on the other, new identities have emerged. These new identities embody what Schrijivers suggests are "ideals that come very close to the Sri Lankan feminist discourse" according to which women assert themselves in the public and the private sphere, renegotiate gender power relations, and increase their autonomy and self-esteem (307). While Rajasingham-Senenayake ("Between Victim and Agent") deals with this debate by stressing that these new roles for women create a sense of "ambivalent agency" in war-time situations, I suggest that these ambivalent agencies risk countering the realities of war in which women suffer intolerably through displacement, widowhood, sexual abuse, and marginalization. Moreover, their experiences cannot be separated from the social stigma that surrounds widows in all three communities, Sinhala, Tamil, and Muslim, which has further marginalized women.[4] Where women do take on greater responsibilities in the community it can also be argued that they subsequently become more vulnerable by nature of their gender and bodies. This reflects the complex realities of everyday life for women living through conflict in which they experience both agency and vulnerability, with the combination of the two constituting the particular nature of women's contribution to survival in dangerous situations and "under fire."

FEMINIST RESISTANCE TO WAR

As previously noted, motherhood has played a central and strategic role in the framing of women's participation in war and in the north and east of Sri Lanka. In Jaffna in the north for example, the Mothers' Front formed in 1984 following the example of the Mothers of the Plazo de Mayo (Madres de Plaza de Mayo) in Argentina and in response to mass arrest of Tamil youth by the state forces. In the east, too, inspired by developments in the north, women set up their own branch of the Mothers' Front. However, despite repeated attempts to demonstrate, protest, and demand the return of their children, the increasing threat and violence directed at the Mothers' Front in the north and east led to its overall weakening as an organization for political change. Increased control by the LTTE, for example, meant that the Mothers' Front was unable to retain its political voice (Samuel). In contrast, de Alwis ("Interrogating the 'Political'") points out that the formation of a Mothers' Front in the south of the island in 1990 to protest the disappearance of their male kin during the 1987-1990 uprising was more successful than its northern and eastern counterparts. Despite being founded and funded by the main opposition party at that time, the Sri Lanka Freedom Party, and therefore implicated in political patronage, the group managed to occupy an important space of protest at the time when feminist and human rights activists were being killed with impunity. By forcing the political sphere to address what was represented as non-political and natural issues of motherhood, the movement continuously "put the parameters of the political itself into question" (de Alwis, "Interrogating the 'Political'" 82). The fate of the northern and eastern Mothers' Fronts reflected a pattern of decreasing space for many women's organizations that attempted to challenge patriarchal norms of war and conflict and sought to replace these with ethics of dialogue, negotiation, and consensus (de Alwis, "Interrogating the 'Political'"; Samuel). There have been many other examples of the work of women and feminist groups and the simultaneous loss of space and silencing of oppositional voices in Sri Lanka. While it is not possible to consider all of them here it is important to recognize the many attempts to push for change and centralize the needs of women particularly and strategically through the identity of motherhood.

Providing a critique of feminist organizations in Sri Lanka, de Alwis ("Interrogating the 'Political'") suggests that many have shifted from strategies of "refusal," which include forms of non-cooperation, civil disobedience, strikes etc. to strategies of "request," such as signature campaigns, charters, and petition. This in turn has rendered many feminist projects often indistinguishable from projects of governance. This understanding is based on the fragmentation of women's activism, where, argues de Alwis, intervention has often been diluted by NGO-inspired projects of "women's empowerment" and "gender sensitization" ("Interrogating the 'Political'" 85). De Alwis notes that, "today, there exists no autonomous feminist peace movement in the country, and the voices of feminist peace activists are rarely heard nationally" (de Alwis, "Interrogating the 'Political'" 85). She attributes this to the same groups of feminists being stretched to support the multiple campaigns on women's issues alongside the institutionalism and professionalization of feminism. The latter in particular can be recognized as a "sticking point" for feminist organizations through co-option and codification of local organizations by larger donor organizations and development aid. While providing funding, they also narrow frameworks forcing the recipients to devise strategies of "request." This pattern of fragmentation and dilution of the work of feminists has been noted not only in South Asia but also as an effect on women's groups globally (see Menon). However, while recognizing the critique of contemporary feminist groups it is also important not to romanticize earlier feminist networks for, as we have seen, they struggled precisely because of their lack of support and protection thereby exposing women to the violence of the state (de Alwis, "Interrogating the 'Political'").

Therefore, between the vulnerability of the less-defined feminist networks and the over-exposure and standardization of women's feminist activism as a "profession" (Menon), there seems to be little sense of what can and is being done by women actively challenging violence and subordination. However, using the experiences of mothers connected to the Valkai group, in this chapter I suggest that rather than assuming work is not being done there is a need to look at the *way* in which it is carried out. In doing so, it becomes clear that the everyday strategies and tactics of negotiation and risk incorporated in mothers' everyday work transcend the categories through which feminist activism has thus far been understood.

THE VALKAI GROUP AND THE AMNAS

The Valkai group formed from a series of weekly meetings amongst residents across the Batticaloa district concerned by the escalating violence in 2005. Some of the local participants worked with international non-governmental organizations (INGOs) and local organizations (NGOs) while others worked independently. A number of individuals from international agencies wanted to find ways, beyond the capacity of their own organizations, to support local citizens. Although the group formed after the tsunami, most of the members had lived and worked on issues of human rights in the north and east for the majority of their lives, focusing on work with torture victims, support for abused and war-affected women, and advocacy work for women's and human rights. Support involved family visits to the relatives of people who had been victims of violence and activities such as meetings for the mothers of forcibly recruited children and tree-planting ceremonies for families whose loved ones had been killed.

While the group intentionally tried to create change through networking, this was done in accordance with and as an extension of the role and strategies that individuals and families across the east were already carrying out, rather than as new forms of activism. Where they pushed at boundaries and sought to reach out to others, they also embedded their work in the crevices of life already present, making it a form of what they termed "active living," rather than what we (as researchers/academics) might label as "activism." Cues were taken from the *ammas* (the mothers) in the villages, the majority of whom had experienced many losses and therefore had themselves spent long periods of time navigating the thin edge of survival in order to deal with the violence. This was what also separated them from many of the local and international agencies in eastern Sri Lanka. Many of these agencies prioritized being known and recognized for their work, reproducing the patronage-client type relationships that tend to define non-governmental work in Sri Lanka, particularly in the aftermath of the tsunami (Walker, "Taking a Back Seat"). The tactics and strategies used by the Valkai group to create close networks of consolation and cooperation as "active living" were not defined by violence nor were they free from it; instead they fluidly moved through and around the violence that existed in everyday forms. Active living therefore transcended a defined and categorized form of action, demanding a broader understanding of what we understand by activism in conflict areas. An example of this kind of activism is illustrated through the activities organized by the Valkai group, such as tree planting ceremonies and the mothers' meetings.[5]

While the Valkai group was predominantly made up of women and it was primarily women from whom they collected information and stories, one of their primary messages was that men also suffered irrevocably through conflict. This was not just as fighters but as grandfathers, fathers, uncles, brothers, and sons; men also grieved for their loved ones and sought out strategies to survive. Lawrence notes that during the 1990s, a disproportionate share of men between twenty and forty-five years of age lost their lives—not only on the frontlines but also due to the fact that men within that age range were always suspected of being militants and therefore risked arbitrary arrest, torture, and disappearance by the SLA throughout the war. Men had to learn to minimize their movements and visibility in order to reduce the risk of arrest; and instead, women took on the tasks they were prevented from doing. The Valkai group, therefore, did not focus exclusively on women but instead took account of the different roles that men and women could play in a context of risk and violence and acted accordingly. Subsequently, women were the ones who formed connections, often against boundaries set by men with guns. This is clearly shown, for example, when in 2005 some of the Valkai members accompanied a group of women whose husbands had been abducted or killed by the LTTE to Kilinochchi, the LTTE headquarters in the north. Here the women demanded information about their husbands and signed statements reporting their cases. This was a perilous move on the part of the mothers and the Valkai members. In a context where one would do anything to avoid being noticed or known by the LTTE, by challenging the LTTE in this way the women were making themselves highly visible and vulnerable to a group well known for callously disposing of anyone who opposed or appeared to oppose their totalitarian rule. As one of the Valkai members put it, "We were all scared ... some women didn't want to make a case. But then we decided together we must do this. We must show it's not okay" (Valkai member). Another stated, "The *ammas* were the focus because they were the ones leading the way. The ones who could do things. That to us is putting women first and being activists for women" (Valkai member).

The mother's meetings, organized by the Valkai group, emerged from the wishes expressed by women and especially mothers to share their experiences with one another. The role of the Valkai group therefore was simply to organize a safe space to meet (often in a local NGO building), provide tea, lunch, and the cost of local transport, and most importantly "to listen to what the *ammas* had to say" (Valkai member). Much of the meeting would be spent sharing stories and discussing particular problems, such as dealing with the army or Tamil militant groups and in particular the problem of the conscription of children by the LTTE (and later TMVP).

Tamil children were vulnerable to recruitment by the LTTE from the age of ten onwards and the practice of demanding one child from each family was widespread in the north and east. Families that didn't comply had children taken by force. Even when children appeared to join "voluntarily," it was often due to poverty, deprivation (particularly in the border areas), abuses, and suffering under the SLA, alongside a sophisticated LTTE propaganda machine (HRW "Living in Fear"). Once recruited, most children were allowed no contact with their families. The LTTE would subject them to rigorous and sometimes brutal training, and public punishment of those who tried to run away was used to discourage other children from trying. The role of external agencies such as The United Nations Children Fund (UNICEF) and Save the Children appeared largely ineffective in holding the LTTE accountable for child recruitment. Families I spoke with across the east expressed disappointment that despite the amount of international attention on child soldiers and the LTTE that in reality there was no protection for their children before and/or after they were conscripted. Ultimately, this meant that the task of trying to protect their children and to find them fell on the mothers, grandmothers, sisters etc.—those who knew were often the most vulnerable in conflict and yet at the same time were able to actively challenge the violence.

During a meeting I attended in 2007, one mother, Radhika, described to the rest of the group her experiences of trying to get her son back from the LTTE. She explained that in January 2006 her son was taken to an LTTE camp in Kokkodaichcholai, which at the time was an LTTE stronghold in the east. Since she knew where he was, Radhika began daily visits to the camp, travelling the long distance from her home and over the lagoon to the gates of the camp guarded by young LTTE cadre: "I would plead with them for my child back," she stated, and continued:

> *I would sit on my legs like this [demonstrating how she would kneel in a praying/begging position] and ask again and again for my son. I would tell them he needed to go to school, to study, and that he wasn't part of this war ... but they wouldn't listen to me. Not to an old woman. Not to a mother.* (Radhika)

Radhika explained in great detail the periods she spent outside the camp and how she eventually decided to threaten to commit suicide in front of the LTTE if her child was not returned:

> *I went to that camp every day—I insulted them [LTTE cadre] so much that they would have had fifty lorry loads of my saliva!*
> *For nine days I did not eat, did not go to the toilet—how*

could I if not eating? Then I went there with a knife—it was actually so blunt that it would not pierce my skin but they [the LTTE] did not know that. I waited at the camp and told them I would kill myself. They said I wouldn't but I told them I had only my son so it did not matter what happened to me. Then they told me they would see me the next day and sent me to stay with a family close by. The family was told by them [the LTTE] to take the knife from me when I went to bathe so that I could not kill myself. I left the knife under my dress when I went to bathe but I saw them do this [take the knife] and I told them, "I will not cause you any trouble—I am not here to trouble you but only to get my child." The next day at the camp I refused to leave until they [the LTTE] gave my son and said I would kill myself if they did not. (Radhika)

Unusually for the LTTE, they finally released Radhika's son. However, what was significant about this particular story was the way in which Radhika used her experiences to map out the landscapes of risk and violence that she faced and the emphasis she placed on pushing against the boundaries of restrictive spaces (literally in terms of the LTTE camp and metaphorically in terms of her own fear) to find her child. Moreover, the significance of this anecdote is that it is not framed as the narrative of a victim or a heroine, but reveals the realities of everyday life for many mothers in eastern Sri Lanka. Located within the space of the mothers' meeting and alongside the work of the Valkai group, the story illustrates the sharing of experiences as a means to strengthen everyday activities and strategies and for women to challenge those who took their children and husbands.

This is supported by other accounts that emerged during my research of mothers and grandmothers who at the time of the LTTE split had physically beat back LTTE cadre to gain access to and release their children from the camps where they were quartered (de Alwis, "Rising in the East"). One teenage girl described to me how her grandmother had stayed outside the LTTE camp for days during the split waiting for her. Finally, with a change of clothing for her under one arm and a food packet in the other the grandmother had marched past the LTTE cadres declaring that she was taking her granddaughter home.

One of the points that Radhika made during the meeting, when explaining how she had fought to get her son back, was that she did not compromise. After finishing her story she had turned to the other mothers in the room and berated them for being too willing to negotiate with those who were holding their children. She insisted that they should keep pushing and finding ways to move forward, and not to listen when they were told to come back the next day or to pay money to people. Many mothers in the meeting agreed with Radhika and stated that they still would go to any length to find their children—and that often involved trying to initiate contacts within the LTTE. Jeeva, another mother present at the meeting, reflected on her search to find her son who had been detained by the LTTE a number of years prior. "I still go to the camp," she stated, "I ask for him every month." Jeeva described how one of the high-level commanders at the camp where she believed her son was being held was a relative of hers. Every time she went there she asked for him and tried to call him but he always avoided her and ignored her calls. Jeeva also said how she had met other women outside of the camp who were looking for children and that they had grown to know one another and tried to help with information or leads they may have: "We try to share … but we are also scared. If they see us talking [referring to the LTTE] they may get angry and not help us." Reflecting on the experience of being a part of the mothers' meeting and sharing experiences, Jeeva noted, "It's important that we know that we all have this problem—it is not just one—we need to fight together" (Valkai member).

However, despite the threads of shared experiences of loss, pain, and struggle that tied the mothers together, there was also much that kept them apart. Relationships and connections amongst the mothers, while held in the moment, were not inherently fixed and pure; they were also fractured from within in terms of individual interests, the need to protect one's family, and fear of others, all within a constantly changing context. This was captured in the words of one mother at the meeting who noted: "If I get my child back I will not let go. Nothing else will matter then. I just want my child." Alongside the pressure of political control, this was perhaps part of the reason why the Mothers' Front also failed. The levels of risk and fear woven through their everyday contexts, and the mothers' ultimate concern for their own children, meant that they could not make promises or fully trust one another or be fully committed to a political cause.

Yet at the same time, we can see how connections of loss and the need to keep pushing forward tied women together, however loosely. Moreover, those who were in relatively safer positions, like members of the Valkai group, could operate as conduits to connect with those facing immediate danger and this was seen in many of the narratives that emerged during the mothers' meetings. Accordingly, we can argue that it is in the spaces of loss, an experience that few families in the east have escaped, that the power of violence and vulnerability has highlighted the strength of connections, which work through and against structures of control. These connections and actions are particularly strong amongst women and mothers.

CONCLUSION

While the "lack of visibility and voice" identified by de Alwis ("Interrogating the 'Political'" 85) is palpable in the working sphere of feminist organizations and NGOs in Sri Lanka, it does not necessarily account for the networks of mothers in eastern Sri Lanka who are carrying out critical and vigorous work and in many ways align with the feminist peace movement. While these networks may not have an obvious voice and remain largely invisible on the surface of everyday life, it is also these very factors that enable them to continue effectively. Therefore, in recognizing the critique of feminist activism and acknowledging the work being carried out actively by women, this chapter suggests that rather than assuming that the space to destabilize and contest politics doesn't exist, perhaps we need to refocus the lens through which we are observing. In doing so we can ask what else might be happening in and amongst the more recognizable spaces of everyday activities and amongst women and particularly mothers. By turning to these spaces and this kind of "active living," we might recognize that what seems to be most effective is that which actively avoids being labelled as activism or as a women's group. Moreover, although my focus in this chapter has been on the role of women, I have shown that the Valkai group itself has not intended to discount the role played by men. Instead the experiences of the group have revealed the extent to which gender shapes Tamil-speaking communities in creating norms and conventions that precede us and which can often shape the limits and possibility of actions and agency. In Batticaloa this has meant that women and especially mothers, while facing increasing vulnerabilities and violence, have become more visible in their negotiation of everyday risk, and in some cases have used this as a strategy to widen spaces for the support of others.

[1]For a detailed analysis of Sri Lanka's political histories see Spencer; Hoole.

[2]Under international law, a state commits an enforced disappearance when it takes a person into custody and denies holding them or refuses to disclose their whereabouts. "Disappeared" persons, hereafter referred to as disappeared, are commonly subjected to torture or extrajudicial execution and cause family members continued suffering. An enforced disappearance is a continuing rights violation—it is ongoing until the fate or whereabouts of the person becomes known (HRW "Recurring nightmare").

[3]In September 2010, the Child Development and Women's Empowerment Ministry claimed there were 49,000 widows in the east and 40,000 in the north, and that of those in the east, 25,000 are from Batticaloa, of which approximately half are below the age of 40 and one third have three or more children (see International Crisis Group 128).

[4]See also Rajasingham-Senanayake ("After Victimhood") and The International Crisis Group.

[5]For a more in-depth analysis of the role and activism of the Valkai group, see Walker ("Enduring Violence").

WORKS CITED

De Alwis, Malathi. "Interrogating the 'Political': Feminist Peace

Activism in Sri Lanka." *Feminist Review* 91 (2009) 81–93. Print.

De Alwis, Malathi. "A Rising in the East." *Polity* 2.1 (2004): 12-14. Print.

De Alwis, Malathi. "Motherhood as a Space for Protest: Women's Political Participation in Contemporary Sri Lanka." *Appropriating Gender: Women's Activism and the Politicization of Religion in South Asia*. Ed. Basu Amrita and Patricia Jeffrey. London and New York: Routledge, 1997. 185-203. Print

de Mel, Neloufer. "Fractured Narratives: Notes on Women in Conflict in Sri Lanka and Pakistan" *Development* 45.1 (2002): 99-104. Print.

Hoole, Rajan. *Sri Lanka: The Arrogance of Power: Myths Decadence & Murder*. Colombo: University Teachers for Human Rights (Jaffna), 2001. Print

Human Rights Watch (HRW). *Recurring Nightmare: State Responsibility for "Disappearances" and Abductions in Sri Lanka*. March 5th 2008. Web. December 15, 2014.

Human Rights Watch (HRW). *Living in Fear: Child Soldiers and the Tamil Tigers in Sri Lanka*. 16.13. November 2004. Web. December 15, 2014.

International Crisis Group. "Sri Lanka: Women's Insecurity in the North and East" *Asia Report* No. 217, December 20, 2011. Web. December 15, 2014.

Lawrence, Patricia. "Work of Oracles, Silence of Terror: Notes on the Injury of War in Eastern Sri Lanka" Diss. University of Colorado, 1997. Print.

McGilvray, Dennis and Mirak Raheem. "Muslim Perspectives on the Sri Lankan Conflict." *Policy Studies* 41 (2007). Print.

Menon, Nivita. *Recovering Subversion: Feminist Politics Beyond the Law*. Delhi: Permanent Black/Urbana and Chicago: University of Illinois Press, 2004. Print.

Radhika. Personal interview, 10 September 2005.

Rajasingham-Senanayake, Darini. "Between Victim and Agent: Women's Agency in Displacement." *Refugees and the Transformation of Societies: Agency, Ethics and Politics*. Eds. P. Essed, G. Frerks and J. Schrijvers. Oxford: Berghan Publishers, 2004. Print.

Rajasingham-Senanayake, Darini. "After Victimhood: Cultural

Transformation and Women's Empowerment in War and Displacement." Paper presented at the *Conference on Women in Conflict Zones*. International Centre for Ethnic Studies (ICES), Colombo: Sri Lanka. 1998. Print.

Samuel, Kumudini. *A Hidden History: Women's Activism for Peace in Sri Lanka 1982-2002*. Colombo: Social Scientists Association, 2006. Print

Schrijvers, Joke. "Fighters, Victims and Survivors: Constructions of Ethnicity, Gender and Refugeeness among Tamils in Sri Lanka." *Journal of Refugee Studies* 12.3 (1999) 307-333. Print.

Spencer, Jonathan. "Introduction: The Power of the Past." *Sri Lanka: History and the Roots of Conflict*. Ed. P. Essed. G. Frerks and J. Schrijvers. London: Routledge, 1990. Print.

Thiruchandran, Selvy. *The Spectrum of Femininity: A Process of Deconstruction*. New Delhi: Vikas Publishing, 1998. Print

Valkai member. Personal interview, 8 March 2006.

Walker, Rebecca. "Taking a Back Seat—The Uses and Misuses of Space in a Context of War and Natural Disaster" *Humanitarianism and Responsibility: A Special Issue of The Journal of Human Rights* 12.1 (2013): 69-86. Print.

Walker, Rebecca. *Enduring Violence. Everyday Life and Conflict in Eastern Sri Lanka*. Manchester: Manchester University Press, 2013.

2.
Holding Everything Together

Palestinian Mothers Under Occupation

BREE AKESSON

OVER THE PAST SEVERAL DECADES, there has been much research exploring the psychosocial consequences of political violence on children (Barber *Adolescents and War*; Boothby, Strang and Wessells; Cairns; Garbarino, Kostelny and Dubrow). Yet, with a few notable exceptions (see Robertson and Duckett, for example), little has been written about mothers' experiences of caring for their children in the context of political violence. Framed by Winnicott's concept of the mother as a "holding environment" (*The Child*) and using data from qualitative research with Palestinian families, this chapter argues that protracted political violence challenges the functions of mothering in Palestine. In this context, mothers may find it difficult to respond to their children's needs, as they struggle to address their own needs in the face of seemingly insurmountable challenges. In this context, Palestinian mothers are essentially making efforts to hold everything together for their families and for themselves.

PALESTINIAN MOTHERING IN CONTEXT

Palestine (which includes the West Bank, the Gaza Strip, and East Jerusalem) has been occupied by Israel since 1967, marking the longest military occupation in modern history (Hajjar). The occupation, deemed illegal by international law (Hollander), has greatly contributed to ongoing violence in the region. The ongoing Israeli occupation and "matrix of control" (Halper 15) create what Abu Nahleh has described as "a sustained multidimensional crisis in Palestinian society" impacting mothers specifically and the Palestinian family generally by sharply reducing household income, which in turn creates widespread poverty (103). This crisis also isolates mothers from their extended kin and social networks, leaving them dependent on their insufficient household resources. In addition to threats to daily livelihoods, mothers have to contend with very real physical threats to their families posed by Israeli settlers and the military. Furthermore, political violence may not be the most pressing form of adversity for mothers (Akesson "War", "Addressing"). They may face additional challenges such as poverty, violence, and the constraints of a patriarchal society.

THEORIZING MOTHERING: THREE FUNCTIONS OF MOTHERING IN THE CONTEXT OF POLITICAL VIOLENCE

Winnicott described the role of mother as a "holding environment" for the child, which involves physically holding the child, protecting the child from harm, and consistently caring for the child (*The Child*). To embody this role of "holding environment," the mother has to have the physical and psychological resources to attend to her child and respond to the child's changing needs. Expanding on Winnicott's theory, Barnard and Solchany suggest there are three functions of mothering: (1) monitoring and surveillance, (2) expected nurturing, and (3) responsive caregiver-social partner (14). This chapter argues that the context of protracted political violence challenges these three functions of mothering, making it difficult for mothers to feel competent. This section will provide an overview of the three aspects of the mothering role drawing connections to the experience of mothers affected by political violence.

In the *monitoring-surveillance function*, mothers' attentions are often riveted to their children, consistently monitoring their children's locations and activities. Winnicott identifies this as "maternal preoccupation" with the child (*Through Paediatrics* 304). In this function, mothers aim to provide security to the child, while supporting children's exploration of their environments by providing predictability, reliability, approachability, and responsiveness. As a baby, the mother holds her child close in order to protect

41

and show love to the child. As the child develops and begins to explore his or her environment, the mother may shift her focus to supporting and assisting the child's development of self-regulatory behaviour. With the child further from his mother, the mother may monitor the child's whereabouts from afar and speculate as to the activities the child may be engaged in. In the context of political violence, mothers may find it especially challenging to monitor their children's activities that may take place under unsafe conditions. In this way, a mother struggles between the dual duties of letting a child explore his or her environment and trying to protect the child from any potential harm.

In the *expected nurturer function*, a mother's role is to ensure the physical survival of the child. This entails providing for the basic needs of the child including nutrition and a safe physical environment (Barnard and Solchany). Providing for children in this way leads to a sense of maternal competence. On the other hand, if a mother is unable to provide for her children's needs, she experiences a sense of maternal *in*competence. A central question related to the expected nurturing function is how a mother can take care of her child when she cannot take care of herself. Emergencies have a profoundly negative effect on the health of women and children (Al Gasseer et al.), and mothers may struggle to meet their own individual needs in addition to their children's needs.

In the *responsive caregiver-social partner function*, the mother exchanges feelings, emotions, and information with her child. Barnard and Solchany claim that a fundamental aspect of this function is contingency or "the ability to monitor, interpret, and respond to the child's behavior in an immediate and appropriate manner" (16), which is key to a child's developing trust in his or her physical and social environment. However, political violence can impact this change. Research shows that mothers model coping skills for their children during war, with children mirroring their mothers' reactions to stress (Aptekar and Boore; Chemienti and Abu Nasr). For example, several studies show that a mother's level of anxiety and depression is the most important predictor of her child's mental health (Laor, Wolmer, and Cohen; Qouta, Punamäki, and El Sarraj; Smith, Perrin, Yule, and Rabe-Hesketh). Similarly, Barber's ("Political Violence") research with Palestinian youth found that a nurturing parenting style protected children's developmental and emotional well-being in the context of political violence. In a study of Palestinian children by Punamäki et al., children who had loving and non-rejecting parents were more creative and efficient in problem-solving, ultimately protecting their children's mental health despite exposure to political violence. Additionally, in Garbarino and Kostelny's research with Palestinian children and mothers, political violence was found to pose a "manageable" threat when children faced danger in the context of healthy functioning and parental well-being; however, it was a critical developmental risk in the context of family dysfunction and violence (43). All of the above studies focus on the role of the parent-child relationship in affecting child development within the context of political violence. There are fewer studies that draw from mothers' actual experience mothering in the context of political violence, a gap that this chapter attempts to address.

METHOD

This paper represents a part of a larger qualitative research project exploring the concept and meaning of place for Palestinian children and families. Data was collected in 2010 and 2012. Eighteen families from various administrative regions of the West Bank and East Jerusalem participated in collaborative family interviews. A minimum of three family members from the *a'ila* (immediate, nuclear family)—including parent, older child (aged 9-18), and younger child (eight and under)—were invited to take part in the research. However, family interviews often included members of the *hamula* (extended family) for a total of 149 individual family members from 18 families. Figure 1 shows the distribution of the study sample, according to age and gender. Of the 18 interviews, 9 were conducted with only the *a'ila* mother, three with only the *a'ila* father, and 6 with both *a'ila* mother and father. The average number of children in the 18 households was 5.4.

Interviews—lasting between one and two hours—were conducted after full and informed consent by each family member was obtained. Participants were guaranteed anonymity and assured that all information would remain confidential and used only for

Figure 1: Family demographics (age and gender)

	Index Family (a'ila)*		Other Family (hamula)**		Total
Adults (18+)	Male (Father)	9	Male	8	17
	Female (Mother)	16	Female	17	33
		25		25	50
Children (<18)	Male	45	Male	10	55
	Female	33	Female	11	44
		78		21	99
Total		103		46	149

*a'ila: immediate, nuclear family
**hamula: extended family

research purposes. The interview consisted of families' experiences living in Palestine, including their daily activities. Parents were specifically asked how they raise and protect their children in the context of political violence. To further ground the data, 32 (22 in 2010 and 10 in 2012) in-depth interviews were conducted with key community informants who work with Palestinian children and families. The data were analyzed using a grounded theory approach (Charmaz). The results of the data are presented below.

FINDINGS AND DISCUSSION

Everyday violence and oppression in the occupied Palestinian territories has stretched and tightened family systems. But how does this stretched family system affect mothers? How do mothers cope with occupation and violence? What activities do mothers engage in to protect their children and themselves? How do mothers interact with the other elements of children's protective environments (home, school, community, nation-state)? In order to better understand mothering under fire, the following section presents data based on the experiences of Palestinian families, organized around three areas: (1) everyday experiences of mothering in the face of uncertainty, (2) the challenge of lone mothering, and (3) communal support for mothering. Winnicott's holding environment (*The Child*) and Barnard and Solchany's three functions of mothering are further explored.

Everyday Mothering in the Face of Uncertainty

Mothers in this study spoke about their daily routines that revolved around taking care of the children as well as the general household. Mothers' efforts were focused not only on taking care of children, reflecting both the monitoring-surveillance and expected nurturer functions, but also on tasks such as preparing meals, washing clothes, cleaning the home, and other daily housework. For example, in the village of Al-Makkah, 30-year-old Umm-Omar cares for her three children—thirteen-year-old Basma, eleven-year-old Omar, and four-year-old Anouar. Describing her daily activities, Umm-Omar explained:

> At six in the morning, I prepare the children to go to school. After they leave, I gather things and organize the house. Then I go to my father-in-law's house. My mother-in-law is very sick, so I help with the sheep. After I help there, I come to my house and organize at home. [When the children come home from school], I give them lunch, after that they rest, and then they have to study.

Mothers' descriptions of their day-to-day activities highlighted the daily demands placed on mothers, as well as selflessness and altruism that indicated mothers put their family's well-being before their own needs. For example, previous research has indicated that women in poor families who prepare food for their families have less food for themselves in terms of quality and quantity, as they prefer to offer it to the male breadwinners and the male children as an act of motherly sacrifice (Kuttab), as well as complying with? Or providing evidence of?] a male-dominated culture.

Mothers did not hide the fact that their everyday lives were extremely difficult, especially when trying to attend to their children's needs in the function of expected nurturer. When asked how they provided for their children, mothers often answered,

"It is difficult, as you see," or "We're forced to live like this," while gesturing to their oftentimes impoverished living conditions. Thirty-four-year-old Umm-Nacer explained the physical challenges she faces when she travels away from her village to collect firewood for her home:

> It's really far away to go to that place, but I am forced to do that to get the wood, and I go by foot. Don't forget that once there, I search for the best wood, break the wood, hold it, and put it on the donkey. It's really tiring for me, and you know, when it's summertime, I have a headache from the sun. You know, when I go back home, I feel really, really tired.

Mothers identified lack of money and material goods as the greatest challenge they faced when trying to fulfill their role as expected nurturer, especially within large families. As Umm-Nacer continues:

> Life is difficult, really difficult. There are no materials, no money. You can see these are all my children.
>
> …We don't have money. We can't fill a jar of gas for the oven. I go to [name of village] to bring wood. Sometimes it takes me one day to go there, and I leave my little child alone. The problem is money.

When asked Umm-Nacer how she provides for her children, she replied:

> To be honest, there are no diapers at all, and she needs milk. Sometimes, I really need money to buy clothes for my children or shoes. Our lives are really difficult … if I need to go to someplace urgently, I don't have money to go there to get important things for my house. See my little child [pointing to four-year-old Säida, crawling on the dirt]. She needs milk, but there is no money. Our situation is becoming worse actually, really difficult.

Through their stories, the mothers conveyed feeling the weight of responsibility for their children and worried about their ability to take care of their children in light of the increasing economic hardship they faced.

These mothers were struggling with their role as expected nurturers, in which they struggle to ensure the physical survival of their children and provide for their basic needs. They expressed not only being unable to provide physical protection because of the violence surrounding them, but also being unable to provide for minimum needs such as nutrition and shelter. Therefore the women felt a sense of maternal incompetence, which is reflected in other research, such as Lipson's study of Afghan refugees and Robertson and Duckett's study of mothers in Bosnia. Like Robertson and Duckett's research, the stories of the mothers in this study revealed a paradox: the mothers described living in situations that greatly impacted the way that they take care of their children thus making them feel incompetent as the expected nurturer. However, they were actually highly competent in their mothering, ensuring the physical safety of their children to the best of their ability in a highly difficult setting. Faced with environmental stress, mothers adapted by conceptualizing their abilities as mothering in the best way that they could under challenging circumstances. This paradox could be viewed as a coping strategy that helps women continue mothering versus giving up.

The Challenge of Lone Mothering

Mothering is especially challenging when the father or husband is absent due to imprisonment or death, which in Palestine is often related to the ongoing political violence. Research shows that mothers face a range of challenges when their husbands are not present, which leaves women with the sole responsibility for the home and children (see Fox, Cowell, and Johnson; Robertson and Duckett; Robertson et al., for example). Lone mothering can result in families becoming more impoverished in communities that are already struggling with the challenges of political violence (Pavlish). Mothers become responsible for fulfilling multiple roles within the family. Not only does the mother have to fulfill the function of monitoring-surveillance, but she must also be the expected nurturer when she may not be able to provide her children with physical protection or basic needs.

At the time of this research, Umm-Omar's husband, Abu-Omar had been in prison for four years, which the family identified as the greatest challenge for them living under occupation. Umm-Omar explained that she was depressed about her husband's (and by extension her family's) situation, dreaming of a day when he would be released and she would see him again. She waited in uncertainty for information about her husband's release, a period characterized by alternately hoping and losing hope that he would return. This finding resonates with Robertson and Duckett who described lone mothers in Bosnia as "living somewhere in-between" (467). Living somewhere in between, Umm-Omar's children were also deeply affected by their father's imprisonment, making statements about longing for their family to be "whole" again.

Imprisonment and/or death were not the only reasons that husbands and fathers were absent. Three mothers interviewed for this study had husbands who had taken another wife and left the home to live with the new wife and start another family. Consider again the story of 34-year-old Umm-Nacer who lived in a small home in the middle of the Al-Jazari encampment with her five children: twelve-year-old Najet, eleven-year-old Nacer, ten-year-old Sofiane, nine-year-old Rayan, and four-year-old Säida. Umm-Nacer's most pressing concern was that of her husband recently leaving her. Umm-Nacer explained that her husband left her and their children and moved next door with another wife, 20-year-old Amana. Despite the everyday violence posed by the nearby settlement and Israeli military, Umm-Nacer explained that her husband's taking a second wife was "the most difficult thing" for her at this time, not only as a mother, but also as a woman. In fact, when speaking about this, Umm-Nacer stopped the interview several times and cried. She described the hardship of being alone to raise her children and having no income. Umm-Nacer's situation was further complicated by financial instability. She explained how her husband could not afford to take care of two families because he was unemployed and had no money, which made it difficult for him to find work and make a living. Umm-Nacer took on the role of the primary caregiver for her five children, primarily in the monitoring-surveillance function and struggled to provide for their basic needs in the expected nurturer function. However, her role in the responsive caregiver-social partner function was compromised because of her own feelings of being overwhelmed due to her husband's absence. For example, because of the emotional stress related to her relationship with her husband, Umm-Nacer explained how her oldest daughter, twelve-year-old Najet, was caring for the children in the family.

Because of the ongoing political violence, mothers in this study found themselves in new roles, oftentimes solely responsible for providing the needs of their families, often with few supports and material means. Lone mothers reported living in limbo, not knowing whether their husbands would return from prison or return to them after taking a second wife. In this environment of uncertainty, mothers were no longer traditional mothers in traditional families, but became the sole heads of households and the protectors of their children. Lone mothers often indicated that they had not only lost the father/husband as the main provider for the family, but also as a source of social support, protection, and independence. This negatively impacted these mothers' sense of self-worth. Mothers were coping with daily household tasks and the unending demands of their children, while worrying about the future, all within the constraints of a male-dominated society.

Communal Support for Mothering

In most cultures, mothers tend to have primary responsibility for childrearing. Mothers may care for their children directly or by ensuring that others, such as those from the *hamula*, will consistently provide nurturance and support to their children (Weisner). This kind of childcare involves "chains of support" managed by mothers and reflected through the *hamula* family structure in Palestine, which is enacted in both everyday practices and in times of extreme stress. Mothers in this study noted the positive impact of communal support for childrearing, especially in a context of uncertainty related to the ongoing political violence. Key informant Marwan explained how the *hamula* functions to protect children:

In our society ... there is a responsibility with the families. The families are related to each other ... members are gathering and they communicate ... if the dad was martyred, there is the granddad, the connected family. So, they will be together to help and assist. This is like, a kind of protection for the children with the families. And there is somebody instead. So if like, somebody died, there is something. They are all connected to each other.

Despite the added layer of protection that the *hamula* provides, engaging others to care for their children was still be a source of anxiety for mothers, especially when those caregivers were outside of their immediate family. Umm-Nacer's four-year-old daughter, Säida, has a neurodevelopmental disability and spends her days crawling on a small piece of plastic covering the ground near the entrance to Umm-Nacer's home. Umm-Nacer described the challenges of leaving Säida alone when she leaves the village to collect firewood:

Don't forget that my daughter, I left her sometimes at my brother-in-law, but you know, they have their own children. I'm always frightened or worried about her. Or sometimes I leave her at my sister-in-law's house. [But my sister-in-law] has other children to take care of.

Indeed, Umm-Nacer's experience indicates that the *hamula* provides social cohesion and economic support. The *hamula* may take on the maternal role of monitoring-surveillance, which serves as a coping strategy for an overwrought mother who is struggling to respond to the multiple needs of her children. However, like the effects of the occupation itself, taking away this maternal role may result in feelings of maternal incompetence.

CONCLUSIONS

Under occupation and in the face of ongoing political violence, Palestinian families continue to live under conditions of increasing insecurity and vulnerability. This protracted crisis that ruptures the social and cultural fabric of Palestinian society does not only result in loss of livelihoods and a decline in household income, but also produces serious threats to Palestinians' physical and mental health. By examining the everyday experiences of Palestinian mothers in the context of protracted political violence, this research found that mothers struggle to hold everything together, juggling the needs of their family against their own needs. Mothers in this study described the everyday challenges of taking care of their children as well as the everyday tasks related to maintaining a home. Lone mothers whose husbands were absent took on multiple roles in the family adding to already challenging circumstances of raising children under occupation. Finally, all mothers indicated that community support—relatives in the *hamula* and neighbours attending to their children—alleviated some of the stress related to raising children, but that it could also raise additional challenges by taking away maternal functions related to monitoring-surveillance, expected nurturing, and responsive caregiver-social partner.

Bergum used the phrase "a child on her mind" to describe the constant emotional connection that a mother has with her child, which contributes to child well-being (xi). This is aligned with Winnicott's conceptualization of the mother as a "holding environment" for her child, where the child feels protected, understood, and loved (*The Child*). But when a mother is also trying to attend to her own needs in times of political violence, her ability to be connected is compromised. In families where there is a high degree of stress, mothers may not be responsive to the immediate behaviour of the child, thereby contributing to discordance between the mother and child. In other words, when mothers' minds are preoccupied with the loss and trauma related to political violence, there is little energy left to devote to their children. Indeed, exposure to political violence places great burdens on mothers and may compromise their parenting ability. Therefore, how can mothers affected by war be supported to assume a maternal role and keep the "child on her mind"? This research shows that mothers may be better able to care for her children with support from the *hamula*. Allowing for others to help raise their children is a way that these mothers cope with the stress of the political violence. However, the research also indicates that engaging others in childrearing activities can add another layer of stress to mothers' experiences. The *hamula* (or others in the broader community) may take away elements of maternal functioning that mothers engage in, thereby contributing to their sense of maternal incompetence.

This research also points to the importance of making mothers' stories visible, thereby contributing to a textured understanding of what it is like to be a mother "under fire" in adverse conditions. As practitioners and policymakers develop initiatives to improve the well-being of those affected by political violence, there is much to learn from the narratives of Palestinian mothers about their struggle to protect their children and families—and address their own needs—in the face of adversity. Those working with populations affected by political violence have the opportunity to gain important insights into the experiences of these mothers and design methods to support mothers. They are in a position to help mothers build positive communal support in their lives in order to provide a safe and healthy social environment that nurtures maternal competence and aids the effective raising of children under adverse circumstances. Indeed, this finding is aligned with other research that emphasizes the value of community-based interventions to strengthen mothers' coping strategies (Dybdahl; Weine et al.; White-Traut). For example, in research with Palestinian and Israeli mothers, Guttman-Steinmetz et al. suggest that the effects of exposure to armed conflict may be ameliorated by a sense of healthy family relationships.

Though there are marked differences among culture and context, the challenges of Palestinian mothering may resonate in other settings of protracted political violence such as Syria and Afghanistan, especially since little is known about the mothering experiences of women in these countries. Therefore, research should look at mothering in different contexts, not only to understand the distinct challenges that mothers face, but also to uncover potential mechanisms of support that might be shared cross-culturally, such as cultural variations of the Palestinian *hamula*. Along these lines, research on mothering should expand its scope to include the experiences of children, fathers, and extended family members in the *hamula* to better understand the complexity of mothers' experiences in political violence.

WORKS CITED

Abu Nahleh, Lamis. "Six Families: Survival and Mobility in Times of Crisis." *Living Palestine: Family Survival, Resistance and Mobility under Occupation.* Ed. L. Taraki. Syracuse: Syracuse University Press, 2006. 103-184. Print.

Akesson, Bree. "'War is Not the Only Trauma': Rethinking Psychosocial Healing in Complex Emergencies." *Columbia Social Work Review* 3.1 (2005): 32–42. Print.

Akesson, Bree. "Addressing the Psychosocial Needs of Pregnant Women Affected by War." *Refuge* 25.1 (2008): 55–59. Print.

Al Gasseer, Naeema, Elissa Dresden, Gwen Brumbaugh Keeney, and Nicole Warren. "Status of Women and Infants in Complex Humanitarian Emergencies." *Journal of Midwifery & Women's Health* 49.4 (2004): 7–13. Print.

Aptekar, Lewis, and Judith Boore "The Emotional Effects of Disaster on Children: A Review of the Literature." *International Journal of Mental Health* 19.2 (1990): 77-90. Print.

Barber, Brian K. "Political Violence, Social Integration, and Youth Functioning: Palestinian Youth from the Intifada." *Journal of Community Psychology* 29.3 (2001): 259–280. Web. 2 Oct. 2014.

Barber, Brian K. *Adolescents and War: How Youth Deal with Political Violence.* Oxford University Press, 2008. Print.

Barnard, Kathryn E., and JoAnne E. Solchany. "Mothering." *Handbook of Parenting: Being and Becoming a Parent.* Ed M. H. Bornstein. New Jersey: Lawrence Erlbaum Associates, 2002. 3-26. Print.

Bergum, Vangie. *A Child on Her Mind: The Experience of Becoming a Mother.* Westport: Praeger, 1997. Print.

Boothby, Neil, Allison Strang, and Michael G. Wessells eds. *A World Turned Upside Down: Social Ecological Approaches to Children in War Zones.* Bloomfield: Kumarian Press, 2006. Print.

Cairns, Ed. *Children and Political Violence.* Oxford: Blackwell, 1996. Print.

Charmaz, Kathy. *Constructing Grounded Theory: A Practical Guide Through Qualitative Analysis.* London: Sage Publications, 2006. Print.

Chemienti, Giovani, and Julinda Abu Nasr. "Children's Reactions to War-Related Stress II: The Influence of Gender, Age, and the Mother's Reaction." *International Journal of Mental Health* 21.4 (1993): 72–86. Print.

Dybdahl, Ragnhild. "Children and Mothers in War: An Outcome Study of a Psychosocial Intervention Program." *Child Development* 72.4 (2001): 1214–1230. Web. 2 Oct. 2014.

Fox, Patricia G., Julia M. Cowell, and Margaret M. Johnson. "Effects of Family Disruption on Southeast Asian Refugee Women." *International Nursing Review* 42.1 (1995): 27–30. Print.

Garbarino, James and Kathleen Kostelny. "The Effects of Political Violence on Palestinian Children's Behavior Problems: A Risk Accumulation Model." *Child Development* 67 (1996): 33–45. Print.

Garbarino, James, Kathleen Kostelny and Nancy Dubrow. *No Place to be a Child: Growing Up in a War Zone.* San Francisco: Jossey-Bass Inc. Publishers, 1991. Print.

Guttmann-Steinmetz, Sarit, Anat Shoshani, Khaled Farhan, Moran Aliman, and Gilad Hirschberger. "Living in the Crossfire: Effects of Exposure to Political Violence on Palestinian and Israeli Mothers and Children." *International Journal of Behavioral Development* 36.1 (2011): 71-78. Print.

Hajjar, Lisa. *Courting Conflict: The Israeli Military Court System in the West Bank and Gaza.* London: University of California Press, 2005. Print.

Halper, Jeff. "The 94 Percent Solution: A Matrix of Control." *Middle East Report* 216 (2000): 14-19. Print.

Hollander, Ricki. *The Debate about Israeli Settlements.* Committee for Accuracy in Middle East Reporting in America. 13 June 2007. Web. 2 Oct. 2014.

Kuttab, Eileen. "The Paradox of Women's Work: Coping, Crisis, and Family Survival." *Living Palestine: Family Survival, Resistance and Mobility under Occupation.* Ed. Lisa Taraki. Syracuse: Syracuse University Press, 2006. 231–274. Print.

Laor, Nathaniel, Leo Wolmer, and Donald J. Cohen. "Mothers' Functioning and Children's Symptoms 5 years after a SCUD Missile Attack." *The American Journal of Psychiatry* 158.7 (2001): 1020–1026. Print.

Lipson, Juliene G. "Afghan Refugees in California: Mental Health

Issues." *Issues in Mental Health Nursing* 14.4 (1993): 411–423. Print.

Pavlish, Carol. "Action Responses of Congolese Refugee Women." *Journal of Nursing Scholarship* 37.1 (2005): 10–17. Print.

Punamäki, Raija-Leena, Samir Qouta, and Eyad El-Sarraj. "Resiliency Factors Predicting Psychological Adjustment after Political Violence among Palestinian Children." *International Journal of Behavioral Development* 25.3 (2001): 256–267. Web. 2 Oct. 2014.

Qouta, Samir, Raija-Leena Punamäki, and Eyad El Sarraj. "Mother-Child Expression of Psychological Distress in War Trauma." *Clinical Child Psychology and Psychiatry* 10.2 (2005): 135–156. Print.

Robertson, Cheryl Lee, and Laura Duckett. "Mothering during War and Postwar in Bosnia." *Journal of Family Nursing* 13.4 (2007): 461–483. Print.

Robertson, Cheryl Lee, Linda Halcon, Kay Savik, David Johnson, Marline Spring, James Butcher, Joseph Westermeyer, and James Jaranson. "Somali and Oromo Refugee Women: Trauma and Associated Factors." *Journal of Advanced Nursing* 56.6 (2006): 577–587. Print.

Smith, Patrick, Sean Perrin, William Yule, and Sophie Rabe-Hesketh. "War Exposure and Maternal Reactions in the Psychological Adjustment of Children from Bosnia-Hercegovina." *Journal of Child Psychology and Psychiatry* 42.3 (2001): 395–404. Print.

Weine, Stevan, Kathleen Knafl, Suzanne Feetham, Yasmina Kulauzovic, Alma Klebic, Stanley Sclove, Sanela Besic, Aida Mujagic, Jasmina Muzurovic and Dzemila Spahovic. "A Mixed Methods Study of Refugee Families Engaging in Multiple-Family Groups." *Family Relations* 54.4 (2005): 558–568. Web. 2 Oct. 2014.

Weisner, Thomas S. "Support for Children and the African Family Crisis." *African Families and the Crisis of Social Change.* Eds. Thomas S. Weisner, Candice Bradley, and Philip L. Kilbride. Westport: Greenwood Press / Bergin & Garvey: 1997. 20-44. Print.

White-Traut, Rosemary. "Providing a Nurturing Environment for Infants in Adverse Situations: Multisensory Strategies for Newborn Care." *Journal of Midwifery and Women's Health* 49.4 (2004): 36-41. Print.

Winnicott, Donald W. *Through Paediatrics to Psychoanalysis: Collected Papers*. London: Karnac, 1956. 300-305. Print.

Winnicott, Donald W. *The Child, the Family, and the Outside World*. Middlesex, UK: Perseus Publishing, 1973. Print.

3.
Giving Birth in War-Torn Afghanistan

CAROL MANN

TODAY IN 2015, DESPITE THE BILLIONS of dollars that have poured into Afghanistan for the purpose of reconstruction, infant and maternal mortality continue to be amongst the most dramatic in the whole world, hardly better than in some Central African states that do not receive even a fraction of the aid directed towards Afghanistan. According to CIA *World Factbook* and the Index Mundi, Afghanistan had in 2012 the highest level of infant mortality, with 122 deaths for 1000 births in 2012 (followed by Niger with 110 and Mali with 109). Until recently Afghanistan also led the statistics for maternal mortality, with the bewildering rate of 1600 deaths for 100,000 births in the province of Badakhshan, the highest ever recorded anywhere. The tragic particularities of this situation make scholarly analysis difficult, even though the author of the present essay is a sociologist and historian, as well as someone who has been engaged in direct humanitarian action for the past thirteen years. With regard to material presented in this essay, the author adopts a dual stance, that of the practitioner and the scholar. Little or no scholarly research exists on birthing in Afghanistan. Humanitarian agencies are mainly tasked with finding facts wherever they may exist in order to devise aid programs, and the lack of ethnographic knowledge often proves to be counter-productive to humanitarian efforts.

In this essay, I shall attempt to evaluate the influence of conflict and its ramifications through economic and social issues on giving birth in Afghanistan. Two particular periods in time will be described: First, the highly influential decades that three million Afghans spent in refugee camps, where most attempted to stay as long as possible, distrusting the offers the Kabul made to them, even after the fall of the Taliban. Then, I shall discuss the problems birthing mothers encounter in rural areas since the NATO intervention up until today, such as the influence of Taliban ideology on traditions of respectability regarding the recourse to available medical facilities. The under-reported link between the increase of child-brides and juvenile mothers and the mass cultivation of opium will also be explained. The fluid notion of culture will be discussed in order to understand some of the seemingly incomprehensible barriers to modern health care. An additional hypothesis will be put forward to explain the downward health trend observed amongst young Afghan children today, linked to the development of the market economy and the simultaneous eroding of traditional nutrition, reinforced by the disappearance of domestic agriculture. The precariousness of the overall situation means that the conditions are there for fully fledged armed conflict to reemerge.

This essay is based on fieldwork conducted between December 2001 and November 2010 in Pakistan and Afghanistan—including refugee camps at the Pakistan-Afghan border. This was the basis of my doctoral thesis at the EHESS (Ecole des Hautes Etudes, Paris) in 2005, and numerous papers published afterwards. Since then, I have been conducting further research as the founder and director of the NGOs, Femaid and Women in War. This paper is a humanitarian reflection, a product of my field work but also my own feelings of anger and helplessness the face of an increasingly desperate situation, made worse by the lack of interest researchers have shown for this area of study.

The vast quantity of aid and investment has not brought expected solutions in Afghanistan because the country lacks a strong central government and a well-established sense of collective citizenship via which national priorities can be developed and implemented through policies and infrastructure. This has made the setting-up of an efficient health system, complete with hospitals and medical training, as well as the implementation of strict criteria for basic hygiene and security, practically impossible. These realities make Afghanistan a regional exception operating very differently from India, Pakistan, or Bangladesh—or Iran where Shah Reza Pahlavi, in the early 1960s, instituted nation-wide health care. As in so many developing and especially post-war societies, the gap between private and public hospitals is very big. Private clinics primarily service occupying forces and the military and offer a high level of care, thereby raising standards for a privileged class, which stands in sharp contrast to the level of care offered in the public health system. The circumstances in the public health sector will likely become even worse as foreign funding will decrease significantly after the final departure of NATO troops.

There is another issue at stake. In Afghanistan, the very notion of giving birth has always been considered a private matter controlled by the husband's family, namely the mother-in-law, and occurring in domestic space. There has been a real and ongoing effort made in private clinics in Afghanistan to bring pre-natal care and birthing into the organized sphere of regular medical surveillance, a transition that has already taken place in the neighbouring countries. The improved survival rate has helped introduce safe birthing as an expected norm, and infant and mother mortality at birth is beginning to be considered an avoidable tragedy, at least by the developing middle-classes who can afford private hospitals in the capital. This attitude has started to trickle down into the public hospitals, sustained by the experience of returnees from refugee settlements in Afghanistan and Iran, as I shall show further on.

The circumstances of birthing in Afghanistan are complex all the more because they cannot be analyzed within the classic logic concerning the suffering of pregnant women in war. Several situations intersect in a unique and contemporary way: modern warfare, ancient honour codes, religion, post-conflict neo-colonialism, globalisation, and the drug trade, all of which intersect in the context of sinister realpolitik. Although Afghanistan today is theoretically at peace, the situation is best described as an ongoing low-intensity war with peaks of violence in rural areas and a climate of fear in the cities linked to security issues. The major urban centres, Kabul and Mazar-e-Sharif, are relatively calm, with suicide bombings constituting the main source of danger. In theory this means that most women can, if the families allow it, give birth in hospitals or call midwives to their home. However, the state of medical facilities for birthing mothers remains globally poor, despite real improvements in the capital. Conditions for the extremely impoverished rural majority are much worse, especially in those areas controlled by the Taliban. My essay focuses primarily on women giving birth in these regions, with the aim of describing the extremely precarious conditions for pregnant mothers and their babies.

The overall outlook for birthing mothers and infants remains bleak. The failure of health policies and the disastrous mortality statistics continue to be blamed on poverty and a host of reasons associated with it, such as the malnutrition of expectant and lactating mothers, absence of hygiene (according to Pasteurian notions), hand to mouth survival necessitating the engaged work of all members of any family unit, as well as some health-threatening cultural traditions (using earth on wounds or rejection of colostrum for newborns). Added to these hardships are the ongoing conflict and violence. Since 1979, the country has continually been in a state of war; in that sense the present issues regarding pregnancy and birthing seen as the result of decades of violence. From armed conflict in the days of the Soviet invasion beginning in December 1979, to the U.S. and Allied intervention from the end of 2002 onwards, continued through drone attacks, war has been on the agenda for the civilian population in every conceivable form, including the phenomenal rise of opium production and trade which has escalated since the beginning of NATO occupation. These factors need to be considered collectively to understand the challenges faced by pregnant women in Afghanistan today.

REVIEW OF LITERATURE

The writings that have appeared since 2002 on Afghan women fall into two broad categories: the sensationalist and the first academic reactions to these sweeping generalizations, rather sensationalist tomes describing the experiences of women under the Taliban regime, supposedly transcribed by well-meaning pen-pushers. Looking back, many of these, which I deliberately do not name, appear to be works of propaganda designed to justify the U.S. intervention, just like the innumerable articles and reports in the same vein that have appeared in the press. As a reaction, some more academic studies have criticized what can be considered a quasi-racist demeaning of Afghan women in particular and Muslim women in general that reduce them to passive objects of fate, rather than the active subject of their own histories. The writings of Lila Abu-Lighod, Leila Ahmed, and Deniz Kandiyoti were essential to put all these readings into a wider context of non-Western feminist thinking and to challenge assumptions embedded in most of the standard references about Islamic society, such as those by Bernard Lewis. This is the balance that Elaheh Rostami-Povey's study, for example, seeks to redress; however, by demonstrating the empowerment of women, she brings out mainly the trajectories of an articulate middle-class she has encountered in urban settings. The experience of those who cannot speak for themselves, because of age, poverty, lack of education, or even the most basic sense of self is the hardest to chart. These also happen to constitute the majority of the often very young women who die in childbirth in Afghanistan. This is what I have been seeking in my own work across the years.

In my own approach to Islam and its ideologies, I have chosen to follow Mahmood Mamdani's position, as I will focus on *political movements that speak the language of religion* in opposition to Islamic Fundamentalism, which can be understood as a purely religious ethic (37). Nevertheless, I do not subscribe to the uncritical cultural relativism sometimes implied in his text, having directly witnessed, through years of humanitarian aid work in the region, the consequences of some of these ideology-driven misogynistic excesses on the health and well-being of women in Afghanistan.

When considering the insufficiently documented field of pregnancy and childbirth in Afghanistan, one necessarily needs to turn to the reports by the major aid agencies, Oxfam, Save the Children, SIDA, Medica Mondiale, and USAID, among others. Likewise, United Nations demographical publications are important but these need to be considered critically as they have their own agenda of which fundraising is an essential part. The political acrobatics of any aid agency caught between a shaky government and occupying troops need to be taken into account because their own survival is at stake, as is the work they are carrying out. Why one needs to be critical if not actually wary of figures produced by various agencies needs some explaining (Viswanathan et al.).

Numbers vary greatly as research is so difficult to conduct in a country where many areas are inaccessible and unsafe. Model projections are more often than not the source for demographic evaluations, which in turn are used to justify the choice of health programmes. Furthermore, women rarely know their own age; births and deaths are insufficiently recorded. Because of the absence of female literate surveyors, agencies have to rely on males who cannot approach the female population and have to rely on approximate information given by the local men. To this it needs to be said that all the statistics ever collected by UN and affiliated agencies compute the fertility of women between the ages of 15 and 49. The desperately young girls who give birth before that age are not accounted for—and yet it is known that child marriage is a prominent issue in Afghanistan, especially linked to the war economy, to which I shall return later in this paper. And finally, it should be noted that aid agencies have repeatedly been under armed attack and are being targeted themselves, including those working specifically with women and infants.

THE AFGHAN REFUGEE EXPERIENCE (1979-2005)

The social consequences of the pro-Communist revolution known as the Saur (April) revolution of 1978 enforced a form of egalitarianism and compulsory secular education in Afghanistan that came as an unacceptable shock to totally unprepared illiterate populations of rural Afghanistan. When a year and a half later, in December 1979, the Soviet army intervened to bolster the Kabul government, these populations began a mass exodus southwards to the North-West Frontier Province (NWFP) and Baluchistan in Pakistan, crossing the Khyber Pass into the nearby frontier regions. Between 1980 and 1990, some six million out of a population of about fifteen million Afghan citizens fled their homeland, migrating primarily in the direction of bordering Iran and Pakistan.

Pakistan became home to approximately sixty percent of the refugees, of which three-quarters resided in the NWFP in the four hundred or so official and unofficial camps and settlements. Urban refugees systematically fled to cities, settling into what became semi-suburban shanty towns, whereas the rural population joined family or village members in camps, in attempts to recreate familiar social units. Families were frequently dislocated: elders were often left to look after land and livestock while the younger generation escaped to refugee camp to avoid conscription. This meant that young pregnant mothers (mostly teenagers) found themselves without the help and advice of older women during pregnancy and childbirth. The sudden deprivation of this most basic form of assistance constitutes one of the least recorded tragedies of war. Yet on the other hand, the lack of pressure of elders gave them a hitherto unheard of freedom to take decisions concerning family health and the future of their children.

In the camps, rural refugees who unlike their urban contemporaries had not benefited from Communist social and health structures experienced their first encounter with standardised Western egalitarian values, as expressed in UNHCR health care and education packages. For the first time in these rural women's lives, trained medical staff was available for basic medical surveillance of pregnancy and delivery. These services were of higher quality than that afforded to the local population, something which created considerable friction between the communities (Bartlett). At the same time, not all refugee women were permitted by their menfolk and mother-in-laws to benefit directly from these facilities for reasons linked to respectability and propriety, especially if the medical personnel were male. Maintenance of collective *gherat* (honour) took precedence over health, especially when it comes to women, considered by nature weaker and thus most likely to threaten the reputation of the whole group. This was reinforced by the Mudjhadin warlords who implemented misogynous policies in the camps they controlled, as a gesture of reassurance to those who feared the liberal influence of the West. So female refugees resorted to the only time-honoured alternative: seeking advice from the *mollah* of which there were several in every camp. In my own fieldwork, there was a shift towards accepting modern medical assistance when it came to the health of male children, even if it meant that the mother would need to speak a male doctor. The same has been observed in the Western-style Kabul children's hospital set up by the French in 2005 where boys appear to constitute the main bulk of the patients.

The availability of medical staff gradually allowed women to express their own problems whilst having their children examined and this was to be highly influential concerning their future attitudes to health care. By addressing vulnerable populations, health programmes challenged the inevitability of pain and suffering as the classic lot of women and introduced a notion of personal, psychological well-being as henceforth being the norm (Mann, "Femmes"). In the words of an aged female correspondent from the remote Farah province with whom I had the opportunity to speak in 2008, about the violence she had endured all her life:

> *We used to think pain was normal, just part of every woman's life. Me and all my sisters-in-law, we were regularly beaten by our men, our mother-in-law, it was normal. When we gave birth of course it was terrible, the doya [untrained midwife] would give us a bit of tariok [opium], nobody thought twice about it. One, she punched my belly to force the baby out. We all suffered horribly and I saw young women die in labour.* (Mann *Femmes d'Afghanistan*)

Unfortunately, the shift of expectations produced a hitherto unknown reliance on medication as the absolute cure for any kind of ailment, physical and mental, encouraged by the increase of self-styled pharmacies selling counterfeit drugs. This situation was imported into Kabul with the mass return of refugees on one side and the new health facilities built by NGOs on the other. According to a medical doctor in the French Medical Institute mentioned above, parents insist on antibiotics for their infants and if he does not prescribe them, they purchase them in nearby pharmacies.[1] The same thing has happened with oxytocin used in hospital births for labour induction. According to doctors in Kabul, untrained midwives have been able to buy it over the counter and are using it indiscriminately as a miracle drug that apparently enhances their reputation, but at the cost of great suffering for the mothers.

The experience of female refugees in Iran presents similarities to those of their contemporaries in Pakistan. Despite continuous discrimination from the Iranian state, women had access to quasi-Western levels of health care. The theocratic Islamic state guaranteed respectability thereby countering any opposition from male refugees. Infant and maternal mortality in Iran are a small fraction of that in Afghanistan or even Pakistan (CIA), raising standards for Afghani women who returned to Afghanistan. Access to health care for birthing mothers could be considered henceforth a natural right, at least for returnees if not for those who had remained in the country. Yet the improvements were often ineffectual in a deeply unjust system made even more unjust by war. These circumstances, as I have shown elsewhere, led to a mass wave of suicides initiated by returnees from Iran and spreading to other parts of the country (Mann, "Female Suicide").

THE INFLUENCE OF THE TALIBAN
ON INFANT AND MATERNAL HEALTH

The sudden explosion of anti-Taliban ire was a reaction in the aftermath 9/11. This came six years after Mollah Omar and his men had swept into power, not eliciting any reaction from major powers. The idea of the "Afghan woman" shrouded in her blue nylon burqa and circulated in the Western media became a world icon and served principally as a propaganda tool to justify the NATO intervention into Afghanistan. The group then known as the Taliban had, in fact, been received with relief by a population exhausted by years of civil wars. They broke up the bloody coalition of Mudjhaddin parties that swept into power after the fall of the Moscow-supported Najibullah regime in 1992. These warlords turned the politics they had instituted in the Pakistani refugee camps into an agenda according to which they ran the country. Henceforth reactionary gender politics served to counter any attempts at secular egalitarianism by the ousted Communist government. The violence of the civil war was worse than anything that had been experienced before; Kabul was destroyed, and for the first time rape was used as a weapon of war in operations of ethnic cleansing.[2] The health service fell apart and only a few foreign NGOs remained operative from bases in Iran and Pakistan. The Taliban government that followed brought a modicum of peace but pursued their misogynous gender politics to an extreme. What remained of state medical institutions collapsed, leaving even fewer international NGOs to provide aid with minimal funding. Through-out these upheavals, refugees were understandably reluctant to return, their hopes of going back to their homeland thwarted by such extremes of violence. As the situation did not improve under the Taliban regime, many women and children remained in the camps, where living conditions were vastly superior to what they would have encountered in their devastated villages. Security and health services, I was told during my research in the camps, were their main motivation to stay, even after the fall of Mollah Omar. For instance, infant mortality was lower among the refugees than among the local rural Pakistani population (Bartlett). It is only in 2005 that most refugees were forcibly evicted by the Pakistani army.

Despite propaganda about the supposed success of the government in Kabul and much celebrated victories of the NATO forces from 2002 onwards, the so-called "insurgent forces" and the Taliban have not been eradicated. The Taliban label loosely describes the powerful warlords (some of which are active politicians) and their chain of command that subscribes to Political Islam and fundamentalist Deobandi ideology rather than solely adheres to tribal codes that are still a major reference in rural areas both in Afghanistan and Pakistan. Deobandi is a movement belonging to Hanafi Sunni Islam originating in India; it preaches an extremely rigorous literal reading of religious texts. It is likely that half of Afghanistan is presently under Taliban governance. They control the largest poppy and cannabis cultivating provinces, and provide seeds and payments for future crops as loans to local cash-strapped peasants who cannot afford to invest in irrigation to plant the orchards that once graced these regions. Since the arrival of NATO troops, Afghanistan has become the world's leading supplier both of opium and cannabis, the production having doubled and scheduled to increase as NATO troops leave (UNODC "Afghanistan Opium Risk Assessment"). Because of the sheer danger and opposition to their efforts, aid agencies have restricted their activities in these areas. The rates of maternal and infants mortality has plunged. But there is another reason.

Because of the fall of heroin prices at street level in the West (UNODC *Afghanistan Opium Survey*), farmers can no longer re-imburse their debts. So when the dealers turn up to collect their dues, they often are paid in kind with extremely young girls given over in lieu of cash, the monetary advance they have received being counted as bride-price paid in advance. If the government theoretically has instituted fifteen as the minimum age for marriage, the Taliban scrupulously follow the Quranic precepts where nine is deemed to be an adequate age. Reports indicate that girls are frequently married off between the ages of ten and fourteen and the age difference between the spouses can be anywhere from ten to fifty years (WCLRF). The author knows, from having researched in rural areas, that these marriages are generally consummated, whether the girls are nubile or not. According to a number of reports, such marriages are on the increase, with an ensuing rise in births. On average, girls are wed significantly younger nowadays than their own mothers were. Not only is contraception unavailable in the rural areas, but there is enormous pressure to produce a child within the first year of marriage, so these child brides find themselves giving birth whilst they themselves are still growing. This is shown in a report that quotes the head representative of the Ministry of Public Health in Badghis province (who happens to be the only surgeon in this area populated by 400,000 inhabitants) as saying that he routinely saw girls as young as twelve having babies ("Afghanistan's child brides").

This complex situation has to be considered a product of modern war with numerous repercussions on women's reproductive health and the health of infants. For a start, the presence of Taliban usually means a likelihood of military confrontation with NATO troops and therefore increased insecurity. Furthermore, the attitude of the Taliban towards humanitarian aid and/or hospitals or dispensaries run by the Ministry of Public Health is problematic. Depending on the local commanders, men seeking medical aid for their wives in labour may be considered an act of treason as such initiative is seen as a sign of recognition and support the Kabul government and its institutions (Jackson). The situation is made worse by the fact that the Taliban disapprove of women working outside the house so female medical staff (including trained midwives) are equally viewed with suspicion and threatened, leaving women no option but to give birth with no trained help at hand.

With the lack of any other medication, opium in different forms (including the novel injectable form) is used during childbirth for pain, contributing to rise in addictions among women and children. Informal discussions I have had with medical doctors over the years reveal that the combination of the youth of the mothers (and therefore an underdeveloped bone structure worsened by malnutrition) and the passivity induced by drug intake contribute to obstructions during childbirth leading to death. But in such a difficult context, real statistics are impossible to establish for reasons explained at the beginning of this paper. So the official story that indicates an apparent drop in the rate of maternal mortality may turn out to be a reflection of underreporting of deaths, especially as the demise of females is not perceived as a tragedy by this society that mainly values males, as other reports have shown (Jackson; Viswanathan et al.).

As well, militant political Islam in war zones has instigated active policies that have had disastrous consequences for mothers and infants, in the fields of public health and education generally, reversing any efforts undertaken to improve the standard of living. In North Eastern Nigeria where the Boko Haram (who are close to the Taliban in so many respects) rule, the consequences are practically identical, all founded in the oppression of women and girls: infant and maternal mortality are even higher than in Afghanistan again for the same reasons (United Nations Children's Fund).

TRADITIONAL CULTURE AND RESISTANCE TO CHANGE

It is only since about 2012 that the concept of "culture" has repeatedly appeared in official reports as a barrier to access to health facilities in Afghanistan. For at least ten years, the blame for maternal and infant mortality was entirely placed on the absence of medical facilities and poverty, yet in view of the visible failure of health policies despite the presence of expensive facilities, specialists were forced to seek answers elsewhere and turned to examining the significance of culture, tradition, and the omnipresence of the notion of honour, understood in a particular way. Although the Afghan rural populations are devout Muslims, Pashtuns, the dominant ethnicity, especially conform to an unwritten pre-Islamic code known as Pashtunwali that provides a sense of collective and personal identity and ethical guidelines (Barth). Variations of this code are also upheld by all other ethnic group in the country, especially when it comes to safeguarding what is considered family honour as represented by female conduct, necessarily passive and submissive. Enforced by councils of village elders (*jirgas*) until today, this framework serves as general reference and takes precedence over any kind of state imposed law or Sharia prescriptions.

Cultures are hardly monolithic, static entities, especially when undermined by dominant politics. Political Islam here and elsewhere has managed to destroy local practices, replacing them by a globalized form of Islam where regional particularities as well as ancient monuments are destroyed. Pilgrimages to tombs of saints used to be particularly important sites of worship for women who considered themselves barren but now such practices are shunned. These customs allowed for a form of acceptable socialization outside family obligations. As a result, domestic space has shrunk, confining women to a degree hitherto unknown. In order to stake their territory, the Taliban have set themselves up as the sole champions of ethnic tradition and authentic religion. By stressing the threat represented by women's rights to patriarchal privilege, they have fuelled local opposition to the occupying Allied forces, NGOs, and the government in Kabul. Reproductive health and safe childbirth have become highly sensitive political issues as they rely on outside expertise to improve standards of survival. All too often, recourse to medical aid for women in labour is considered an act bringing shame on the family. It is said locally that Bin Laden preferred to have one of his daughters-in-law die in childbirth at Tora Bora rather than call for outside help.

War was the traditional way in which Afghan warriors could display male honour and virile prowess. The punitive raids of Taliban or the confrontations with the U.S. and allied military are not considered a valid outlet for visible heroism. As a result, the control of women remains the sole marker of the efficient application of criteria of respectability

Aid agencies and health workers are continuously targeted, all in the name of an imagined tradition, purporting to defend male honour. Taliban politicians, manipulating local anger at ISAF military presence have indeed managed to harm the populations that sustain them, with the paradoxical support of the most corrupt elements of the Afghan government.

There is a new financial aspect to this as well. Since the NATO intervention, in a previously frugal society, wealth and financial success have become the markers of nouveau-riche honour. This trend has expanded through an economy based on war profiteering and narcotics and bolstered by the warlords' direct handling of massive U.S. financial aid. Marriage is now essentially a financial transaction with extreme pressure exerted on girls and regulated by bride-price (i.e. money given by the groom's family to the bride's father) rather than the dowry system. It is therefore essential for fathers to maintain their daughters' economic worth on the marriage market, which is judged solely on criteria of conformity to stringent standards of respectability.

Having no other assets, the poorest have to fall back on the maintenance of family honour and extreme restrictions imposed on women and young girls. This goes a long way in explaining the persistence of so-called "honour" killings throughout the country (including against girls trying to run off to the new shelters set in towns) with reference to tradition that seemingly confers to such practices some kind of fraudulent legitimacy. The same mechanisms apply to birthing and explain the under-use of hospital facilities put in place by aid agencies under the aegis of Ministry of Public Health.

It was in the World Health Organization (WHO) office in Kabul that this author was told about a breach birth which a traditional midwife did not know how to handle. In the end, she wrenched the baby's body out, severing it from its head which remained inside the mother's womb. It took the family six days to get to a hospital in nearby Jalalabad. The woman was operated on and barely survived, with major health complications including permanent fistula. Yet, apart from the sheer horror of the tale, what was astounding was that the WHO officer (a high-ranking one at that) had not inquired why the young woman had not gone to the hospital in the first place, especially as her village was situated a few miles away. As soon as the midwife saw that the baby was coming out feet forward, she must have known that there was little she could do to save either mother or child. Even before that, she would have noticed that the child had not turned properly and that major problems were on the way. This means that some-one—a husband or mother-in-law—had taken the decision *not* to send the young woman to the hospital and kept her in inhuman suffering for nearly a week. Possibly fearful for her own safety or uninformed about the extent to which the concept of honour matters in Afghan culture, the WHO officer was not asking these questions. Afterwards, I spoke to her Afghan assistants, asking them why they had never brought up such cultural issues. Their reticence betrayed their social insecurity: wanting to be considered as equals by their Western counterparts and employers, they had chosen to distance themselves from traditional practices at least in the workplace. I have encountered similar behaviour in other humanitarian agencies in Afghanistan.

Once again, the preponderance of rigid norms of honour as a sole principle for safeguarding male property and privilege explains the reservations towards imported health care. Out-side intervention, especially in a hospital situated on territory not owned by the clan, is seen as an encroachment on the right of ownership and as a strategy to display the incapacity of the male group to look after "its" women. This may be a reason for under-reporting maternal and infant deaths in rural provinces, but it also needs to be taken into account when attempting to comprehend the numerous maternal deaths actually occurring in areas where health facilities are available. The issue is territorial on more than one level. It is deemed essential for women to give birth especially to their first-born on paternal territory. Identity is inextricably wound up with inherited land that exclusively belongs to the male clan into which women marry. Many other examples abound, but health politics and politicians receive no anthropological guiding; practically no research on traditional practices has been undertaken or made publically available. The trend is to develop more inclusive health policies and use local resources, including the community *mollahs*. But financing such projects is a complex political matter. Sponsors still prefer to pay for highly technological improvements which at best will land in a private hospital in Kabul, to be used by the elite.

THE PRICE OF PEACE

Recent statistics show that since official hostilities have ceased, infant and child mortality is actually on the increase in Afghanistan, reversing the trend that had been observed in the refugee camps. The main cause is severe malnutrition. Based on a UNICEF report of 2012, Save the Children has stated that 33 percent of under-fives are stunted and over eight percent actually wasted (mainly in the 6 to 29 month age bracket), of which there are 20 percent more girls. They stress that a quarter of lactating mothers are undernourished and are more likely to bring forth low-weight babies. They could have added that Afghanistan is one of the few places on earth where women actually die younger than men. All these factors are linked, even though experts are seemingly puzzled. Whilst feeding programmes are being put together, presumably on the same basis as what is used in famine-stricken areas in Africa, it might be more instructive to consider certain traditional aspects as interdependent with a post-war modern economy.

As in India, Pakistan, and Iran, the Ayurvedic medical tradition largely prevails and still dominates in popular thinking about nutrition. Food is conceptualized in categories known as "hot" and "cold," which are then consumed according to age, gender, sickness, temperament, and season. Men are thought of as "hot" and women as "cold"—something which recurs in many cultures where "passive" women are associated with the moon and "active" men with the sun. In order to preserve health, each sex has to restrict the intake of specific foods that could be detrimental to what is considered their immutable nature, whatever their size and condition. For instance meat, eggs, nuts, and sweets generally are thought to be hot and generally unsuitable for women, a practice that, unless regulated, can lead to protein deficiencies. Even pregnant women, thought to be temporarily in a "hot" state, are worried about overheating so further restrict intake of vital nutrients, especially in early pregnancy. Why the tenets of the traditional diet have never been taken into account by health authorities is not clear.[3]

Before the Soviet intervention, *mollahs* received a certain amount of traditional medical training that could guide their communities. With the rise of Political Islam, however, the stress has been put on rote learning of texts, excluding any further education. As a result, unlike in India and parts of Iran where this tradition is regaining favour along with traditional herbal medicine, in Afghanistan it has been passed on in a fragmentary way, more as a form of superstition than real medical practice. When the local markets became swamped with junk food and carbonated drinks, these needed to be fitted into ancient categories. So Coca-Cola and other such beverages are considered "hot" (because they are sweet) and they are routinely being fed to babies and infants, especially boys in lieu of more nutritious foods.[4] From babyhood onwards, girls systematically receive less food because it is thought that males will need greater strength in their adult lives. One correspondent informed me that in rural areas, he had seen farmers sell their own produce to be able to buy these comparatively expensive goods for his children. In the West, the consequences of junk food are mainly obesity. In Afghanistan, it leads to severe malnutrition. Can one blame the war on this? A few years after President Karzai came to power, heavily backed by the U.S., he opened a gleaming Coca-Cola factory in a Kabul area that had neither running water nor electricity. The day chosen for the ceremony was September 11, 2006, exactly five years after the attacks on the Twin Towers. This was doubtless his way of expressing gratitude to the U.S. for its presence and the personal power bestowed on him. Free access to natural resources and facilitated opening of the local market to multinationals are the usual pay-off for supposedly humanitarian armed intervention.

It could be further argued that in a globalized capitalized economy, Coca-Cola has sufficient marketable prestige to be desirable for populations worldwide, including the most remote village in Afghanistan, sustained by the media and shrewd advertising. Unregulated sub-products equally abound, flowing in from neighbouring Pakistan. Taking into account the present trend in child mortality and its relationships to diet and the ideas surrounding junk food, the consequences could be disastrous.

CONCLUSION

Much that has been described in the present chapter did not occur in an active battle zone but they need to be understood in a larger context of modern warfare, the venomous hydra of our time, which presents so many lethal aspects that add up to veritable war against civil populations, especially women and children. Armed conflicts today do not cease with the signing of peace treaties or even with the trial of war criminals in The Hague. None of these have occurred in Afghanistan and warlords with heavy criminal records are over-represented in the government. Clausewitz famously defined war as "the continuation of politics by other means"—here one may say that the present low-intensity quotidian violence is the continuation of war by other political, social, and economic means. The mix between pronounced gender inequality, the ready availability of carbonated drinks, and agricultural under-development in favour of opium production can be said to be a lethal by-product of modern armed conflict. This conflict is underscored by a purported reconstruction and state building economy based on investors' profit rather than true development. Add to this the lack of education, increase of malnourished child brides and their stunted infants, as well as the rise of substance use and the contemporary Afghan battlefield appears in its full horror. No guns necessary.

[1]Personal interview at the French Medical Institute, Kabul, May 2008.

[2]The leader of one of the factions responsible, Abdul Rasul Sayyaf, was elected to parliament in September 2005 and has been in power since. For more information, see Gossman.

[3]In the West, however, it is only since World War II, that women have become more carnivorous, as steaks and the like were—and in parts still are—considered "male" food.

[4]Thanks to Parka Khushal for talking to Afghan refugees in Quetta (April 2014).

WORKS CITED

Abu-Lighod, Lila. "Do Muslim Women Really Need Saving? Anthropological Reflections on Cultural Relativism and Its Others." *American Anthropologist* 104.3 (2002): 784-790. Print.

"Afghanistan's Child Brides: Pawns in a Desperate Business." *World Vision, Afghanistan.* 2014. Web. 13 April 2015.

Ahmed, Leila. *Women and Gender in Islam: The Historical Roots of a Modern Debate.* New Haven: Yale University Press, 1993. Print.

Barth, Fredrick. *Ethnic Groups and Boundaries.* Boston: Little, Brown & Company, 1969. Print.

Bartlett, Linda. "Maternal Mortality among Afghan Refugees in Pakistan, 1999-2000." *The Lancet* 23.2 (2002): 643-649. Print.

Central Intelligence Agency (CIA). *World Factbook. Afghanistan.* Web. 13 April 2015.

Gossman, Patricia. "Afghanistan." Crimes of War Education Project. 2011.

Jackson, Ashley. "Taliban Policy and Perceptions towards Aid Agencies in Afghanistan." *Humanitarian Exchange Magazine* 58 (2013). Web. 13 April 2015.

Kandiyoti, Deniz. "Identity and its Discontents: Women and the Nation." *Millennium Journal of International Studies* 20.3 (1991): 429-443. Print.

Lewis, Bernard.*Political Words and Ideas in Islam.* Princeton: Princeton University Press, 2008. Print.

Mandani, Mahmood. *Good Muslim, Bad Muslim: America, The Cold War and the Roots of Terrorism.* New York: Doubleday, 2005. Print.

Mann, Carol. *Femmes d'Afghanistan.* Paris: Le Croquant, 2010. Print.

Mann, Carol. "Female Suicide in Afghanistan." *Crimes Against Women.* Ed. David Wingeate Pike. Paris: American Graduate School of International Relations and Diplomacy, 2011. 203-209. Print.

Reuters. "Pepsi to March In, As Foreign Troops Leave Afghanistan." *Reuters. Kabul.* May 20 2013. Web. 13 April 2015.

Rostami-Povey Elaheh. *Afghan Women, Identity and Invasion.* London: Zed Books, 2007. Print.

United Nations Office on Drugs and Crime (UNODC). "UNODC Afghanistan Opium Risk Assessment 2013." *Public Intelligence.* April 2013. Web. 13 April, 2015.

United Nations Office on Drugs and Crime (UNODC) and Islamic Republic of Afghanistan Ministry of Counter Narcotics. *Afghanistan Opium Survey 2013: Summary Findings.* November, 2013. Web. 13 April, 2015.

United Nations Children's Fund (UNICEF). "Mother, new-born and child health mortality in Nigeria." UNICEF Web. 13 April 2015.

Viswanathan, Kavita, Stan Becker, Peter Hansen, Dhirendra Kumar, Binay Kumar, Haseebullah Niayeshi, David Peters and Gilbert Burnham. "Infant and Under-five Mortality in Afghanistan: Current Estimates and Limitations." *Bulletin of the World Health Organization.* 2010. Web. 13 April 2015.

Women and Children Legal Research Foundation (WCLRF). *Early Marriage in Afghanistan.* Research Report. Menlo Park, CA: Flora Family Foundation, 2008. Web. 13 April 2015.

4.
Mothering in the Context of Isolation and Insecurity

Tracing the Experiences of Young Women Formerly Associated with Armed Groups in Columbia

LINDSAY JONES AND MYRIAM DENOV

THE PERSISTENT ASSOCIATION BETWEEN WAR and masculinity in popular culture and mass media continues to blur the presence of women and girls in situations of armed conflict, despite increasing evidence to the contrary. It has now become well substantiated that women and girls are a significant part of the war machine in armed conflicts across the globe (McKay and Mazurana). A recent surge of attention to gender and war in research and scholarship is gradually painting a more accurate representation of the reality of girls and women in armed groups.

The importance of shifting attention to the uniquely female experience of wartime participation is vital. Girls' post-war needs are separate and distinct from those of their male counterparts, in some cases requiring specialized assistance as they leave armed groups. Nonetheless, there are subgroups of war-affected girls that remain invisible. In particular, very little is known about the experiences of motherhood among former girl soldiers. What challenges and barriers do they face? How is their reintegration experience shaped or influenced by their roles as mothers? Importantly, what are the intergenerational effects of war and violence on mother and child? In this chapter, we aim to shed light on the post-demobilization experiences of a small group of young mothers in Colombia who were formerly associated with armed groups. As these women share intimate details of their personal lives, of hardship and hope, they introduce us to the realities of mothering in a context of isolation and insecurity. Their perspectives help to shed light on motherhood in the aftermath of armed violence, drawing attention to both their vulnerabilities and the way in which they overcome adversity.

The chapter begins with an overview of the history of children's involvement in Colombia's armed groups and specifically, the presence of girls. We then explore the gendered realities of disarmament, demobilization, and reintegration (DDR) in Colombia. Following a description of the study's methodology, and drawing upon the voices of ten female participants, we highlight the realities of motherhood following demobilization. In particular, we address the meaning of motherhood for participants, the realities of family separation, post-conflict stigma and marginalization, psychological challenges, and economic vulnerability. We conclude with key implications for policy and practice.

HISTORY AND CONTEXT: CHILDREN'S INVOLVEMENT IN ARMED GROUPS IN COLOMBIA

The current armed conflict in Colombia involves multiple actors, including the Colombian government's National Army, or Ejército Nacional, guerrilla groups (the National Liberation Army or Ejército de Liberación Nacional (ELN), and the Revolutionary Armed Forces of Colombia or Fuerzas Armadas Revolucionarias de Colombia (FARC-EP), and a national umbrella association of paramilitaries called the United Self-defense Forces of Colombia or Autodefensas Unidas de Colombia (AUC). More recently, narco-paramilitary groups also known as *Bandas criminals* (BACRIM) are beginning to take up a prominent place in the conflict.

At the early stages of the armed conflict, there was very little evidence to suggest that children were used in hostilities. However, as the armed conflict has progressed, paramilitary and guerrilla groups began to adopt new recruitment strategies that included the mobilization of children. Due to the perceived benefits in using the young, vulnerable, and obedient, the recruitment of children became endemic in the 1990s. By 2003, Human Rights Watch estimated that there were at least 11,000 children recruited into armed groups in the country (Human Rights Watch). Children are now said to compose 30 percent of all members of armed groups in Colombia, while over 60 percent of those in urban militias are believed to be children (Burgess).

A multitude of studies and reports have documented the profound deprivation, as well as the physical, sexual, and psychological violence and abuse against children that occurs within Colombia's armed groups (Bjorkhaug; Cortes and Bechanan ; Save the Children; Watchlist, *No One to Trust*; Thomas). The United Nations Security Council Report of the Secretary General on Children and Armed Conflict in Colombia (2012) provides information on grave violations against children, including the recruitment and use of children by armed forces and groups, killing and maiming, sexual violence, abductions, attacks on schools and hospitals, and the denial of humanitarian access. The report highlights that armed groups continue to perpetrate these violations in Colombia, and emphasizes the need to implement specific measures to prevent and address grave violations against children and combat impunity for such violations. Within armed groups in Colombia, the use of violence against children is far from sporadic and has become a habitual practice that is an integral part of the armed conflict.

Girls in Armed Groups

Often subsumed within the category of *children* (who are assumed to be male in the context of soldiery), girl soldiers have been subjected to a double invisibility (Denov and Ricard-Guay). Officials, governments, and national and international bodies have frequently concealed, overlooked, or refused to recognize girls' presence, needs, and rights during and following armed conflict (McKay and Mazurana). Despite this overall invisibility, girls are currently embroiled in armed conflict far more widely than is reported. While the proportion of females in armed groups and forces varies according to geographic region, it generally ranges from 10 to 30 percent of all combatants (Bouta). In Colombia, Springer (qtd. in Giraldo) notes that among all recruited children, 57 percent are male and 43 percent are female.

Girls in fighting forces contend with overwhelming experiences of *victimization, perpetration, and insecurity* (Denov, "Girls in Fighting"). In the context of Colombia, girls in armed groups perform an array of tasks to support the activities of the armed group. Their duties often vary according to their age, physical strength, and the circumstances of the armed group. Importantly, girls' roles are often multiple and fluid, most often carrying out a variety of roles and tasks simultaneously. They act as combatants, porters, cooks, bursars, spies, managers, radio operators, and medical assistants. Girls are often socially or economically dependent on the group. Although rape and overt sexual harassment are said to not be tolerated (Human Rights Watch), many male commanders use their power to form sexual liaisons with under-age girls.

DISARMAMENT, DEMOBILIZATION AND REINTEGRATION: GENDERED REALITIES

While the challenges that these youth face in the context of armed groups and armed violence are significant and undeniable, the challenges do not abruptly end upon exiting an armed group, but instead change shape. The difficult and complex transition from a militarized life in an armed group to a civilian life has been well documented (Helmus and Glenn). Given the extended periods of time that children are often associated with an armed group, upon exiting, they are faced with the need to be reintegrated into norms and institutions from which they had been isolated, often for years. To ease the transition, national and international efforts have sought to conceptualize and implement post-conflict development assistance projects and programs. What is known as "*disarmament, demobilization* and *reintegration*" (DDR) programming is regarded as vital to increasing security, public safety, and protection in the aftermath of conflict, as well as promoting peace.

Disarmament processes usually occur following formal peace accords and involves the surrender, registration, and destruction of weapons and ammunition. *Demobilization* refers to the process by which armed forces and/or armed groups either downsize or completely disband, as part of a broader transformation from armed conflict to peace. And finally comes *reintegration,* which is the process that aims to assist those formerly associated with armed groups and the community in the difficult transition to civilian life, supporting those formerly associated with armed groups to be productive members of society by providing alternative employment support options, and seeking to promote broader social acceptance and reconciliation.

In Colombia, the DDR program has been conceptualized and created within the logic and framework of a "post-conflict" context. However, in reality, DDR programming is actually occurring within a context of on-going armed violence (Ruiz Serna and Marchand). This adds a unique complexity to long-term reintegration whereby "the government is attempting to implement mechanisms of reparations and reconciliation in a 'pre-post conflict' context, and to implement DDR on the terrain of transitional justice" (Theidon 67).

To assist with child soldier reintegration, since 1999, the Colombian Family Welfare Institute (ICBF) has provided assistance to former child soldiers from all armed groups who have been captured by the Colombian army or have deserted and handed themselves into the authorities. A total of 4,811 children were assisted through this program between 1999 and 2011, of which 72 percent were boys and 28 percent were girls (Watchlist, *Columbia's War on Children*).

As noted by Jaramillo, Giha and Torres, *prevention* and *care* are the two core aspects of the ICBF's DDR program. The aspect of prevention is coordinated within the ICBF's ongoing child protection projects and programs, but has a particular focus in areas where there is high risk for recruitment by armed groups. For a child who has been demobilized from an armed group, the care aspect of ICBF programming involves support and protection of demobilized youth within an institutional or family setting. Here, programming focuses on psychosocial care, return to schooling, job training, and support for productive initiatives through Centers for Specialized Care (Centros de Atención Especializada) (CAES) and Youth Homes (Casas Juveniles) located in different regions of the country. Protection and care of demobilized children within a social/family setting can take one of two forms, depending on whether the child in question has a family to return to. If a child is able to return to their family, the ICBF ensures that the child's fundamental rights are met and secured within the family context, and provides a subsidy, depending upon the family's resources and ability to meet the child's needs. If the child does not have any family or they are unable to return to their family, the ICBF selects a foster home (*hogar tutor*) trained to receive children on a voluntary and temporary basis.

Girls and Demobilization

Despite the growing recognition of girls in armed groups, there are clear indications that girls continue to be marginalized within DDR programming (McKay and Mazurana). In many contexts, girls may actively choose to avoid DDR programs as a result of gender-based violence and insecurity in DDR camps and fear of stigmatization as former soldiers, as well as lack of medical or hygienic facilities (Denov, *Child Soldiers*). More recently, young mothers have been identified as being the most underserved population within DDR programs. The overall inattention to the needs of girls and girl mothers by national governments and the international community is seen as systemic and discriminatory by both researchers and advocates for girls (Worthen et al.).

To explore the gendered realities of demobilization in Colombia, we trace the experiences of ten young women formerly associated with armed groups, examining the challenges they experienced, as well as the realities of mothering post-demobilization. Before doing so, however, we address the study's methodology.

METHODOLOGY

This study, funded by the Social Science and Humanities Research Council of Canada, examined the reintegration experiences of a group of demobilized youth who had been associated with various armed groups during the course of the armed conflict. A key aim of the research and fieldwork was to gain not only an understanding of girls' experiences following demobilization, but also their reflections and interpretations of these experiences, as well as their psychosocial effects.

To be included in the study, participants were required to have been associated with an armed group in Colombia (whether through force or non-force) while under the age of 18 years. No stipulations were made regarding the length of time that the youth were associated with an armed group, or their assigned role within the group. Participants were purposively selected with the assistance of two professionals working in Colombia's DDR program who had ongoing contact with the youth through their daily work. The two professionals introduced the research team to young women currently involved in the DDR program and those who were interested in participating in the study were interviewed.

To explore participants' experiences of reintegration, in 2010, the second author conducted semi-structured interviews in Spanish with ten young women who had been formerly associated with an armed group in Colombia. At the time of the interviews, all the female respondents were over 18 (ranging from 20-23 years) and living in an urban context in the province of Quindío. The in-depth interviews were audio-recorded with permission and subsequently transcribed and translated into English. All respondents had been recruited by an armed group when they were under 18 (ranging between eight and sixteen years old) and had remained with the group for an extended period of time (ranging from 18 months to eight years). Nine participants became mothers following demobilization, while one entered an armed group with an infant.

The ethical implications of this research were significant. Participants were being asked to share potentially traumatic and painful events, which could evoke varying levels of distress. Given the profound potential for re-victimization, support structures were put into place to ensure that participants were provided with ongoing support and assistance during and in the aftermath of interviews. This came in the form of assistance from local professionals and social workers who worked with the youth on an ongoing basis through the DDR program.

Analysis of the translated interview transcripts was essentially a phenomenological process that involved careful reading and annotation of the collated information so as to ascertain the meaning and significance that the youth attributed to their experiences following demobilization. Through this inductive analytical process, we were able to discern the realities and implications of mothering in the post-demobilization context. Importantly, however, given the small sample size, the findings of the study can in no way be generalized to the larger population of former girl soldiers in Colombia.

MOTHERING POST-DEMOBILIZATION:
REALITIES AND CHALLENGES

While DDR supports in Colombia address key issues of education, employment, and trauma among ex-combatants, the issue of motherhood and caring for a child in the context of post-demobilization is largely absent from programming. For the most part, young ex-combatants are left to navigate the transition from *soldierhood* to *motherhood* on their own. Due to the hostile reception often given to former combatants in Colombia, this heightens concern for the health and safety of both mother and child and raises questions around the potential for the intergenerational transmission of trauma and violence. Although the reintegration realities among our participants are unique, many common threads can be identified. Here, we outline participants' perspectives on motherhood as they move from militarized surroundings to civil society, and as they adapt to a new set of social norms and way of life. Key themes articulated by participants included becoming a mother, family separation, stigma and social exclusion, psychosocial challenges, and economic vulnerability. Yet in responding to these challenges and barriers, these women display an incredible amount of courage, strength, and love for their children.

Becoming a Mother

The women that we interviewed had different experiences of becoming a mother. One participant had children very young, prior to joining an armed group, while others had children within the months and years that followed demobilization. However, despite these different trajectories of motherhood, all women faced similar challenges to mothering in the post-demobilization context. The experience of becoming a mother had varied consequences on the emotional and psychological states of the women. Participation in an armed group disrupted gender norms, roles, and responsibilities for many young women coming from traditional Colombian households. Within armed groups, many women reported being treated as "equals" with their male counterparts. Within this context of hyper-masculinity, this meant an abandonment of traditionally feminine qualities and roles:

> *When one goes over there [to war], one does men things and does not have women's intimacy. It gets lost. You do men things and you are with men…. The punishments are equal. We have to open trenches, go through the same training and wear the same camouflage. Everything, everything…. One acts the same and gets used to it, and loses the feeling of being a woman.* (Ana)

For some participants, entering motherhood jolted them back in touch with their femininity, restoring a sense of purpose:

> *When I got pregnant, I was very happy from the first time that I found out until the end … my baby. When I found out, it brought me such happiness, such an internal satisfaction just to know that I was going to take care of a little person for whom I would live. That made me feel many things and in a way I feel that my son is the final touch in feeling like a woman and a good one. I felt that.* (Ana)

For this participant, becoming a mother reportedly gave her more confidence and certainty over who she was: "It gave more security, I would walk on the streets and feel safer, safer about what I could say or affirm as a woman" (Ana).

Becoming a mother also represented hope for a new start during a difficult period in their lives. For many, the journey from war to civil society was bitter and lonely. Many participants did not return to their families and their communities, but were forced to relocate, due to fear of retaliation by armed groups. Becoming a mother offered some women the chance to redefine themselves with renewed hope and purpose: "It was a unique experience, an experience that emanates a lot of tenderness. A lot of hope, one feels that one has someone to fight for, someone who will accompany you, part of you that will start living, a hope" (Ana).

However, not all participants viewed motherhood in a positive fashion. Some participants perceived becoming a mother as more of a burden than a blessing. For this participant, after she found out she was pregnant, the father of the child left her when she refused to have an abortion. As such, she was left to raise her baby alone: "I had screwed up. I was too young, and now that he left me pregnant, my life was going to be worse because I had no education ...with nothing ... and then with a child" (Paola).

Despite having experienced challenging lives as a result of the armed conflict, all participants interviewed shared their love and adoration for their children and expressed their dedication to giving them the best life they could. When asked who they are closest to, all women named their children: "[Because of what I went through during the armed conflict] I am a person who is very depressed ... wanting to kill myself. What keeps me going is them [her children]" (Emilia).

Family Separation

One of the more common themes among the women interviewed was the lack of contact with family members as they returned to civilian life. Most of the young women we spoke with shared that they had little or no contact with their family members. After leaving armed groups, girls under the age of eighteen were typically placed in temporary homes or in foster care through the DDR program. None of the women we spoke with returned directly to their own families. In some cases, understanding the post-mobilization stories of these women begins with an understanding of their childhoods, for which many was a history of abuse and neglect. Most of our respondents disclosed deeply personal stories of physical violence, neglect, and emotional and sexual abuse at the hands of their trusted relatives, often mothers, fathers, uncles, grandfathers, and cousins. Escaping the torture of repeated abuse was cited as a principal factor pushing these girls to leave home. In fact, many joined armed groups with the illusion of freedom and emancipation. For example, one young woman left home when she was only ten years old to escape repeated physical and sexual abuse. She explained that this abuse was perpetrated by her father, grandfather, and male cousins and that her aunts and own mother denied that this was happening: "They would say that I was a liar ... that I was bored, because no one supported me, no one would help me. I was alone. I was like the black sheep in the family" (Violeta).

Emotional neglect and physical and sexual abuse figured prominently in the childhood of this young woman as well: "The truth is that my mother didn't take care of me. She left me in the care of some men in an apartment here in Colombia. Over there, they mistreated me. They hit me and raped me" (Paola).

The above participant explained that her mother abandoned her when she was only six years old, for reasons that she still does not understand, and that the sexual abuse that she endured began when she was nine years old at the hands of her mother's male cousins. Eventually, at fourteen, she ran away to escape the abuse and became pregnant one year later. Soon after, she was swept up into the paramilitaries, together with her baby girl of just four months. Following their exit from hostilities, a history violence and abuse prevented many of these girls from actively seeking out their families and reuniting with them.

The decision not to return home was also made to protect family members from the violence of armed groups. For this participant, acts of retaliation by armed groups towards her family led to her decision to abandon the hope of family reunification:

> When they killed my brother, I was in the program in Bogota.... My mom called the program and said they have killed my brother. I continued communicating with them and one day my mom said, "Gloria, I can't call you again," and I said, "Why?" and she said, "Because they are threatening me, I can't call you again." (Emilia)

For other girls, separation from family was not entirely their decision, but a decision made for them. For many families, a daughter's participation with an armed group was seen as a great insult or threat to the family's security. In these cases, many young women were not welcome to return home after they demobilized:

> My family does not forgive me for what I did [joining the armed group]. ... I talk a bit with my mom because we understand each other. With my sisters, I tried but it is hard because we are like strangers to each other. We were not raised together because I left my house when I was young.

So it is hard to build a relationship after so many years, more than ten years. So it is very difficult.... (Rafaella)

Some women shared that they did not want to put their families in danger and thus kept distance from their loved ones. One woman tried desperately to keep distance from her family to protect them, but despite her best efforts, she discovered that armed men captured and killed her sister.

Family cohesion and support has been strongly linked to improving resilience to cope with and recover from wartime violence (Villanueva O'Driscoll et al.). Family support often acts as a protective factor, serving to shield children from the experiences and exposures of armed violence. Villanueva O'Driscoll et al. link a strong familial bond to the prevention of child soldier recruitment and re-recruitment. The lack of ties and connection to family may increase the vulnerability of these young mothers as they face a multitude of challenges to reintegrating into society while caring for their children.

The Stain of War: Stigma and Marginalization

The issue of social exclusion and stigmatization has wide reaching effects for ex-combatant mothers, making meaningful reintegration extremely challenging. Frequently without the support of family, they are forced to build a new social support network, and they must do so within a hostile context. Often relocated to new communities following demobilization for security reasons, these women often begin their lives anew with no friends and relatively few contacts. Because of their former association with an armed group, this is not an easy task, as they may face profound stigma and rejection from family and community members (Denov and Marchand, in press). The realities of stigma and marginalization push many women to live "underground," concealing their status as an ex-combatant. The fear of being discovered and found out prevents many women from opening up and forming new relationships:

I am someone who doesn't share her problems with just anyone. I keep my problems to myself and resolve them alone. I hardly talk to anyone about my problems and I

think that being alone is better for me because I don't like
telling people my problems. Personally, I like to be alone
... more isolated. (Rafaella)

Most women shared that they are closest to their children. Many said that their only "friends" were other girls they had met through the DDR program, and that these were the only people they felt safe with. As they had experienced similar things during the armed conflict, they could relate to each other and understand each other.

Respondents reported significant barriers in terms of finding employment and a safe place to live because of the stigma they experienced. When being assessed for a new job, an ex-combatant status becomes very difficult to hide, given the years spent off the grid. With minimal education and a lack of references, qualifying for a job is extremely challenging. Renting apartments can be just as difficult, as landlords often request proof of income and a financial background check. As one woman explained, as an ex-combatant that has passed through the DDR program, one receives a small subsidy from the High Council (government). Receiving this subsidy may alert community members of an individual's former participation in the conflict, and subsequently act as a barrier to securing housing and employment. One woman shared that she was forced to move from her home when her neighbours discovered her ex-combatant status. Neighbours associated with local militias broke her window and sent threatening letters, forcing her to flee her home with her children. This highlights the powerful relationship between stigma and motherhood and the intergenerational aspects of stigma and marginalization.

The Emotional Toll: Psychological Challenges

Participation with an armed group does not affect all women in the same way, although exposure to wartime violence can have major emotional and psychological consequences. As such, many women were offered psychosocial support through the DDR program in the form of counselling. Most women reported benefiting from this support, highlighting the value of being able to talk through their experiences with a psychologist. Many continued to experience lasting emotional and psychological effects of witnessing and participating in wartime violence:

> *I had to see a lot of things over there. If someone does not want to work, they kill him in front of everybody. They ask you to line up, and in front of everyone, they kill him. If someone rebels, they kill him in front of you and during the time that I was there, I had to see three men fall down because of that. So one prefers, at times, one prefers to die.* (Paola)

Nightmares, flashbacks, suicidal ideation, and sleep disturbances were commonly reported among our respondents, even years after their time spent with armed groups: "You cannot forget so easily so there are nightmares. If I am sleeping while it rains and there is lightening, it is horrible for me because I wake up disturbed, I think of things that are not related. I feel paranoid" (Rafaella).

Many participants carry a heavy burden of regret and self-blame because over what they did during their time with armed groups, whether under the threat of violence or not:

> *It makes me sad to remember those things, because perhaps if I have had another chance, that may have never happened. ...There are very horrible things that happened that I had to do over there, like take the life away of one or another person. The memories are like a little box full of explosives. All together they make a team but if one explodes, they all explode. ... So, I try not to tap on the box.* (Ana)

During the armed conflict many young women not only witness acts of violence and cruelty, but also engage in them. As such, forgiveness can be a long and arduous road for many ex-combatants, given the acts of violence that many were trained for and instructed to carry out. Despite being children who were under many circumstances kidnapped and forced to do the things they did, many women found it difficult to absolve themselves. This speaks to the complexity of having been simultaneously a victim and a perpetrator in hostilities. This may incite confusion of identity, and can lead to a sense of responsibility and self-blame: "I did forgive myself but there are many things about my past … knowing that one has arrived to kill another person … is nostalgic and sad. … It does hurt despite forgiving oneself" (Ana).

Ex-combatants in Colombia must also confront a continuous threat to their safety and security, as they remain potential targets for re-recruitment and retaliatory violence long after they have demobilized. The stress and fear of being discovered can also act as a powerful force in driving young mothers underground, living with pseudonyms and keeping very little company.

War-related trauma experienced by the mother has the potential to impact the health development and growth of the child (Devakumar et al). Symptoms of depression, insomnia, guilt, and regret can affect a woman's ability to care for and bond with her child. Within the context of minimal resources and poor support networks, and where mothers often avoid critical self-care, the risk of a negative impact on the child may increase. Intergenerational transmission of trauma and violence may be a serious concern under these circumstances.

Economic Vulnerability

As girls leave armed groups, one of the key challenges to successful reintegration is financial stability and security. Many women receive a subsidy from the government through their participation in the DDR programs, which does assist them with basic living expenses. However, most women must find additional sources of income to be able to fully provide for themselves and their children. According to our respondents, these subsidies are intended for an individual, and rarely account for the presence of children.

Among the women interviewed, some shared creative strategies that they had used to find a way to provide for their children. One woman made paintings and sold them for money. Another woman opened a café with her husband using start-up funds from the government. And other women shared that they were studying to fulfill their goals of becoming a nurse, doctor, or lawyer. However, childcare was commonly cited as a barrier to advancing in an educational or professional capacity. With the government assistance, there was scarcely enough money to cover basic expenses, leaving nothing left for childcare expenses. Given the absence of family members and friends for many young mothers, staying at home with the children was often their only choice.

The level of isolation appeared to be a strong predictor of how well a woman was able to cope financially. Those who were more isolated from family members and who did not have a trustworthy partner struggled to support themselves and their children. These women were forced to make difficult choices in order to provide for their children in the best way possible, at times relying on a male companion to ensure financial security. For some, this meant staying in high risk and abusive situations to ensure that there was enough to eat: "I found out through the woman who takes care of my child that he touches my daughter. It was very hard because I cannot count on my family.... I continue to live with him because I don't have anyone else here. I am alone. And if I leave, I cannot manage economically" (Violeta).

Lack of resources and opportunities for this group of women forces impossible choices to be made, which can have detrimental consequences on the well-being of the child and mother. This young woman was appalled at the knowledge of her daughter's abuse, and disclosed the situation to social workers in the DDR program, yet she continued to stay with the perpetrator, believing that there was no other way for her and her daughter to survive financially. She explained: "My goal is to finish my studies and have a financial base to leave and leave him because that is what I could not do economically. If I leave, I will have to leave my daughter with someone I don't know and that could be a bigger risk" (Violeta).

This example also points to the risk to the health and safety of the child in situations where ex-combatant mothers are left with no support. Despite educational and vocational opportunities through DDR programming and subsidies that are distributed, many women continue to struggle in the aftermath of their experience with an armed group.

MOTHERING IN THE CONTEXT OF ISOLATION AND INSECURITY: IMPLICATIONS FOR POLICY AND PRACTICE

Understanding the experiences of former child soldiers requires a multifaceted lens that acknowledges not only the presence of girls in armed groups, but of the many roles and categories of girls that exist. In this case, we have examined the presence of girl mothers in a demobilized context. The shared stories of these young women help to widen our collective understanding of the realities of mothering in the context of isolation and insecurity, reminding us that for many ex-combatants, the impact of participating with an armed group extends far beyond the reach and scope of current DDR programming and support. From the bravely told narratives of our participants it is clear that ex-combatant mothers experience multiple and intersecting levels of vulnerability, which act as barriers to meaningful reintegration. Separation from family, stigmatization and social exclusion, economic insecurity, and the psychological impact of armed conflict represent some of the key challenges facing young mothers in the aftermath of hostilities. Unlike other young mothers in Colombia, these women begin motherhood at a disadvantage, often lacking support and under the constant threat of violence.

Despite incredible obstacles and adversity, these women continue to demonstrate a tremendous amount of courage, strength, and above all, love for their children. Without adequate resources or support, these women go to great lengths to ensure that their children are given the best possible life. Most women expressed concern and fear that their child would live to endure the pain and suffering that they did and vowed to do everything they could do lead them down a different path. The actions they took, some with tragic consequences, were in the name of love for their children as they are indeed the source of their strength, purpose, and joy.

The issue of demobilized motherhood needs to be a more thoughtful consideration within the context of DDR programming and support. Without ignoring the significant progress that has already been made in gendered support, much more work is needed. Greater attention needs to be paid to ensure that ex-combatant mothers are properly supported in caring for their children. For the most part, they are alone, and while their love for their children is undeniable, additional support would help them provide better protection and security for their children to ensure their healthy development. As a global community, we have a responsibility to these women, who were just children themselves when they were swept up into armed conflict. Their rights were violated, whether they were forcibly recruited or made a decision to join, and they deserve to be supported as they attempt to make a new life themselves and their children.

DDR policies and programs need to evolve with a clearer understanding of the scope of post-demobilization life and its challenges. Programs and services need to be implemented to respond to the multifaceted needs that ex-combatant mothers uniquely face. In particular, having access to additional funding to help provide for their children and gaining assistance with childcare would be important. These women may also benefit from peer support groups in order to help break the social isolation that accompanies post-demobilization life. A key building block of future programs and services tailored to the needs of these women should be the recognition of their resilience and the qualities that make them strong. These girls and young women need to be directly included in program development. The participants in our study demonstrated ambition, courage, motherly devotion, and an ability to make the best of their situation. Ex-combatant mothers should be approached from this viewpoint, and not understood only for their vulnerabilities. Successful policies and programs around this group will work with their strengths and harness their potential.

> How does it affect me now? I think everything in life teaches you, in a more personal way, in a profound way, a lesson. Everything that I have learned there I will not repeat. I can choose because I know how to, it was a personal growth, a learning process. I think that it has been a unique experience. (Ana)

The long-term effects of mothering in isolation and insecurity, for both mother and child, remain poorly understood. Further research is needed in order to help clarify the nature of the experience, not only in Colombia, but also in situations of armed conflict around the world. The stories of these women help to capture a snapshot of the issue, but more in depth exploration is indeed needed.

WORKS CITED

Ana. Personal Interview. Colombia, February 2011.

Bjørkhaug, Ingunn. "Child Soldiers in Colombia: The Recruitment of Children into Non-state Violent Armed Groups." MICROCON Research Working Paper 27, Brighton: MICROCON. 2010. Print.

Burgess, Ryan. "Colombia's Children at Risk of Recruitment into Armed Groups: Exploring a Community-based Psychosocial Pedagogy." *Journal of Education for International Development* 4 (2009): 1-11. Print.

Cortes, Liliana. and Marla Jean Buchanan. "The Experience of Colombian Child Soldiers From a Resilience Perspective." *International Journal of Advanced Counselling* 29 (2007): 43-55. Print.

Denov, Myriam. *Child Soldiers: Sierra Leone's Revolutionary United Front*. Cambridge: Cambridge University Press, 2010. Print.

Denov, Myriam. "Girls in Fighting Forces: Moving Beyond Victimhood." Report Prepared for the Government of Canada through the Canadian International Development Agency 2007. Print.

Denov, Myriam and I. Marchand. "'One Cannot Take Away the Stain': Rejection and Stigma Among Former Child Soldiers in Colombia." *Peace and Conflict: Journal of Peace Psychology* 20. 3 (2014): 227–240. Print.

Denov, Myriam and A. Ricard-Guay. "Girl Soldiers: Towards a Gendered Understanding of Wartime Recruitment, Participation and Demobilization". *Gender and Development* 21.3 (2003): 473-488. Print.

Devakumar, Delan, Marion Birch, David Osrin, Egbert Sondorp, Jonathan CK Wells. "The Intergenerational Effects of War on the Health of Children." *BMC Medicine* 12.57 (2014): 1-15. Print.

Emilia. Personal Interview. Colombia, February 2011.

Giraldo, Viviana Patricia Montoya. *Former Girl Soldiers in Colombia: Young Voices That Need to be Heard*. Diss. Dalhousie University, 2014. Print. .

Helmus, Todd C. and Russell W. Glenn. "Steeling the Mind: Combat Stress Reactions and Their Implications for Urban Warfare." Santa Monica, CA: Rand Arroyo Centre, 2004. Print.

Human Rights Watch. "'You'll Learn Not to Cry': Child Combatants in Colombia." *Human Rights Watch*. 1564322882. 18

September 2003. Web. 1 April 2014.

Jaramillo, Sergio, Yaneth Giha, and Paula Torres. *International Center for Transitional Justice, Transitional justice and DDR: The case of Colombia.* New York: Research Unit International Centre for Transitional Justice, 2009. Print.

McConnan, Isobel and Susan Uppard. "Children, Not Soldiers: Guidelines for Working with Child Soldiers and Children Associated with Fighting Forces." Save the Children, 2001. Web.

McKay, Susan and Dyan Mazurana. "Where are the Girls? Girls Fighting Forces Northern Uganda, Sierra Leone and Mozambique, Their Lives after The War." Canada. International Center for Human Rights and Democratic Development, 2004. Print.

Paola. Personal Interview. Colombia, February 2011.

Rafaella. Personal Interview. Colombia, February 2011. Ruiz Serna, Daniel and Inez Marchand. "Agape: A Reconcilation Initiative by Members of Civil Society and Former Child Soldiers." *Intervention* 9.1 (2011): 35-43. Print.

Theidon, Kimberly. "Transitional Subjects: The Disarmament, Demobilization and Reintegration of Former Combatants in Colombia." *The International Journal of Transitional Justice* 1(2007): 66–90. Print.

Thomas, Virginia. *Overcoming Lost Childhoods Lessons Learned from the Rehabilitation and Reintegration of Former Child Soldiers in Colombia.* London: Y Care International, 2008. Print

United Nations. "Report of the Secretary-General on Children and Armed Conflict in Colombia." New York. 2012. SC S2012/171. Print. Web. 3 March 2014.

United Nations Inter-Agency Working Group on Disarmament, Demobilization and Reintegration. "Blame It On the War? The Gender Dimensions of Violence in Disarmament, Demobilization and Reintegration: Report and Recommendations for Action." 2012. Web. 10 March 2014.

Villanueva O'Driscoll Julia, Gerrit Loots, Ilse Derluyn. *Children disengaged from armed groups in Colombia: Integration Processes in Context.* London: Versita, 2013. Print.

Violeta. Personal Interview. Colombia, February 2011.

Watchlist. *Colombia's War on Children.* February 2004. Web. 1 March 2014.

Watchlist. *No One to Trust: Children and Armed Conflict in Colombia. Field Monitors Report.* 2012-2015. Web. 13 April, 2015.

Worthen, Miranda, Susan McKay, Angela Veale and Mike Wessells. "Reintegration of Young Mothers." *Forced Migration Review.* Refugee Studies Centre, University of Oxford. 2012. Print.

5.
Maternal Pedagogies in
Swat Valley, Pakistan

Mothers' Perspectives on Faith, *Jihad* and Peace

LUBNA N. CHAUDHRY

THE YOUNG PEOPLE MOVED GENTLY, their arms held in graceful arcs in rhythm with their feet. A few of them danced close to each other but the rest were scattered around the courtyard. The music blared from two large speakers, but the women sitting on the cots in the verandah continued to chat with each other, eating dry fruit, and occasionally clapping in sync with the dancers. "We are celebrating the New Year, my brother's daughter's wedding, and coming back to our homes after six months," one woman told me as she made space for me to sit down. It was December 31, 2009, my first evening in Swat as an ethnographer, and my hostess had brought me to her friend's house to witness the wedding festivities.

The song finished and there was a round of applause for the dancers. Some dancers remained in the courtyard dancing to the new song, while others returned to the veranda. One of the girls who had been dancing sat on the cot next to me. I smiled at her and complimented her on her dancing. To my horror, she started crying. Amidst her tears she murmured:

> I did not want to dance, but my mother sat me down and explained to me the importance of moving to the music. I was very close to my uncle—he was both my mother's and father's cousin. We found his body with his identity card on top of his severed head. The Taliban slaughtered him. How can one dance when one's heart is so full of sorrow? My mother told me that's the best time to dance. We have to be grateful that we came home after long months in

Peshawar. We have to be grateful we are seeing a happy occasion again. Life is pain, life is happiness. Dancing helps us see that.

Her mother came over to us, laughingly chastising her daughter for being too sensitive, even as she pulled her into a warm embrace.

The objective of this chapter is to analyze the role of mothers in guiding their children, sons, and daughters of all ages in the context of the armed conflict and reconstruction phase in Swat Valley, Pakistan. From 2007-2009 the Swat Valley, a lush district in Northwestern Pakistan, with a population of around two million, was under the control of the Pakistani Taliban, who had begun to create a base for themselves from 2003 onwards (Akhtar). During this period, the Taliban presence elicited resistance from some local leaders and intermittent retaliation from Pakistan armed forces, but a significant number of Swatis also supported the Taliban and their reign of terror (Akhtar). In the spring and summer of 2009, after evacuating the Swatis, the Pakistan military launched a massive operation disabling and dispersing the Taliban (Chaudhry).

Drawing on ethnographic data collected from 2009 to 2012, I delineate how mothers expressed their views, with the intent to teach and advise, on a range of topics. More specifically, I focus on what mothers had to say about faith, *jihad* (which is an Arabic word that translates to "struggle"), and peace through interviews with twenty-five women between the ages of thirty and sixty, and their twenty-five daughters and sons aged fifteen to forty-five. This exploration of "maternal pedagogies" (Byrd and Green) blurs the theoretical distinction between motherhood and mothering on the one hand and education and teaching on the other. Watt draws a parallel between motherhood and education systems as patriarchal and controlling, with the potential to be oppressive, and mothering and teaching as "practitioner-defined and potentially empowering" (56). While in the Swat context maternal pedagogies remained influenced by motherhood and patriarchal systems of education, they simultaneously reflected mothers' efforts at enacting transformative praxis based on visions of alternative societal possibilities. Both women who aligned themselves with the Taliban and those who opposed them generally promoted worldviews anchored in Islam

99

and tried to channel their children in directions they saw as "potentially empowering" within the particular set of options available to them. I attempt to read mother's pedagogies and perspectives from within the specificity of their epistemologies as Muslim women located in particular temporal and spatial backgrounds as well as participants in a conflict where their contribution cannot be cast as exceptional or marginal.

Maternal pedagogies in the Swat context of conflict remained circumscribed by power relations: as mothers disseminated knowledge to guide their children they at times resisted relations of domination and subjugation, while at other points they complied with them. In some instances, given that power relations are multi-layered and contradictory, there was both resistance and co-operation. I have tried to refrain from positioning women as either dupes in patriarchal relations or as above such relations, choosing instead to use their words to meticulously map their shifting subjectivities and their rejection or acceptance of prevailing choices. In such an analysis, class, ethnicity, and age as axes of power and difference emerge as salient in shaping the distinctive contours of maternal pedagogies.

While Swat is a patriarchal society, with quite rigid demarcations of duties, entitlements, and spaces, mothers are highly revered. Mothers of all class and ethnic backgrounds have a strong influence in molding behaviours and options in life, including careers. A good number of fathers spend years at a time working internationally, mostly in Saudi Arabia and the Gulf states; this absence of fathers means that bonds with mothers are even stronger. Mothers figured prominently in peoples' reflections about the choices they made with respect to their relationships with the Taliban, their roles in the armed conflict, and their paths to healing after the armed conflict ended. Both interviews with mothers and interviews that discussed mothers put forth a conception of mothering that transcended customary perspectives on maternal care in Swati and Pakistani society: Swati mothers were lifelong guides whose interventions into their children's lives were not contained by the boundaries that demarcated the purview of most women. While most Swati mothers I met had little or no formal education, the scope of their maternal pedagogies encompassed the myriad dimensions of their children's lifeworlds, and their children had especially begun to appreciate these pedagogies during the course of the turbulence in Swat.

HISTORICAL SNAPSHOT

Swat was an independent state before 1969 when it became part of Pakistan. Yusufzai Pathans (also known as Pashtuns), who came from Afghanistan in the sixteenth century and occupied Swat, are the majority population and represent the most powerful segment of Swat society (Chaudhry). Other communities referred to generally as the artisan communities are in the minority, both numerically and in the sense of power relations (Chaudhry).

The local leader for the Taliban in Swat, Fazlullah, was a charismatic Yusufzai Pashtun who managed to establish the foundations for the Taliban rule both through his connections with his own clan and through an appeal to the sense of disenfranchisement faced by non-Pashtuns in Swat (Chaudhry). Between 2004 and 2006, Fazlullah and his colleagues used face-to-face instruction and several illegal FM channels to spread their word (Akhtar). In these broadcasts Fazlullah used a vernacular that was favoured by women and interspersed Islamic injunctions with recipes and other tips for the running of the household.

As the Pakistani Taliban began to control Swati institutions, challenging the writ of the state and setting up parallel structures to govern the area, the violence they deployed became intensified (Zalman). For instance, between 2007 and 2009, most girls' schools and women's colleges in Swat were destroyed (Zalman). The military managed to dislodge the Taliban from Swat in the summer of 2009. Since then the Pakistan army has continued its visible presence in Swat.

METHOD

The larger ethnographic study from which the present project evolved concentrated on peoples' constructions and experiences of the armed conflict in Swat. The 25 women I chose to interview as mothers were identified through the interviews with their sons and daughters for the larger study. Of the 25 mothers I interviewed, five came from affluent Pashtun families, six from middle income Pashtun families, seven from working class or relatively poor Pashtun families, two from middle income artisan families, and five from poor artisan families. Seven mothers were between the ages of 30 and 40; nine mothers were between 41 and 50; and nine mothers were between 51 and 60. All the mothers had been married: at the time of data collection three of the women were widows.

MATERNAL PEDAGOGIES/MOTHERS' PERSPECTIVES

On Faith

All the mothers I interviewed, with the exception of one upper class Pashtun woman and one poor artisan woman, identified as staunch Muslims who had raised their children as good Muslims. Faiqa Begum,[1] a woman in her early fifties who runs her own business, stated that she was far too interested in fashion to be ever a good Muslim, and she had tried to raise her children to be independent of religious doctrine as well since she thought religion was a limiting force. Jannat, a poor artisan woman, said that she had been too busy all her life just trying to get two meals a day: "Religion was a luxury I couldn't afford." For all the other mothers religion was a strong force in their lives, although they differed in the nuances of what they saw as religious practice and beliefs, differences that got translated into varied messages to their sons and daughters.

Nine women, three from wealthy Pashtun families, four from middle class Pashtun families, and the two from middle income artisan families, did not believe that their relationship with God should be mediated by a third party. Interestingly, these women were all above forty-five years of age. They all felt that *mullahs*, Muslim religious leaders, had too much power in Swat society and this power had been used to delude and exploit the common people. These women were therefore skeptical of the Taliban project in Swat right from its inception.

"If your faith is strong you can obtain guidance from the Koran and the elders in your own family is what I told my children and daughters-in-law. The FM radio was forbidden in my household.

"I told my sons not to interact with Fazlullah," said Jamilah, a woman from a middle class Pashtun family. Sardar Begum, another woman from a middle-class Pashtun family said:

> *I told my children, how can Fazlullah teach us anything about Islam? He is just a chair-lift operator wearing lots of gemstone rings who used to be on drugs when he was younger. I did not listen to the FM channel and advised my children to do the same. I told my sons not to go to his madrassah.*

Shabnam, a woman from a middle income artisan family said:

> *Right from when they are young I have taught my children the difference between the words of God and the interpretations that other people have of what God says. I have no education, but God gave me a mind, and I could tell the Taliban were cheaters and trouble-makers. So many boys from our communities wanted to be part of the Taliban. I had to work hard on my sons. Every day I talked to them, made sure they were safe from the Taliban web.*

Most children chose to follow their mothers' advice and example when it came to the Taliban's teachings. Shabnam's nineteen-year-old son, for example, said to me, "Many of my friends would go listen to the Taliban. They said they were becoming good Muslims. I told them I already was a good Muslim, and needed no further teachings than those I received at home" (Rubab Ahmad). Other sons and daughters also revealed how they learned to be critical of the Taliban from their mothers even before the Taliban rule in Swat. Naghmana, a 25-year-old woman who came from an affluent Pashtun family, said:

> *I kept a distance from the Taliban activities: the FM channel, the discussions, everything, but like my mother I observed it all carefully and saw how people were being manipulated. My mother said women were made to compete with each other to see how much they could give, as if that could*

*determine how good a Muslim they were. My mother
said only those who were not good Muslims had to prove
something, and I saw that what she said was true.*

A few of the children, however, also rebelled at least during the
earlier part of the Taliban's time in Swat, before the violence escalated and became particularly gruesome. As Shakeela, Sardar
Begum's forty-year-old daughter shared with me:

*I thought for once that my mother was wrong. Fazlullah
must have had some magic. I gave a gold ring to Fazlullah's
cause, which at that time was just the building of a madrassah. My mother quarreled with me and told me that instead
of giving funds to mosques it would please God more if
I bought something one of my children needed. And then
those government officers started to be killed. They were
not American agents, but the Taliban slaughtered them.
My mother turned out to be right after all.*

For these nine women it was quite clear that class intersected
with age to create particular subject positions. In general people from upper and middle class backgrounds in Swat tended
to view the power of clerics with disfavour, perhaps because
this power undercut their own power. This was especially true
of people from Pashtun backgrounds who tended to have more
control over non-Pashtun bodies: the resistance towards the
Taliban exhibited by these upper and middle class women, to a
certain extent conceivably signified an acceptance of historical
hierarchies in Swat society. Furthermore, women from upper
income and middle income families were more likely to have
received a thorough religious education when they were growing
up as opposed to those from poorer backgrounds who were put
to work when they were quite little. Poorer families also could
not afford the fee or gifts needed to contract teachers for their
daughters. People in Swat also shared that religious education
used to be more comprehensive and sound before Swat became
part of Pakistan. Possibly these factors enabled older mothers
from wealthier families to be confident challengers of Fazlullah's

words and positions. From 2007-2009, some of these women and their families received death threats because they did not support Taliban policies: Sardar Begum's son, for instance, had a job in a non-government organization (NGO) and was issued a death threat for working in a "Western outfit." Sardar Begum merely advised her son to continue his work, saying that their faith in God would protect them.

The other group of 14 women, one from an upper class Pashtun family, two from middle class Pashtun families, and the rest from poor Pashtun and artisan families, were of the view that the public face of religion was important. For them religious leaders had the potential to steer people on the right path. As one woman, Jahaan Paas, a 45-year-old woman from a poor artisan family put it, "We don't have the time to study religion closely. When someone who knows more is trying to teach you, I told my children they have to be grateful. Fazlullah taught us through the radio and that made it easier to listen to him as we went doing our daily work. I wanted my son and daughters to learn more about Islam. God had sent us the way." Fareeda, a 30-year-old woman from an upper class Pashtun background said, "I thought the Taliban were re-creating the earlier years of Islam when people were devout followers and there was no crime. My children were quite young then, but I send my two boys to Fazlullah's *madrassah* to learn even when it was still under construction."

These mothers encouraged their sons and daughters to benefit from Taliban teachings, even when their husbands and other family members did not support this. Except for Fareeda, none of them thought they had received adequate religious education themselves: some of them confessed that their religious practice was inconsistent in that they did not pray five times a day before Fazlullah's influence. While some like Fareeda saw the Taliban as the harbingers of a true Islam, thus romanticizing the Taliban project, others took a more realist approach to the situation. Shahnaz, a 50-year-old woman from a poor Pashtun family said:

I told my children that in order to practice Islam well we need to follow some guide. Fazlullah and his colleagues seemed to have the best resources of all the mullahs. They had good madrassahs, FM channels that taught useful things, and they might train one of my sons to be a mullah. Mullahs make a good living and they are good Muslims as well.

A number of women also praised the Taliban for their attempt to give women a more important role in religion and everyday religious practices. Thirty-eight-year-old Laiq Begum who belonged to a middle income Pashtun family said:

I was overjoyed that someone was recognizing women's place in Islam. When Fazlullah said it was our duty as mothers, wives, and daughters to get our men to the mosque, he gave us rights no one gives us in Swat society. I told my daughters to learn about the respect that Islam gives us women. Yes, we should cover ourselves up, wear a burka, *but in our homes we have a lot of authority that was acknowledged because of Fazlullah's teachings.*

Noorana, a woman in her mid-40s from a poor artisan family complicated Laiq Begum's analysis further by adding a classed element to her interpretation. "My daughters and I have never had the time to learn about religion. No one teaches poor women about their faith. I did pray sometimes, but I was always calling on God. Because of Fazlullah poor women like my daughters and I got to know something about our place in Islam."

Within the ideational context of the Swat scenario where religion is seen as a strong foundational block of society (Akhtar), the Taliban's teachings and discussion on faith-related issues resonated strongly with these fourteen mothers. Some went so far as to say that Fazlullah and his colleagues provided a strong complement to their mothering: the Taliban were quite nurturing in their early interactions with communities in Swat. As the Taliban's project unfolded through the years, some of these women did lose their trust in them, but as I show in the next section there were others who continued to support the Taliban especially through their maternal pedagogies.

On Jihad

Fazlullah and his associates began talking about the urgency of *jihad* to set up an Islamic order in Swat in late 2006 and early 2007. Naila Begum explained to me:

> *I used to listen to Fazlullah's radio regularly. He talked about issues in religion and the sayings of the Holy Prophet. I thought this education on religion was useful till he started to categorize people as either* mujahidin *[literally meaning ones who struggle]* or *non-*mujahadin. *These two groups then started to fight with each other. I could tell Fazlullah was instigating the conflict. He was trying to create an army of mujahidin for himself. That is when I backed off from the Taliban and persuaded my children to do the same.*

Shahnaz expressed similar sentiments:

> *I wanted my son to get religious training and grow up to work in a peaceful Swat. The talk of* jihad *was frightening. At first my son got carried away by the excitement of getting a chance to be part of the* mujahideen. *But, God be thanked, I calmed him down and he listened to me and dissociated himself from the Taliban. I had to be very vigilant and keep and eye on him and talk to him regularly. But he remained safe.*

Fareeda was more understanding about the need for *jihad*; what she could not understand was why *jihad* included destroying girls' schools and stopping children from taking the polio vaccine:

> *My children were confused when I told them they would no longer go to the* madrassah. *My older son who was twelve needed a lot of explanation for why I did not like Fazlullah anymore. It was quite difficult to relate why my perspectives had changed and why he [the son] should not think of Fazlullah as a proper guide anymore. My son's father did not help me with this task because he had not trusted Fazlullah all along.*

Of the fourteen women who initially appreciated the teachings of Fazlullah and his colleagues, only seven, all from poor backgrounds, continued to support the Taliban once their *jihadi* intentions became clear. All seven women convinced their children to join the Taliban in different capacities.

Rehana Begum, from an artisan family, told me that she supported the Taliban because the Taliban supported class struggle in Swat. For her, the *jihad* was for her family's rights:

> *I have had a hard life. My two sons did not do well at school, so they had to go into wage labor as small boys. I just work, work, and work. My children and I talked about the pros and cons of joining the Taliban. I decided that they were not to be part of any direct violence, but it was to our advantage as a family if they worked for the Taliban.*

Rehana's older son worked as a driver for the Taliban, and the younger one carried a gun for them for 50 rupees a day.

The other six women engaged in similar deliberations with their children, especially their sons. Noorana's son was only fifteen when it was decided that he would join the Taliban as a combatant. "We spent a good many hours for a few days talking about the issue. My heart was heavy because I was exposing my son to danger, and my daughter was quite upset about it. But I made it clear to my children that if we wanted to participate in true *jihad* we cannot play safe. There was no point if we were not going to fight for religion to exist in its true form." Noorana's 19-year-old daughter said, "I was very confused but I stopped disagreeing with my mother. She has always looked after us" (Shaheena).

While Rehana mostly believed in the *jihad* for her personal upliftment and Noorana claimed that she was motivated by religious fervour, the other five Taliban supporters said that for them their support of the Taliban *jihad* was a result of both a desire for the redistribution of wealth and the hope that an Islamic state could be formed in Swat. Shandana, a 36-year-old mother from a poor Pashtun family said:

I gave the Taliban all my savings, but mostly I gave them my most precious item, my 20-year-old son. I wanted the richer Khans to be challenged. They rule the poor as if they are animals. I wanted a rule in Swat that was based on Islamic equality. I made it clear to my son that he had to fight for Islamic values. I reminded him of the verses in the Koran that he needed to recite every day during the jihad. *If other mothers had done their job and taught their sons well, the movement would have succeeded.*

The two mothers who did not believe in religion and the nine mothers who had chosen to resist the Taliban continued to work with their children when the Taliban were soliciting, and even coercing, people into their *jihad*. Shahzia, a woman from a middle class Pashtun family told me how her son became attracted to the guns and almost became a Taliban combatant:

His father, his uncle, his grandfather all tried to talk to him, but he lectured them about Islam. He was only eighteen but he spoke so well that he embarrassed them. Pashtuns are such fools when it comes to Islam. He finally came to me. I locked the door. We talked all night. My tears did not convince him, but my words did. I showed him the weakness of the Taliban jihad, *how it was based on violence and their self-gain. The next day we had to arrange to take him out of the country because the Taliban would have killed him for defecting. He only came back after the army liberated Swat.*

I interviewed Shahzia's son Ahmad, who said that he was indeed fascinated by the idea of becoming a hero in the Taliban army. "My mother's teachings that night before I left saved my life. Her arguments were very strong, stronger than any of the men's. She should be a General in the Pakistan Army. She would be very successful."

Other children of the women who resisted the Taliban also spoke of their mother's superior intellect and analysis. While most of these mothers felt a politics of non-interference was the best modus operandi, three mothers, one from an upper class Pashtun family, and two from middle-income Pashtun families, did espouse a message of counter-*jihad*. "My mother said that *jihad* was actually fighting back the Taliban. While I did not pick up a gun, I did work with the army to point out Taliban allies and hide-outs," said 36-year-old Alam Din. Shahbano's family, however, did engage in *jihad* against the Taliban by using guns provided by the Pakistan army: at that point in 2007-2008 part of the military strategy was to create armed militia among civilians. Shahbano said she convinced her sons to volunteer for such a role. In a vein similar to other mothers, she thrashed out the issues with her sons in a conversation that lasted for hours. "She has always raised us to stand up for ourselves. She has also raised us as good Muslims and as patriotic Swatis. She said our way of life was endangered if we did not take up arms. The men in our extended family discussed the issue but I did not choose any sides before my consultation with my mother," said 28-year-old Nawaz Shah.

On Peace

The interviewees were asked to respond on what they considered "peace" and how mothers transmitted knowledge pertaining to peace to their children. The research participants utilized a broad and complex definition of peace as both *aman* (which means absence or cessation of conflict) and *sukoon* (which refers to peacefulness and peace of mind). Talib Ali, a 45-year-old man shared:

> When I came back to Swat, I was full of rage. I wanted revenge from those who had terrorized us. I knew some people who had worked with the Taliban as spies but received no punishment. I wanted to destroy them. My mother sat with me for hours every night explaining to me again and again why I had to be at peace with myself. I did not have to forget, just be at peace and trust God.

The majority of mothers and their children expressed the opinion that despite the cessation of armed hostilities and the dispersion of the Taliban from Swat the peace was fragile, perhaps even deceptive. According to Shahbano, whose family had participated in armed combat against the Taliban, antagonism between those who had actively supported the Taliban and those who had openly resisted them was very much alive:

> *I have told my children to be very careful. This peace is not real. Just a little while ago we used arms against our neighbors and they used arms against us. Yes, the military had armed us, and the Taliban had armed them, but we were the ones who picked up the weapons. It would be naïve of us to think that there is no anger in our hearts anymore. So I tell my children to tread lightly, to not to trust anyone yet, but wait for a while before being neighborly. Perhaps we can never be neighborly again, who knows?*

Some of the mothers, both those who had sided with the Taliban and those who had not, also spoke of the need for mediation. Sardar Begum, a Taliban opposer, said:

> *I have been suggesting to my children that we somehow need to have third-party mediation if we want enduring peace in Swat. I have especially been discussing the matter with my older son, who has been involved in the reconstruction of Swat after the conflict, that he bring it up with the authorities. There might be still be aggression in peoples' hearts and this needs to be brought out in the open.*

Noorana who had been pro-Taliban said something similar but from her positionality as a poor artisan woman:

> *Someone from the outside needs to intervene and bring lasting peace and forgiveness to people in Swat. At present, it is difficult to function in society. People know and remember whether you were part of the Taliban or not. This has implications for how they treat you and your children. If poor people like me and my children are to survive here*

we have to erase the past to bring in a new era.

The ongoing enmity among people has been especially difficult for poor Pashtuns and the artisan community since they rely on the middle class for sale of their goods and services. Mothers spoke of instructing their children in negotiating their way through persistent hostilities. Jannat, a poor artisan woman who had purposefully remained neutral through the conflict said:

> *My children complain that no one wants to work with them. Because of me, because I taught them not to take sides, the Taliban supporters and the anti-Taliban people stay away from them. I tell them not to worry and just work for the few who are willing to move on. Gradually, things have been changing, as people are learning to forget. I have also told my children to go outside into new areas for work. It will be difficult for a while but then they can come closer to home once time has healed more wounds.*

While seven mothers—one from an affluent Pashtun family, three from middle income Pashtun families, two from middle income artisan families, and one from a poor artisan family, felt that the army is required in Swat to ensure that the cease fire continues, the remainder felt that it was best if the army slowly reduced its numbers in the Valley. Interestingly, the first group consists entirely of mothers who were anti-Taliban, with the exception of Jannat who chose to remove herself from both parties in the conflict. The second group, on the other hand, was comprised of Taliban supporters, those who had initially supported the Taliban and changed their minds and also Taliban resisters.

The women who saw the military presence as a deterrent to armed conflict spoke of instructing their children to be respectful towards members of the army. "I tell my children that we need to treat the officers like our guests. They helped get rid of the Taliban. If they leave, the Taliban will come back," said Jamilah. "My children sometimes complain about the check-posts and body searches by the soldiers. I explain to them that these measures are for our own security. I ask them if they see any other choice. If we don't have the army, we will have the Taliban," said Jannat.

With respect to those that perceived the military presence as unnecessary, two themes emerged. First, they complained about the security measures taken by the military, seeing the body searches and identity card checks as humiliating. Military attitudes towards Swatis were seen as symbolic of the manner in which the rest of Pakistan viewed the tribal belt. "The soldiers from other parts of Pakistan treat us like animals, as if we were uncivilized and backward," said Jamilah. Far from creating peace, the military presence in Swat was seen as adding another layer to the conflict. "The military puts our children on edge. Our freedom has been compromised," said Sardar Begum. "We are afraid of both of them, the army and the Taliban. They both looted our homes. They both mistreat the weak," said Shahnaz. Second, the women believed that the presence of the army stifled opportunities for actual peace between the various factions in Swat. They felt that Swatis needed to take responsibility for bringing in lasting peace and the army by staying on in Swat increased tensions. Mothers from upper and middle class backgrounds focused more on the second theme, whereas mothers from the lower classes focused more on their fears of the army and the disrespect they and their children experienced at the hands of the soldiers. My participant observation backs up the poor mothers' claims that the soldiers handled those as perceived as poor more harshly.

Strategies shared by the women with their children in the face of the situation with the soldiers also have a classed dimension. The upper and middle class women did instruct their children to be tolerant of the army, but they also insisted that their children not accept any insults or humiliation. As Shahbano said, "I tell my sons to keep their heads cool, but if a soldier misbehaves take his name down and report him to his superior. We have had reports of soldiers hitting people. If we don't report misbehavior they will keep on getting away with it." Poor mothers spoke of feeling powerless in relation to the military. Shandana said, "The army can do anything. I instruct my children to keep their eyes lowered. Even if a soldier says something, just don't respond, and focus on getting away from them as soon as possible."

Meanwhile, Swatis continue to negotiate with the military to arrange for a timeline to leave Swat. Some of the mothers, again from upper and middle class backgrounds, spoke of how they communicated their input to the negotiators through their sons and husbands.

CONCLUSION

This chapter has mapped women's perspectives on faith, *jihad*, and peace, as well as their communiqués with their children on these matters in a manner that tries to transcend the binary between dominant systems of meaning and systems of meaning that challenge relations of domination. Women's power to influence their children stemmed, to a large degree, from the power ascribed to motherhood and mothering within Swati society, but the manner in which women used the specific nuances of their roles to teach their children remained contingent on their intersectional subjectivities and individual histories. Building on Mahmood's (112) definition of agency as "a capacity for action that historically specific relations of subordination enable and create," I seek to analyze mothers' choices and strategies at different points in the armed conflict to share the diversity and complexity of maternal pedagogies. While women remained motivated by what they saw as the well-being of their families and children, their constructions of well-being, which in some instances was linked to violence, does bring us face to face with the uncomfortable reality of mothers' complicity with war-mongering agendas. On the other hand, the chapter does not want to discount the allure of a utopian yet patriarchal Islam for most of the mothers I talked to, whether they linked that utopia to the Taliban or not. What is key is to understand the genesis of mothers' desires, to locate mothers' desires and the transmission of desires to their children as the conflict unfolded within the particularity of their gender, class, ethnicity, and religious realities, and ultimately to recognize these desires as generative of particular situations and circumstances within the Swat conflict and its aftermath.

[1]The names of research participants have been changed to protect their confidentiality

WORK CITED

Ahmad. Personal interview. 7 November 2012.

Ahmad, Rubab. Personal interview. 22 November 2012.

Akhtar, Aasim Sajjad. "Islam as Ideology of Tradition and Change: The 'New Jihad' in Swat, Northern Pakistan." *Comparative Studies of South Asia, Africa, and the Middle East* 30.3 (2010): 595-609. Print.

Ali, Talib. Personal interview. 6 July 2010.

Begum, Faiqa. Personal interview. 9 November 2012.

Begum, Laiq. Personal interview. 8 November 2012.

Begum, Rehana. Personal interview. 1 November 2012.

Begum, Sardar. Personal interview. 16 November 2012.

Byrd, Deborah Leah, and Fiona Joy Green. "Introduction: Maternal Pedagogies: In and Outside the Classroom." *Maternal Pedagogies: In and Outside the Classroom.* Eds. Deborah Leah Byrd and Fiona Jay Green. Bradford: Demeter Press, 2011. 1-20. Print.

Chaudhry, Lubna N. "Researching the War on Terror in Swat Valley, Pakistan: Grapplings with the Impact on Communities and the Transnational Knowledge Industry." *Social Issues* 69.4 (2013): 713-733. Print.

Din, Alam. Personal interview. 5 January 2011.

Fareeda. Personal interview. 10 November 2012.

Jamilah. Personal interview. 20 November 2012.

Jannat. Personal interview. 17 November 2012.

Mahmood, Saba. "Feminist Theory, Agency, and the Liberatory Subject." *On Shifting Ground: Muslim Women in the Global Era.* Ed. Fereshteh Nouraie-Simone. New York: The Feminist Press at the City University of New York, 2005. 111-152. Print.

Naghmana. Personal interview. 3 January 2011.

Noorana. Personal interview. 5 November 2012.

Paas, Jahaan. Personal interview. 11 November 2011.

Shabnam. Personal interview. 22 November 2012.

Shah, Nawaz. Personal interview. 14 July 2010.

Shahbano. Personal interview. 15 November 2012.

Shaheena. Personal interview. 28 December 2011.

Shahnaz. Personal interview. 7 November 2012.

Shahzia. Personal interview. 2 November 2012.

Shaista. Personal interview. 11 November 2012.

Shakeela. Personal interview. 16 November 2012.

Shandana. Personal interview. 4 November 2012.

Watt, Jennifer. "Re-Searching Mommy: Narrating my Inquiry of Maternal Pedagogies." *Maternal Pedagogies: In and Outside the Classroom*. Eds. Deborah Leah Byrd and Fiona Jay Green. Bradford: Demeter Press, 2011. 53-65. Print.

Zalman, Amy. "Terrorism Timeline: Pakistan and the Global War on Terror." *about.com* n.d. Web. 8 Sept. 2013.

6.
Mother'hood

Mothering Amidst Gang Warfare

LILIANA CASTAÑEDA ROSSMANN

THIS CHAPTER EXAMINES THE INTERSECTION between gang membership and motherhood in a large metropolitan area in western United States. In analyzing interview data, I argue that being a gang-impacted mother is similar to being a "mother under fire." Thus, I offer the term "mother'hood" (Rossmann) as encompassing a number of painful and debilitating patterns that such a mother experiences, and the ways in which she can envision a future beyond the gang. Mothers in gangs experience violence in particularly troublesome ways due to the disadvantages they face— being unskilled, uneducated, under-age, and oftentimes having extremely low socio-economic status or/and being undocumented. Additionally, these mothers not only face violence and aggression from rival gang members, as well as oppression by police and the criminal justice system, they also encounter violence or oppression in their homes (Hunt and Joe-Laidler). Girls' reasons for joining gangs include experiencing domestic violence and suffering sexual abuse (Moore and Hagedorn). Because the perpetrators of these types of violence also include fathers, step-fathers, or uncles, gang violence, like violence in conventional warfare, is gendered (Joe-Laidler and Hunt). I utilize the notion of "Gang Wars" to describe this particular type of violence (Mydans; Morales; Greene and Pranis; de Córdoba).

GANG WARS

Barrett describes gang activity as urban warfare and Hayden refers

117

to it as "street wars." Here, I am using "war" as a metaphor for situations of extreme violence encountered by gang-impacted and gang-involved mothers. As Shaw shows, "gang girls often describe themselves as fighters"; she conceptualizes them as

> …warriors, attempting to defend themselves, their families, their homegirls and homeboys, their neighborhoods, their small plot of turf against structural oppression and exploitation. Gang girls learn to approach life in the warrior mode, always prepared for a battle, always ready for a fight. Living in warrior mode is how they have constructed their survival femininity. (223-4)

Specifically, in such violent circumstances, where endemic and pervasive attacks on their minds and bodies are the norm, the "enemy" is not just the members of rival gangs. The enemy is in their neighbourhoods that present them with multiple marginalities (Vigil). The enemy is their sexual partner and father of their child(ren), for these relationships often include an element of violence (Dietrich; Fleisher; Valdez). The enemy is their own peers, sisters in mother'hood, for these women often see each other as competition as they vie for the attention of the men in the gang—often the same men who mistreat them (Miller; Molidor). The enemy is their own families, as they chastise these young women for their early pregnancies and unmarried status (Whitehead; Wiemann et al.). The enemy is law enforcement personnel, even when police may try to enforce domestic partner violence ordinances and other laws that might benefit the women but would land their men in prison (Fleisher). The enemy is school personnel who, already overworked and underpaid, lack the capacity to address so many young individuals whose academic skills are challenged by dangerous living conditions and who, thus, end up reproducing hegemonic masculinity (Shaw). The enemy is themselves, for they often must battle addiction while pregnant (Moore and Devitt). The enemy is the child, for s/he limits the mother's ability to maintain her status in the gang on the one hand, while forcing her to opt out of legitimate activities, such as getting a job or attending school, on the other (Varriale). While some women may see being pregnant and having children as a practical way to exit the gang, they face more threats to surviving gang warfare (Cepeda and Valdez).

Indulging in creative punctuation and alternative spelling, I am offering the term "mother'hood" to signify the storying process that these women engage in relating to their pregnancies, childbirth, and childrearing. Although they may see themselves as warriors, these women invariably tell parallel stories about treasuring their children, supporting the notion that many women in gangs hold traditional beliefs about parenting (Campbell; Valdez). Their stories are not unusual, for as Moore and Hagedorn have observed, "regardless of the cultural context, there is one constant in the later life of most female gang members: most have children" (200). I will elaborate below how "mother'hood" signifies a particular kind of experience for mothers in the context of gang warfare.

The current chapter draws from an earlier work (Rossmann) that described how Latinas used storytelling as a way to transcend gangs; that is, to leave the gang habits because and despite of their previous experiences. The data are drawn from qualitative interviews with women who were either gang-involved (they were active in the gang) or gang-impacted (the fathers of their children were gang-involved; they lived in a neighbourhood where there was gang presence; or both). Where the interviews were conducted, warfare involves a number of 'hoods or *barrios* (often spelled by them as *varrios*) belonging to two major gangs: Norteños and Sureños. Three women's stories fit the warrior mentality of mothers under fire: they had children while still involved/impacted by the gang. Gracia became a mother at fifteen and Florencia at fourteen, both while still involved, and neither left the gang until they were in their twenties. Both women temporarily lost custody of their children—Gracia while in prison and Florencia due to her drug addiction. The third story by Serenity illustrates the nature of violence for mothers in gang warfare from their sexual partners.

The theoretical framework that informs this analysis owes a great deal to the Social Construction paradigm (Berger and Luckman; Pearce and Cronen), to transcendent storytelling and transcendent communication (Pearce and Pearce; Littlejohn), and to the feminist poet Adrienne Rich, who wrote that "... in all cultures, it is from women that both women and men have learned about caresses, about affectionate play, about the comfort of a need satisfied—and also about the anxiety and wretchedness of a need deferred" (126). Mother'hood then encompasses the deferred need to engage in self-identity while tending to the need to survive gang warfare. Ultimately, I agree with Geertz that "it is explication I am after, construing social expressions [that are] on their surface enigmatical" (5).

I aim to introduce another key word in this study: *storying*. By taking "story" and converting it into a verb, I hope to denote the active signifying performed through the linguistic process of creating one's image to oneself and to the world. Therefore, I propose that *storying* used as a verb highlights its ongoing nature. My concept of an individual's choice to "story" one's identity resonates with theories of identity formation, such as Erikson's theory of psychosocial development, as he addresses the emergence from role confusion into ego identity: "We can study the identity crisis [...] in the lives of creative individual who could resolve it for themselves only by offering to their contemporaries a new model of resolution such as that expressed in works of art, or in original deeds, and who furthermore are eager to tell us all about it in diaries, letters, and self-representations" (134). Specifically, there are similarities with the continuum between ego identity and role confusion that occur during adolescence and my notion of transcendence. As individuals visualize their purpose or role in society, they story their role confusion into ego identity. The stories presented in this chapter emerge from remnants of the stories lived before. These women take stories previously untold, unknown, unheard, unimagined, and unthinkable and release them in hopes of transforming their mother'hood identity in the context of gang warfare.

Although mother'hood presents challenges to a woman's level of gang involvement, for these gang warriors, mother'hood functions as a harbinger of their descent into gang obscurity. Mother'hood also can improve the life of a gang-involved woman (Fleisher and Krienert) by re-storying her identity out of gang warfare and into a new, less risky, and more honourable role of caregiver. Pregnancy motivates the mother to stay away from the gang, avoid using drugs and alcohol, get on with her education, and pursue healthier relationships (Rossmann), as it could amount to a "life-changing event" (Lesser, Anderson and Koniak-Griffin 11). What follows here are their mother'hood stories—redacted for relevance—with commentary. Italics show when these mothers speak in Spanish, either translated or left in the original.

GRACIA

Although Gracia had her daughter at fifteen years old and her son at seventeen years old, she continued involvement in gang warfare until her early twenties. There are several distinct prefigurative forces in this story (Pearce and Cronen) that obligate her to perform certain actions and prohibit her from certain others. Namely, Gracia continued storying herself a warrior, regardless of practices such as the "mommy track" and "glass ceiling" that prevent professional women from achieving top leadership positions. Likewise, while the armed forces of most countries prevent women (whether mothers or not) from serving in active combat (Israel as the most notable exception), Gracia felt no obligation to keep herself or her children away from active duty. While initially Gracia saw herself in control of her own destiny, the birth of her first child began to erode her influence vis-à-vis her peers. Like many teen mothers, Gracia's pregnancy forced her to leave school to care for her child; unlike many mothers, regardless of age, her reluctance to forfeit her leadership position placed her own children directly in the war zone:

> *I didn't resent having the baby but I was really emotional because a lot of my freedom was taken away. Wasn't able to do a lot of the stuff anymore.... I noticed that I had to spend a lot of time at home with my baby while my boyfriend was still out there kicking it with all the homeboys, homegirls, and partying; of course all the homegirls are still there, and I couldn't be there no more ...because I couldn't be running around the streets with my baby.*
>
> *And so, a lot of the homegirls wouldn't come around to visit me.... I was there when they needed me, but when I needed them to hang out with me, keep me company and stuff, they weren't really so much around. So I wasn't able*

to go to the same neighborhood or go to those same houses because I had my baby. A couple of times I'd do it, but every time I'd take my baby with me, there was either a fight or they were leaving somewhere and I couldn't take my baby along because there was either going to be guns or some kind of weapon like that in a vehicle or the people were going to be carrying it. Of course if there was going to be a gang fight I couldn't take my baby, so I couldn't go.

And so I just started noticing that I had a whole different role. I had to be, I couldn't be who I was anymore. Not only because I had a baby, but because when I really needed them, they weren't there for me. Like if I needed money to buy my baby milk, they didn't give me any money, they couldn't help me. They didn't have it or …but they were still young too. But they still had money to buy beer and buy drugs though.

But … we got into fights, there was nobody to help me, you know, protect my baby. And I started thinking a lot about, "Was it worth me losing my child over the color red? Over gangs, was it worth it?" And again, when I started weighing things out, I'd do all this for them, but what are they doing for me and my child? So, I couldn't think of me anymore. I brought a life into this world, and she's the one I had to think about. She's the one I had to put first.

There appears to be no equivalent expression among gang members to describe how Gracia's fair-weather friends excluded, disappointed, and ignored her during her pregnancy and after the birth of her children, although this is a common phenomenon (Becerra and de Anda; Hunt, Joe-Laidler and MacKenzie). Thus, I also offer the term "mother'hood" as encompassing alienation from Gracia's fellow warriors and a demotion from being a leader in her own gang to being a non-warrior:

So I started taking my baby places with me. I started taking her to hang out with me at the liquor store.… And so, there was one incident where we were at the liquor store. There was a huge gang fight. I had to push my baby into

*the liquor store ... and when that happened, I remember
fighting and at the same time still trying to keep an eye
on her and I remember seeing some guys walk into the
liquor store. First thing I thought about was, "My baby is
in there," you know, and I started yelling for the girls, or
even the guys, even my boyfriend, I was like, "Go get my
baby, somebody help me," 'cause I'm still fighting at this
time, and I even see some girls run away like they were
just running away from the fight and nobody thought
about my baby. Nobody thought about getting my baby
and protecting my baby.*

*And when I had my child that is when I saw that I
needed to be the one to make something different. And it
didn't really take place until I had my second one, where
I encountered a drive-by shooting.... We were all hanging out in a front yard of my friend. The older one was
in the front room and my son was in the bedroom, in his
crib.... So they just started shooting wherever and, um,
all I remember was ducking for cover and, um, seeing my
boyfriend duck for cover too. He was yelling my name
and first thing, the only thing I could think of was, "My
kids. My baby is in that room, in that front room." So I
made my way to the front room and all I could, and she
was on the couch and was just thinking, "Oh, she's going
to get it, they're going to get her, the bullets are going to
get her" [cries]. And that is when I made up my mind,
when I got to her, I just kept hoping that, that she was
fine, that nothing happened to her, and it was really hard
for me because I had to go to her and then I had to run
to my son. And my boyfriend was outside running to get
revenge. And here I was going to go help my babies. And
here I'm thinking, "I'm not going to go out there to see if
any of the homeboys or homegirls are okay!" You know,
all I could think about was my kids! None of them came
in to see if my kids were okay.... And so, that's where I
made up my mind, I was done. I was done. From that day
on, that's when I started deciding that I wanted to live life
differently and that I didn't want to be in gangs no more.*

Indeed, mother'hood entails a conflict between a woman's wish to continue participating in gang activities and the care she must provide for her children (Moloney et al.). By leaving the gang, Gracia's identity changed from warrior to mother. Mother'hood also presented a practical challenge for Florencia in terms of reconciling her hard-core warrior image with the desire to do right by her children.

FLORENCIA

Pregnancy and mother'hood among gang-impacted girls often occur through sexual relations with older males (Hunt, Joe-Laidler and MacKenzie) because the social standing of a girl is directly influenced by the reputation of her sexual partner generally (Joe-Laidler and Hunt) and by the father of her child(ren) specifically (Cepeda and Valdez). Florencia's story fully corroborates these research claims:

> *...a really good friend of mine ... introduced me to this guy who had just got out of prison, and he was twenty-five and I was thirteen. So that ... I ended up being with him, he was my boyfriend, and everybody knew he was my boyfriend. That was like a big thing when you're a young girl like that, being with an older guy like that, all tattooed down, done prison time, he was from the neighborhood; that was like a big deal for a girl. You were looked at with more respect.*
>
> *Then I got pregnant. I had my first baby when I was fourteen, and she was born with spina bifida and hydrocephalus. He went back to prison and stayed in prison. Getting pregnant changed something inside me. I wanted to love my baby and be a mom to her and take care of her. And I thought that was going to change everything, but it actually got worse. I stayed clean my whole pregnancy. I didn't do a whole lot of drugs before I got pregnant, but after I had my baby, I got really badly into drugs.*
>
> *But I'd take care of her, in my own way. When she was born, they wanted to take her away from me. They said,*

"No, you can't have her! She's going to have to go into a home; she'll be taken care of." But I fought for her, I said, "No! I want to keep her! You can't take her away from me!" I was like, "There's no WAY you're taking her away from me!" I fought and fought and they had to release her to me. She had a big hole in her back and I would bandage it every day. I took the best care that I knew how, as a kid having a kid.

Although Florencia claimed she was changed by the pregnancies and birth of her children, like many teen mothers—perhaps by being in denial about her pregnancy—she was able to indulge her willingness to remain in active duty in her gang (Kivisto). She also told a competing story about being a hard-core Norteña, willing to engage in combat even while pregnant:

I did a carjacking when I was three months pregnant.... I was at this bar and there were these guys they were Sureños and they were talking about me, they were speaking Spanish. They didn't know I spoke Spanish. They were saying, "Yeah, let's get that girl." ...They were in my neighborhood. Somebody found out and called me "Hey, there's two Scraps [a derogatory term for Sureños] at the bar, go handle them." They were not allowed to come into our neighborhood and they were in our neighborhood. I went over there to take care of it and I didn't know who they were. I went over there by myself and had two screwdrivers in my back pocket and had one in the front. I didn't even take a gun. I was just thinking, "Oh, just go over them, hit them up, ask them what they're doing and just split." So I went down there and when I walked in, I just walked up and started talking to them. At first I just wanted to see what they were about. I seen one of them had a blue paño [bandana] in his back pocket. "Oh, they are 'Scraps.'" So, I was like, "Hey, what you guys doing here?" And they're like, "Oh, we're just here." I had a red Pendleton on so they knew I was a Norteña. One of them starts telling the other in Spanish, he said, "Yeah, let's ... um... let's tell her to go party with us and we'll rent a room and we'll rape her, tie her up, face down on the bed." He was using other language and he goes, "We'll cut her up, we'll cut her from top to bottom." That got me so mad and I thought, "You know what? I'm going to get in that car and do to you what you say you'll do to me." Because I would flip, when they started talking that way about me, I flipped into another person. I didn't care.

At that point, I was just supposed to tell them to leave, rough them up. Sounds funny, a girl, but I was crazy like that. I'd popped their tires, took a knife to slice ... guys before if they came into the neighborhood, I didn't care, "I'll cut your face, I don't care, you gotta get out of here." Well, instead I was like "No, I'm going to go with them. I'm gonna get in their car and I'm going to go." This girl had been coming around our neighborhood, and she was what we called a "wannabe." So I was like, "Oh, you want to be in the neighborhood, you gotta do this jale [job] with me, this job and if you don't, if you back out, whatever I'm going to do to them, I'm going to do to you." So the guys, they didn't know I spoke Spanish, so are talking real bad about us. I slipped her one of the screwdrivers and I had the other. They pulled over to this house and this guy came out. They told him, "Yeah, we got these two girls, tenemos dos chapetas." That's what they call Norteños, they call them chapetes. They're like, "This is what we're going to do to them and vamos." And they guy looked at me... 'cause he hated us. He was a [sic] older guy. He told the one guy, "Vamos adentro, I'm going to get a piece." They're telling us, "Oh, we're going to get some dope." It was like do or die. "Man, they're going to do something to us, we gotta do something to them." They park and the guy tells the other guy, "I'm going to get a piece," and they leave the one guy in the front. I looked and seen they left the keys, so I thought "This is it, I'm going to split with this one guy." So I told this girl, "Okay, stick that screwdriver in his neck and I'm going to jump in the front seat and I'm

*going to drive." And that's exactly what we did. I drove
off with the car and we pushed him out of the car in the
freeway and I took the car....*

After having her children taken away, being rejected by her
homies, an overdose and subsequent recovery from a severe drug
addiction, and a momentous experience with religion, Florencia's
current situation—a former hard-core Norteña warrior who
married a Sureño—shows how previous warring factions can be
united in peacetime and do ministry to keep youth out of gangs.

SERENITY

Up to now in this chapter, the warrior mentality of the gang-involved mother has been useful to understand the contradictions
in lived and told narratives (Davies and Harré) as they reconcile
their warrior identity with their changing role as mothers. To
look at Serenity's story, I turn to the writings of Adrienne Rich
to illustrate the violence committed by a male gang warrior toward his pregnant partner and his own child. Rich argues that in
post-Freudian psychology, a "man's contributions to culture are
his way of compensating for the lack of the one, elemental, creative power of motherhood" (113). The "penis envy" that women
feel, according to Freudian psychology, is not envy for the male
sexual organ, but for the power that having such organ implies.
Ubiquitous male power and dominance engenders not only a
misogynistic civilization but phallocentric thinking that devalues
motherhood in order to account for this residual envy. In this sense,
it is perhaps more appropriate to talk about "uterus envy" that men
feel about the power of women to carry life within their bodies,
for "besides the very ancient resentment of a woman's power to
create new life, there is fear of her apparent power to affect the
male genitals" (Rich 114). In the following, italics denote where
Serenity spoke Spanish.

*My mistake was, when I got together with Marco, I didn't
get to know him well. He was very strict, jealous, I don't
know. His mother came from an abusive relationship. I*

didn't know what I was myself getting into. I was just wanting to be loved. I was always by myself and I finally had someone, you know? I like, knew it was wrong for me getting pregnant. I didn't want to get pregnant. But he ended up convincing me to get pregnant.... I don't know why, maybe because he wanted to keep me under control. I don't know why he wanted that, but I ended up pregnant at the age of eighteen and had my baby girl at nineteen. I can still remember when the nurse showed me and I started crying because I had through all my pregnancy, I had a hard time. I was getting hit, I almost had a miscarriage.... He was kicking me even when I was pregnant. But no, she survived. He didn't care. I don't know if it was because he was tweaking behind my back.

When the nurse showed me my baby, I started crying because that was my baby. That was part of me. That was the only thing I had that I knew was mine. And when I saw her I knew I couldn't be with him no more. I knew right there and then. I knew because I didn't want my daughter to suffer for anything. I started working back up at [a restaurant]. I just wanted to save money and leave. I wasn't happy no more. I didn't wanna get hit no more. I knew pretty much that I was done. But he had that over me, I couldn't leave. He had my daughter.

One day, [the owner] called me to cover a shift and told me that if I came in, I'd get a raise. It was my day off. And I said okay. I decided to leave the baby with [Marco]. And when I left the baby, I left her sleeping and I hugged her. And I went to work. I got a call like around four, I don't remember the time. He told me that the baby had fallen. I said, "Is she okay?" he was like, "Yeah." "Okay just put her to sleep. Give her Tylenol or shower her." But he told me like, "She has a bruise." I didn't think it was a big bruise you know? I asked if she was asleep. He goes, "Yeah, she already fell asleep." I go, "Is she okay?" He goes like, "Yeah." I get another call another hour after that, that the baby was not responding. He didn't want to call the ambulance. I was, "Call them or I'll call the ambulance." He tells me that, when the ambulance got there, that the baby was responding. And he hanged up because the officer told him to hang up. So I went to the hospital.

I then was waiting in a room with my aunt in the hospital and the doctor comes in and tells me that ...that she was gone, that she was already dead by the time they were in the home, that they couldn't do anything, that she was not responding. I never saw my baby girl after that day. They never let me see her after that, even when they took her to the morgue or anything. Um, he ... they let him out after like three days because they didn't have enough proof; they needed the autopsy. And I tried asking him what happened. He told me that he didn't remember anything. So, on Monday, he got locked up. The officers told me that the baby was murdered. They were asking so many questions, I didn't know [cries].... She was just a baby [sniffles]!

During the courts [sic], I couldn't even ... the judges wanted me to see the papers, her pictures, I didn't wanna see because I knew he did it. Something deep inside me told me but I didn't want to believe. I was all messed up from all the abuse, the punches he had given me. I didn't want to see it. And then he manipulated me to getting married, which was the biggest mistake I've ever done. After I while, I'd had enough. I never went to see him again. I told him that it was over. I didn't want to. I married him after he got locked up. I made a huge mistake. I kept on thinking that maybe if I kept going, he'd tell me what really happened to the baby. I never got a ... I got no answer, like he never told me, like ... I actually when I saw the death certificate and saw that she'd been abused ... and murdered.

I'm not embarrassed what happened to me no more. It just made me stronger. I thought I wasn't a good mother. That I should have stayed with her. That's what I was ashamed of: that I didn't protect my daughter like I should have. That's what I carried with me.

LILIANA CASTAÑEDA ROSSMANN

A pregnant woman may choose to continue acting as warrior, like Gracia and Florencia. But a pregnant woman who suffers violence at the hands of her gang-involved partner, like Serenity, is made painfully aware that she is powerless to protect not just her life, but the life growing inside her. The pregnancy places her in even more danger as both she and the fetus suffer from a grotesque version of "friendly fire." With every punch and every kick, she encounters the possibility of losing her reproductive autonomy and losing not just her child, but any future relationship with it. Taillieu and Brownridge write that in the literature of violence against pregnant women, scant attention has been paid to "perpetrator characteristics that may impact the risk of violence and virtually no studies include the male partners' perspectives in their analyses" (26). As Fleisher poignantly observes:

The fantasy of independent living is accompanied by [gang] girls' love-escape fantasy, in which a boy who's now in prison will rescue the girl and together they'll ride off into the sunset and live happily ever after. These fantasies are by far the best relationships with boys ... girls ever have. Real lovers beat and exploit them and leave them alone, penniless, and pregnant. (99)

The war metaphor provides a richer view into situations of violence for the gang-involved mother, as the male gang member views her pregnancy as an increasing threat to his warrior mentality. He seeks to control his own multiple marginalities (Vigil), for the only things he has control over—his own body and the body of his sexual partner—have transmogrified into an unborn child that now threatens his warrior identity. I argue that the identity of these male gang warriors undergoes a transformation which they are ill-prepared and ill-equipped to adopt. "The one aspect in which most women have felt their own power in the patriarchal sense—authority over and control of another—has been motherhood; and even this aspect ... has been wrenched and manipulated to male control" (Rich 67).

Misogynistic and patriarchal society provides few cultural and interpretive resources for such male gang warriors to author a

130

story of their lives from which gang warfare is absent, much less a story of being a law-abiding provider for their offspring (Joe-Laidler and Hunt). The challenge comes intrinsically from the relational shift that the gang member must make for "even in our private reveries, we are in relationship" (Gergen 63). Although he is a male warrior, powerful in the gang and over his female partner(s), he is powerless vis-à-vis society writ large. The pregnant woman and their unborn child—in their implied dependency on him for survival—remind him of his obligations, for "our mental vocabulary is essentially a vocabulary of relationship" (Gergen 70). In highlighting his inability to protect them, they become his enemy.

In point of fact, Charles and Perreira found that a pregnant woman whose male partner uses illegal drugs suffers an increased risk of partner violence during her pregnancy. Additionally, in Moloney et al., nine out sixty-five pregnant teenagers interviewed who were gang-involved "specifically recounted stories of the fathers behaving violently toward them after the pregnancy was announced" (12). For the male gang member, the unborn child is less his "own" and more like a rival who takes the mother's attention and therefore undercuts his power. Rich reminds us that the "powerful person would seem to have a good deal at stake in suppressing or denying his awareness of the personal reality of others; power seems to engender a kind of willed ignorance, a moral stupidity, about the inwardness of others, hence of oneself" (65).

TRANSCENDING GANG WARFARE IN MOTHER'HOOD

In summary, mother'hood entails a particular form of pregnancy, childbirth, and maternity experience within gang warfare. It portends alienation from one's peers and a limited ability to participate in gang warfare. Yet, mother'hood also functions to rewrite one's identity from gang warrior to mother, and to engage in relational practices that support this newly authored self. Shaw writes that gang-involved girls perennially inhabit a warrior mentality, always ready to fight, and that it "is not easy for gang girls to relinquish their well-learned, much practiced habits of survival" (223). The paucity of knowledge about how such healthier relationships may form and how to engage in them complicates this process for the teenage-mother storyteller. Again, the words of poet Adrienne Rich provide some insight:

> The mother's battle for her child—with sickness, with poverty, with war, with all the forces of exploitation and callousness that cheapen human life—needs to become a common human battle, waged in love and in the passion for survival. But for this to happen, the institution of motherhood must be destroyed.... To destroy the institution is not to abolish motherhood. It is to release the creation and sustenance of life into the same realm of decision, struggle, surprise, imagination, and conscious intelligence, as any other difficult, but freely chosen work. (280)

There is yet another feature of mother'hood: the struggle both within her and against the discursive forces that the young mother must face in order to become something for which she has no exemplars. When the female gang warrior becomes pregnant, in her *barrio* she is no longer expected to engage in gang warfare but to go on to clean living to provide for her child. Mother'hood earns respect and gives the storyteller wider storytelling latitude. But how can she tell a story that for her is unlived, unimaginable, and unavailable? How can she, as Rich suggests, "release the creation and sustenance of life into the same realm of decision, struggle, surprise, imagination, and conscious intelligence" (280)? How can she freely choose the work of mothering given all that is outside her realm of surprise, imagination, and conscious intelligence?

Quoting Scott, Shaw offers an alternative: the move from reacting and surviving to being liberated by our choices relies on ensuring that "habits be identified, acknowledged for their pluses and minuses, and relegated to the realm of the conscious and the chosen" (Scott qtd. in Shaw 224). In transcending the warrior mentality, a mother must avail herself of useful odds and ends, bits of linguistic resources from old stories and from stories heard from others but not yet lived to re-construct a story of mother'hood. This new mother'hood story helps young women forsake gang warfare because it entails a re-storying of her own identity vis-à-vis the gang. It includes going through a challenging and sometimes alienating—yet helpful—maturing process in which she acknowledges the consequences of their choices, a reevaluation of relationships (with the father of her child or children, their families, and their friends), and a struggle to avail herself of linguistic resources to facilitate her new life story.

WORKS CITED

Barrett, Beth. "Gang Violence is Urban Warfare." *Gangs*. Ed. Scott Barbour. Detroit, MI: Greenhaven Press/Thomson Gale, 2006. 56-63. Print.

Becerra, Rosina and Diane de Anda. "Pregnancy and Motherhood among Mexican American Adolescents." *Health and Social Work* 9.2 (1984):106-123. Web. 18 March 2014.

Berger, Peter and Thomas Luckmann. *The Social Construction of Reality: A Treatise in the Sociology of Knowledge.* New York: Penguin Books, 1966. Print.

Campbell, Anne. *The Girls in the Gang.* 2nd ed. Cambridge, MA: Basil, 1991. Print.

Cepeda, Alice, and Avelardo Valdez. "Risk Behaviors Among Young Mexican American Gang-associated Females: Sexual Relations, Partying, Substance Use, and Crime." *Journal of Adolescent Research* 18.1 (2003): 90–106. Web. 15 August 2010.

Charles, Pajarita and Krista Perreira. "Intimate Partner Violence during Pregnancy and 1-Year Post-partum." *Journal of Family Violence* 22 (2007): 609–619. Web. 1 July 2014.

Davies, Bronwyn, and Rom Harré. "Contradiction in Lived and Told Narratives." *Research on Language and Social Interaction* 25.1-4 (1991): 1-35. Print.

de Córdoba, José. "The Violent Gang Wars Behind Your Super Bowl Guacamole; Mexican Growers in the World's Avocado Capital Chase off Violent Extortionists." *Wall Street Journal*. 31 January 2014. Web 22 February 2104.

Dietrich, Lisa. *Chicana Adolescents: Bitches, 'Ho's, and Schoolgirls.* Westport, CT: Praeger, 1998. Print.

Erikson, Erik H. *Identity: Youth and Crisis*. New York: W.W. Norton, 1968.

Fleisher, Mark and Jessie Krienert. "Life-course Events, Social Networks, and the Emergence of Violence Among Female Gang Members." *Journal of Community Psychology* 32 (2004): 607-622. Web. 15 April 2009.

Fleisher, Mark. *Dead End Kids: Gang Girls and the Boys They Know*. Madison, WI: The University of Wisconsin Press, 1998. Print.

Geertz, Clifford. "Thick Description: Toward an Interpretive Theory of Culture." *The Interpretation of Cultures: Selected Essays*. Ed. Clifford Geertz. New York: Basic Books, 1973. 3–30. Print.

Gergen, Kenneth. *Relational Being: Beyond Self and Community*. New York: Oxford University Press, 2009. Print.

Greene, Judith and Kevin Pranis. *Gang Wars: The Failure of Enforcement Tactics and the Need for Effective Public Safety Strategies*. Justice Policy Institute. 2007. Web. 6 December 2013.

Hayden, Tom. *Street Wars: Gangs and the Future of Violence*. New York: New Press, 2004. Print.

Hunt, Geoffrey, Karen Joe-Laidler and Kathleen MacKenzie. "Moving Into Motherhood: Gang Girls and Controlled Risk." *Youth and Society* 36 (2005): 333–373. Web. 7 February 2009.

Hunt, Geoffrey and Karen Joe-Laidler. "Situations of Violence in the Lives of Girl Gang Members." *The Modern Gang Reader*. Eds. Arlen Egley, Jr., Cheryl Maxson, Jody Miller, and Malcolm Klein. Los Angeles: Roxbury, 2006. 244–257. Print.

Joe-Laidler, Karen and Geoffrey Hunt. "Accomplishing Femininity among Girls in the Gang." *British Journal of Criminology* 41.4 (2001): 656–678. Web. 19 April 2009.

Kivisto, Peter. "Teenagers, Pregnancy and Childbearing in a Risk Society: How do High-risk Teens Differ from their age Peers?" *Journal of Family Issues* 22.8 (2001): 1044-1065. Print.

Lesser, Jana, Nancy Anderson and Deborah Koniak-Griffin. "Sometimes You Don't Feel Ready to Be an Adult or a Mom: The Experience of Adolescent Pregnancy." *Journal of Child and Adolescent Psychiatric Nursing* 11 (1998): 7–16. Web. 6 February 2009.

Littlejohn. Stephen. "The Transcendent Communication Project:

Searching for a Praxis of Dialogue." *Conflict Resolution Quarterly* 21.3 (2004): 337–359. Web. 17 October 2005.

Miller, Jody. "Gender and Victimization Risk among Young Women in Gangs." *Journal of Research in Crime and Delinquency* 35 (1998): 429–453. Web. 5 February 2009.

Molidor, Christian. "Female Gang Members: A Profile of Aggression and Victimization." *Social Work* 41.3 (1996): 251–257. Print.

Moloney, Molly, Geoffrey Hunt, Karen Joe-Laidler, and Kathleen MacKenzie. "Young Mother (in the) Hood: Gang Girls' Negotiation of New Identities." *Journal of Youth Studies* 14.1 (2011): 1-19. Print.

Moore, Joan and Mary Devitt. "The Paradox of Deviance in Addicted Mexican American Mothers." *Gender and Society* 3.1 (1989): 53–70. Web. 5 February 2009

Moore, Joan and John Hagedorn. "Female Gangs: A Focus on Research." *The Modern Gang Reader*. Eds. Arlen Egley, Jr., Cheryl Maxson, Jody Miller, and Malcolm Klein. Los Angeles, CA: Roxbury, 2006. 192-205. Print.

Morales, Gabriel. *Varrio Warfare: Violence in the Latino Community*. Seattle, WA: Tecolote Publishing, 2000. Print.

Mydans, Seth. "Trophies from the Gang Wars: Wheelchairs." *The New York Times*. 6 December 1990. Web. 9 March 2014.

Pearce, W. Barnett and Vernon Cronen. *Communication, Action, and Meaning: The Creation of Social Realities*. New York: Praeger, 1980. Print.

Pearce, W. Barnett, and Kim Pearce. "Transcendent Storytelling: Abilities for Systemic Practitioners and their Clients." *Human Systems* 9 (1998): 167–185. Print.

Rich, Adrienne. *Of Woman Born*. New York: W.W. Norton, 1976/1986. Print.

Rossmann, Liliana Castañeda. *Transcending Gangs: Latinas Story their Experience*. Cresskill, NJ: Hampton Press, 2013. Print.

Shaw, Bonnie. *Schoolgirls Out of School: The Education of Girls in the Gang*. Unpublished dissertation, University of Utah, 2004. Web. 5 March 2009.

Taillieu, Tamara, and Douglas Brownridge. "Violence Against Pregnant Women: Prevalence, Patterns, Risk Factors, Theories, and Directions for Future Research." *Aggression and Violent*

Behavior 15 (2010): 14–35. Web. 12 October 2013.

Valdez, Avelardo. *Mexican American Girls and Gang Violence: Beyond Risk*. New York: Palgrave Macmillan, 2007. Print.

Varriale, Jennifer. "Female Gang Members and Desistance: Pregnancy as a Possible Exit Strategy." *Journal of Gang Research* 15.4 (2008): 35–64. Web. 11 September 2013.

Vigil, James Diego. *Barrio Gangs: Street Life and Identity in Southern California*. Austin: University of Texas Press, 1988. Print.

Whitehead, Elizabeth. "Teenage Pregnancy: On the Road to Social Death." *International Journal of Nursing Studies* 38 (2001): 437-446. Web. 14 January 2014.

Wiemann, Constance, Vaughn Rickert, Abbey Berenson, and Robert Volk. "Are Pregnant Adolescents Stigmatized by Pregnancy?" *Journal of Adolescent Health* 36.4 (2005): 352. Print.

7.
We Are Also Mothers

Rwandan Women With Children Born of Genocide

CLAUDINE UMULISA

IN RWANDA, 1994 REMAINS AN unforgettable year. Over the course of approximately one hundred days, from the assassination of Habyarimana Juvenal on April 6 until mid-July, at least one million Tutsis and moderate Hutus were brutally murdered (Koster). Individual and mass rape formed an "integral part of the process of destroying the Tutsi minority and rape was often intentionally carried out by HIV positive perpetrators" (De Brouwer 9). Tutsi women were systematically raped by Hutu militias as a consequence of the genocidal campaign and an estimated 5,000 children were born as a result of that rape (Mukangendo). The children born of rape are known as *les enfants mauvais souvenirs* (children of bad memories) and often their own mothers have called them "little killers" (Mukangendo).

Since the 1994 genocide, a body of research has emerged that focuses on the experiences of genocide in general (see Nowrojee). Much has been speculated about how rape has been used as a weapon of war in Rwanda and elsewhere (see Baaz and Stern). There is much excellent scholarship addressing the challenges that survivors of wartime sexual violence face in the aftermath of violence in the Rwandan context (see Brouwer). But we know little about the effects of war on women survivors who are parenting children born of rape.

Therefore, the aim of this paper is to explore how the impact of sexual violence and the resultant pregnancy associated with bearing a child shape the motherhood of rape victims in post-genocide Rwanda. To achieve this, ten mothers of children born of genocidal rape were interviewed during the period of 2011-2013. I explored motherhood through the narratives of these mothers of children born as a result of genocidal rape in the Rwandan context. For the purpose of this paper, I refer to the ten women in the study as "mothers," as they bore the children through rape and play the mothering role. My analysis of their narratives aims to provide some preliminary answers to the question: What are the challenges of mothering children born of rape in context of Rwanda?

The paper proceeds as follows: The first section offers a synopsis of the Rwandan history and gives an overview of what we know about rape as a weapon of genocide in the Rwandan case. It does so in order to set the stage for making better sense of the narratives of that category of mother. In the second section, I introduce my methodology before I turn to the narratives gathered from the women themselves.

SYNOPSIS OF RWANDAN HISTORY

During one hundred days of 1994, Hutu extremists known as "*Interahamwe* militias" slaughtered almost a million people, mostly Tutsi, in the Rwandan genocide.[1] The Rwandan conflict has been defined in different ways by both Rwandan and foreign scholars. To understand more fully why ethnicity mattered in terms of genocide and the effect of the sexual violence on Tutsi women who bore children during 1994, I deliberately choose to reflect on how some historians explain the 1994 Rwandan genocide as an identity-based conflict.

The history of Rwanda shows that before its colonisation, the country was divided into many small kingdoms in which the three tribal groups—Hutu, Tutsi, and Twa—coexisted. At that time, Twa, Hutu, and Tutsi were perceived as social classes rather than ethnic groups (Koster). They were defined by their activities and properties: "Tutsi's main activity was herding cattle (with numbers of cows indicating richness and prestige), while Hutu were mostly dealing with agriculture" (Koster 3), although both groups did both activities. The Twa group was engaged in pottery. As Uvin argues:

> The most widely accepted interpretation is that cattle rearing
> Tutsi arrived in Burundi and Rwanda and neighbouring
> regions in successive waves from the North during the fif-
> teenth and sixteenth centuries, fleeing famine and drought.
> The agriculturist Hutu they met in Rwanda had emigrated
> to these fertile region centuries earlier from central Africa.
> The longest-standing inhabitants of the region are the Twa,
> a small marginal group (only 1 percent of the population)
> engaged in pottery making and hunting. (qtd. in Rangira 12)

These social positions were interchangeable, with mobility among the three groups based on economic perspectives. This meant that it was easy for a rich Hutu/Twa to become a Tutsi[2] and for an impoverished Tutsi to become a Hutu. The patrilineal system in Rwanda of that period did not allow women to change classes as men did.

The Berlin Conference of 1884 assigned Rwanda to Germany, marking the beginning of the colonial era. Belgian forces took control of Rwanda, Burundi, and Ex-Zaire during World War I. Belgians attributed "racial" superiority to the Tutsi group; instead of being perceived as social classes, Hutu and Tutsi became fixed ethnic identities and racially constructed (Vansina).

The Europeans were quite smitten with the Tutsi, whom they saw as definitely too fine to be "negroes." Since they were not only physically different from the Hutu but also considered themselves socially superior, the racially-obsessed nineteenth-century Euro-peans started building a variety of hazardous hypotheses on their possible, probable, or, as they soon became, indubitable origin (Prunier).

Tutsi women were assigned exceptional physical beauty com-pared to Hutu women, in the same way that Tutsi men were seen as more attractive or superior to Hutu men. Hutu were "deprived of all political power and were materially exploited by both the whites and the Tutsi in a kind of double colonialism" (Prunier 39). Mamdani argues that:

> Examples of the racial privilege enjoyed by a small Tutsi
> elite included exclusive access to higher education and Tutsi

supremacy in the local administration felt most strongly in
the Belgian administration's coerced effort to Tustify the
chief ship as an institutions when in the 1920s all Hutu
chiefs were systematically deposed and replaced by Tutsi
chiefs. (qtd. in Mibenge 153)

In 1962, Rwanda had become an independent country, following
the overthrow of the monarchy in what was called "the Revolution
of 1959." However, it was Hutus who governed the new state
exclusively, with some support from Belgium (Rangira). The government adopted colonial ethnic definitions of its population and
engaged in the prosecution of Tutsis as revenge for the earlier Tutsi
domination. In a 1973 coup, President Habyarimana took over
the Rwandan government from Gregoire Kayibanda "who had
overseen the persecution and large-scale flight of Tutsis, especially
to Uganda and also to other neighbouring countries" (Rangira 6).
As president, Habyarimana and his Akazu (inner circle, literally
"small house") from the North of Rwanda (the former territories of Hutu kingdoms) exercised a monopoly of power and was
initially popular especially among the Hutu majority, who at the
time made up an estimated 85 percent or more of the Rwandan
population (Rangira).

By the late 1980s, the exiled Tutsi population that found refuge
in Uganda launched an offensive on Rwanda from Uganda as
the Rwandan Patriotic Front (RPF). In 1990, the same year when
RPF started a war against the Rwandan government, the "Hutu
Power" issued the infamous Hutu Ten Commandments calling
for the exclusion and extermination of Tutsis. The so called "Ten
Commandments of the Bahutu," published in the hate-mongering Rwandan newspaper of Hutu power, *Kangura Journal* No.
6 (December, 1990), prohibited the "mixed sexual relations"
between Tutsi and Hutu. Tutsi women were described as objects
of temptation for Hutu men and threats to the homogeneity of
Hutu blood (see Hintjens for details).

When RPF invaded Rwanda in 1990, Habyarimana started
arresting Tutsis and some Hutu moderates and mass killings of
Tutsis began in Bugesera and elsewhere in the country. Preparations
were conducted for the extermination of Tutsis by organizing and

arming Hutu militias and through the systematic use of the media (especially Radio Television des Mille Collines) to spread hatred and propaganda against the Tutsis population.

On April 6, 1994, when Habyarimana's plane was shot down, the RPF was blamed and Hutu militias, as well as the general population, began killing Tutsis and moderate Hutus (who refused to adhere to the racist hatred of Tutsis). One of the first prominent victims was the Prime Minister, Mrs Agatha Uwiringiyimana, who was an outspoken Hutu woman who opposed the politics of hatred. Hutu militias (*Interahamwe*) had been trained to kill by militias and other forces loyal to the Hutu Power bloc in the Habyarimana regime. In just 100 days, at least one million Tutsis were murdered in the presence of UNAMIR forces, the UN peacekeeping troops stationed in Rwanda.

In the following sections, I will discuss rape as a weapon of genocide and the politics of ethnicity in the Rwandan context as a backdrop to understanding the significance of the politics of identity in the mothers' narratives.

RAPE DURING THE 1994 GENOCIDE IN RWANDA

International conventions, especially the Geneva Conventions of 1949 and the Convention on the Elimination of All Forms of Discrimination against Women of 1979, provide special measures to protect women and girls from gender-based violence, especially rape, sexual abuse, and all other forms of violence (Mukangendo). However, during the genocide, the Rwandan government led by members of the MRND party (National Revolution Movement for Democracy and Development), used the local media, and particularly RTLM, a hate-mongering radio station established by the Hutu a hate-mongering radio station established by Hutu leaders, to incite the Hutu militias to rape Tutsi women and girls (Mibenge 153).

In the years preceding the genocide, the identity of Tutsi women was employed as an element of propaganda and creation of ethnic differences. As noted above, Tutsi women were attributed exceptional physical beauty compared to Hutu women, in the same way that Tutsi men were seen as superior to Hutu men

(Mibenge). During the genocide, the word *Kubohoza* (loosely translated as "to liberate") was used as propaganda of the Hutu movement to sensitize men to rape Tutsi women. Rape against women was not only planned to "humiliate Tutsi people but also to spread HIV—and thus ensure the end of the Tutsi people" (De Brouwer 19). However, some rapes were directed at Hutu women who were considered to be political moderates.[3] The acts of rape were often combined with beating and severe genital mutilation of the victims (Mibenge). Pregnant Tutsi women were eviscerated (Taylor), Tutsi girls and women were forcibly impregnated with "Hutu babies," and pregnant Hutu women married to Tutsi men were killed (Mukangendo). Most rape victims were killed immediately; others were forced to flee to neighbouring countries with Hutu militias as "wives" (Mukangendo). War rape occurred all over the country and was frequently perpetrated in plain sight of others, at sites such as schools, churches, roadblocks, government buildings, or in the bush (see Norwrojee). While some women committed infanticide, others decided to keep their babies. These children are referred to by names that pejoratively connote their identity as children of killers and products of the genocide (see Carpenter; Seto). Sexual violence did not occur randomly, nor was it merely a side effect of the genocide. Rather, rape was used strategically and consistently by Hutu militias to humiliate and destroy the Tusti community (Brouwer).

I explored the lived experiences of rape survivors through the narratives of ten Rwandan mothers with children born of rape. In my analysis of their narratives I was concerned to provide preliminary answers to the question of what issues their testimonies of bearing/parenting children in a post-genocide era bring to light.

METHODOLOGY

As I come from the same country and culture being researched, I have had opportunities to speak to rape victims, especially after having lived, studied, and worked almost six years in the country. My experience as a survivor of genocide, educator, and researcher in the Rwandan context has given me insight into the difficulties and desires of women caring for children born of rape. My feminist studies background enabled me to analyse rape-related issues not just in terms of the physical effects borne by the rape survivors, but also to examine the impact of rape from a socio-cultural perspective by considering the complexities of bearing a "child of the enemy" in a period of post-genocide.

The extreme sensitivity of the topic, the unresponsiveness of affected communities, and the lack of reliable data on issues related to children born of rape and their mothers represent only a few of the impediments against a better understanding of the challenges of conducting research on such a subject. Many researchers are interested in the lives of genocide widows, but not in the specified category of mothers with children born of rape. This means that there is a lack of reliable data on the issue. As far as I know, I was the first to investigate this matter in this context, and it caused me some concern that I was venturing into a previously unexplored and politically-charged set of issues.

Data Collection

A narrative inquiry was undertaken as a lens into the complexities of lived experiences of the Rwandan mothers with children born of rape. I was interested in what the stories tell us about each mothers' experience of mothering a child from rape in the context of post-genocide Rwanda.

The only way I could gain access to the mothers was to use a local NGO supporting them. I interviewed ten women members of the Kanyarwanda Association during the period of 2011-2013. The Kanyarwanda Association supports all categories of women—including survivors of rape. After receiving the list of NGO beneficiaries, I chose to contact women who were who were labelled and self-defined as "mothers of children from rape." Initially, twelve mothers were included in the interviews with facilitation from Kanyarwanda Association. Two of the mothers withdrew owing to personal issues that emerged at the time of the fieldwork. Ten women-mothers of children born of rape freely agreed to participate in my study. I envisaged that a small sample would enable a focused understanding of the experience of mothering a child born from rape. In order to understand each woman's individual perspective, I organized in-depth individual interviews, structured in a manner where women were encouraged to openly tell stories of their lives in the aftermath of the genocide.

The interviews began with the question: "Can you tell me the story of your experiences of being a mother to a child born of rape?" The mothers had the liberty to speak from their own perspective and to tell their stories of their lived experiences. In general, they decided to start with the genocide, the birth of the child, and told their stories chronologically. A set of open-ended questions was provided as a guide to the conversation. As noted above, participation in the study was voluntary. Ethical principles of anonymity, confidentiality, and the right to withdraw from the interviews at any stage were shared with the participants. Pseudonyms are used to protect the identity of the participants.

The stage of data analysis involved reading and reviewing the transcripts for commonalities in the lived experiences of the ten mothers, as well as for differences on issues they raised. I extracted certain themes from the narratives based on the perspective of shared experiences.

It is important to mention that I do not claim the women's narratives as "truth"; rather, they are the personal reflections of ten mothers speaking of their lives in post-genocide Rwandan society (Stern). Furthermore, the mothers likely told me only what they wanted me to hear, given who they thought I was and for what purposes I might "use" their stories (Stern). Nonetheless, the narratives provide valuable insight into the ways in which the narrators, *as* mothers of children born of genocidal rape, make sense of their experiences of mothering children born of rape in post-genocide Rwanda.

CHALLENGES AND ETHICAL DILEMMAS

In dealing with individuals who have undergone traumatic experiences, it is not easy to avoid personal emotions, especially after listening to different participants in this study. It is very difficult to represent someone's experience in this matter, and to write as a scholar about what the respondents were expressing during the interviews.

The most difficult and most problematic characteristic to deal with in this research was ethnicity. In Rwanda, ten years after genocide, the government of Rwanda lead by RPF banned ethnic affiliations in identity cards and in public discourse, introducing the Ndi "Umunyarwanda program," loosely translated as "Rwandan-ness," which attempts to define identity through collective citizenship rather than ethnicity. However, in everyday life the majority of people I encountered still take ethnicity as a given and refer to each other as Tutsis or Hutus. They know through the regional or social context who belongs to what group now and during the genocide. The history of genocide is still very important to the way people look at each other, trust each other, and accept or reject each other. At the same time, people seldom use the words "Tutsi" or "Hutu." Instead, the words "genocide survivor" have come to mean Tutsi, excluding Hutus who were also targeted during the genocide. I have also been acutely aware of the ethnic origins of the people I met (as well as my own ethnicity), even when I struggled not to reduce the individuals to their ethnicity. At all times, ethnicity was difficult to deal with—be it as a concept of analysis or as a very acute element of lived realities. I have not solved how to deal with ethnic categorization. I have, however, noted when and how it was perceived as relevant by my informants, for the lives of mothers and their children.

WOMEN TELL THEIR NARRATIVES

As noted above, it is well established that rape functions as a weapon of war in conflict settings and particularly in the 1994 genocide in Rwanda. However, as also noted above, little is actually known about its effects on the mothering a child born from rape in the longer term and in particular contexts. How might the testimonies of mothers of children born of rape contribute to understanding how motherhood is understood and practiced under such circumstances with what we commonly assume to know?

The women in the study spoke of their experiences of mothering a "child of enemy" in complex ways. In reading the mothers' testimonies I paid attention to how they recounted their experiences of bearing children of rape. From multiple readings of their narratives, it became clear that all the narrators felt that they were rejecting their children and that they were marginalized due to their children's identity. Furthermore, they conveyed that understanding their children's identity was vital for grasping the long-term effects (as described by them) of being subject to rape during the genocide. Their testimonies underscored that the identities of the children are central to both mothers' and their children's marginalization. Three key themes that emerged from my analysis are presented in the following sections.

PARENTING A CHILD OF INTERAHAMWE

I saw him as a killer, a son of a killer. Yes, he is a son of Interahamwe[4]—*a Hutu militia. A man who repeatedly raped me, I hate him.* (Agnes)

The mother of the child born of genocide is a survivor of sexual violence. Being subjected to sexual violence has affected mothers emotionally, physically, socially, and economically. This also has a profound impact on their children. It was clear—as portrayed in the in the mothers' narratives—that the way that children identify themselves is related to the emotions of the mothers. The narrators often drew attention to the politics of rape during the genocide and the ethnicity of rapists and highlighted the feelings of bearing/parenting a "child of enemy." The mother-child bond appeared to have been impacted negatively due to the rapists' identity. Ange describes her feelings as follows: "Whenever I see my son, I remember the man, who raped me. It would have been better to die in 1994 than live as a survivor with a child of rape" (Ange).

The women noted that they had a hard time bonding with their own children because of the rapist's identity. All the narrators conveyed that they perceived their children as a living reminder of rape, as they are reminded of the ordeal that they endured during the genocide. In some cases mothers committed suicide rather than attempt to raise a child of *Interahamwe* within their communities. Women reported being ashamed of bearing a child of Hutu militias in post-genocide settings, where their children are considered "children of *Interahamwe*." Like Ange, three others said that they wished they had died during the genocide. Some wished to abort the pregnancy, as Mado describes: "When I knew that I was pregnant, I had the idea of aborting the pregnancy. I ate some traditional medicine to abort but in vain. When my daughter was born, I didn't want to breastfeed my child. My neighbours had to give her cow milk. I used to beat her every day; I hated her lot."

Like Mado, mothers have been known to seek abortions and abandon or kill their baby immediately after birth (Mukangendo). They explained that social stigmatization coming from the mothers' family members caused them to view their lives as worthless, as we shall see below. This happened especially to mothers with limited resources who had to address problems related to survival. They reported being placed in a situation where they had to choose between the child and their own families. The narratives tell us that in Rwanda children of rape have been a source of conflict amongst their families/communities.

FAMILY, COMMUNITY, AND THE CHILDREN BORN OF RAPE

Neither Tutsis nor Hutus like our children; they are there "in-be-tween." Our children are perceived as "children of killers" and they are marginalized in our communities. But the problem is that some of the mothers do not like their children. (Jeanne)

In the Rwandan context, like in so many cultural settings around the globe, family is central to the life of people, and childhood is interlinked with the family and the community (Mukamana and Brysiewicz). Furthermore, the "legitimate" child is defined by customary and Rwandan civil laws as child born to parents who are legally married. This legitimacy is solidified in terms of rights of property and inheritance. As we shall see in the discussion below, mothers conveyed that when their relatives know that the child has been born out of such rape, the child is considered illegitimate and stigmatized, as is the mother.

Rwanda is a patrilineal society. This means that children are typically identified with the lineage of their fathers. The generally patriarchal sociocultural context corresponds with a patrilineal social system such that inheritance passes through the father both in terms of property and in terms of "ethnicity," as well as in the notion that the "child bears the fathers sins" (Goodhart 307). In Rwanda, as in other post-conflict countries where forced pregnancy was used as a strategy of war, children might be seen as indirect perpetrators of genocide (Goodhart). This continues to disturb mothers who think the perception in some cases does not reflect reality. The idea that the child bears the father' sins sends a very powerful message about identity—how it is perceived, constructed, and imagined especially in a patriarchal society like Rwanda. It reflects how the child's identity is tied to the father, even if the child never meets the father, and even if the child's mother cares for and raises the child.

The mothers' narratives tell us that the children are rejected because they are viewed as the enemy, given the circumstances of their conception. Their children are typically identified with the lineage of their fathers. One can surmise that families, community, and society in general perceive children born out of rape as children of killers. Cathy, one narrator, describes the following: "My daughter resembles her father ... the Hutu man who raped me ... and whenever my sisters see her, they remember the man who killed their parents. ... They hate her ... they call her a child of hate ... they call me a wife of a killer." Cathy maintains what other women had also stated during the interviews. Referring back to the discussion of parenting a child of enemy, women narrated that how having a child fathered by an *Interahamwe* is a problem in Rwandan society.

As Carpenter notes, the success of mass rape and forced impregnation as a weapon of war depends not on what identity is ascribed to children by the perpetrators, but on how the affected community views the children. This was also reflected in mothers' narratives. They described the social effects of bearing a child from rape in different ways. Martha explains, for instance:

I am ashamed ... I feel like live in a bush. ... It is not easy to live with a child of enemy in my community. My relatives cannot accept my child and my in-laws cannot recognize him. I am the one who has to carry the burden. ... Caring for a child of Interahamwe *is a heavy burden ... and I know I will not be happy for my whole life.*

Martha emphasizes that after being raped she was not valued by her family and her community. Martha's story illustrates how women still feel as if they live in an insecure environment (they are still "hiding in a bush") and are marginalized by their neighbours and must flee into "anonymity." Martha spoke of the isolation she suffered and the burdens she endured while caring for a child who is neither recognized by his/her family nor accepted, as he/she is "a child of *Interahamwe*." She is destined to a life of unhappiness because of the isolation of bearing these burdens alone.

As noted above, the narrators explained that the rape mainly targeted Tutsi women, not only to physically harm them, but also to send a message to the whole Tutsi community. The narratives of mothers show how, in the context of the genocide and ethnicization of communities, having a child fathered by Hutu militia remains to be perceived as a problem in the community despite the government's effort to ban ethnicity in the post genocide Rwanda.

WE ARE NOT "NORMAL" MOTHERS

I am not a girl because I have a child born of rape. Yet I do not have a husband. I am something in-between. My neighbours call me Indushyi. *(Jeanne)*

In Rwandan cultural settings, *Indushyi* means a woman who is miserable, vulnerable, and sometimes rejected. In this context, marriage is accepted as a traditional and powerful institution (Mukamana and Brysiewicz). The narrators discussed the patriarchal ideologies of Rwandan society and the cultural norms that dictate who is the "good mother." In Rwanda, a woman is often reduced to being viewed as a tool for procreation of future generations, and the term "good mother" is attributed to a woman who is married and bears children in ways the community considers "official."

Like Jeanne (cited above), many narrators reported that both mothers and the children born of rape are still facing stigmatization in their daily lives because society refuses to integrate them and accept their children as part of the community. Given the above, since women *as mothers* are traditionally at the centre of family and are responsible for the cultural reproduction of the family, Tutsi women as mothers or potential mothers became the strategic targets of Hutu men. Baines explains, for instance, that the stigma associated with rape puts the women-victims of rape at risk of being labelled as unmarriageable. The single mothers and girls who have lost their virginity through rape often suffer the problem of social belonging: "I was single and virgin before Hutu militias raped me. Now I have a child but I am still single. I know that I will not be married for the whole of my life" (Olive). In Rwandan culture, a raped woman is seen as an "outcast" and because the rape was done in public, women victims of rape face social stigma and thus political and economic exclusion by the community.

Women conveyed that they are shamed for being raped during war because their experience stands in contrast to the norms of heterosexual sex within the marriage unit. Mariam described as follows: "In order to secure my marriage, I had to leave my daughter, born as a result of rape in my aunt's home. My husband did not like her at all" (Nadia). Like Nadia, several of the narrators highlighted that the pressure from partners contributed to the mothers' losing their marital status, and leaving their children born from rape in order to secure their marriage. The testimonies of the narrators shed light on what life is like in Rwanda for mothers with children born of rape. Mothers are obliged to marry in order to integrate back into the community. As Cathy mentions (below), sometimes new partners pretended to adopt the children born of rape and accept them as their own. But several women interviewed indicated that there was fighting between their children and the step-fathers. Cathy explained: "After genocide, I left my baby at my mother's place when I got married. When my husband knew that I had a child from rape, he divorced me." Cathy, like other narrators explained that the raped woman loses all the support of her partner not just because she was raped, but specifically because she was raped and impregnated by an ethnically defined "enemy." This, in turn, keeps children permanently excluded from the family and keeps their mothers in an in-between position—acknowledged as members of *"survivors of genocide"* by the family and community, but marginalized nevertheless as *mothers of enemy children.*

CONCLUSION

While the Serbs sought to transform the Bosnia Muslim population by forcibly impregnating its women, in Rwanda, the Hutu men used rape as a weapon to torture, to punish, and to destroy the Tutsi community. However, genocidal rape increased the risk of unwanted pregnancies and abortion was/is a crime under Rwandan law. This chapter explores how ten Rwandan mothers of children born of wartime rape recount their experiences of mothering children born of rape in the post-genocide era. Becoming a mother is commonly imagined to be a joyful life event. The testimonies of mothers in this paper are different. Their experience is compounded by the child's identity as well as cultural and patriarchal notions of who is a good mother. The community calls the children, "children of killers." Socio-culturally they do not know where they belong, and this complicates the life situations of their mothers who have to take care of the children in such environment. Mothers in this study show that the consequences of rape and forced impregnation are aggravated by the specific intersection of gender and ethnicity in Rwanda, and the country's specific form of patriarchal relations, where children are typically identified with the lineage of their fathers. This means that a large part of the society will perceive children of wartime rape as belonging to the enemy. This is reflected in the local discourse casting the babies as "little *Interahamwe*" (McKinley qtd. in Mukangendo 42).

In Rwandan culture, a woman is often reduced to being viewed as a tool for procreation of future generations, and "motherhood" is attributed to a woman who is married in the ways the community considers "normal." Pregnancies resulting from mass rape of Tutsi women during the genocide are not considered normal. The mothers' identity as "good" women is tightly locked into motherhood and yet living with "children of enemies" they are unable to become what society considers "good mothers." The narrators in this study have suffered during/after the 1994 genocide and have had to cope with myriad cultural and emotional problems which have made their motherhood journey a difficult path. It was clear—as portrayed in the mothers' narratives—that the way children identify themselves is related to the emotions of the mothers. Some described feelings of anxiety and rejection towards their children. As Carpenter points out, in some countries "there are alternative means of care for those mothers wishing to give up the children" (5). None of these measures, however, exist in Rwanda on the level of state provisions, and very limited resources are provided by non-governmental organizations.

It is crucial to recognize that the narratives of the mothers in this study may not necessarily be pertinent to all mothers with the children born of rape in the Rwandan context. This paper can only be considered an introduction to an immensely complex issue that requires resources far beyond the means of this study. However, provisionally, based on the narratives of mothers in this study, it can be concluded that mothers with children born of genocidal rape have experienced physical and emotional challenges within family, community, and society in general.

[1]The Republic of Rwanda is a landlocked country of 26.338 square kilometers situated in Great Lakes Region, bordered by Burundi in the south, Democratic Republic of Congo (formerly Zaire) in the west, Tanzania in the east, and Uganda in the north (Koster). [2]The best known case is that of a Twa named Busyete, who was promoted as Tutsi by the nineteenth century, and became chief of province and married the king's daughter. His descendants became Tutsis known under the name of Basyete (Vansina). [3]Hutu moderate means Hutu people who did not support the ideology of the MRND and the Hutu women who had married Tutsi men or were the daughters of mixed marriages. [4]*Interahamwe* is loosely translated as "those who stand together." It was a group of Hutu militia licenced by the Hutu extremist government in 1994 to eradicate the Tutsi minority.

WORKS CITED

Baaz, Maria Eriksson, and Maria Stern. *Sexual Violence as a Weapon of War?: Perceptions, Prescriptions, Problems in the Congo and Beyond*. London: Zed books, 2013. Print.

Baines, Erin K. "Body Politics and the Rwandan Crisis." *Third*

World Quarterly 24.3 (2003): 479-93. Print.

Carpenter, R Charli. *Born of War: Protecting Children of Sexual Violence Survivors in Conflict Zones.* Sterling, VA: Kumarian Press, 2007. Print.

De Brouwer, Anne Marie L.M. *Supranational Criminal Prosecution of Sexual Violence: The Icc and the Practice of the Icty and the Ictr.* Antwerp: Intersentia, 2005. Print.

Hintjens, Helen M. "Explaining the 1994 Genocide in Rwanda." *The Journal of Modern African Studies* 37.02 (1999): 241-86. Print.

Kagoyire, Ange. Personal interview.15 April 2012.

Kaneza, Mado. Personal interview. 5 May 2013.

Kayitesi, Agnes. Personal interview. 14 April 2012.

Koster, Marian. *Fragmented Lives: Reconstructing Rural Livelihoods in Post-Genocide Rwanda.* N.pub, 2008. Print.

Mamdani, Mahmood. *When Victims Become Killers: Colonialism, Nativism, and the Genocide in Rwanda.* Princeton: Princeton University Press, 2014. Print.

Mibenge, Chiseche. "Gender and Ethnicity in Rwanda." *Gender, Violent Conflict and Development.* Ed. D. Zarkov. New Delhi: Zubaan, 2008. 145-179. Print.

Mukamana, Donatilla, and Petra Brysiewicz. "The Lived Experience of Genocide Rape Survivors in Rwanda." *Journal of Nursing Scholarship* 40.4 (2008): 379-84. Print.

Mukangendo, Marie Consolee. "Caring for Children Born of Rape in Rwanda." *Born of War: Protecting Children of Sexual Violence Survivors in Conflict Zones* (2007): 40. Print.

Nowrojee, Binaifer. *Shattered Lives: Sexual Violence During the Rwandan Genocide and Its Aftermath.* Vol. 3169. New York: Human Rights Watch, 1996. Print.

Prunier, Gérard. *The Rwanda Crisis: History of a Genocide.*New York: Columbia University Press, 1995. Print.

Seto, Donna. *No Place for a War Baby: The Global Politics of Children Born of Wartime Sexual Violence.* London: Ashgate Publishing, Ltd., 2013. Print.

Stern, Maria. *Naming Security-Constructing Identity: Mayan-Women in Guatemala on the Eve of "Peace."* Manchester: Manchester University Press, 2005. Print.

Taylor, C. "A Gendered Genocide: Tutsi Women and Hutu Extremists in the 1994 Rwanda Genocide." *Political and Legal Anthropology Review* 22.1 (1999): 42-54. Print.

Uvin, Peter. *Aiding Violence: The Development Enterprise in Rwanda*. Sterling, VA: Kumarian Press, 1998. Print.

Vansina, Jan. *Antecedents to Modern Rwanda: The Nyiginya Kingdom*. Oxford: University of Wisconsin Press, 2005. Print.

8.
Raising Children Born
of Wartime Rape in Bosnia

A Maternal Philosophy Perspective

TATJANA TAKŠEVA

B ETWEEN 1991 AND 1995 BOSNIA was one of the deadliest
regions in the wars triggered by the disintegration of the So-
cialist Federal Republic of Yugoslavia. Under the banner of the
old Yugoslav army, all sides, but particularly Serbian nationalist
forces, engaged in campaigns of ethnic cleansing of Bosnians of
Moslem faith and ethnic heritage, also called Bosniaks (*Bošnjaci*
(Sharratt). A significant aspect of this strategy was the massive,
organized, and systematic use of genocidal rape and enforced
impregnation of primarily Bosniak and Croat women. The UN
commission investigating the rapes emphasized that it found
"victims among all ethnic groups involved in the conflict," and
Amnesty International supports this finding based on their own
investigations (Mazowiecki 71). However, looking at the issue in
terms of numbers and scale, it is estimated that between 25,000 and
40,000 Bosniak women and girls—the majority of victims—were
victims of genocidal rape and enforced impregnation by Serbian
forces, released from the rape camps only after their pregnancies
had progressed beyond the possibility of a safe abortion (Allen;
Sharratt; Skjelsbaek; Erjavec and Volčič).

Rape survivors who spoke about what happened to them reported
being told by Serbian soldiers that the purpose behind the rape
was to impregnate them with "Serb children" or "little Chetniks,"
that is, nationalist Serbian soldiers who will later turn against their
biological mothers. The massive and organized scale on which these
rapes were taking place and the existence of the rape camps, im-
provised but purposefully utilized spaces where the women, if they

were not killed, were kept and abused for several months, suggests that even during early investigations in 1992 and 1993 there was likely a politically and ideologically motivated agenda behind the acts. There is now scholarly consensus that there was a genocidal intention behind the enforced impregnation whose purpose was manifold: to cause the rejection of raped mothers and their children and thus destabilize their social and ethnic group (Erjavec and Volčič); to persuade and prepare victims to hate and eventually to destroy their own children or be destroyed by them; to also create a situation where the paternal lineage of the child—seen as decisive in determining ethnic and national identity—would perpetuate and increase the ethnic group of the aggressor and destabilize the social cohesion of the maternal communities.

Sexual and gender violence such as wartime rape is used as a weapon that degrades and dominates not only the women but their communities as well. The sexual violation of women is an attack on female subjectivity and often results in the destruction of that subjectivity (Seifert). At the same time, it disrupts family and social structures and symbolizes the destruction and rape of the community of the enemy force (Seifert). The "perception of public ownership of women's sexuality ... makes it possible to translate an attack against one woman into an attack against an entire community; the impact is multiplied when the woman becomes pregnant" (Shanks and Schull 1153). This perception operates in a post-conflict context as well. Surviving wartime rape results in social stigma against the rape survivor as well as her child as the community often sees the child as an "insult" and a continual reminder of collective violence and the enemy. The gravity and complexity of this particular form of sexual abuse is acknowledged by the Rome Statute of the International Criminal Court, which explicitly recognizes rape and forced impregnation as crimes against humanity (Rome).

The number of Bosnian women who gave birth to babies conceived through rape is difficult to estimate partly due to the reluctance of many survivors to speak of the rapes (as the topic is still seen as taboo in many communities) and partly due to poorly kept statistics. Many survivors chose to abort the pregnancy, if that was possible, in safe as well as unsafe conditions. Many of those who did not have access to abortion or who saw no other alternatives killed their children upon birth. Many others chose not to raise their children and gave them up for adoption. According to Fadila Memiševic of the Association for Threatened Peoples of Bosnia, many of those women would have wanted to keep their children but the pressures they were placed under were intolerable (Beširbašić).

The number of women who found the courage to care for the children—courage, as both often face rejection and abuse from close and extended family, as well as prejudice and discrimination from the wider community—is equally difficult to estimate, but it is a small minority. While there has been some attention paid in international law, social and anthropological studies, and humanitarian policy to the effects of rape and the psycho-social and protection needs of women and girl survivors of wartime rape, there is marked paucity of studies dealing with how the conflict shapes the mothering practices of women raising children born of wartime rape, the children themselves, and the relationships between mothers and children. Based on a small body of recorded narratives by the mothers who, despite overwhelming social pressures, had the courage to keep and raise their children, as well as narratives by their adolescent children, in this chapter I wish to highlight the experience of Bosnian women who have kept and raised their children, some of whom have testified that the choice to raise their child was a means of overcoming the horror of the rape (*War Babies*). Drawing on their narratives, this chapter describes what is known about their lives together and the nature of mothering in which they and their children have been engaged. In my investigation, I adopt a maternal philosophy perspective as articulated by feminist philosopher Sara Ruddick and others as a critical lens through which some aspects of their mothering practice can be contextualized and understood. At the same time, I adapt this perspective with respect to the particular social, cultural, and psychological contexts of Bosnian mothers and children. My aim is to shed light on some of the factors that inform the maternal work of Bosnian wartime rape survivors and their relationship with their children and provide a new framework for understanding their experience.

MATERNAL PHILOSOPHY PERSEPCTIVE AND AIMS

Rather than discussing mothering as a natural activity defined by biological imperatives, Ruddick argues that maternal practice is a conscious and thoughtful endeavour focused on meeting the demands of children in three main areas that are often informed by conflict among the three. These areas are: preservation, nurturance, and training in social acceptability. Ruddick's views enabled the emergence of a perspective according to which the status of mother is not necessarily or solely determined through conception, gestation, and giving birth, but through the mothers' thoughts, intentions, and actions. It also posits the study of maternal practice as a worthwhile pursuit based on her understanding of the complexity of that practice. Mothers are mothers "just because and to the degree that they are committed to meeting the demands that define maternal work" (Ruddick 17). I will apply aspects of each one of the three areas stipulated as demands as they relate to the recorded narratives of Bosnian rape survivors and their children.

It has to be noted that the women and children whose narratives are recorded in existing studies and reports are a self-selected sample and not representative of the entire population of mothers who are rape survivors and children born of wartime rape. However, it is my belief that methodological concerns such as these should not preclude efforts to focus attention on important and understudied issues. The willingness to rely on illustrative cases rather than seeking, often without success, to create a "representative sample" is a step toward the examination of issues pertaining to the rape survivors and their children that often slide off the academic and media radar.

At no point in this discussion do I intend to imply that women who chose to keep their babies fall into the category of the proverbial "good mother," while those who did not are "bad mothers," or that there is something inherently either positive or negative about either group of women. Recent feminist psychiatric discussions of motherhood, for example, clearly point to the importance of maternal subjectivity. Rather than theorizing the mother as an "object" of the baby's desires or "depicted through the containing or transformative function she performs," the mother as a person, her psycho-social history, the specific circumstances of this particular conception, as well as the subjective meaning a woman assigns to the experience of mothering, must not be neglected from any consideration of motherhood (Raphael-Leff, "Mothers" 11). Thus I am not willing to assign ethically-charged, reductionist, and simplistic labels to motherhood or mothering since as a condition and a process neither possesses universal manifestations. To that effect I embrace the premise that people become mothers and practice mothering in particular historical, social, and personal circumstances, and that investigations into mothering practices should be grounded in particular individual, social, and historical contexts. Conscious that there are great personal variations among the interviewed women dependent on their class and educational background, the question I am seeking to provide preliminary answers for is: What does it mean to keep and raise a child born of wartime rape in post-conflict Bosnia? My aim is to engage with the maternal practice of Bosnian rape survivors, both women and children, and the extent to which records of their narrated identities support or contradict aspects of the maternal philosophy here adopted as a critical lens and a tool for critical reflection.

Preservation

In defining preservative love, Ruddick emphasizes the conceptual links between thought and feeling, noting that "thoughtful feeling, passionate thought and protective acts together test as they reveal" the nature of the demand for preservation (70). While her definition applies to the activity of mothering as performed by parents who are raising a child out of choice and a priori desire to do so, in this context, I extend the definition of preservation to include the decision of a small number of raped mothers in Bosnia to keep and raise their children rather than place them in an orphanage or give them up for adoption.

In the current Bosnian context, considering the experience of gestation and birth as separate from the experience of mothering is enabling in at least two ways, both of which serve to underscore the complexity of the mothers' circumstance. On the one hand, the split between the two roles focuses much needed attention on the individual agency of the women who chose to keep and raise their children in adverse circumstance, and highlights a particular kind of personal determination that repositions and redefines their status as victims. The media and consequently the public often portray and construct rape survivors as victims of childbirth who "cannot bear the shame of giving birth to babies they cannot possibly love" (Carpenter, "Fresh Crop" 28). While the violent victimization of rape survivors is indisputable, emphasizing that some women despite the violence, victimization, and the promise of lasting social stigma chose to keep their children reframes their experience and choice in an agentive manner and provides a more complex understanding of the experience of wartime rape survivors in Bosnia. In this sense, the women exercised their choice with respect to what they perceived to be a demand for preservation of their children, regardless of the manner of their conception. The decision to keep and raise their children was seen by some women as helping them overcome their own trauma regarding the rape.

On the other hand, the separation between the experiences of gestation and birth and mothering as a committed practice may negate the reality of some of the mothers whose choice to keep their babies may have been based on their understanding of a profound connection that exists between the two processes—the biological and the social—based on which the biological process is a precondition for the other. Some Bosnian mothers hold an essentialist view of motherhood, which proved helpful in allowing them to negotiate the painful memories of their trauma and the claiming of the children as their own, the products of themselves and their own bodies, and in this way "deserving of" and "demanding" the motherwork that followed their birth. In this sense, it is useful to see the biological aspects of reproduction on the one hand, and maternal caregiving practice on the other, as two processes that, while separate, in some circumstances inform each other in productive and instrumental ways. Both perspectives illustrate the diverse orientations that exist in maternal beliefs and behaviours, women's subjective approaches to pregnancy resulting from rape, the baby, birth, and motherhood, and how "different challenges interact with each expectant mother's personal belief system, self-esteem and mental health" (Raphael-Leff "Mothers" 13).

Answering a perceived demand for preservation and protective care is never straightforward and much less assumed as "naturally" present in any mothering context, but for rape survivors it is even more complex. The matter of preservation with respect to the pregnancy itself was enforced upon the women by the rapists. Many rape survivors had no choice but to carry the pregnancy to term and give birth. Many subsequently gave the babies up for adoption. Few chose to keep their children. Medical research shows that "antenatal emotional experience primes postnatal interactions" and that "pregnancy is a blending of three intertwined systems: biological, psychological and social" (Raphael-Leff, "Mothers" 11). For the rape survivors this reality is even further complicated due to the fact that their antenatal experience includes not only severe emotional trauma, but physical trauma as well, combined with the acute cultural awareness that any children born of such circumstances are likely to be shunned and ostracized along with the mother herself. In the cases of pregnancy resulting from rape, psychiatrists agree that women's mental health is endangered by her pregnancy (Solomon). Even in the best of circumstances, what is usually referred to as "mother love" is "intermixed with hate, sorrow, impatience, resentment and despair" as "thought provoking ambivalence is a hallmark of mothering" (Ruddick 68). The intensity and prevalence of these emotions is especially emphasized for mothers engaged in raising children born of rape.

Jasmina, a rape survivor raising a daughter born of wartime rape committed by a Croat, had a very difficult pregnancy according to a local psychologist, because "like other girls and women in her situation, she did not accept that she was pregnant ... she somehow disassociated herself mentally from the child she was carrying and even when the baby was born, wanted to do little with her" (qtd. in Toomey). Seven days after her daughter's birth, the staff of Medica Zenica, the center for providing medical and psychological help for traumatized and raped women, arranged for a traditional Muslim naming ceremony to be held for the child. Very slowly, Jasmina came to accept her daughter, Elma, despite the fact that her own mother cursed her for not abandoning the baby after birth. Jasmina articulates how her mother came to accept her decision and the reasons why she decided to keep the child: "It was only after she saw how determined I was to keep the child that she began to change her mind. Now I realize it was my daughter who helped me back to some sort of normality. Perhaps that is why I love her so much" (qtd.in Toomey). At the same time, Jasmina's reality shows that in her case, protective love and answering the demand for preservation required a great deal of conscious effort and perseverance. In describing the interaction between herself and her infant daughter in the early days she says: "I used to block out the sound [of her daughter's crying] and just leave her, walk away…. I had to work very hard to love my child" (qtd. in Toomey). Jasmina's words point toward maternal ambivalence and the effort required in accepting her child. In this case, walking away can be seen as an act of preservative care. Her narrative also shows a fundamental attitude that she adopts toward the vulnerable, a protectiveness Ruddick calls "holding … a way of seeing with an eye toward maintaining the minimal harmony, material resources, and skills necessary for sustaining a child in safety" (78-9). Learning how to see Elma as a "separate individual endowed with personal characteristics and changing mental states" resulted in an interactive awareness on Jasmina's part and, evidently, a greater self-understanding (Raphael-Leff 20).

Jasmina admits that the child's gender contributed to her decision to keep her. She feels that the possible physical resemblance and gender identification between the child and the rapist/biological father would be too much to bear. Of her daughter, Jasmina says:

Even now, when my daughter gets angry, there is something in the expression of her face that reminds me of the one who did this to me. I feel like hitting her in those moments. I have to walk away to calm myself. Imagine what that would be like if I had a boy. (qtd. in Toomey)

Jasmina articulates the presence of "intense, ambivalent, thought-provoking feelings," which according to maternal philosophy are typical in most if not all mothers (Ruddick 78-9). In her situation, these feelings are amplified exponentially due to the traumatic nature of her daughter's conception and her own coming to terms with an unwanted pregnancy. At the same time, her actions, walking away when her daughter's behaviour and appearance trigger traumatic memories, demonstrate a form of thoughtful mothering governed by "a *commitment* that perseveres through feeling and structures the activity" of mothering (Ruddick 78-9). Nadia's story demonstrates a similar perspective. One of the few women who have been raising a child born of war, she notes: "I love my son. Sometimes I look at him and feel very angry though—I see him as a focus for what has gone wrong with my family and our lives" (qtd. in Holt and Hughes).

Safeta's experience of mothering a child born of rape by a group of Serb volunteer soldiers shows both similarities and differences. Like Jasmina, Safeta was unable to prevent the birth; after the birth she refused to look at the baby, claiming she would strangle him. For Safeta the child's gender was also an important factor in her decision to keep him, but for different reasons. In her view, she was glad that her child was a boy. To an interviewer she said: "I was afraid that it would be a girl, and that what happened to me will happen to her" (qtd. in Tremonti). Her infant son was deposited in an orphanage in Tuzla (Bećirbašić). However, six months after giving birth, haunted by thoughts of the baby, Safeta set out to find her son: "I couldn't sleep for four months. After six months it became unbearable. If I hadn't found him when I did, I probably wouldn't be alive now" (qtd. in Bećirbašić). The intensity of her feelings toward her child and the connection she makes between her own life and wellbeing and his, echoes Jasmina's experience. It took seven years for Safeta to summon the courage as well as the financial means to take her son, Edin, out of the orphanage. Without employment and without any means to support herself, Safeta took her son to her parents but they refused to accept him. Welfare services from Sarajevo were also unable to provide her with the help she required. Until she was able to secure work and a place to live, Safeta visited Edin regularly and was driven by a vision of the two of them living together under the same roof. She describes this vision as being the sole purpose of her living: "That was what I lived for, the moment when darkness would turn into light. And if people disapproved, I couldn't care less" (qtd. in Bećirbašić). Safeta's ordeal also demonstrates not only the conjunction of "passionate thought and protective acts," but also that her understanding and experience of mothering was governed by a "commitment that perseveres through feeling and structures the activity" (Ruddick 78-9).

One of the aspects of protective love defined by Ruddick as constitutive of answering the demand for preservation is what she terms mothers' "cheerfulness." Cheerfulness is "a matter of fact willingness to accept having given birth, to start and start over again, to welcome a future despite conditions of one's self, one's children, one's society, and nature that may be reasons for despair" (Ruddick 74). While neither Jasmina's nor Safeta's experience can be understood as "a matter of fact willingness to accept having given birth," their daily, years-long fight for their children's survival amidst bigotry, rejection, poverty, and ongoing struggle with their own precarious mental health can be termed cheerfulness in a philosophical sense, as through their mothering practice they do show a willingness to start and start over again, and to welcome an uncertain future in psychologically and socially adverse conditions.

Nurturance and fostering growth

According to Ruddick, to foster growth means "to nurture a child's gradually developing humanity and spirit" (82). She states that "the mind of a mother fostering growth is marked by a sense of children's complexity and of the difficulties of responding confidently to them. ... Many mothers engaged in the practice of preservation do not recognize a distinctive task of fostering growth" (83). The already cited narratives of Jasmina, Safeta, and Nadia indeed indicate that the two are closely intertwined in their own mothering contexts. The mothers' awareness of their children's complexity and the difficulties of responding confidently to those complexities, while common to many mothers, are especially complex and difficult for women rape survivors raising children born of war and violence. In their case, the mothers' awareness of their children's complexity is not marked only by a loving and protective insight into the child's own mental and moral developing world that may be different from the mothers'.

The mothers' loving and protective insight is also often mitigated by her awareness that the physiological origins constitutive of that world clash violently and threateningly with her own. The children's complexity in this case may be perceived as an agent of alienation between mother and child, a potential trigger for the mother's most traumatic memories, whose embodiment the child appears to be.

At the same time, the children's complexity is also marked by their own "outsider" social status and the difficulties that they are facing not only because they are the product of rape by the "enemy," but also due to the cultural perception of their mother's own culpability. The children's complexity here is also marked by their awareness of their mothers' own suffering, and in some cases, their awareness that this suffering is closely linked to their existence and identity. Jasmina's words demonstrate a mother's protective and empathetic awareness of this complexity, as well as her own difficulty in responding confidently to them. Of her daughter, Jasmina says through tears:

> She is a very, very good child, very, very smart, very intelligent. But I feel sorry for her because she is feeling my pain. That is why I am sorry, because she doesn't have her own life, she lives mine. She feels sorry for me all the time. I tell myself, maybe if she was somewhere else, maybe it would be different, maybe if she was with another family maybe she would not feel all this pain. But nobody can love her the way I love her. (qtd. in Tremonti)

Jasmina is worried that her daughter's personal needs for nurture and growth are stifled by her sympathetic response to her mother's own suffering. From Jasmina's words it is clear that she does not see the practice of preservation as distinctive from the task of fostering growth.

The only existing study on the narrative self-representation of adolescent girls born of war and raised by Bosnian rape survivors indicates that the complexity of the children's experience is to a large extent influenced by their "intuitive" feeling of the mothers' suffering (qtd. in Erjavec and Vočič). Three out of the eleven interviewed girls show that they assign guilt to themselves though their relationship with their mothers since they perceive themselves as a "live reminder of rape" (qtd. in Erjavec and Volčič 372). Two of the girls in particular express a close connection to their mothers, using formulations such as "I am one with my mother" and "I am inseparable from my mother" (qtd. in Erjavec and Volčič 372). They feel close to their mothers since "the mothers suffer more" and suffer because of them. As Satka says: "My mother is all about pain and suffering and my hugs bring her even more pain. It's so hard to describe this relationship—I know she loves and hates me at the same time" (qtd. in Erjavec and Volčič 372). While children may reawaken in their mothers earlier conflicts experienced even as far back as childhood (Ruddick), and while maternal ambivalence is the unspoken hallmark of mothering even in circumstances that may be considered more ordinary, most children remain unaware of these complex emotional and psychological realities. In this case, the concern for nurture and growth for the child is mitigated and influenced by the children's acute awareness of maternal ambivalence, the complexity of the mothers' response, and the complexity of their relationship. To some extent, the concern for nurture is here redefined through role reversal, a dominant theme that emerged through the girls' narratives. Meira's understanding of herself and her life is focused on her relationship with her mother; she defines herself as a "mother," claiming that "I am a mother to my mother" (qtd. in Erjavec and Volčič 374). Because her mother had difficulty with managing everyday tasks outside the home, such as shopping or paying bills, Meira took on these and other responsibilities, and in some sense, become her mother's nurturer. Meira and the other girls do not blame their mothers for how they are treated by their community and the ostracism they face; on the contrary, they focus positively on their mothers and see themselves and their mothers as an emotional "unit," a close team of "us" against "them," everyone on the outside (qtd. in Erjavec and Volčič 374).

While many mothers "recognize and presume in their nurturing a child's efforts to create coherence and the shame and confusion he feels when he and the world together cannot find a satisfactory identity" (Ruddick 92), for Bosniak mothers who are rape survivors this practice carries particular challenges. The children's efforts at creating coherence with regard to the most basic narrative concerning their identity in all recorded cases result in an even greater degree of ostracism and social exclusion, and personally constitute the most traumatic event in their lives. Many mothers who are rape survivors chose to conceal the narrative of their children's conception and the identity of their biological father when it is known, precisely because they know intuitively that maternal conversations and maternal stories are important "instruments of self-confidence," and that sharing and elaborating on their observations, making a coherent, dramatic, or poignant story of their children's particularities, establishes continuity in their ongoing nurturing activities (Ruddick 92). Their concealment, while denying the children the possibility of piecing together a sense of continuity and coherence about who they are, is a thoughtful and deliberate effort to protect the child from experiencing trauma. Safeta is one of those women; she and her son live in a small, remote village where most of the men were killed in the war. Her teenage son has never asked about his father and Safeta sees no reason for telling him that his father is not one of those men who lost his life fighting in the war, which is what he assumes (Tremonti).

In many cases, however, people in the community will press for disclosure. For Jasmina this meant being called in by Elma's teacher who wanted to know why her daughter did not want to take part in telling stories about fathers in class (Toomey). Jasmina felt very offended by what she perceived to be an intrusive intervention into their private lives: "I told them they had no right to ask such questions, and told my daughter that if anyone asked her, she should say I am both her mother and her father, that her father is killed in the war" (qtd. in Toomey). Once children reach adolescence, many start asking questions about their fathers, and sometimes they will find out on their own. No matter how protective mothers like Jasmina are, children will have picked up unspoken messages form those around them that the subject is not to be discussed. While "ideally, a mother's stories are as beneficial to her children as they are to her" (Ruddick 98), in this case, far from ideal, the story of the child's conception and origin can be considered beneficial only in the sense that it provides access to an important but painfully experienced truth. Some mothers who have survived rape, like Jasmina, feel that it is important to let their children know the truth about their biological father, and they display extraordinary amounts of thoughtfulness and worry about the conditions and timing of when this knowledge can be revealed to their children. Jasmina is determined that she will tell Elma the truth: "Perhaps when she starts to attend high school, then I'll tell her what happened. I am raising Elma to believe that we should have no secrets. I want her to hear the truth from someone who loves her" (qtd. In Toomey). Jasmina's belief echoes the philosophical perspective that "however realistic they are, maternal stories should also be compassionate" (Ruddick 99).

Social Acceptability

The demand for training the children for social acceptability is a very problematic and complex area of maternal practice for mothers who are rape survivors in Bosnia. Provided that the desire for social acceptance for them and her children is among primary human concerns for mothers and children, the realities of Bosnian society and the hostility of the mother's own community preclude and frustrate any attempts to achieve this acceptance. Children born of wartime rape are marginalized as subjects of human rights law and there is a tendency to "identify them with the perpetrators rather than the victims of genocide" (Carpenter, "Surfacing" 403). The dominant cultural discourse constructs them as "children of the enemy" and "children of hate" and represents them as tools of genocide within already victimized communities.[1] As the victims of rape at the hands of the enemy and whose proverbial chastity has thus been doubly violated, the women themselves are perceived as "damaged goods" and often rejected by their close and extended families. The women's own psychic state and thus their capacity to mother authentically are furthermore complicated by the facts that "the child is frequently seen by her family and/or other compatriots as proof of the woman's collaboration with the enemy, or as evidence of her immoral behavior" (qtd. in Nikolić-Ristanović 70). So while it is true that "many mothers find that the central challenge of mothering lies in training a child to be the kind of person whom others accept and whom the mothers themselves can actively appreciate" (Ruddick 104), this perspective acquires a particular profundity in the case of mothers rape survivors.

In more ordinary circumstances, the articulated challenge lies in reconciling the mother's own values and beliefs with those of her society, since aspects of the two often find themselves in conflict. According to a philosophical understanding of maternal practice, mothers who negotiate this challenge with a degree of confidence are said to be able to mother authentically. In the context of mothering children born of rape in Bosnia, there are many factors that can prevent mothers from mothering authentically. One such factor contributing to the loss of maternal authority is the gaze of others as represented by "teachers, grandparents, mates, friends, employers, even anonymous passers-by who judge a mother by her child's behavior" (Ruddick 111). In this context, the mother is judged not only by her child's behaviour, but also by her child's very identity and her own past traumatic experience. These conditions can make mothers lose confidence in their own personal values and their own effectiveness as mothers and lead to a "loss of self" (Ruddick 111). In cases where mothers are themselves economically impoverished, stigmatized, and excluded from the broader community and battling their own untreated Post-Traumatic Stress Disorder, this loss of self prevents them from mothering from a place of confidence and social agency. Mothers are also rendered powerless in children's eyes because they are treated with contempt by others—fathers, landlords, welfare workers, teachers, therapists, and numerous other authorities who insult mothers even in front of their own children (Ruddick). This happens to many mothers, but it is something that happens habitually to Bosnian mothers who are raising children born of rape.

Anecdotal evidence and press reports show that children born of rape are routinely subjected to stigmatization, that is they are deeply discredited based on their being reduced to the "children of hate" and thus socially discounted (Erjavec and Volčič). Their mothers are left powerless in trying to help the children feel accepted by the society around them. A total of six out of eleven interviewed girls born of war define themselves as the object into which society can channel frustration. Zerina's statement embodies these feelings: "I see myself as a scapegoat because I have Serbian blood and in this way, I am kind of ... available for everyone to hate me. I am a channel for their sadness ... I am guilty for their pain. I am guilty for their misery that lives on. And no one likes me, everyone avoids me, everyone hates me" (qtd. in Erjavec and Volčič 367). The girls spoke about their physical abuse and social exclusion in public spaces, such as schools, shops, and streets, indicating that they are "not afforded the social respect that is commonly accorded to others," saying that in everyday contexts they have been attacked and discriminated against by community, neighbours, teachers, classmates, relatives, and close family (qtd. in Erjavec and Volčič 368).

It is often that the persistent stigmatization and abuse by the community precipitates the moment when the children discover the truth about their identity. Beba's narrative illustrates at once the harshness of her social exclusion, the traumatic moment of discovery for both mother and daughter, the complexity of the mother-daughter relationship, and the compassion the mother experiences for her daughter's situation:

> Well, that's when I asked my mother why I was being attacked, and that's when she told me the truth about it. I thought it was the end of the world.... I understood why we have no family, why we are alone. This was the day that transformed me and my life forever.... I remember we both cried, not just one day, it was a period of several weeks when we were both crying, not going out ... she is on pills from that day. (qtd. in Erjavec and Volčič 370)

Hoping to protect her daughter from the traumatic truth about her identity, the mother tried to keep the silence; her being silent also signals her hope that not naming the truth will increase her daughter's chances of seeing herself as part of their society. Faced with the realization that she would have to tell her daughter the truth for her daughter's sake, since it explains the source of their social exclusion, and being aware of the effect this will have on her daughter, as well as her future in this society, the mother is placed in an almost untenable psychological position, forced thereafter to rely on medication for continued survival.

In view of the severity and apparent omnipresence of social hostility and having being pushed to abdicate maternal authority in some cases, mothers rape survivors, rather than being "free to comfort and protect" their children (Ruddick 112), are not free at all, but rather imprisoned by multiple oppressors that work against her and her children and often turn inward, into a state of passivity. Thus, on the one hand, Beba's mother may have experienced loss of self with the realization that she has no way of protecting her daughter and sparing her not only the truth but also the continued social ostracism that the truth carries. On the other hand, however, she provided the most authentic form of mothering available to her at the time: a compassionate narration about what happened to her during the war and the truth of her daughter's identity, and a compassionate response to her daughter's own trauma triggered by the discovery. Ruddick notes that "her children's differences require the most demanding of a mother's many balancing acts: alongside her own convictions of virtues and excellence she is to place her children's human need to ask and answer for themselves questions central for moral life" (108). With her decision to tell her daughter the truth and her compassionate response to her daughter's suffering, Beba's mother placed her child's human need to ask—and answer for herself—questions central to moral, as well as ethical life. In this case both mother and daughter exist as social "outsiders," and the mother's task becomes not so much to train her child in social acceptability, but to train her child to first understand the reasons for her outsider social status, and then to find ways of reconciling herself to this difficult reality. Ruddick further points out that "often the demands for nurturance of the child's spirit and the demand to shape that spirit in socially acceptable ways pose a challenge" (105). In Beba's mother's case, the challenge exists not between nurturing and honouring the child's spirit and shaping that spirit in socially acceptable ways, but between trying to nurture the child's spirit and helping it unfold in ways that will prevent it from being broken by social exclusion and ostracism.

Rather than training their children to be socially acceptable, for some Bosnian mothers who are raising children born of war maternal practice depends upon successfully training the children to resist dominant social discourses that marginalize them. Seada is one girl who speaks of how her mother's explicitly agentive maternal practice enabled her to find a constructive way of dealing not only with the truth of her own identity, but also the social response that that identity elicits:

> You have to know that my mother is ... a fighter. She just has a strong character. When my grandparents were upset with her, because she talked very openly about what a woman was not supposed to talk about, at least that's what my grandparents thought, she did not surrender, but she left the city, and we came to Sarajevo. Just us two. No one helped us, we started anew. She is even more active here, and even more people listen to her. Zlatko [Seada's stepfather] and I support her. Yes, I guess we are all active, and we feel that we have to support her. Three years ago, when my mother went to The Hague, she told me what really happened to her. She told me how she and many other women have suffered in the camp, and she also told me who my father is. I kind of ... started to understand what the meaning of my life is. While having this discussion with my mother and all the family, we concluded that all this suffering has to have some meaning. It has to serve some purpose. Maybe to help others in similar situations? My mother decided to go public with her story—not just witnessing in The Hague but also to tell her story to a wider community here in Bosnia. I also decided to not be ashamed of it—and I started to talk about it to my friends in my school.... We all have to make sure this does not happen again. We have to assure there will be no repetition of these acts of violence.... We have to connect and build Sarajevo for all of us. (qtd. in Erjavec and Volčič 379)

Seada and her mother differ economically from the other interviewed girls since they live a more financially stable, middle-class life. Her mother is a teacher, who after the war got married to a man who officially adopted Seada. She is the only girl in the study who at the time of the interview lived with a father and siblings (qtd. in Erjavec and Volčič). In her narrative, Seada acknowledges her mother's status as outsider, as someone who stands against social, and in this case, family pressure, and chooses to live in a way that is deemed rebellious and dismissive of social expectations, including her decision to "go public with her story." At the same time, her mother's outsider status in Seada's narrative is redefined: instead of being seen as a source of weakness, it is identified with the authoritative position of someone who fights for the right cause. Her mother showed determination and strength in rebuilding her life after the war for herself and her daughter, without deference for social customs that may have kept her back from this goal. The mother's determination to take control of her own life and to place her wartime experiences in a wider perspective is evidenced in her testifying at the International Court Tribunal for the Former Yugoslavia in The Hague, in speaking about what happened to her during the war, as well as in the manner in which she let her daughter know the truth about her identity. Letting her know that "she and many other women suffered in the camp," the mother identifies the events that led to Seada's conception and birth in a broader wartime context that affected a large group of other women in the same way.

By situating the traumatic events in a broader context, the mother provided Seada with the conceptual tools that enable her to understand what happened in a way that is not focused on some imagined form of individual shame or culpability for mother or daughter, which is how women rape survivors and their children are commonly constructed in Bosnian society. In fact, the mother models for her daughter how a traumatic event can be transformed into a source of power, self-confidence, and authority, as well as an activist stance in the service of peace and rebuilding of society. Seada recognizes her mother's authenticity and authority in noting that "she is even more active here, and even more people listen to her." It is through this model that she herself can decide "not to be ashamed" about who she is, but to use it as a teaching tool, a way to overcome and prevent future violence. The mother, through her own example and perspective, trained her daughter to successfully negotiate various social pressures and hostilities and emerge as an agent of her own destiny, helping mold social opinion instead of being molded by it or in deference to it.

CONCLUSION

The experience of mothers who are wartime rape survivors in Bosnia investigated here shows that maternal practice is profoundly shaped by armed conflict that involves sexual violence against women and girls. In the context of their experience, conflict takes on a broader meaning. It obviously refers to the conflict that precipitated the sexual atrocities the women were subjected to, including their enforced impregnation. But it also acquires a more extended meaning, as it refers to the sometimes profound ambivalence and conflict the women experience within themselves as mothers of children conceived of wartime rape. It also refers to the continuous conflict the women feel between themselves, their choices, and their children on the one hand, and their communities on the other, which persist in constricting their identities in ways that challenge and undermine their maternal practice.

The records of their lived experience both support and challenge aspects of the maternal philosophy perspective adopted in this chapter. They show that mothering is cognitively, interactively, emotionally, and often physically one of the most complex practices humans engage in, and to simplify its manifold manifestations, or reduce it to one or two aspects for the sake of a sentimental appeal, profoundly misrepresents its rich reality and its diverse forms in particular individual, social, and historical milieus. Investigating the experience of some Bosnian mothers raising children born of wartime rape through this perspective provides an alternative framework for understanding their lives and decisions, different from the dominant media narratives that define them almost exclusively in terms of their victimhood, and medical and psychiatric discourse that tends to pathologise them and their relationship with their children, often implying a normative bias. Looking at the complexity of their maternal practice through a philosophically informed perspective offers the potential to humanize their experience, reframe them as survivors rather than victims, and situate their mothering within the context of a broad and varied spectrum of mothering practices.

I am very grateful to Inger Skjelsbaek for reading earlier drafts of this chapter.

[1]Erjavec and Volčič; also Allen. Intolerance and discrimination toward children born of rape is not confined to Bosnian society. Similar trends can be perceived in most conflict zones around the world where there are children born of wartime rape, such as Uganda, Sierra Leone, Rwanda, and Vietnam (see Carpenter *Born of War*). At the same time, a similar attitude informed by stigma and prejudice follows children born of rape in the U.S. today (see Solomon *Far from the Tree*). These findings show that rape is still a taboo topic in most societies, including those that consistently represent themselves as "progressive" and as leaders in human rights protection.

WORKS CITED

Allen, Beverly. *Rape Warfare: The Hidden Genocide in Bosnia-Herzegovina and Croatia.* Minneapolis: University of Minnesota Press, 1996. Print.

Bećirbašić, Belma. "Invisible Casualties of War." *Institute for War and Peace.* September 6, 2006: n. pag. Web. 12 September 2014.

Carpenter, Charli R. "A Fresh Crop of Human Misery: Representations of Bosnian 'War Babies' in the Global Print Media, 1991-2006." *Millennium—Journal of International Studies* 38 (2009): 25-54. Sage. Web. 9 April 2013.

Carpenter, Charli R., ed. *Born of War: Protecting Children of Sexual Violence Survivors n Conflict Zones.* Bloomfield, CT: Kumarian Press, 2007. Print.

Carpenter, Charli R. "Surfacing Children: Limitations of Genocidal Rape Discourse." *Human Rights Quarterly* 22 (2000): 428-477. Print.

Erjavec, Karmen and Zala Volćić. "Living With the Sins of Their Fathers: An Analysys of Self-Representation of Adolescents Born of War Rape." *Journal of Adolescent Research* 25 (2010): 359-386. Web. 3 February 2012.

Holt, Kate and Sarah Hughes. "Bosnia's Rape Babies: Abandoned by Their families, Forgotten by the State." *The Independent*. 13 December 2005. Web. 2 September, 2014.

Mazowiecki, Tadeus. "Situation of Human Rights in the Territory of the Former Yugoslavia." *United Nations Economic and Social Council*. 10 February, 1993. Web. 2 September 2014.

Nikolić-Ristanović, Vesna. *Women, Violence and War: Wartime Victimization of Refugees in the Balkans*. Budapest: Central European University Press, 2000. Print.

Raphael-Leff, Joan. "Mothers' and Fathers' Orientations: Patterns of Pregnancy, Parenting, and The Bonding Process." *Parenthood and Mental Health: A Bridge between Infant and Adult Psychiatry*. Eds. Sam Tyano, Miri Kereen, Helen Herman and John Cox. Hoboken, NJ: John Wiley & Sons, 2010. 9-22. Print.

"Rome Statute of the International Criminal Court." Section A: Preamble to Part 3.

General Principles of Criminal Law. *Prevent Genocide International*, 2008: n.pag. Web. 1 September 2014.

Ruddick, Sara. *Maternal Thinking: Toward a Politics of Peace*. New York: Ballantine Books, 1989. Print.

Seifert, Ruth. "The Second Front: the Logic of Sexual Violence in Wars." *Women Studies International Forum* 19.1/2 (1996): 35-43. Print.

Shanks, Leslie and Michael J. Schull. "Rape in War: The Humanitarian Response." *The Journal of the Canadian Medical Association* 163.9 (2000): 1152-1156. Web. 1 September 2014.

Sharratt, Sara. *Gender, Shame and Violence: The Voices of Witnesses and Court Members atb War Crime Tribunals*. Farnham: Ashgate, 2011. Print.

Skjelsbaek, Inger. "Victim and Survivor: Narrated Social Identities of Women Who ExperiencesRape during the War in Bosnia-Herzegovina." *Feminism & Psychology* 16 (2006): 373-403. Web. 3 February, 2012.

Solomon, Andrew. *Far from the Tree: Parents, Children and the Search for Identity*. New York: Scribner, 2012. Print.

Solomon, Andrew. "The Legitimate Children of Rape." *New*

Yorker. 29 August 2012. Web. 1 September 2014.

Toomey, Christine. "Cradle of Inhumanity." *The Sunday Times*. 3 November 2003. Web. 17 September, 2014.

Tremonti, Anna Maria. "Born of War." Audio blog post. *The Current*. CBC Radio, 3 Apr. 2012. Web. 10 September 2014.

War Babies. Dir. Raymonde Provencher. Macumba Productions, 2002. Film.

PART II:
IMMIGRATION, DISPLACEMENT, REFUGE

9.
Fractured Mothering

The Impact of U.S. and Arizona Immigration Policies on Mexican Immigrant Mothers with U.S. and Non-U.S. Children

SALLY STEVENS AND ROSI ANDRADE

O VER THE PAST THREE DECADES the United States (U.S.)/Mexico border region has increasingly become a place of conflict specifically with regard to cross-border mobility and immigration. Increases in border crossing regulating policies along with heightened policing has created harsh conditions for those with family members living on both sides of the border as well as for mixed citizenship-status families living in the U.S. This chapter addresses the unique struggles of non-U.S. citizen (immigrant) mothers living in the U.S. who have U.S. and non-U.S. citizen children and the challenges they face to effectively mother in the adverse conditions of this border region. Following an overview of the U.S./Mexico border region and reasons for the relatively recent disruption in trans-border mobility, we give voice to immigrant mothers with U.S. and non-U.S. citizen children and the pervasive fear they endure and the hardships they encounter as mothers. As feminist researchers, our approach entailed a critical liberatory pedagogy centred on the mothers' lived experiences with an emphasis on their participation in the research process. We share aggregate data with regard to the 20 mothers who participated in the study along with example narratives that succinctly articulate the adverse mothering conditions and their consequences—including fractured mothering. The immediate and intergenerational negative impacts of such hostile mothering conditions are discussed along with a call for further examination of U.S. policies and practices affecting immigrant mothers, specifically studies that embody the voices of immigrant mothers.

INTRODUCTION

Immigrant mothers without U.S. citizenship live in constant fear—particularly those situated in the conflict-ridden Arizona U.S./ Sonora Mexico border region. Fear permeates their lives—fear of being deported, fear of being separated from their children, fear of threats, all stemming from the daily reality that she or another family member may be targeted and asked, "Are you a U.S. citizen?" "Show me your papers." "Give me your social security number." The scenarios play out in encounters like that of a minor traffic stop, whether the target is driver or passenger; on a walk to work, at the bus stop; or at a doctor's office or government agency requesting care or benefits for a U.S. citizen child. This fear is pervasive as noted by a participant in the current study:

> *Not being able to go out. With fear of any, any mistake. That shouldn't have to happen, but any small driving infraction can end in something very serious. You have no fear until you see it, what happens with the people you know and you say, "Well, I have children too." That really does scare me.* (Interview 2007)

The words quoted above from a 33-year-old mother of two U.S. citizen girls, ages five and three, succinctly captures her realization of the fear of persecution and separation from her daughters. She and her husband have been living in Tucson, Arizona for eight years. Forced to leave Mexico, even with a university degree, due to the bleakness of the economy and lack of viability for the future, she and her family live in a constant state of fear, cautious not to draw attention to themselves or give anyone a reason to question them or retaliate against them. Yet she, like the other women in this study, wants to be heard.

THE U.S.-MEXICO BORDER REGION

Historically, the U.S.-Mexico border region was open, with a relatively obscure border. For southern Arizona, the line between Nogales, Sonora and Nogales, Arizona, remained a more symbolic gesture to denote the physical demarcation between one side and the other, with individuals crossing the border to and from work, shopping, or visiting family. The history of this border region has been one of *los dos Nogales*, the two Nogales, with an ebb and flow all its own that reached deeper into southern Arizona, as evidenced in the language and cultural practices of the region, so markedly different from its neighbours to the north.

That flow has been disrupted more and more since the 1980s with 1) concerns about the growing drug trade in the U.S.-Mexico corridor, 2) changes in economic, social, and health policies, and 3) heightened security and the passage of laws that criminalize immigrants and those providing services for them. This collusion of forces has resulted in greater violence and exploitation and increasingly higher death rates for those crossing the border. While these may appear unrelated in the mind of the reader, they are related in the prevailing attitudes about migrants as criminals, where drug trade violence and loss of economic and job opportunities are frequently blamed on the non-U.S. citizens travelling to and living in the U.S., without consideration of the high demand for illicit drugs and lax gun policies in the U.S..

Given concern over the increase in illicit drug smuggling, the policies and programs coming out of the U.S.-driven War on Drugs have resulted in increased violence and aggression in the border region. One such example is that of counter narcotics efforts to trace U.S.-made weapons falling into cartel hands, where "roughly 70 percent of recovered cartel weapons originated in the United States" (Wilkason and Fogel 29-30). The strategy to capture the U.S. weapons in the hands of cartel played out near the Nogales, Arizona/Nogales, Sonora border (i.e., "Operations Fast and Furious" arms program [Bureau of Alcohol]). Smugglers crossing the border shot and killed U.S. Border Patrol Agent Brian Terry with a U.S. weapon put into circulation by, and being traced as, part of the Fast and Furious program. Tragic outcomes of programs like Fast and Furious, place the migrant as a suspect of criminal activity on one side of the border, and victim of criminal enterprises on the other side. Given changes in policies and practices along the U.S.-Mexico border, which have created a violent and untrusting climate, migrants are often forced to rely on the criminal enterprise to cross the perilous desert. Crossing the border has become a minefield of sorts with migrants having to pay "coyotes," professional border crossers, who in addition to human trafficking may also include drug trafficking and violence in their enterprises.

Economic policies such as the 1994 North American Free Trade Agreement (NAFTA) expanded free trade between Mexico, the U.S., and Canada. This accelerated greater migration to the U.S.from Mexico and created a wake of shrinking opportunities and lack of financial stability for workers through the movement of jobs and industry across borders. With the loss of jobs in the U.S., a growing climate of hostility toward migrants (and immigrants) became a call to arms for political groups and extremists alike, leading to movements to criminalize, incarcerate, and deport them. Concern over illegal activities such as "alien" smuggling and fraudulent immigration documents propelled the 1996 legislation—the *Illegal Immigration Reform and Responsibility Act*. Among other facets, this legislation sought to enforce legal immigration through restrictions in the employment and benefits as well as through heightened surveillance (Saint Germaine and Stevens). Moreover, the 1996 Personal Responsibility Work Opportunity Reconciliation Act (i.e., Welfare Reform Bill), which emphasized self-sufficiency, divided immigrants into two categories: qualified and non-qualified "aliens" (Viladrich). These policy changes reduced opportunities and increased fear among immigrants to seek employment and services for themselves and their children—even when benefits were warranted.

Since the September 11, 2001, attack on the World Trade Center, border security has been tightened with the creation of the Department of Homeland Security (DHS) in 2002. DHS combined twenty-two different federal agencies with a mission to "secure the nation from the many threats we face," including threats related to border security (Department of Homeland Security). In 2003, DHS created the U.S. Immigration and Customs Enforcement (ICE) to enforce the protection of the U.S. and its citizenry. With the added strength of the U.S. Customs and Border Patrol, the National Guard Reserve, and local law enforcement agencies, the U.S.-Mexico border region became heavily "policed," creating a conflict zone where tensions were and continue to be fierce and in which immigrant and mixed-status families live in fear. This intensive policing of the border pushes migrants, including many who have historically crossed back and forth across the border with ease, to cross in areas that are difficult to police—through mountain ranges and dangerous desert lands with perilous heat (Luibheid, Andrade and Stevens). While perhaps an intentional strategy to decrease the number of border crossings, the practice has resulted in hundreds of deaths of migrants, often abandoned by the coyotes and left to suffer the severe consequences of the extreme heat—further fracturing families and intensifying the level of trauma, grief, and loss experienced by migrant families.

Adding to this hostile border conflict zone are recently enacted Arizona laws such as Senate Bill 1070, which was signed into law in 2010. This highly contested law is the strictest anti-immigration law in recent U.S. history. Among other requirements, SB1070 requires that state law enforcement attempt to determine a person's immigration status when there is reason to suspect the person is an illegal immigrant, which endorses and increases problematic racial profiling. The law also imposes penalties on those hiring, transporting, or sheltering illegal immigrants. This law brings the border-related hostility to all of Arizona—in both rural and urban areas and in multiple venues. Fear is pervasive for immigrants, resulting in mixed-status families restricting their movements, inhibiting families from visiting each other or being able to provide extended family support. Additionally, these families are inhibited from seeking health care as well as education and employment opportunities. In a culture that has a history of extended family support in mothering practices, these added constraints on immigrant mothers to effectively mother are acutely troublesome.

The Kids Count Dataset reports there were 437,000 children in immigrant families in Arizona in 2011 (27 percent of all children), which is less than the 513,000 (30 percent of all children) reported in 2009 (Annie E. Casey Foundation). While the housing and job market are, in part, reasons for this decline, Arizona's harsh immigration laws and immigration raids are also factors (Sunnucks). Still, the numbers are high and thus the magnitude of those experiencing disrupted mothering conditions is enormous.

Understanding mothering in the context of immigration in the hostile region of the U.S./Arizona-Mexico borderland needs to be examined not only through numbers but through their lived experiences. Yet, the exclusion of women in the discussion of migration has been noted in the literature, specifically as it relates to methodology and centric views (e.g., collecting information on women from men) that excludes women's authentic participation or voice (Gil; Velasco). In our own work we found that immigrant mothers in southern Arizona want to speak out against the policies and practices that incite others to treat them and their families as criminals, as less than, as unworthy—but they have not had the opportunity to do so. They are silenced by the potential consequences. One participant commented:

> ... and immigration practices? I've always wanted to say this. That I watch and I think it's wonderful, that this country and on all the news on national television, if there was a sanctuary established for the ducks that are migrating, if there was a reserve established for monarch butterflies that are migrating. If something was done for the seals or the whales or any other species in danger of extinction, but in general for, for the animals that migrate. I'm talking about animal rights, and it's very good. And it's fine, I'm not saying that it's a bad thing. But I'm asking to be allowed to make the comparison, how is it possible that it appears on national television, that something so good is praised, while human beings are treated worse than animals? (Interview 2007)

RESEARCH CONTEXT AND METHODS

As feminist researchers committed to the respect and support of all mothers and their children, our approach entailed a critical liberatory pedagogy centered on the marginalized voices and lived experiences of immigrant mothers with U.S. citizen and non-U.S. citizen children. Feminist pedagogical principals and methods (Fonow and Cook; Hammarsrom) were employed along with participatory action research (McTaggart) in which the participants engaged in the research process, including assisting in the interpretation of the data.

Immigrant mothers are highly vulnerable facing devastating consequences should they be discovered, including long-term imprisonment, separation from their children, loss of mothering rights, and deportation. If they are arrested or held, women often disappear in the legal system while their children end up in the child welfare system with little or no communication between the two systems (Rabin). Thus, utmost protection of the study participants was called for. For this study, all materials, protocols, and assessments were reviewed and approved by the University of Arizona's Human Subjects Internal Review Board and a federal Certificate of Research Confidentiality was secured to give added protection to the mother's identities and their corresponding data.

The authors' past experience collaborating with Mexican immigrant mothers on other participatory action projects allowed us establish the interviews for the present project. Immigrant mothers with at least one U.S. citizen child were recruited through a local elementary school that serves a high number of immigrant families. Those consenting to participate were given a choice to conduct the interview in English or Spanish, with all participants selecting Spanish. With the exception of one interview, conducted at a fast food restaurant, all interviews were conducted in the home of the immigrant mother, which was viewed as a safe and confidential location for the participant.

Participants included immigrant mothers who migrated to Tucson, Arizona from Mexico—each telling her own experiences of mothering in a mixed status family. They ranged in age from 27 to 49 years (average = 37 years). The mothers had lived in the U.S. for 4 to 22 years (average = 9.4 years). Most (85 percent) were high school graduates, 35 percent had income from paid employment and 80 percent had income from a spouse or partner in the previous 30 days. The mothers reported having 1 to 5 children (average = 2.9 children) ranging in age from 1 to 26 years (average = 10 years). While the percent of household members who were U.S. citizens ranged from 20 to 80 percent, the percent of children who were U.S. citizens was 67 percent.

We employed a mixed-methods design that included a semi-structured interview with quantitative items and scales along with open-ended questions that allowed for discussion between the interviewer (second author) and the participant. The interviews were audiotaped with the quantitative questions also being documented on the interview form. The audiotapes and questionnaires were transported to the authors' university office, where the recordings were transcribed and translated and the quantitative data entered into an SPSS database by the second author and university students. The data was reviewed to ensure that all identifying information was deleted. A grounded theory approach (Pope, Ziebland and Mays) for the qualitative data analysis allowed for the identification of common responses and themes. One of the most salient themes to emerge was the concept of fractured mothering in which the mothers spoke articulately and emotionally about the difficulties of mothering their children in the conflict-ridden U.S.-Mexico borderlands.

FRACTURED MOTHERING

Fractured mothering was most evident in the area of accessing and receiving healthcare. Access to healthcare for Mexican immigrant families of mixed status living in the U.S. varies by the citizenship status of the family members. U.S. citizen family members can access healthcare, although there is evidence of a "chilling effect" in which family members who are eligible to receive services do not attempt to access them due to fear, feelings of being undeserving, and other reasons (Viladrich). Immigrant mothers who have children who are U.S. citizens and others who are not citizens report being distressed about the inequities between her children in terms of what services they can access. Mothering becomes fractured. A 35-year-old mother of five children, four non-U.S. citizens (ages ten, eleven, and twelve) and two U.S. citizens (ages seven and eight), spoke about how she could obtain medical care for her U.S. citizen children, while she could not access care for herself and her three non-U.S. citizen children:

... when my [U.S. citizen] children have gotten sick, I call a taxi and it comes to pick me up, it takes me to the ap-

pointment, I get to the doctor. But with the others [non-U.S. citizen] no, and they tell me, "Mami, why can you take them to the doctor and not us?" And I tell them, "Well, it's because they can and we can't." (Interview 2008)

Unable to secure the care and resources needed to treat the oldest non-U.S. citizen child, a daughter, she relied on remedies and the medicine cabinet to treat the child. This "care" did not adequately treat the underlying infection that eventually led to a medical crisis. At the sight of her daughter's worsening condition, including growing inflammation and pain, the mother then relied on her only other option: to bring care to her daughter by summoning a relative living in Mexico to provide the care she could not access in the U.S. Current laws and policies preventing equal access to healthcare and establishing certain criminalization for the non- U.S. citizen are at the crux of frequent medical crises and set the stage for further criminalization of immigrant mothers who must parcel out crucial health resources to some of their children and not to others.

Lack of access to healthcare not only results in pain and suffering for the child, but it also creates anxiety and frustration for the mother. Additionally, finding other resources for healthcare is financially costly to the immigrant families. A 31-year-old mother of two children, one a non-U.S. citizen (fourteen years of age) and the other a U.S. citizen (seven years of age) talked about being unable to access medical treatment for her son:

...the U.S. citizen, he got a little lump of fat in his neck and I took him to the doctor. They sent me to the specialist ... I paid the appointment with the specialist and they sent me to the hospital because they had to remove it surgically but they didn't want to give me an appointment because I had to have AHCCCS [state-sponsored healthcare insurance].... So the same doctor told me, get AHCCCS. So she never gave me the appointment, she kept putting it off, putting it off, so what I did was, I sent him to Nogales [Sonora]. At home, the situation with my sisters is the same. Some of us are from here; some of us are from over there. So

*my citizen sister took him for me, they operated on him
and she brought him back…. In fact, I had to wait some
time to gather the money to be able to send him, have him
operated on, and to bring him back.* (Interview 2003)

In Arizona, the review and decision on paperwork submitted
for AHCCCS can take up to two months and documentation,
including a birth certificate, is needed with the application. Even
if the child is a U.S. citizen, the process is challenging and the
wait-time lengthy. Not knowing what the application requires,
many immigrant mothers are swayed from applying for fear that
their own immigration status will be questioned. In spite of the
frustration of not getting a medical appointment and the delay
in treatment, the mother was able to get the needed care for her
U.S. citizen son by relying on her sister. Still, the anxiety and
stress along with the financial burden for the mother and her
family is troublesome.

Stress, anxiety, and fear were also discussed by a 46-year-old
mother who has lived in the U.S. for thirteen years. She has two
daughters, one a Mexican citizen (25 years of age) and the other
a U.S. citizen (eleven years of age). She spoke about the oldest
daughter who returned to Mexico, and the pull, with neither
mother or daughter able to travel to see one another, "When you
have a child over there, and, and she can't come and I can't go
because neither of us have a visa, yes. It's hard."

Listening to the conditions that led to her older daughter leaving
the U.S. after living here for twelve years, we garner insight into
the cloud of daily stress and fear that followed the non-U.S.citizen
daughter. When a 22-year-old niece, detained at a traffic stop,
was deported, "Well, the little one cried. She is very emotional.
And the older one? Well, fear. She would say, 'Here none of us
are safe. Any day they can stop the car and [say] let's see, *You're
not carrying your papers?* and the same thing will happen.' A lot,
a lot of worries."

The impact of Arizona's anti-immigration state bills was immediate, as her then 24-year-old daughter, for example, began to
show signs of stress, "She started seeing so many things. She was
so ill at ease that she couldn't even go to work … it was all nerves.

That this or that could happen, so it was better [that she left]. 'I'm getting sick from nerves,' she would tell me" (Interview 2010).

Mexican immigrant mothers in this study frequently talked about the fear they and their family members have about being stopped by the police, questioned, detained, and/or deported. Many of the women chose to walk to the store, to their children's schools, or other relatives' homes, avoiding spaces, such as a traffic stop, where they might be questioned. The impact of such a traffic stop can be devastating and may lead to lengthy detainments in immigration detention facilities, deportation, separation from children, and/or a financial crisis. A 41-year-old mother of three children, all U.S. citizens (ages eight, six, and three) talked about her reaction to her husband being stopped by the police:

> He called me ... he was coming from work when the police stopped him ... and they asked for everyone's license and legal documents ... he told me, "You know what?" He said, "The police stopped me and they're going to call immigration. I am here at this address. I am on Pima here in Green Valley," and he said, "So you can call my dad so he can come for the car."...It affected me a lot because well, I had just given birth through a C-section ... the world crashed around me ... I wasn't working and I said, "What am I going to do with the bills, with my children?" (Interview 2002)

The husband quickly warns his wife of the situation so she knows that he may disappear into the U.S. judicial system from which he may not be able to contact her again for a long time. While her father-in-law may be able to retrieve the vehicle, concern for her household and children becomes paramount and the mothering of her children is situated squarely on her shoulders.

CONCLUSION

Given the impact of recent reforms of U.S. and Arizona immigration and welfare laws since 1996, immigrant mothers are reluctant to seek benefits for their children, including their U.S. citizen children.

Not surprisingly, U.S. citizen and non-citizen children with immigrant parents are more likely than children in families headed by U.S. citizens to live in poverty, lack health insurance, and struggle in school. As discussed by the participants in this study, mothers and their family members live in fear, report extensive stress, and patch together solutions—working around the system—in attempt to meet the health care and other needs of their children. In the hostile space of the U.S.-Mexico border, mothering practices among Mexican immigrant women is fractured. The inequities experienced at the macro level contribute to intercultural tensions and mistrust while inequities at the micro level between family members (citizen versus non-citizen) result in family disparities—all of which contribute to border-related conflict and the resulting threat to international relations, local communities, and families—including women's ability to effectively and equitably mother.

Under these hostile conditions, effective mothering is intensely problematic. Yet, the immigrant mothers in this study found creative solutions and engaged in unconventional practices to successfully mother their children. The struggle in doing so is apparent and comes with a price, including financial, psychological, and physical health consequences. The financial constraints are multi-faceted and come from policies that keep non-U.S. citizen immigrants from being able to engage in employment, and policies that keep children of immigrant mothers from seeking health care. While many non-US citizen immigrant mothers often work in the informal economy, these jobs do not provide health insurance coverage. When a child needs medical care, the financial burden is placed on the parents: costs for home remedies that often result in an additional medical crisis; travel to Mexico for medical treatment; payment to others to make the border crossing with the child; and out-of-pocket medical treatment costs.

Recent research indicates the increased involvement of police in immigration enforcement has heightened the fears that many Latino/a immigrants have of police, resulting in mistrust, isolation, and the underreporting of abuse and other crimes against them (Theodore). Thus, fear, anxiety, and stress is intensified with the knowledge that not only might they be detained, deported, and separated from their children, but that they do not have recourse for injustices committed against them. The impact of constant fear and resulting stress on immigrant mothers and their families living in this hostile environment is not well known, although the field of neuroscience indicates that trauma affects the brain in multiple ways, including learning and coping abilities (Horsman). Moreover, such stress has been known to affect one's physical health in negative ways contributing to documented health disparities among immigrants (Derose, Escarce and Lurie; Ku and Matani). Further, a study of cumulative experiences of trauma and stress of women enduring extreme poverty, addiction, incarceration, loss of parental rights, and domestic violence points to the women's social location and their identities and predicts that PTSD is likely to increase by 40 percent with each traumatic experience brought on by these stressors (Kubiak). Finally, while the impact of the immigration-related stress experienced by the mothers in this study on their children is not yet known, the negative impact of historical and intergenerational trauma has been noted in other populations (Substance Abuse and Mental Health Services Administration; Stevens et al.).

Health disparities are closely associated with social, economic, and/or environmental disadvantages. Those who have systematically experienced greater obstacles to health care based on race or other characteristics linked to discrimination or exclusion are negatively affected (Windsor, Jemal and Benoit). While the U.S. Department of Health and Human Services aims to reduce health disparities and defines health equity as "attainment of the highest level of health for all people," until immigrant mothers are able to and are not fearful about seeking services for themselves, their non- U.S. citizen as well as their U.S. citizen children, achieving the highest level of health for all people is not possible. Policies and practices must change so mothers can access care without fear or threat of being separated from their children through detainment, incarceration, and/or deportation.

In summary, we argue for examination of policies and practices affecting immigrant mothers who are living in the U.S., especially as they have come to create a hostile environment and a de facto police state, like those in other regions of the world, targeting individuals on the basis of race, political beliefs, gender, sexual orientation, and/or religion. Moreover, we advocate for additional studies where the stories of immigrant mothers are heard, which will, in turn, assist in shaping policies and practices that diminish the lived experiences of fractured mothering.

WORKS CITED

Annie E. Casey Foundation. *Children in Immigrant Families in Arizona: Fact Sheet*. 2014. Web. 21 May 2014.

Bureau of Alcohol, Tobacco, Firearms and Explosives. *Operation Fast and Furious and Related Matters*. Web. 4 June 2015.

Department of Homeland Security. *About DHS*. 27 February 2014. Web. 21 May 2014.

Derose, Kathryn Pitkin, Jose J. Escarce and Nicole Lurie. "Immigrants and Health Care: Sources of Vulnerability." *Health Affairs* 26.5 (2007): 1258-1268. Print.

Fonow, Mary Margaret and Judith Cook. *Beyond Methodology: Feminist Scholarship as Lived Research*. Indianapolis: Indiana University Press, 1991. Print.

Gil, Carmen Gregorio. "Los Movimientos Migratorios del Sur al Norte Como Procesos de Genero." *Globalizacion y Genero*. Ed. Paloma Villota. Madrid: Editorial Sintesis, 1999. 259-288. Print.

Hammarsrom, Anne. "Why Feminism in Public Health?" *Scandinavian Journal of Public Health* 27 (1999): 241-244. Print.

Horsman, Jenny. *Too Scared to Learn: Women, Violence, and Education*. Mahwah: Lawrence Erlbaum Associates, Inc., 2000. Print.

Interview 2002. Personal Interview. 17 February 2011.

Interview 2003. Personal Interview. 17 February 2011.

Interview 2007. Personal Interview. 18 February 2011.

Interview 2008. Personal Interview. 21 February 2011.

Interview 2010. Personal Interview. 22 February 2011.

Ku, Leighton and Sheetal Matani. "Left Out: Immigrants' Accesst to Health Care and Insurance." *Health Affairs* 20.1 (2001): 247-256. Print.

Kubiak, S.P. "Trauma and Cumulative Adversity In Women of a Disadvantaged Social Location." *Am J Orthopsychiatry* 75.4 (2005): 451-65. Print.

Luibheid, Eithne, Rosi Andrade and Sally Stevens. "Fractured

Mothering: The Impact of U.S. and Arizona Immigration Policies on Spanish-speaking Immigrant Mothers with U.S. Citizen and Non-citizen Children." Women's International League for Peace and Freedom (WILPF). 9 May 2014. Presentation.

McTaggart, Robin. *Participatory Action Research, International Context and Consequences.* Albany: State University of New York Press, 1997. Print.

Pope, Catherine, Sue Ziebland and Nicholas Mays. "Qualitative Data in Health Care: Analyzing Qualitative Data." *British Journal of Medicine* 320 (2000): 114-116. Print.

Rabin, Nina. *Disappearing Parents: A Report on Immigration Enforcement and the Child Welfare System.* Report. The University of Arizona. Tucson, 2012. Print.

Saint Germaine, Kate and Carly J Stevens. *Summary of 1996 Illegal Immigration Reform & Immigrant Responsibility Act.* 30 September 1996. University of Washington-Bothell. Web. 21 May 2014.

Stevens, Sally, Rosi Andrade, Josephine D. Korchmaros, and Kelly Sharron. "Intergenerational Trauma: Family Loss Experiences of Substance Using Native American, Latina, and Caucasian Mothers Living in Southwestern United States. Special Issue: Examining the Relationship between Traumand Addiction: Etiolog, Treatment, and Social Policy." *Journal of Social Work Practice In the Addictions* (Under Review). Print.

Substance Abuse and Mental Health Services Administration. "Trauma-Informed Care in Behavioral Health Services." Treatment Improvement Protocol (TIP) Series 57. HHS Publication No. (SMA) 13-4801. Rockville: SAMHSA, 2014. Print.

Sunnucks, Mike. "Arizona's Immigration Population Continues to Decline." *Phoenix Business Journal* 24 June 2013. Print.

Theodore, Nik. *Insecure Communities: Latino Perceptions of Police Involvement in Immigration Enforcement.* Chicago: University of Illinois at Chicago, 2013. Print.

U.S. Department of Health and Human Services. "The Secretary's Advisory Committee on National Health Promotion and Disease Prevention Objectives for 2020. Phase 1 report: *Recommendations for the Framework and Format of Healthy People* 2020 (Internet). Section IV: Advisory Committee Findings and Recommendations. Web. 4 June 2015.

Velasco, Diana G. Palmerin. "'I Feel Like a Different Woman': Negotiating Gender and Motherhood in the Context of Transnational Migration from Axochiapan, Morelos to Minneapolis, Minnesota." *Journal of the Motherhoold Initiative* 4.2 (2013): 47-59. Print.

Viladrich, Anahi. "Beyond Welfare Reform: Reframing Undocument Immigrants' Entitlements to Health Care in the United States, A Critical Review." *Social Science & Medicine* 74 (2012): 822-829. Print.

Wilkason, Colby and Mikhaila Fogel. "Cartel Weapons and their Provenance." *The War on Mexican Cartels: Options for U.S. and Mexican Policy-Makers*. Final Report. Institute of Politics. Cambridge: Harvard University, 2012. Print.

Windsor, Liliane Cambraia, Alexis Jemal and Ellen Benoit. "Community Wise: Paving the Way for Empowerment Reentry." *International Journal of Law and Psychiatry* 37.5 (2014): 505-511. Print.

10.
When Tragedy Is Not Enough

Female Syrian Refugees in a New Homeland

DAVID EICHERT

We left Syria to escape death and we found something worse than death. If we had stayed in Syria to die it would have been more honorable. There death is fast, here it is slow. (Damon)

SINCE ITS BEGINNING IN 2011, the Syrian civil war has created one of the largest refugee crises in history. While the United Nations no longer tracks death toll statistics (in July 2013 the UN capped deaths at 100,000 because of their inability to verify information), there is no end in sight to the war or the ever-expanding refugee population (UN Women, "We Just"; Karimi and Abdelaziz). While gridlock has blocked any further debate on political ends to the conflict, Syrian refugees are finding themselves increasingly abandoned by the international community. At the end of August 2014, it was announced that three million Syrian refugees had registered with UN agencies outside Syria, with an additional 6.5 million individuals displaced within Syria (Nebehay). Most of these refugees—over a million—have settled in Lebanon, with hundreds of thousands living in refugee camps or cities in Turkey, Jordan, and Iraq (UNHCR, "Syria"). Despite the fact that the number of those in need is continually increasing, funding for these refugees is shrinking. Relief efforts by international aid agencies like UNHCR have never been fully funded and as of September 2014, UN aid efforts lacked almost $2 billion in needed funding. This has put greater stress on refugee families, as food parcels and non-food items have become scarce (Ki-Moon; UNHCR, "Syria").

While survival is difficult for all Syrian refugees, Syrian mothers must deal with the greatest struggles. It is critical that aid agencies address the fact that Syrian refugee mothers face unique difficulties, given that around 80 percent of refugees and internally displaced Syrians are women or children ("Syrian Women's"). In addition to the normal stresses of refugee life, refugee mothers must deal with unique economic and social challenges such as a lack of childcare or employment options. These realities of refugee life increase the gendered responsibilities of women and the workload they must shoulder. Female refugees are also at a much higher risk of sexual violence, which is compounded by the patriarchal nature of Arab culture. Gender-based violence is also especially prevalent in the region (UN Women, "We Just").

The first part of this chapter is dedicated to discussing the day-to-day economic problems faced by displaced Syrian mothers, including the struggle to find employment and housing while dealing with trauma-induced psychological disorders. The second part of this chapter will discuss various forms of gender-based violence faced by Syrian refugee mothers, including domestic violence, sexual harassment, rape, and early child marriage. Finally, the chapter will conclude by offering several solutions to these problems. While a more permanent solution to the refugee crisis will not be found until the end of the conflict in Syria, the international community must act to provide gender-based services and protect the needs of Syrian women and mothers.

ECONOMIC AND PSYCHOLOGICAL CHALLENGES

> I am a mother, my children were getting dizzy from the lack of food, one said I can't lift my head, the other said I can't move my legs. ... I want my children to be independent, I worked very hard for their education, I worked a lot in this life for them to be able to reach university. (Damon and Razek)

In general, Syrian refugees face discrimination from a reluctant host population when looking for employment and housing. While locals are mostly sympathetic to the Syrians' plight, one observer noted that many locals are "apprehensive that the Syrians will stay for a long time because they are their rivals when it comes to employment ... because Syrians accept employment at lower wages" (UN Women, "Gender-based" 22). As refugee populations grow, more locals blame the Syrians for their country's economic problems, which place further economic and social pressure on refugee families (Murray).

Moreover, cultural forces which disfavour women exacerbate the many problems faced by Syrian refugees. For example, while many female refugees are the heads of their households (their husbands having been killed or separated from the family because of the war), they must still navigate a patriarchal society that restricts their participation in civil society and the economic market. Female refugees and mothers without the protection of a husband are socially marginalized and denied justice by oppressive societal norms that favour men.

Among Syrian refugees, female-headed households are consistently worse off financially than male-headed households. In a Jordanian camp, for example, 34 percent of all households reported no income, while 55 percent of female-headed households had no monthly income at all. Of the remaining 45 percent of female-headed households with some income, 25 percent reported an income from a working son in the household (CARE). Many mothers cannot work due to family commitments to young children or concerns about safety. Cultural and patriarchal norms also make it more difficult for mothers to work outside the home, as employment in many fields is often reserved for men (CARE).

In other cases, refugee women have reportedly turned to prostitution or survival sex in order to meet their needs. The lack of alternative employment opportunities for female refugees, coupled with health problems, childcare, and cultural stigmas against women working, sometimes force female refugees to make this drastic decision. The number of women arrested for prostitution has sharply increased, and many of these women charge a relatively low fee, suggesting that they are selling their bodies out of desperation instead of economic gain (Hadid).

While selling sex is much harder to do inside refugee camps, it is very lucrative in neighbouring cities. Women are paid in goods or money in exchange for sex (Sherlock and Malouf). Another serious problem relates to the predatory nature of some aid workers. Some women have reported that they put on makeup and flirt in order to receive assistance from aid workers, while others reported knowing girls who had sex with men in order to receive aid (CARE). Rumours about prostitution also plague female refugees who do not sell their bodies for sex. A number of women in a recent survey said that they were treated differently when others found out they were Syrian because of the stigma of Syrian prostitutes. One mother in Jordan under threat of eviction even had to produce a marriage certificate proving that she was not "living in sin" (CARE 31).

Moreover, there are not many opportunities for education for children, which further hinders Syrian refugee mothers. In pre-war Syria roughly 94 percent of boys and 93 percent of girls were enrolled in primary school, whereas only 40 percent of school-age Syrian refugee children currently attend school (El-Masri, Harvey, and Garwood). Furthermore, a recent survey found that 100 percent of mothers felt that their children do not have "safe spaces in which to play" (CARE 33). Because mothers must constantly provide for and protect their children, it leaves them less time to find suitable employment, housing, or medical care. This in turn worsens feelings of helplessness for mothers and impairs their ability to be a good parent and employee (Charles and Denman).

Another challenge faced by many is the fact that fleeing Syria leaves most refugees impoverished. For this reason refugee families rely partly or wholly upon charitable handouts for survival. While many families receive support from aid agencies in the form of food vouchers or non-food items, these donations do not cover all of their needs. The primary need of most refugees is cash in order to participate in the local market economy and meet basic household needs. The majority of monetary aid goes towards paying rent and some mothers have reported selling some or all of their food vouchers at less than face value in order to pay for rent (Margolis).

The scarcity of adequate housing for Syrian women and families is also perhaps one of the greatest challenges faced by refugees. The ever-increasing numbers of refugees has created very limited housing markets in Beirut, Amman, and other neighbouring cities. Many refugees live in tents or makeshift settlements while they search for appropriate housing. During winter the urgency of having appropriate housing increases drastically (International Federation).

It is even harder for families with female heads of households to find accommodation for several reasons. Mothers often lack the skills and experience necessary to work, which makes affording good accommodations difficult. Furthermore, cultural stigma often disfavours mothers looking for housing, which forces them into unsafe or uncomfortable living arrangements. Landlords are reluctant to rent to unaccompanied women because they are culturally perceived as being "socially problematic" (CARE 37), and in a tight housing market it is much more advantageous for landlords to rent to a man. Some women have even been reported to the police for running supposed brothels because they had both male and female family members staying with them (CARE). Charities distributing cash payments for rent and other services such as healthcare often give aid only to men, which conforms to and perpetuates traditional gender roles in these societies. Because of gaps in funding, these charities choose to help the individuals in society who are traditionally responsible for a family and ignore the plight of mothers and female-headed households (El-Masri, Harvey, and Garwood).

Paying rent is cited as the largest problem faced by almost 100 percent of refugees. A majority of these refugees owned their own houses in Syria and are therefore not accustomed to paying rent costs (El-Masri, Harvey, and Garwood). Most mothers report being unable to pay rent and utility costs, or being in debt to landlords for rent payments. Rent prices have also increased drastically in these cities, which has resulted in some families and individuals renting cramped locations in garages or shacks. Often landlords will impose limitations on the number of people allowed in one house and unfairly increase rent under the flawed assumption that all refugees receive cash assistance for rent. In some instances, refugees are sleeping with twenty people in a room (El-Masri, Harvey, and Garwood; International Federation).

Many female refugees must also deal with debilitating psychological trauma, which makes survival even more difficult. Many Syrian refugee women suffer from trauma-induced psychological conditions like PTSD or depression. Even though these women have escaped the immediate threat of civil war and found a secure environment, the memories of violence often haunt survivors. These problems are compounded by the lack of professional psychological treatment for refugees and few monetary means that would make finding care possible. In some instances, refugee women were tortured by the Syrian government or subjected to violent treatment at the hands of rebels. For example, one reporter told the story of Selma, a middle-aged refugee mother, who fled Damascus after being tortured for months by the regime on allegations that she aided the rebels. She was "blindfolded, beaten with an electric rod, and told lies that her son had been killed and her home destroyed." Now a refugee in an overcrowded housing structure in Lebanon, she must deal with the psychological trauma alone: "The other day I couldn't deal with anyone," she said to reporters, "so I went to a gravesite and just talked to the dead" (Murray).

In other cases, refugee mothers must help family members and especially children cope with traumatic experiences and memories from Syria. One mother named Maryam told reporters that her son saw a dog eating the corpse of a man killed by rebel fighters. "Because of that," she continued, "he started having nightmares. He clings to his dad, so that he won't flee. There is nothing good about this situation" (Murray). The lack of psychological treatment coupled with sparse resources and few employment opportunities worsen already existing psychological problems and put undue stress on mothers to hold families together.

Anger is also a common feeling, as many male refugees struggle to find work or resolve simple challenges faced by their families. Men, however, are not the only ones struggling with feelings of violence and anger in these situations. Feelings of resentment and frustration as well as the loss of what was familiar and safe have been reported by many Syrian women and mothers. For example, the UN Population Fund published a study of 452 Syrian women aged 18-45 which revealed that 74 percent of those surveyed "could not manage their anger and frustration and admitted to beating their children more than usual as a form of release" (Charles and

Denman 105). The same study also revealed that only nine percent of the women had access to mental health services (Charles and Denman 105).

SEXUAL AND GENDER-BASED VIOLENCE

> When I first arrived here he came to me and said, "You can give me a bath and I'll give you a bath. Come home with me to have some fun. You can live in the shelter for free if you do this."... Ten days before the rent is due he comes to me and asks again. When I say no, he starts yelling. (Margolis)

In Arab culture, a woman's honour and sexual purity are all-important, and in many cases more valuable than the life of the woman. Because of this, the bodies of female Syrians have become an extension of the Syrian civil war. For example, a recent Amnesty International report asserts that "each and every refugee has a unique story of suffering and survival, but most [female Syrian refugees have] said that their main reason for leaving Syria was fear of rape and sexual assault" (1). The International Rescue Committee recently found that rape as a weapon of war is a "significant and disturbing" part of the civil war in Syria (Sherlock and Malouf). Even escaping Syria is much more risky for women and mothers than for men. Female refugees must navigate a complex cultural and political climate that threatens sexual assault and exploitation by armed forces, border authorities, and even refugee camp officials (Deacon and Sullivan). Mothers must guard not only themselves but also the physical integrity of their children.

Even after fleeing Syria, however, a woman is not free from the threat of gender-based violence. Many refugee camps are poorly equipped to deal with the needs of female refugees, which worsen threats to financial and physical security. For example, Amnesty International reported that many communal toilets are unlit (either because of lack of funds, or because the lights are stolen by other individuals in the camp). Women feel unsafe using them after dark—one mother told Amnesty, "There is no light, if we come in here there could be a guy hiding or something." Because these women are forced to wait until daybreak to use the toilets, there have been serious health consequences (Amnesty International 2).

In other instances, living facilities do not conform to culturally acceptable norms of privacy, which puts further stress on Syrian women. One mother described sharing the same shower and cooking area with several families: "It is very public and I feel shame walking by all the men. Mohammed [her husband] is very angry everyone can see me" (Murray). Sharing bathing facilities also results in a higher rate of sexual violence. Some refugee women have also reported that sanitary items received from aid agencies are not of good quality, which causes discomfort and health problems (El-Masri, Harvey, and Garwood).

Sexual harassment and violence are daily challenges for many refugee mothers, and harassment charges often go uninvestigated. A recent UN Women report found that 82 percent of female refugees interviewed "lived in daily fear of abuse or aggression," and 68 percent said that they knew someone who had been sexually abused (UN Women, "We Just" 6). Much of this harassment arises because these refugees are foreigners and are perceived as vulnerable targets by non-Syrian men. Women have reported men saying things such as, "We know you are Syrian, we have money" (UN Women, "We Just" 6). Non-Syrian men will also "accidentally" enter a tent in an attempt to find these women alone or undressed. Even more seriously, refugee mothers are sometimes blamed or punished by male relatives when they learn about the unwanted harassment. UN Women reported that in a particular camp, seven women reported being physically abused because relatives had learned that they were being harassed ("We Just").

Sex trafficking is also a threat to refugee women, although there is little evidence of sophisticated networks of traffickers like in other parts of the world. Nonetheless, traffickers are able to exploit the economic injustices and social marginalization that these women face for their own profit. For example, one mother told reporters that a man promising free housing for refugees had taken her and her daughter to a house outside of their city where the girls inside were scantily clad. Upon realizing the situation, they were both able to flee the situation (Damon).

In male-headed households, Syrian women face the threat of

domestic violence, which occurs at a much higher rate in refugee families. One explanation for this is that while a greater reliance on tasks traditionally performed by women—such as caring for family or finding and preparing food—has increased the burden of work for mothers, the workload of men has decreased. Many men cannot find work and do not take on any of the more "feminine" household duties, which results in boredom and a feeling of disempowerment for the men. Other causes for an increased rate of domestic violence outside of Syria include crowded and subpar living conditions, economic stress, and unresolved mental health problems (Charles and Denman).

Many women have rationalized and accepted the violence that they face as being a normal part of the refugee experience. Interviews with these women have revealed a sense of empathy towards the violent men. They feel that women need to understand the stressful circumstances that drive these men to violence. Many of these women also expressed the feeling that nothing could be done to stop the violence (Charles and Denman; Usta and Masterson).

One of the biggest problems in reporting domestic violence is related to the women's status as refugees in a foreign country. Some women have reported that they fear being sent back to Syria if they reveal they have been abused (Charles and Denman). Many refugee women are unfamiliar with their surroundings and the laws of their new country. There is also a clear need for shelters and temporary safe havens for survivors of intimate partner violence (UN Women, "We Just"). Furthermore, 35 percent of women were not allowed to leave their homes for fear of attack (UN Women, "We Just").

Even when refugee women can leave their homes, they must change their behavioural patterns in order to protect against harassment and rape. Many women in a recent survey reported pretending to call a close male relative or family member in order to feel more secure outside (Charles and Denman). In another report, one mother interviewed had thirteen children; two daughters are teenagers and their mother was so concerned about leaving them alone that "she hasn't been able to leave the house to vaccinate her baby" (Damon).

In addition to domestic violence, for safety and financial reasons many refugee mothers and fathers marry off their daughters at a young age. In fact, so many girls are being married that early marriage is now the norm for many refugee families. For example, over half of all Syrian refugee women married in 2013 were under the age of 18 ("Syrian Women"). While child marriage was rare in Syria before the war, rates of early marriage have sharply increased among refugee populations, and mothers who wish to protect their young daughters face intense pressure to marry them off (Damon). For example, in one instance a woman told reporters that her 15-year-old granddaughter had received over 25 marriage proposals during her first year in a refugee camp (Stoter).

Many mothers in desperate situations are willing to give into the demands of these wealthy men for several reasons. Marrying off a daughter means that there is one fewer mouth to feed. The family also profits financially from the dowry. For example, in one area 4.2 percent of respondents said that dowries were their family's primary or secondary source of income (UN Women, "Gender-based"). Parents also believe that marrying off a daughter will guarantee her financial security and a higher quality of life (Charles and Denman). When girls are under constant threat of rape or sexual harassment, it is worth it to some parents to save the honour of their family by marrying off girls to strangers at a young age. Parents are also concerned that they will not survive long enough to see their daughters married, and thus act drastically in order to ensure the safety of their children (Charles and Denman). Echoing this desperation, one mother said of her decision to marry off her daughter:

> Zeina's father is not here, so she doesn't have male protection.... Especially at night, Za'atari [refugee camp] can be dangerous for young girls. I heard some horrible rumours about girls getting raped or kidnapped. So, when we found out that this young man had a college certificate and good potential to support and protect her in the future, we decided to say yes. (Stoter)

One of the most perverse forms of sexual exploitation present in Syrian refugee camps relates to the pre-Islamic custom of pleasure marriage. These are marriages that end after a predetermined span of time, where the man is under no obligation to care for the woman or any offspring. More often than not the girls who enter into pleasure marriages are under the age of 18, and it is usually the girl's parents who arrange the union (UN Women, "Gender-based"). Pleasure marriages are legally acceptable in Shi'a Islam, and several Muslim clerics, including Saudi Arabia's highest sheikh, have even issued declarations permitting this form of sexual exploitation of minors (Toameh; "Young Saudi"). In a culture where honour is central to social acceptance, pleasure marriages are seen as a more acceptable form of buying sex. However, the practice exploits young girls and ultimately harms Syrian refugee families (Damon).

At an increasingly frequent rate, Arab men from Saudi Arabia and other wealthy Middle Eastern countries are coming to areas dense with Syrian refugees to buy sex. Under the pretext of being charitable, these men arrange with refugee parents to marry Syrian refugee girls. The parents contracting the marriage usually mistakenly believe that the marriage is permanent; however, in some cases these marriages are seen by parents as a solution for daughters who have been raped and their honour lost (Sherlock and Malouf; UN Women, "Gender-based"). The men often rent rooms near refugee camps where they consummate their "marriages" before returning the girls to their families. Often these men promise to send for the girl upon returning to their country, but never deliver on their promises.

This phenomenon of pleasure marriage is becoming a culturally acceptable norm. For example, in Zaatari refugee camp in Jordan, UN officials estimate that at least 500 underage Syrian girls are married every year. The exact number is unknown, since many parents conceal the marriage of their daughter if it ends up being temporary in order to preserve family honour (Sherlock and Malouf; El-Masri, Harvey, and Garwood). One in ten respondents to a recent survey said they knew a girl who had been in a temporary marriage.

SOLUTIONS

While the challenges faced by Syrian refugee women are immense, there are simple solutions available to aid agencies, host countries, and the international community that will do a great deal to resolve many regional problems. By providing innovative gender-based services that address the economic and security needs of Syrian mothers and women, these groups can alleviate much of the suffering borne by refugee families. Gender must also feature prominently in any data collection or project implementation.

While various UN agencies (UNHCR, WFP, WHO, UNICEF, etc.) maintain a vital presence in refugee camps, many non-governmental aid agencies are also present and play an important role. Many of these NGOs identified the need for gender-based humanitarian responses and have responded by creating programs that provide hygiene products, counselling, and cash assistance to women in need. Other agencies have created safe spaces where mothers can discuss sensitive topics like domestic abuse or poverty, free from traditional social stigma. The establishment of recreational programs and religious services also helps refugee families to deal with frustration and feelings of helplessness.

However, aid agencies must continue to focus on countering traditional systemic forces that discriminate against women and mothers. Gender-balanced distribution systems must be created and constantly monitored to prevent corruption or exploitation. Aid programs should employ equal numbers of female staff and ensure that aid reaches women as well as men (UNHCR, "Sexual and Gender-Based").

Governmental and non-governmental agencies working with refugees should devote more resources towards providing education for school-age refugees. This will help children deal with psychological trauma and free up time for women to generate income or address personal health needs. Greater funding should also be provided to alleviate the gendered responsibilities of women by providing easier access to things like clean water and laundry services (Charles and Denman).

Many refugees bring valuable, marketable skills with them from Syria. Host countries must remove legal barriers to refugees working (for example, Syrians in Jordan must pay a fee of 275 Jordanian dinars for a work permit). This would improve the Syrians' abilities to create safe and secure lives for their families. Financial problems could be alleviated by giving small investment grants to Syrian families, which would grow the local economy. These should be directed at helping women. For example, in one focus group, many Syrian women expressed interest in home-based income-generating activities to support their families (CARE). Men and women should have equal access to all charitable donations and income-generating activities.

Governments should also create a system of housing vouchers or cash assistance to help refugee mothers find adequate housing that meets the needs of their families. Alleviating problems of over-crowding and unsafe accommodations will help prevent domestic and gender-based violence, reduce feelings of frustration and help-lessness for mothers and families, and help individuals heal from traumatic experiences. It is particularly important that this system of rent subsidy give special attention to the needs of disadvantaged Syrian mothers and female-headed households (Miks).

Reports of sexual violence need to be investigated and impunity for sexual assault must be eradicated. This must include allegations of misconduct by individuals working for humanitarian organi-zations in the area (UN Women, "We Just"). Camp facilities will be improved as aid agencies consider a gendered perspective on humanitarian work. Police officers can be stationed near toilets to prevent vandalism of lights and sexual harassment in a way that would minimize the threat to women and girls during the day and night (Amnesty International). Women must also be made aware of the rights and services available to refugees, and aid agencies should work with local and national legal systems to prosecute perpetrators of gender-based violence (UNHCR, "Sexual and Gen-der-Based").

Programs that aim at preventing gender-based violence must be incorporated into existing aid programs and should include men as well as women. Too often programs that focus on violence prevention ignore the fact that men perpetrate the majority of incidents of gender-based violence. Men must therefore be part of the solution to these problems (UNHCR UNHCR, "Sexual and Gender-Based").

In response to greater media coverage of early marriages and pleasure marriages, several clerics in the region have issued dec-larations condemning the twisted religious logic used to justify such unions. However, more is needed. A greater awareness of the problem both inside and outside the refugee camps will ultimately stop the further exploitation of Syrian women (Zarzar). Empowering mothers through vocational training, micro-credit investment, and leadership roles will also provide alternatives to early marriage all while promoting the economic self-reliance of women (UNHCR, "Sexual and Gender-Based").

However, the greatest solution by far to these problems will be unity at the international level to fully fund aid efforts and end the Syrian conflict. Because there is no end in sight to the refugee crisis, governments and other international actors have been reluctant to commit to fully funding refugee services. Aid agencies are struggling to provide for an ever-increasing number of refugees while being billions of dollars short of their funding requirements. If the needed amount of aid is not given to fund humanitarian projects for Syrian refugees, the growing refugee crisis will continue to have a destabilizing effect on the entire region (Damon). The international community should commit to fully funding refugee services while working together to find a solution to the Syrian civil war. Women must be a part of the peace process and should be at the center of all reconstruction projects.

Syrian mothers and women, while often the victims of exploitation and discrimination, are also the solution to many of the region's problems. By guaranteeing that the needs of female Syrian refugee are met, the international community can ensure a healthy and stable population that will one day return to rebuild Syria.

WORKS CITED

Amnesty International. "Syria: Safe Access to Toilet Facilities for Women Girls in Za'atri Camp."

Amnesty International USA's Women's Human Rights Coordination Group, n.d. Web. 8 January 2014.

CARE Jordan. "Syrian Refugees in Urban Jordan." CARE, April 2013. Web. 21 January 2014.

Charles, Lorraine and Kate Denman. "Syrian and Palestinian Syrian Refugees in Lebanon: the Plight of Women and Children."

Journal of International Women's Studies 14.5 (Dec 2013): n.p. Web. 25 January 2014.

Damon, Arwa. "No Sanctuary for Syria's Female Refugees." CNN. 26 June 2013. Web. 25 January 2014.

Damon, Arwa and Raja Razek. "Syria refugee's desperate act: 'They burned my heart before they burned my body.'" CNN. 3 April 2014. Web. 30 May 2014.

Deacon, Zermarie and Cris Sullivan. "Responding to the Complex and Gendered Needs of Women." *Affilia: Journal of Women and Social Work* 24.3 (Aug 2009): 272-84. Print

El-Masri, Roula, Claire Harvey, and Rosa Garwood. "Shifting Sands: Changing Gender Roles among Refugees in Lebanon." *Oxfam International*. September 2013. Web. 25 January 2014.

Hadid, Diaa. "Syrian Refugee Women Face Sexual Exploitation." *Associated Press*. 1 August 2014. Web. 30 September 2014.

International Federation of Red Cross and Red Crescent Societies. "Syrian Refugees Living in the Community in Jordan: Assessment Report." ReliefWeb. September 2012. Web. 21 January 2014.

Karimi, Faith and Salma Abdelaziz. "Syria Civil War Deaths Top 160,000, opposition group says." CNN. 20 May 2014. Web. 30 May 2014.

Ki-Moon, Ban. "Remarks at Meeting on the Humanitarian Crisis in Syria." United Nations. 6 September 2013. Web. May 30 2014.

Margolis, Hillary. "Want to Save Syrian Lives? Step Up Humanitarian Aid." *Human Rights Watch*. 23 September 2013. Web. 30 May 2014.

Miks, Jason. "How World Can Respond to Syria's Refugee Crisis." CNN. 12 May 2014. Web. 30 September 2014.

Murray, Rebecca. "Syrian Refugees Struggle with Trauma." *Al-Jazeera*. 5 November 2013. Web. 21 January 2014.

Nebehay, Stephanie. "Syrian Refugees Top 3 Million, Half of All Syrians Displaced: UN" *Reuters*. 29 August 2014. Web. 13 September 2014.

Sherlock, Ruth and Carol Malouf. "Syrian Girls 'Sold' into Forced Marriages." *The Telegraph*. 23 January 2013. Web. 8 January 2014.

Stoter, Brenda. "Teenage Syrian Refugees Wed 'For Protection.'" *Al-Jazeera*. 12 November 2013. Web. 8 January 2014.

"Syrian Women Refugees Face Forced Early Marriages and Restricted Mobility: UN Women Report." *UN Women*. 20 June 2013. Web. 21 January 2014.

"Syrian Women's Joint Statement on Engagement in the Syrian Political Process." *UN Women*. 13 January 2014. Web. 21 January 2014.

Toameh, Khaled Abu. "How Muslim Men are 'Helping' Syrian Refugees." *Gatestone Institute*. 11 September 2012. Web. 9 March 2014.

"UN: Syrian refugee's murder of son highlights desperation." *The Daily Star*. 22 January 2014. Web. 22 January 2014.

UN Women. "Gender-based Violence and Child Protection among Syrian Refugees in Jordan, with a Focus on Early Marriage." *ReliefWeb*. July 2013. Web. 21 January 2014.

UN Women. "'We Just Keep Silent': Gender-based Violence amongst Syrian Refugees in the Kurdistan Region of Iraq." *United Nations*. April 2014. Web. 1 May 2014.

UNHCR. "Syria Regional Refugee Response." *UNHCR: The UN Relief Agency*. n.d. Web. 30 May 2014.

UNHCR. "Sexual and Gender-Based Violence against Refugees, Returnees, and Internally Displaced Persons." *UNHCR*. May 2003. Web. 30 September 2014.

Usta, Jinan and Amelia Reese Masterson. "Assessment of Reproductive Health and Gender-Based Violence among Displaced Syrian Women in Lebanon." UNFPA Lebanon, Power Point presentation. Web. 21 January 2014.

"Young Saudi Girl's Marriage Ended." *BBC*. 30 April 2009. Web. 9 March 2014.

Zarzar, Anas. "Syrian Refugees: Forced into Marrying off their Daughters." *Al-Akhbar English*. 11 September 2012. Web. 31 May 2014.

11.
Motherhood Out of Home and Hearth

Experiences of Pakistani Mothers in Displaced Families

ANWAR SHAHEEN AND NAZISH KHAN

FOR MOTHERS, PAKISTAN HAS BEEN declared the second most dangerous place in the world. Beside poverty, malnutrition, poor healthcare, disaster, and social exclusion, armed conflict has enhanced the danger in recent years. In the aftermath of the Soviet withdrawal from Afghanistan in 1990, and Pakistan's involvement in the U.S.-led "War on Terror" in 2001, militancy and insurgency have left millions of people injured, killed, or displaced. In 2012, Pakistan had the largest number of people, i.e., 15 percent of its total population, directly affected by conflict and living with violence, fear, and deprivation (Save the Children Foundation). On 15 June, 2014, an extensive and decisive military operation, namely "Zarb-e-Azb" was launched against terrorists in North Wazirastan area, and the operation was later expanded to other areas, for curbing the menace once for all. The total estimate of internally displaced peoples (IDPs) after this operation alone was over one million. Though camps were set up, IDPs mostly preferred to live at places of their own choice, such as friends'/relatives' homes or rented homes. The stakeholders in various operations included the local population, local *jirgas* (tribal council), *lashkars* (private armies), the government, and the militants-turned-insurgents with links and targets inside and across the border. Pakistani motherhood in crisis and conflict, therefore, needs to be understood in the context of this background. This context also highlights the relevance of the present study for Pakistan.

This chapter is based on conversations with a sample of 20 mothers in two conflict zones in Pakistan with different administrative status—FATA (Federally Administered Tribal Areas) and PATA (Provincially Administered Tribal Areas). The insurgency and militancy rooted in the strategic location and governance of these two regions was curbed through a series of operations by the government that effectively destroyed the lives of security force personnel and innocent people, as well as physical infrastructure, crops, and and other means of livelihood. Those most affected by the consequent displacement were the women, children, the elderly, and the disabled. The present study explores the experiences of mothers during their displacement from FATA and PATA. We argue that the suffering of IDPs, especially women (IDWs), has close links to their socioeconomic status, the strategic location of their homes, and the conditions and time of exit. The findings of the study show that motherhood duties in Pakistan are undergoing change because the concept and dynamics of the roles mothers play in various segments of Pakistani society[2] are exposed to rapid change, geared by various political and economic factors, including displacement.

THE BACKGROUND

The province of Khyber Pakhtunkhwa (KP) has three regions that have evolved with different histories: PATA, FATA, and settled districts. FATA is divided into seven agencies—Bajaur, Khyber, Kurram, Orakzai, Mohmand, North Wazirastan, and South Wazirastan (see map). PATA comprises the four former princely states (Swat, Chitral, Dir, and Amb) which opted to join Pakistan in 1947; their status as "states" was changed to a provincially administered zone, PATA in 1969. Swat was a fairly developed state as compared to other regions of KP. In PATA, the Swat population increased by 49.5 percent during 1998-2011, while the KP province showed a 51.6 percent increase (Khan). The FATA is overwhelmingly tribal in character, whereas Swat society tends to adopt more modern/capitalist norms. On the whole, agencies in FATA can be located variably towards the traditional side of the locus of traditional-modern; Swat occupies the modern extreme. The isolation of FATA is a myth; only the very poor and agriculturist families do not leave their areas; otherwise men are fairly mobile. The recent wave of militancy and conflict has forced more people, particularly women, to move out of their areas. International, national, and non-governmental agencies are actively involved with the conflict-affected population.

THE CONFLICT CAUSING DISPLACEMENT

The crisis in KP was caused by a complex set of factors. The FATA has been chronically marginalized, underdeveloped, and used as a buffer zone between the British and Russian powers in the colonial period. Later, it turned out to be a hiding place for the Al-Qaeda militants from the region and the world who share a homogenized worldview and an ideology of martyrdom (Hussain). In the case of Swat, weakening of political institutions and militarization from the 1970s onward promoted autocracy. Petro-dollars and Wahabi interpretation of Islam have infused the society since the 1980s. Jihadist interpretation of Islam gained popularity and its proponent Fazalullah became popular through his illegal FM radio in Swat. He started curbing women's freedom but, ironically, gained the support of older women who supported his version of Islam. Meanwhile his groups' links with militants in Afghanistan became instrumental in challenging the government in the valley. When terrorism and brutality heightened, counter-operations became inevitable.

The first operation began in November 2007 in Swat when the residents of Khyber agency were found suffering under threats and terrorist attacks by the militants, mostly from Afghanistan. Many fled to Peshawar, Nowshera, Charsadda, Mardan, and nearby locations (SEED). The government tried to provide relief to them during and after displacement in many ways. After an operation in Mohmand Agency, when about 8,000 displaced families returned home they were supplied basic needs for few months till they were able to restart their routine life (*The Nation*).

About half a million people live in Kurram Agency, 40 percent of whom belong to the Shia sect, the largest ratio in the FATA region. The sectarian conflict heightened due to influx of anti-Shia people and Taliban into the agency. Due to breach of peace deals and persistent trouble with the Tehreek-e Taliban Pakistan (TTP), Shias, and Hqqani Network, Operation Koh-e-Sufaid was launched in Kurram Agency on 4 July 2011, and was declared successful on 8 August (Jan and Worby). There were 51,582 registered IDPs by 7 June 2013. Forty-five percent of women were deported, and 87 percent families were reportedly in off-camp locations (Shaheen). IDPs from Orakzai Agency protested in the neighbouring Hangu district over inadequate arrangements by the government (*The News International,* 8 August 2010).

North Wazirastan Agency (NWA) has remained a strong centre for terrorists and insurgents since the turn of the century and efforts were made to break their influence. It was once again under the threat of military operation in early June 2014 that people were fleeing. Almost 60,000 left before the start of the operation (Gul), including the militants against whom the operation was meant, so the utility of the announced operation became questionable (AFP). South Wazirastan Agency (SWA) also proved difficult to be cleared of militants during Operation Rah-i-Nijat in October 2009 (Mahsud). There were more 40,000 registered Mehsud families living in host communities of Tank and Dera Ismail Khan Districts waiting for aid and/or clearance to go back (Ali).

The estimate of IDPs in 2010 was 1.23 million (IDMC). In total, the number of registered families displaced from FATA since 2008 is 281,754. In all cases of displacement, more IDPs stayed in the camps than with host communities because of fear of renewed violence, since the camps were not always safe and many of them bombed.[3]

WOMEN IN PATA AND FATA

The status of women in the two sample communities is different because FATA has been observing a stricter form of Pakhtunwa-li—the Pakhtun tribal code—than the PATA region, which is now modified into a feudal-cum-capitalist culture. Pukhtunwali confines women to the traditional roles of wife and mother. Due to observing strict purdah—segregation of sexes—women do not participate in activities in the public domain. The tribal region lies adjacent to PATA and settled districts, so men do go there for business and come back; women rarely go. The difference in class and family background determines the amount of freedom for women in terms of education, mobility, economic, and political participation, and decision-making about their lives.

The Swat region is more integrated into the modern world. Swat valley has fertile land, and agriculture, trade, transport, industry, forestry, and tourism are major economic sources. For the men, it has been common to immigrate to other parts of the world, such as Germany, Dubai, and Canada, to amass personal wealth. The women of Swat have greater chance to pursue education, and are generally more affluent compared with FATA women who face more hardships in their daily lives. Swat has highly class-specific subcultures and women's status frameworks. Recently, the *parachkaan* (workers/labourers), *dhekaan* (peasant), and *chamyar* (cobbler) families have started to encourage their daughters to become educated. After getting education, the women become teachers and professionals, and gain the respect of landowning families. Lower class women who work in fields are exposed to contact with un-related men, so command less respect. Normally women maintain purdah by using a wrapping robe (*chador*), and travel in curtained wagons. The lower class girls usually attend nearby school and those from wealthier families are transported. Women's attendance of college and professional institutions is becoming acceptable. Socio-economic indicators show that FATA has been much more deprived than PATA regarding facilities of education, health, roads, communication, modern sector of production, and urbanization. The experiences of displacement in Swat and FATA communities, therefore, inevitably proved different.

Militant insurgence, however, stopped the growing process of women's rights. Under the militants' threats, women's appearance in the public domain, mobility without male chaperon, shopping in the market squares, and going out for education, all became significantly more difficult. The number of schools destroyed in Swat, KP, and FATA areas ran into the hundreds. The attack on Malala Yousufzai, a young girl from Swat, was intended to prevent her from advocating for the rights of children to education; she survived the attack and became an icon of courage and the demand for rights to education at the global level.

In contrast, FATA has variegated economic structures. Green and fertile lands in the northern part and barren hills in the south

Base Map for Khyber Pakhtunkhwa & FATA with Tehsils

give rise to difference in livelihood patterns. Due to FATA's strict tribal norms, its women remain relatively more disenfranchised. However, with the introduction of *Political Parties Act* in 2011, the recent elections saw noticeable participation of women as voters and candidates. In lower class Pakhtun families, marrying

off girls in their early teens has been very common. Joint families
are gradually thinning out. In the absence of husbands, women
with small children usually live with the joint family, where an
adult male is responsible for their social affairs. However, many
mothers prefer to live separate from in-laws when the children
grow up and they can afford a separate house. The control of the
mother-in-law is maintained in the traditional manner. The young
spouses cannot express their mutual affection openly. Domestic
violence against women is accepted generally as a norm, and wom-
en's work in the public domain is generally not allowed. Due to
limited opportunities for education and personal growth, girls in
both FATA and PATA internalize becoming a wife and a mother as a
supreme goal of their lives. Love marriages are rare, but the dower
amount and conditions of a marriage contract make the wife a
strong economic partner. Men, socialized to be sturdy, brave, and
to take pride in masculine traits, usually do not express sympathy
for their wives, even when they are in trouble, as this would be
against the "man's pride."

Women work in fields, fetch water from long distance, and go
to streams for washing clothes. Strict purdah keeps them off the
busy roads, transport, and away from markets. Their access to
modern urban facilities is restricted due to poor infrastructure.
Mules and donkeys remain the only feasible transport. The high
cost of transportation on hilly terrain has denied access to health
and family planning workers for people living in scattered houses
and hamlets. Visits to hospitals for antenatal and post-natal care
are rare, thus causing high incidence of maternal mortality—about
260 recently (Government of Pakistan). The people have been under
the influence of orthodox religious leaders, more so in the recent
upsurge of religious extremism, that condemns contraception, so
the population has increased in FATA faster than other parts of
the country.

Preference for sons is high in the FATA tribal and patrilineal
system. Sons also affirm masculinity and masculine pride, which
are seen as damaged by daughter's birth. Traditionally, upon
giving birth, a woman expects to receive, apart from other gifts,
about forty hens and ten kilograms of pure ghee, an item of gold,
clothes for herself and baby, and a feast for her in-laws from her

parents. Similar traditions are followed by all classes depending upon affordability. Glorification of motherhood and marriage with a well-earning man are the preferred ideals of women's lives. Childless women are regarded as unfortunate. A girl, if she is not studying, gets married in her teen years; however, mothers have started disliking this practice. Contraception is practiced but not openly admitted. The proof is the average number of children, which is now dropping to four or five. Now women are more likely to refer to the number of children as being the husband's choice; earlier, the couple would refer to it as being "up to God."

CONDITIONS OF INTERNAL DISPLACEMENT IN PAKISTAN

Pakistan has been facing large-scale humanitarian emergencies during the past five years due to combined menaces of armed conflict. Mothers, newborns, and children, therefore, have been facing challenges of health and survival more than the rest of the people even in new destination in cities (Yousafzai). Pakistan has become a fragile state as well, due to persistent high-intensity internal conflicts and terrorism, with FATA being the most vulnerable region. Of the total 125,832 IDP families in KP in northwest Pakistan, only 16,316 (13 percent) are currently registered in camps (excluding fresh wave of Zarb-e Azb operation). Data collected in a recent multi-agency rapid assessment reveals that many IDP families are living in off-camp areas and have few income-generating possibilities. They place an immense strain on housing and water, sanitation, and hygiene facilities of the host communities (ACTED). Moreover, those who were affected but did not leave the area also have special needs. The stream of displaced persons has continued, so that while in one part of South Wazirastan the families are returning, in another part they are under serious threat to leave to avoid being trapped in a conflict zone. There have been at least 1.6 million internal refugees in FATA (Mohsin).

METHODOLOGY

In our approach, we have been mindful of the sensitive nature of data gathering, the curb on women's voices, the risks in disclosing identity, the scattered nature of respondents, and the surveillance of FATA women who come into contact with any unknown person (male or female). Motherhood is not a very private matter but women prefer talking about it only with women. The survey population was defined as "mothers having experience of conflict-related displacement in recent years along with children, newborns, or pregnancy." The FATA sample was still largely displaced in various cities, including Karachi. Data was collected through personal contact and telephone for families accessible to the researchers in Swat and Karachi, and for others acquaintances were used to build rapport. In case of Swat all the families had settled back, so they were contacted in their homes. The general circumstances of women in both populations were already well known to the authors due to past research with these communities on subjects other than motherhood. We used purposive sampling, but we ensured representation of socio-economic variety and geographical coverage among a large number of possible respondents. The narratives reflect this variety. The Swat sample of respondents posed no difficulty, but the FATA respondents, especially from Wazirastan, were the most difficult to contact and interview because they belonged to remote tribal areas and had little exposure of the world out of their villages. Pushto-speaking interviewers were arranged. Contacting FATA women without the permission of men was very difficult; however, men themselves were helpful in giving general information about displacement. Their hesitation was caused by recent incidents of IDP harassment in the city of Karachi. Complete anonymity was ensured to the respondents.

FINDINGS

There were ten mothers each in the FATA and PATA samples. The 20 sample mothers belonged to different socioeconomic strata and their biographical conditions varied. Respondents' mean age at the time of migration was 29.9 years, whereas their age groups were 20-25 (eight); 26-30 (three); 31-35 (two); and over 35 (six), showing that a range of young and older mothers (20-45) was included. Their average number of children was 4.45, whereas the age range was one to eleven. Most mothers (17 out of 20) had children less than ten years. Out of 89, 24 children were one to five years old; 21 were in six to ten years old; 22 were eleven to fifteen years old; and the rest were above fifteen. Mothers' education was very low: illiterate nine (45 percent); Quran literate one (five percent); up to primary nine (45 percent); and only one to seventh grade. Only one woman was employed as a school helper; the rest were housewives. All the households spoke Pushto as their first language; only 25 percent lived in joint families. The major sources of family income included labour (30 percent); driver (20 percent); agriculture, government service, remittance from abroad, and business (15 percent each); security guard and property rent (five percent each). Their houses, to which they returned or were living in state of displacement, were of variable sizes—from 16 square yards to 2500 yards, with mean size at 430 square yards. Of the total, 30 percent of houses were less than 100 square yards. Two houses of 2000 and 2500 square yards indicated affluent families (of Swat). The number of rooms ranged to one to eleven rooms; houses having one or two rooms were 15 percent each; and three and four rooms, 25 percent each.

Displacement

The year of migration in the case of Swat sample was mostly 2009 (45 percent of total sample); only one family of Buner migrated in 2010. The FATA residents migrated between 2007 and 2013. One Swati family had to migrate twice. Ten FATA mothers belonged to North Wazirastan (2), South Wazirastan (3), Mohmand (1), Khyber (2), Orakzai and Bajaur agencies (1 each).

Only one mother reported being confident to travel alone, while others reported never having travelled alone before the displacement (65 percent), but had travelled along with children (55 percent); many reported being afraid of travelling alone (30 percent). The first safe point of transit stay was outside the zone of operation; in Swat it was the border district, and in FATA, it was in areas where no shelling or attack by any side was feared. Only three (15 percent) reported going to the IDP camp; others had preferred to go to their relatives (60 percent) or live in a rented house (60 percent). Two families went to a school shelter in Charsadda; from there one family shifted to rented house and the other returned after three months. Only one family stayed in camp for 5 months (the longest stay in sample) and then after receiving a call from government officials went back home in Orakzai Agency. One family from Buner and eight from FATA did not return; mostly they went a long way to Karachi and decided to stay there. The Buner family reported, "We went to see our house after two years, it was all broken so we came back to Karachi." The Khyber agency family found their home occupied by militants and they were unable to retrieve it, so the family went back to Karachi.

Travelling was done on foot, on vehicles, on animal carts, on push-carts, or on bicycles. The distance between home and the point of first stay was not known by most women; they could report only the time taken in travel. This was true mostly for the FATA women, who just followed men's instructions. The distance was estimated at 50 km in the Orakzai case, 600-2000 km in FATA-Karachi travel, and 3-48 hours due to blocked roads and having to hide while fleeing. The trouble and time depended on the family status and the exit conditions, as some affluent families could arrange their own vehicles and managed escape largely safely due to early departure or quick mode of travel; many families, however, had to walk on foot for long distances due to unavailability of vehicles. This was the case of most of the Swat residents. FATA residents were poorer hence encountered more trouble.

Mothers' Experience of Displacement

Among the 20 sample women, fifteen were pregnant at the time of departure, two were nursing infants, and three had older children. The length of pregnancy was two and four months (one each); six months (two); seven and eight months (four each); nine months (two); and unknown length (one). The order of pregnancy in months was eighth (3), seventh (two); fifth (two); fourth (3), third (two); second (two); and first (one). Later the women gave birth at hospital (seven); clinic (one); at the birth attendant's home (two); and at relatives' home (five). The birth was attended by a trained doctor/nurse/midwife in thirteen cases and no trained person in two cases. Delivery was normal in eleven cases, needed blood in one case, and was complicated in one case. Newborn weight was normal in 50 percent of cases. One fetus was still-born, one was aborted, and one baby died after three days.

Newborns were fed breast-milk in all live cases, and health problems developed in all newborns, and were treated with difficulty in all cases. These problems included jaundice, diarrhea, coughing, skin problems, boils, and prickly heat, but ranged in severity. Main reasons for the health problems were homelessness, exposure to intense heat, unhygienic conditions, and inability to take precautions. Mothers' also faced problems related to the general health of older children and their own reproductive and general health. Travel was also difficult due to food scarcity and the sickness of children. A mother of eleven children reported that her children all "fell sick one by one." The older children also faced health problems during the displacement due to intense heat, skin diseases, accidents like slipping, and children's common ailments.

Travel was an ordeal for mothers also due to their lack of experience in any kind of travel. Many walked on foot wearing men's slippers; a sufficient number of vehicles were not available. One mother reported: "The vehicle was so full of people that on every ascending men have to get off, and I used to pray, as if I had alighted, slipping or walking uphill was risky for my pregnancy. My children started vomiting due to such a rough journey." The conditions of hijab and segregation were difficult to maintain while travelling and in camps. Mothers reported no harassment during their travel or stay in camps, likely because they were accompanied by men from the family, as well as the risks they would face after reporting of any such incident.

Few men and women in Swat stayed back in severe risk due to serious illness or disability. In most cases they were to take care of crops, gardens, cattle, shop, house, etc. Also the love of land and home was strong in older generations. A young mother reported: "My old mother cooked chicken for us and packed for travel but she stayed back due to old age." Most IDPs returned home at their own cost, but some were supported financially by the government (Rupees 25,000 in Swat). "This money was given to men but not women," a woman complained. Returnees were given rations for two or three months. Getting ration card was not easy at the camp or even upon coming back home. Such facts show that the mother's job of caring for the family remained difficult for long time. Very few houses remained undamaged. One sample family fell sick due to drinking water from a contaminated home-well after returning. Both the government and NGOs helped people to resettle by providing for their immediate needs, partial compensation for damages, and building materials in South Wazirasatn case.

Feelings of insecurity still prevail among returnees in both PATA and FATA cases. The people are still afraid of speaking against the government, army, militias, or the militants, due to previous suffering. The children had recurring bad memories: "They seemed to be mentally sick at times," a mother reported. The militants were never crushed to extinction, and civilians remain vulnerable. Night watching had to be arranged by people themselves. Even their old sympathy for Taliban was of no use now. The crisis still casts its shadows.

Economic problems were mostly faced by returning families due to disruption of business and routine economic activities. Even then women were not allowed to earn for their families. However, in response to the harsh economic conditions, recently a few women had started businesses at home. For those who did not return, economic problems grew due to having to pay house rent and utility bills at the new destination. Education was also a casualty of this process, as in the crisis phase the schools were either completely destroyed or not functioning properly. Returnees found it difficult to resume education, due to the break, fearful memories, impoverishment, and the presence of militants. One mother reported loss of two years of schooling. The private sector schools resumed teaching faster than government schools, which are mostly still in need of repair. A number of girls dropped their studies and boys became child labourers.

Motherhood in Privation: Mothers' Voices

All mothers reported that travel was extremely difficult, and that the conditions in the camps were inadequate. In many cases these conditions influenced the outcomes of their pregnancies and the health of their children. The mothers recounted the case of a newly married girl, who was full-term pregnant with her first baby, and who had to leave urgently as the villagers were all leaving.

Accompanied by her husband, mother-in-law, and few females, she could only find space sitting on the floor of a truck already full of people. On the road she went into labour and the women put a *chador* around her as a privacy curtain. She bled before and after the baby was born. The people in the truck could not help her as everyone was worried about their own life and family, no one could stop the truck, nor was it possible or useful, since there was no medical facility. By the evening both mother and newborn were dead, and later buried in a graveyard they finally found along the road.

In this section we provide some of the displaced mothers' own narratives:

I was newly married, eight months pregnant, travelled on foot and on many vehicles, whoever agreed to give us a ride. In the camp, life was very difficult, as if hell broke loose. The baby was delivered at a hospital nearby but the doctor put more stiches than needed and I still feel agony of that. In fact the doctor was in hurry because we reached the hospital at two am and she wanted to leave. She spoiled my case.

We went to the nurse/doctor's clinic, who had worked in an army hospital. She was very cooperative and charged a small fee (rupees 1500) for the normal delivery. My older child became sick in night and was seen by a doctor, who perhaps was not qualified, so we were given the wrong medicine, in reaction to which the boy became seriously ill. The next day we went to the clinic again and the other doctor explained that the medicine from the previous night was wrong. Then he gave proper treatment.

I was fourth months pregnant, expecting my second child, but I had a miscarriage due to miserable travel conditions. No one could do anything. After that I could not conceive again. It was painful to lose my baby.

We are poor. The nurse in the hospital who attended birth

wanted more money as she saw that we are in trouble. Perhaps it was God's will, so we complied silently.

It was my eighth baby and a full-term pregnancy. We were not allowed to go to hospital due to curfew at night, so we waited. In the morning I reached the hospital and delivered a stillborn. There was only one nurse available and we were very late.

The narratives show feelings of misery, helplessness, and dependence on relatives, friends, government authorities, and non-governmental sources. Women suffered due to pregnancy and the delivery happened mostly in difficult circumstances, either due to unavailability of proper staff and healthcare facility, or non-professional care or high fees demanded by the available staff. Women who could not go to hospital in time had a stillbirth or a very weak newborn who could not survive. One mother miscarried due to poor travel conditions. The accompanying family members in most of the cases could not help or did not try it as the norms of shame, honour, purdah, and privacy were all intensified in out-of-home situation. A strong feeling of shame overpowered mothers due to conditions of helplessness. Mothers mostly suffered in silence or protested in a few cases. The mother's dream of raising children in comfort and peace was shattered. Psychological troubles, loss of education, and health problems accompanied them back home. Family was always there but all kept suffering together. Leaving home and hearth meant misery in all cases.

Mothers' Feelings

The tribulations mothers experienced were expressed by respondents as follows:

We had to change vehicles, walked on foot endlessly, and the thought of babies being delivered on their way was horrifying. We prayed to God to keep us in dignity.

I could not walk on foot due to fatigue of pregnancy. My mother-in-law and husband were scolding me to cover myself. I was wearing burqa, was hot and feeling sick, too. I responded to my husband: "I have covered myself; it is your deed which is so obvious now."

My husband was abroad and I had to tell everything about my illness and pregnancy and delivery to my brother-in-law who accompanied me. That was so shameful, but I had no choice. My husband should have been there with me in the hour of need. He did not care for me. A folk tappa says: "Pa ma di zan da inzar gul ko boi di razi, Rang di pa istargo na inam (You have made yourself a flower of fig for me, whose fragrance comes but cannot be seen with eyes."

I was seven month pregnant when we had to walk out of Bajaur for about two days thirsty and hungry, so my baby suffered. When I got to the doctor, he operated me due to complications that emerged during travel. Lot of my blood was wasted and the baby could survive only for three days. It was given oxygen, was very pale, and looked like a lump with little chance of survival. After that, I was unable to walk for about three months due to weakness. I had to travel with this shame, and, alas! My baby also died.

For a new bride it was a real shame to travel with a big belly. I was enraged and shouting at my husband. But what could I do if God had given me this heavy load. People kept watching me and I kept walking.

We travelled on foot and on different vehicles. Every jumping in rickshaw gave serious signals to me with full term pregnancy. We had just reached one place then we were ordered to vacate that place as well. Finally, I was with some relatives. During nighttime curfew, we were not allowed to go out to the doctor, so my mother-in-law cut the umbilical cord. It got infected and my baby still feels its pain. The doctor came in the morning to give one injection. "Male doctor came and I [the mother] was feeling so much shame, but having no option, I closed my eyes

and he gave me the injection." The newborn was in pain
for weeks and little medicine lying in people's home was
used. I had weakness, pain, and anemia for months on, as
no treatment was available properly when it was needed.

CONCLUSION

Pakhtun women of Pakistan have multiple roles—household man-
ager, caregiver, house worker, mother, wife, daughter, daughters-
in-law, and earner, depending upon their stage of life and marital
status. The roles adopted once affect later stages, too. At all stages
they are expected to comply with the traditional norms and values
of Pakhtun womanhood. As mothers, they are highly respected,
glorified, and protected. The overall family and kinship affinities
have been operative in supporting the displaced families. In many
cases, friends and relatives proved helpful during the crisis. The
cultural context for FATA and PATA mothers was similar but the
socio-economic context varied. The variety purposively maintained
in this study sample was to represent the situation of thousands
of other mothers and families. Women with younger children
experienced more difficulty.

Some women avoided travel due to old age or disability and men
stayed to tend the fields, gardens, business, or disable/sick person.
In cases where no one stayed back, the people found their home and
belongings in wretched state on returning. Broken houses needed
maintenance or rebuilding. Resuming normal life was very hard
for all sample families except for those holding government jobs
or receiving help from abroad. Many of the FATA IDPs refrained
from going back; they are still waiting for improvement in conditions back home or have found better survival places. Those who
stayed with host families were in trouble due to crowding, sense
of dependence, and lack of privacy. Displaced women in cities
were very uncomfortable due to having to interact with strangers,
little space, poor knowledge of the locality, ethnic difference, and
language barriers.

The experience of displacement has extensive implications for
Pakistani motherhood and women's status in the future. In extensive conversations with most mothers we could see that the sample

women draw their identity and strength from motherhood. They are socialized to do so. They never condemned their children; even the full-term pregnant mothers when faced with humiliation and trouble, did not complain about the baby, but the husband. Motherhood makes their lives meaningful, confident, proud, secure, and empowered. The women showed a desire to become perfect mothers. If they failed in it, they regretted it; even when being totally helpless and not at fault for displacement, they regretted the wrongs done to their status as mother and the well-being of children and family. Though most are not breadwinners, their sense of integration within the family keeps them alert to fulfillment of family needs, so much so that if men cannot provide, women feel guilty for it. In this sense it is a shared parenting. The twin role of being a mother and provider is for them not worth-emulating as per the traditions and cultural norms. Whenever they had to assume the role of both mother and father, the women reported feeling uneasy.

Respondent women's ideals of motherhood were shaped by the dominant culture of their community. Mothers of Swat were concerned about loss of children's education but FATA mothers did not mention it, and the same was the attitude of fathers from FATA. Altruism prevailed undoubtedly but mothers asserted their own needs as well, especially health and fitness needs, because, if not fulfilled, these needs would prevent them from performing motherhood duties. In crisis, however, they did not care much for their personal needs as long as their children were provided for properly. The company of children was a source of safety for them, since they reported never travelling alone but only in the company of children before this migration. In the sample families, women were not considered confident, safe, and clever enough to move about in the public domain, except for their familiar routes to regular shopping areas in nearby towns. The same women would not step out without men's chaperoning in an alien environment. What this shows, however, is that displacement has contributed to the confidence of such women.

Gradually one can see that with good income from remittances and the waning of joint family structures under the pressures of displacement, the wives'/mothers' control on men's/sons' income, is strengthening. The control of in-laws is dwindling. The family size is shrinking and women's concerns about their own health and reproductive choices are being asserted more often. With exposure to and stay in cities, the isolation of tribal women is also broken, resulting in some personality changes. How they conceive of their motherhood role is likely to change, as well.

The FATA and PATA societies are similar in their ethos derived from Pakhtun code, but changes observed in Swat society are expected to come to the FATA society as well. The tribal social structure is gradually transforming to adopt modern structures of economy, polity, and society. The recent disruption in the FATA belt has facilitated breaking up old norms and practices. The recent displacement has boosted this process of transformation by breaking many taboos regarding gender. We expect that mothers in future societies of FATA and PATA will become more assertive as persons when their ideas of both motherhood and personhood undergo changes.

[1]*Zarb-e-Azb* has been the 162nd operation since 2003 when the army first entered FATA. The achievements before its start included killing over 3,000 terrorists and 14,000 security forces men. The issues emerging from Zarb-e Azb are not within the scope of this chapter.
[2]These segments can be identified as lying on a continuum of tribal to capitalist modes, and the displaced women of the sample belonged to the remotest or most backward tribal region as well as a fairly modern capitalist region.
[3]IRIN reported that on 17 April 2010, there was bombing on Kacha Pukha IDP camp near Kohat killing 41 IDPs. Later, other incidents of violence and bombing were also reported in various such camps.

WORKS CITED

Abbasi, Zaheer. "Pakistan Sinks to 146th in HDI: UNDP". *Business Recorder*, 29 March 2013. Web. 1 May 2014.

ACTED. "Pakistan: Dramatic Increase in Number of IDPs Causes Greater Strain on Host Communities." *Agency for Technical*

Cooperation and Development. n.d. Web. 10May 2014.

AFP. "North Waziristan empties out as foreign fighters flee." *Dawn. com*. Dawn Media Group. 13 June 2014. Web. 13 June 2014.

Ali, Zulfiqar. "South Wazirastan Operation: Only Sararogha Cleared in Three Years". *Dawn.com*. Dawn Media Group, 06 August 2012. Web. 14 May 2014.

Asif Bashir Chaudhry, "Zarb-e-Azb May Conclude This Month". *The Nation*. 8 August 2014. Web. 30 September 2014.

Government of Pakistan. *Pakistan Economic Survey 2013-14*. Islamabad: Finance Division, Economic Advisors' Wing, 2014. Print.

Gul, Pazir. "Panic-Gripped Waziristan Tribesmen Fleeing to Afghanistan." *Dawn.com*. Dawn Media Group, 26 May 2014. Web. 29 May 2014.

Hussain, Khadim. *The Militant Discourse: Religious Militancy in Pakistan*. Islamabad: Narratives, 2013. Print.

IDMC. "Pakistan: Millions of IDPs and Returnees Face Severe Crisis." *International Displacement Monitoring Centre*. International Displacement Monitoring Centre. 2 December 2009. Web. 12 April 2014.

Jan, Reza and Sam Worby. "Limited Goals, Limited Gains: The Pakistan Army's Operation in Kurram." *Critical Threats*. 6 September 2011. Web. 2 May 2014.

Khan, Abdul Sattar. "KPK Population Increases by 51.6 Percent in 13 years, Data Shows." *The News International*. 3 April 2012. Web. 12 May 2014.

Mahsud, Saifullah. "Combating Militancy in Bajaur and North-Waziristan Agency in Federally Administered Tribal Areas (FATA) of Pakistan- A Comparative Analysis." *Tigah*. 11 (2012): 149-64. Web. 17 May 2014.

Mohsin, Zainab Rubab. "The Crisis of Internally Displaced Persons (IDPs) in the Federally Administered Tribal Areas of Pakistan and their Impact on Pashtun Women." *Tigah*. 3.2 (2013): 92-117. Web. 23 April 2014.

Personal interviews with survey respondents.

Save the Children Foundation. *State of the World's Mothers 2014*. Save the Children Federation, Inc., 2014. Web. 6 June 2014.

SEED. "Emergency Assistance to IDPs from the Conflict in Khyber

Agency, Khybe Pakhtunkhwa, Pakistan." *SEED*. 2013. Web. 10 May 2014.

Shaheen, Sikander. "Operation Displaces 51,000 in Kurram: UN." *The Nation*. 7 June 2013. Web. 8 June 2014.

The Nation. "90 percent of Mohmand Agency Cleared of Militants; IDPs Return Home." *The Nation*. 16 September 2011. Web. 8 June 2014.

Yousafzai, Wisal. "1.6 Million Fata IDPs Living in Peshawar". *Reliefweb*. 2013. Web. 27 May 2014.

12.
Refugee Mothering, Resettlement and Mental Health

JACQUELINE CICCIO PARSONS, REBEKA R. PENDER
AND LARRY V. PARSONS

A MOTHER IN A WAR-TORN country will often attempt to flee the atrocities and violence. In order to escape, she may apply for political refugee status in another nation. If the mother is extremely fortunate, she may be granted asylum in a different country that is not experiencing political upheaval, after what is typically a long, drawn-out process. However, the opportunity to escape oppression can come at a significant price. The refugee mother may even be forced to leave behind some or all of her family, including her children, regardless of age. Even though the refugee mother can physically escape from political oppression and danger, it is not atypical for the stressors and the emotional torment of the conflicted area to follow her to the nation granting resettlement status. Long after a mother from a nation of conflict settles in a new country, she may still experience the psychological impacts of her past trauma. Mental health-related issues, including post-partum depression (PPD), fear, depression, anxiety, paranoia, psychosis, complicated grief, guilt, and post-traumatic stress disorder (PTSD) are often part of the refugee mother's reality.

This chapter is concerned with refugee mothering, resettlement, and mental health, and will focus on refugee women relocated to Canada and the United States, although refugee mothers resettled in other parts of the world experience similar issues. In the chapter we will discuss the migration process, refugee mothers' negotiation of a new culture and homeland cultural traditions, her fear for personal safety, and the physical and mental health challenges refugee mothers may experience when relocating to a new country for political asylum. Finally, the chapter will conclude with some suggestions on how mental health practitioners in the host county can offer counselling services to refugee mothers that are respectful of the mothers' own culture and customs. This chapter is unique because refugee mothers and mental health-related issues are virtually absent in existing literature.

CIRCUMSTANCES LEADING TO REFUGEE STATUS

Effective mothering requires safety, stability, shelter, succor, and schools. Refugee mothers typically flee their native lands because they can no longer provide safety, the most basic of these needs, for their children. Along the way, many mothers tend to lose their ability to provide for these basic needs, resulting in both mothers and children perishing as refugees. Other mothers are forced to leave children behind because of circumstances or because they cannot physically locate or move their children. This separation, or course, is one of the greatest possible affronts to the mother-child relationship. Conflict situations pose a number of challenges to daily mothering tasks. Only one example of this would be the deplorable conditions in which Afghani mothers must walk many miles each day just to acquire water and firewood, all while providing food and shelter and protecting their children in a very dangerous environment (Tramz).

As of 2012, there were over forty-five million displaced persons in the world (UNHCR). Two-thirds of these people were displaced within their own countries, while another third were displaced outside the borders of their native lands, and therefore were considered refugees. People are displaced from their homes for a variety of reasons. Sometimes people are displaced due to natural disasters and famine, but the primary causes are war, genocide, and the resulting anarchy. Currently, more refugees leave from Afghanistan than any other country, and there are more refugees living in Pakistan than in any other country (UNHCR). Women and children represented eighty percent of these displaced persons (International Rescue Committee).

Many refugees apply for asylum in a new country. Most countries grant asylum to people based on physical danger. If it is clearly unsafe for a person to remain in her native country, it may be possible for her to immigrate to another country and attain refugee status. Unfortunately, the number of people living in mortal danger in the world far exceeds the number of places they can go. Most displaced persons initially flee danger by moving short distances, travelling to adjacent towns or regions within their native countries. If they find themselves to be still in danger, they may flee to neighbouring countries. This is rarely a good solution, as dangerous, poverty-ridden countries tend to be surrounded by other dangerous, poverty-ridden countries.

When a refugee moves into an adjacent region, she often finds herself in a refugee camp, a place where huge numbers of desperate people crowd together with insufficient food, water, shelter, and medical care. Refugees in these camps are often at the mercy of the "host" nation, which may or may not have the means and motivation to care for them. Because these nations are often impoverished themselves, the support they provide is usually very limited. Non-governmental organizations (NGOs) like the United Nations may provide additional support, but the amount of support that actually reaches the refugees can vary widely. Unfortunately, the food, money and medicine contributed by the NGOs to help refugee populations does not always reach those populations. And the circumstances leading to the formation of these camps usually involve violent political upheavals like civil wars or long-term anarchy, so a host nation can actually be partially responsible for the violence, or may even benefit from it. As a result, refugee camps around the world are always hellish places of squalor, starvation, disease, and crime. Any refugee who enters one of these camps will want to leave as quickly as possible, either returning to her home, or fleeing farther away from the violence. As a general rule, the best refugee camps may offer some modicum of safety and basic needs, but jobs, schools, and child care are far out of reach. For mothers and children who are forced to languish in these camps for decades, there is almost no hope for long-term prosperity and independence. Because complications of pregnancy and childbirth are so much more common in this environment, the United Nations High Council on Refugees has developed a specific program targeted at improving maternal fetal health among refugee women

(UNCHR). In conditions like this, it is not uncommon for a refugee mother to experience anxiety and depression, as well set up future scenarios for PTSD.

If a refugee is fortunate, she will find transportation to one of the more prosperous countries that accept applications for asylum. These countries include the European countries, Australia, and, chiefly, the United States, which accepts about 70,000 refugees annually. U.S. policy on refugees has fluctuated depending on numerous factors. For example, after 2001, refugees began facing increased scrutiny, as the Department of Homeland Defense (DHD) formed and began screening them. Until 2009, terrorists and criminals had substantial success in entering the U.S. to commit crimes and acts of terrorism; for example, Somalis were able to come to the U.S and kidnap Somali refugee children, returning them to Somalia to serve as child soldiers. But in 2009, the FBI and DHD were able to significantly improve their ability to detect criminals and terrorists attempting to enter as refugees; since that time there has been far less criminal and terrorist activity by refugees. This is extremely important from the perspective of the typical, law-abiding refugee, who suffers even more prejudice and xenophobia when so many criminals and terrorists are finding ways of entering the country.

MIGRATION PROCESS

Each country granting asylum has a complex set of rules governing application for asylum, with heavy emphasis on ensuring that the asylum seeker is not a criminal or terrorist. In the U.S., the DHD checks carefully for these two characteristics, but does not check the health, education, or ability of the asylum-seeker. Most refugees rarely have money available to pay for transportation, temporary sustenance, and administrative costs. Female refugees are especially vulnerable to human trafficking, sexual slavery, and other forms of exploitation. In 2011, women and girls accounted for seventy-five percent of the victims of human trafficking (UN-ODC). In this way, asylum seekers are usually far better off than refugees who do not seek asylum, for the host nation often has a political reason for providing asylum seekers with some support.

Conversely, refugees who are not granted asylum may not even be allowed to stay in the host country.

Refugees receiving asylum in the U.S. are allowed to work and go to school, and can apply for citizenship after five years. They are not, however, allowed to vote. New refugees in the U.S. are supported by Refugee Resettlement Agencies (RRAs), which work for the federal government, specifically the Office of Refugee Resettlement. RRA staff members are paid by contract to provide certain services to newly arriving refugees. The RRA staff will meet the new arrival at the airport, obtain an apartment and pay the first six months' rent, take the refugees to the doctor, enroll the family for food stamps, and enroll the children in school. From a practical standpoint, most of the support a newly arriving refugee mother will receive is from her fellow refugees, especially those from her native or neighbouring countries. Part of this process is a phenomenon called secondary migration in which refugees move within the host nation in order to cluster with other immigrants of the same origin. This clustering can improve a refugee's functional ability to find a job, obtain healthcare, and educate her children (Geltman et al.). A refugee has very little time to learn a new language, get a job, generate an income, and so much more, so this support can mean the difference between success and failure. Because of these issues, a refugee can feel like a second-class citizen in her new country, resulting in self worth issues or depression.

DISRUPTION IN FAMILY SUPPORT SYSTEMS

It is obvious that the family support system of a refugee mother undergoes tremendous stress during the immigration process. A refugee family can be fractured in numerous ways. It is typical for a refugee family to experience the deaths of numerous family members. Separations are also very common and many families spend years attempting to locate a missing family member who may be dead or alive. Given the circumstances from which these families come, various family members may be injured or ill, and thereby less able to contribute to the mutual support of the family. In fact, in many cases, a disabled family member can pose an extra burden, which increases the stressors on the family system. Each of these situations can disrupt the family support net in some hard-to-define way.

HEALTH ISSUES: REFUGEES AND HIGH LEVELS OF STRESS

Refugees often experience enormous amounts of stress. This may be because they do not know where their relatives are, or because they feel insecure about their future, or for various other reasons. Refugees may continue to be distressed even when there is no direct threat. Because of this, their muscles may feel tense all the time. This tension can cause physical complaints, which may in turn worry them. These worries may then increase the tension in their muscles and make the physical complaints worse. In other words, they get caught in a spiral of increasing anxiety and increasing physical complaints.

Refugee mothers and children frequently arrive in the new country suffering from numerous physical and mental illnesses. They have left environments of violence, crime, famine, and disease. These maladies cover a very wide range of medical issues, including oral health and dental problems, which are the most common (Geltman). These health concerns reduce the mother's ability to find work and generate sustainable income. The children, of course, are affected the most. It is common for refugee children to suffer from cognitive disabilities due to their lack of sufficient nutrition (Corbett and Oman). In the U.S., refugee women and children receive healthcare under the Medicaid system, which varies widely from state to state, and could never be considered optimal.

Refugee mothers of children with disabilities face even more difficulty during the resettlement process (Beatson). Despite access to Western medicine, refugee mothers will often seek assistance for their children from healers native to the mothers' home country. Mothers sometimes report that Western medicine is not effective in meeting the needs of their children and are often disappointed when healing practices that were common in their native countries are not available (Beatson). If familiar practices are available, money may not be available to perform the ritual. Refugee mothers may also blame Western immunizations for causing their child's disability

(Beatson). It may be difficult for someone providing mental health services to bridge this cultural gap.

Not surprisingly, behavioural health issues are common and frequently very severe among refugee mothers and their children. The disruption, upheaval, violence, and uncertainty they have endured have almost always traumatized these mothers and children. Common diagnoses among refugee mothers include depression, anxiety, PPD, psychosis, obsessive compulsive disorder, and PTSD.

MENTAL HEALTH ISSUES

The majority of refugees, if not all, have been exposed to some form of traumatization in their home country. Specifically for women, experiences can range from emotional torture and multiple rapes, to female genital mutilation (Harris; Teodorescu et al). As refugees transition from their home countries, they face hunger and poverty, continued sexual violence and abuse, and finally unemployment and the stress of adjustment upon resettlement (Schubert and Punamaki). The consequences of these experiences, even after resettlement, can impact a woman for the remainder of her life if not properly addressed through mental health interventions. In general, there are high levels of PTSD, depression, pain, and anxiety among survivors of torture who seek asylum and resettlement from areas such as the Middle East and Central Africa (Schubert and Punamaki). Not widely available are mental health care services that have been adapted to serve the refugee population.

Based on previous reviews of the literature, there is a dearth of research regarding mental health concerns of refugees and especially how best to treat refugee women. The stressors of resettlement often depend on the host country and the opportunities and services available in those countries (Vergara et al.). Much of the research addresses the stress refugees experience on their way to resettlement camps, but not many studies exist on the mental health stress they experience once they are in the camps. Very few studies have examined the impact of gender on stressors, such as refugee women and the difficulty of adjusting to the Western culture. Refugee women tend to experience more stress than men during pre-migration, in transit, and the in resettlement process (Perera et al.). Women also seem to have a more difficult time learning the English language in addition to adjusting to American culture (Perara et al.). This is perceived as being due to culturally-conditioned differences in gender roles. Refugee women and adolescent girls are considered the "keepers of the culture" and so are not encouraged to learn English or acculturate in that sense (Ellis et.al). Additionally, refugee women face much different gender norms when arriving in certain countries such as the U.S. Often, refugee women come from patriarchal societies and find adjustment to cultures that stress independence or freedom for women much more difficult than men (Perara et al.). Additionally, refugee women are limited by pre-migration access to education and post-immigration access to valuable resources such as vocational training, education, and social involvement (Watkins, Razee, and Richters).

Services provided to refugees are time-limited and require multiple facets of integrative care and responsiveness (Murray, Davidson, and Schweitzer). The limited research that has been conducted indicates that mental health services that are provided to refugee women should include adjustment to the host culture and the consideration of cultural concerns (Murray, Davidson, and Schweitzer). The mental health professional providing the services should avoid cultural stereotypes and over-generalizations and should provide psychoeducational services that include resources for housing, employment, and information for daily living (e.g., food markets, laundry facilities, transportation, currency exchange, etc.) (Murray, Davidson, and Schweitzer). Additionally, due to the stress of resettlement, adjustment to a new culture, and symptoms of stress, depression, and anxiety, mental health interventions should also focus on fostering a supportive community and connections with others to allow for support systems to be built (Murray, Davidson, and Schweitzer). This would be especially important for single-parent mothers who have come alone with their children.

CULTURAL COMPETENCE

One of the most important things for mental health providers when working with someone of a different culture is to be culturally responsive. A culturally responsive counsellor acknowledges cultural differences and appreciates those differences and is willing to learn as much as he or she can about that culture in order to provide the best services possible (Arredondo et al.). When working with refugee mothers, a culturally responsive counsellor would seek to understand the cultural implications of motherhood for that cultural group. This may include seeking indigenous wisdom from community leaders and learning the role of mothers and children within that group (Beatson; Papadopoulos). Culturally responsive counsellors must also consider incorporating the use of native healing practices in mental health treatment, performed of course by a native healer (Beatson).

Another mental health concern that can be overlooked in refugee women due to a difference in conceptualization is post-partum depression (O'Mahony et al.). Within the female refugee population, there is generally lack of knowledge about PDD and a lack of understanding of the symptoms associated with it, such as depression. The symptoms of PDD are often not validated within the family or community and there is a stigma associated with seeking help (O'Mahony et al.). Newly immigrated refugee women may be afraid to even admit that they are suffering from depressive symptoms at all. Culturally speaking, it may be deemed inappropriate to seek external help for depressive symptoms (O'Mahony). If depression is not considered a medical condition within the refugee's culture, medical assistance of any kind may not be sought. Here again, cultural responsiveness of the mental health professional is of great importance as some refugee women who have pursued treatment have faced insensitivity, discrimination, and a lack of knowledge of cultural and religious practices that meet their needs.

On the other hand, if refugee mothers come from cultures that revere women, value them, and support them after giving birth, postpartum symptoms can be exacerbated if that support is not available once the mother has been resettled (Barclay and Kent). In this way, cultural values and beliefs are considered protective factors when the mother uses customs and rituals to strengthen her system of support. When the culturally responsive counsellor values and respects the mother's role within her culture, the symptoms of PDD can be improved (Barclay and Kent).

Culture can be a tremendous barrier to addressing mental health issues for refugee populations. A refugee mother's native culture may stigmatize and deny behavioural health concerns so much that the mother may not seek treatment for herself or for her children. And if she does decide to seek treatment, her cultural mores may lead her to rely more on traditional forms of healing not practiced as commonly in the new culture. For example, she may prefer herbal, spiritual, or holistic cures to those espoused by Western medicine. Culture and language can make treatment more difficult as well. Even the spiritual culture of a refugee mother can impede her treatment by a mental health professional. For example, many refugees from Burma and Nepal follow spiritual traditions such as animism, which professes that a person can commune with spirits, such as the spirits if dead relatives. There have been cases in which followers of animist spiritual belief systems are perceived by Western mental health practitioners as experiencing hallucinations, even though an animist culture might describe the same experience very differently, for example, as a common response to a stressful event.

Role-shifting can also be a threat to refugee health. For a family that comes from a culture in which the mother is typically responsible for ensuring the health and well-being of family members, it can be very disruptive when the children take on additional responsibility due to their faster acculturation and language-skill acquisition (Edberg, Cleary and Vyas). The mother can feel like a failure, which brings on additional stressors, challenging an already complicated situation.

In the U.S. and Canada, there are agencies to help with the mental health of refugees, but some receive federal funding and funding is being cut. The Vancouver Association of Survivors of Torture (VAST) is one such Canadian agency whose funding was recently cut. The cuts resulted in there being only three members of staff offering mental health counselling to refugees in this agency, which significantly reduces the number of refugees they can help, creates backlogs, and impedes the effective delivery of programs. Before the cuts, there were six full-time mental health workers offering free services to refugees in British Columbia, Canada. A similar program, called the Refugee Well-Being Project (RWP) is intended to improve mental health among refugees in the U.S. (Hess et al.).

ACCULTURATION

Behavioural acculturation is a "measure of such factors as with whom people spend time, the types of media they are exposed to, the language in which they feel most comfortable conversing and reading, and with whom they identify" (Geltman et al. 1516). Acculturation "comprehends those phenomena which result when groups of individuals having different cultures come into continuous first-hand contact, with subsequent changes in the original cultural patterns of either or both groups" (Redfield, Linton, and Herskovits qtd. in Pender 22). An expanded definition is offered by Cuellar, Arnold, and Maldonado (qtd. in Pender) and includes both macro and micro levels of the values, language, beliefs, behaviours, and practices of the group to which the individual is acculturating.

Acculturation is usually associated with higher levels of functionality, but this is not always the case. For example, medium levels of acculturation can lead to poor functionality, as the refugee finds herself operating in both cultures simultaneously, with little effectiveness in either (Geltman). Sometimes low levels of acculturation can be associated with better health. Africans with sickle cell disease often report a worsening of symptoms when they convert to a less natural, highly processed Western diet. Dental health can also worsen for people who adopt a Western diet high in sugars and acids (Geltman). And, possibly because Western culture promotes unhealthy body images, women who acculturate to Western societies often experience an increase in body image distortion (Pender).

Additionally, a 2012 study of young Serbian refugees showed that higher acculturation levels were associated with lower levels of self and family satisfaction (Lazarevic, Wiley, and Pleck). When one becomes more acculturated to the dominant culture, one often has to lose aspects of one's home culture in order to "fit in," which may cause emotional conflict and issues with life satisfaction. Additionally, "acculturation to the heritage culture may be less of a resource for those immigrating without family" (Birman et al. 69) and with no previously established community. On the other hand, a refugee who is working in a business that is operated by a person from her own home culture may feel less inclined to acculturate to the dominant culture as there is an ethnic enclave already in place that supports the culture of the refugee (Birman et al.).

Discrimination is also a factor in acculturation and has been associated with poorer physical and mental health among refugees (Ellis et al.). This discrimination can lead to a negative self-identity if the refugee feels rejected or stereotyped by the dominant culture.

The World Health Organization's handbook, *Mental Health of Refugees*, lists five simple rules for providing mental health services to refugees. The practitioner is advised to learn the names the refugee's culture uses to identify behavioural health issues as well as the way the culture describes symptoms of mental health concerns. The handbook further recommends visits to the refugee at home, using simple language, and reassuring the client about confidentiality (World Health Organization).

WORKS CITED

Arredondo, P., R. Toporek, S. P. Brown, J. Jones, D. Locke, J. Sanchez, et al. "Operationalization of the Multicultural Counseling Competencies." *Journal of Multicultural Counseling and Development* 24 (1996): 42-78. Print.

Barclay, Lesley, and Diane Kent. "Recent Immigration and the Misery of Motherhood: A Discussion of Pertinent Issues." *Midwifery* 14.1 (1998): 4-9. Print.

Beatson, Jean E. "Supporting Refugee Somali Bantu Mothers with Children with Disabilities." *Pediatric Nursing* 39.3 (2013). Print.

Birman, D., Simon, C. D., Chan, W. Y., Tran, N. "A Life Domains Perspective on Acculturation and Psychological Adjustment: A Study of Refugees from the Former Soviet Union." *American Journal of Community Psychology* 53 (2014): 60-72. Print.

Corbett, Mary and Allison Oman. *Acute Malnutrition in Protracted Refugee Situations: A Global Strategy.* UNHCR/WFP Report. January 2006. UNHCR/WFP Global Nutrition Strategy. Web.

Edberg, M., S. Cleary and A. Vyas. "A Trajectory Model for Understanding and Assessing Health Disparities in Immigrant/ Refugee Communities." *Journal of Immigrant Minor Health* 13.3 (2011): 576-84. Print.

Ehntholt, Kimberly A. and William Yule. "Practitioner Review: Assessment and Treatment of Refugee Children and Adolescents Who Have Experienced War-Related Trauma." *Journal of Child Psychology And Psychiatry, and Allied Disciplines* 47.12 (2006): 1197-1210. Web. 8 June 2014.

Ellis, B. H., Lincoln, A., MacDonald, H. Z., Klunk-Gillis, J., Strunin, L., and Cabral, H. J. "Discrimination and Mental Health Among Somali Refugee Adolescents: The Role of Acculturation and Gender." *American Journal of Orthopsychiatiry* 80.4 (2010): 564-75. Print.

Geltman, Paul L., et al. "The Impact of Functional Health Literacy and Acculturation on the Oral Health Status of Somali Refugees Living in Massachusetts." *American Journal of Public Health* 103.8 (2013): 1516-1523.Print.

Hess, Julia M., et al. "Reducing Mental Health Disparities Through Transformative Learning: A Social Change Model With Refugees And Students." *Psychological Services* (2014). Web. 9 June 2014.

Kaczorowski, Jessica A., et al. "Adapting Clinical Services to Accommodate Needs of Refugee Populations." *Professional Psychology: Research and Practice* 42.5 (2011): 361. Print.

Lazarevic, Vanja, Angela Wiley, and Joseph H. Pleck. "Associations of Acculturation with Family and Individual Well-being in Serbian Refugee Young Adults in the United States." *Journal of Comparative Family Studies* 43.2 (2012): 217-236. Print.

Murray, Kate E., Graham R. Davidson, and Robert D. Schweitzer. "Review of Refugee Mental Health Interventions Following Resettlement: Best Practices and Recommendations." *American Journal of Orthopsychiatry* 80.4 (2010): 576-585. Print.

O'Mahony, Joyce Maureen, et al. "Cultural Background and Socioeconomic Influence of Immigrant and Refugee Women Coping with Postpartum Depression." *Journal of Immigrant and Minority Health* 15.2 (2013): 300-314. Print.

Papadopoulos, Renos K. "Refugees, Trauma and Adversity-Activated Development." *European Journal of Psychotherapy and Counselling* 9.3 (2007): 301-312.Print.

Pender, Rebekah. "A Study of the Relationship of Acculturation and Body Image of Mexican-American Women Attending College: A Dissertation." Diss. St. Mary's University, 2012. Web.

Perera, Sulani, et al. "A Longitudinal Study of Demographic Factors Associated with Stressors and Symptoms in African Refugees." *American Journal of Orthopsychiatry* 83.4 (2013): 472-482. Print.

Schubert, Carla C., and Raija-Leena Punamäki. "Mental Health among Torture Survivors: Cultural Background, Refugee Status and Gender." *Nordic Journal of Psychiatry* 65.3 (2011): 175-182. Print.

Teodorescu, Dinu-Stefan, et al. "Posttraumatic Growth, Depressive Symptoms, Post-traumatic Stress Symptoms, Postmigration Stressors and Quality of Life in Multi-Traumatized Psychiatric Outpatients With a Refugee Background in Norway." *Health Qual Life Outcomes* 10 (2012): 84. Print.

Tramz, Mia. "The Faces of Afghan Refugee Mothers." Time.com, 8 May 2014. Web. 06/07/2014.

United Nations High Commissioner for Refugees (UNHCR). "World Refugee Day: Global Forced Displacement Tops 50 million for First Time in Post-World War II Era." Office of the United Nations High Commissioner for Refugees, 20 June 2014.

United Nations Office on Drugs and Crime (UNODC). *Global Report on Trafficking in Persons.* UNODC, 2014. No. E.13.IV.1. Web. 08/16/2014.

Vergara A. E., J. M. Miller, D. R. Martin, and S. T. Cookson. "A Survey of Refugee Health Assessments in the United States." *Journal of Immigrant Health* 5.2 (2003): 67-73. Print.

Watkins, P. G., Razee, H., and Richters, J. "I'm Telling You ... The Language Barrier is the Most, the Biggest, Challenge: Barriers to Education Among Karen Refugee Women In Australia." *Australian Journal of Education*, 56.2 (2012): 126-141. Print.

World Health Organization (WHO). "Mental Health of Refugees." UNHCR/WHO 1996. Web. 6 June 2014.

13.
Mothers' Decision-Making Power

A New Vision for Working with Internally Displaced People in Uganda and Kenya

TUSHABE WA TUSHABE AND BESI BRILLIAN MUHONJA

T HIS CHAPTER EXPLORES IN TWO parts—relating to Uganda and Kenya respectively—the complex nature of the social institution of motherhood and how its position in the processes of creation, production, and distribution of resources can be effected in resource and community development for internally displaced people (IDP). Each section, on Uganda and Kenya, analyzes ways in which collective motherhood is a site of tension that can aid in the implementation of government and non-governmental organization (NGOs) services, international aid organization policies, and delivery of resources to communities living in camps of IDP. The two parts are written independently to engage and accommodate unique historical and political contexts within which mothers in East Africa perform motherhood under conditions of displacement. Our choice to address the issue from two very different perspectives highlights intricacies that may otherwise be perceived as unessential or remain unrecognized by refugee agencies. Focusing on mothering networks as locations for alternative knowledge and decision-making power will greatly enhance agencies' needs assessment protocols and service delivery.

WORKING WITH INTERNALLY DISPLACED PEOPLE IN UGANDA

A little over three decades ago feminist activist and African American scholar bell hooks called for a "revolutionary motherhood" in her powerful book, *Feminist Theory: From Margin to Center*. hooks was not articulating a utopian vision, but expressing a lived

248

experience in the African American community where collective motherhood is a significant component of family life. hooks' call for revolutionary motherhood was necessary in the face of changing family dynamics in the U.S. Revolutionary motherhood, hooks hoped, would open up new possibilities in family relations and the distribution of resources in the American social approaches to family. hooks states:

> Child rearing is a responsibility that can be shared with other childrearers, with people who do not live with children. This form of parenting is revolutionary in this society because it takes place in opposition to the idea that parents, especially mothers, should be the only childrearers. Many people raised in black communities experienced this community-based childcare. (144)

hooks' idea has the potential to enrich the experience of motherhood for an array of people in a number of global communities, but it also advocates for a shift in family paradigms, from hierarchies of patriarchal power embedded in the concept of the nuclear family to a space of shared responsibility where mothers matter as producers of knowledge and decision-makers.

hooks's crossing of cultural and national epistemological borders to highlight a community-based mothering provides a relevant framework for my own (Tushabe) witnessing of how mothers made decisions just after the Allied Democratic Forces (ADF) entered Uganda through eastern Democratic Republic of Congo and randomly killed dozens of people in Bundibugyo in western Uganda. Based on my observations of mothers during this time, the notion that the biological mother plays only a small part in childrearing, and that the community has a social and cultural responsibility to take part in the raising of children, was clearly embodied and practiced both in stable family life and in disrupted family life, such as in camps for internally displaced people. This experience foregrounded the sense of community and responsibility that a mother has to the child and community, and vice versa as a never-ending kind of interdependence, something obscured by the hierarchies of patriarchy.

As the ADF made their way through eastern Democratic Republic of the Congo to Uganda, they terrorized Congolese families and forced them to flee to their relatives in Bundibugyo. When the ADF rebels entered Bundibugyo, they started to randomly kill people, which further forced the Congolese and their families in Bundibugyo to flee as one group to their extended relatives near Fort Portal in Toro district. The Uganda People's Defense Force (UPDF) fought the ADF from Ntoroko, near Fort Portal, to Bundibugyo. In the meantime, displaced people were maneuvering the Rwenzori Mountains to find a place they could temporarily call home. I was trapped in Bundibugyo the entire week of random killings by ADF until the UPDF secured the area. To prevent abductions and killings, men often separated from women, which automatically left children under the care of their mothers. It was powerful and challenging to see how mothers kept saying to themselves and to each other, "*Bana bange, bana bawe,*" meaning, "My children, your children." The question of children's safety was a determining factor in the decisions mothers made—whether to mourn neighbours who had been killed in the night or to risk making fire to cook something for the children. By mid-week, mothers had decided to flee Bundibugyo for their own sake and that of their children. Mothers made these decisions without their husbands, prepared to bear all the uncertainties involved in finding refuge, food, and shelter for their children. The ways in which the mothers made the decision to travel in search of refuge, and the care the mothers expressed for one another's children, were not something new to them, but part of the practice of collective mothering.

War disrupts family life in many ways, whether directly or indirectly. In 2006, the Internally Displaced Monitoring Center (IDMC) reported that 24.5 million people were displaced in their own countries due to armed conflict (IDMC, "The Global Overview"). The 2014, IDMC report shows that 33.3 million people worldwide are displaced due to armed conflict or violence, of which 12.5 million come from sub-Saharan Africa. In Uganda, armed conflict has displaced over 2.5 million people from their homes since 1986, when rebel leader Joseph Kony started fighting against Uganda government (IDMC "The Global Overview").

Western Uganda has experienced an influx of refugees from Congo, Rwanda, and the briefly displaced people in Bundibugyo district, Hoima, and Kisoro, while northern districts including Gulu and Acholi have faced more prolonged displacement of people from their homes than any other part of the country in Uganda's history. When people are displaced, they relocate to different parts of the country and adjust to homelessness, landlessness, and to the sheer reality of displacement within new surrounding cultures in their new locations.

Because mothers in indigenous settings mother collectively by relying on relatives and other women to rear children, they experience particular obstacles in refugee camps where the family structure is reorganized to suit the structure of the nuclear family, with a father as the assumed head and provider of the family. Mothers face obstacles in planning a meal for their children when they do not know how much food they have or when the food rationed out to them is not the kind they are used to eating. When mothers in Bundibugyo kept saying to themselves and to each other, "*Bana bange, bana bawe*," they were hinting at critical questions of feeding their children and looking after them effectively in the context of collective motherhood. Mothers realized that displacement was inevitable and they were going to leave their land, gardens, and crops behind. How would mothers continue doing their collective motherhood without the necessary recourse? How do childhood and motherhood nurture each other when both are experienced in battlegrounds? What are the intricacies of motherhood when the relationship between a mother and her children is cut short or transformed by abduction, or when there is loss of her children's father or loss of limbs of her own body or of her children's, while homelessness and landlessness remain a reality in their life? How are they to continue to mother collectively when a grandmother or aunt has nothing to give the child (food, space to play, or time to listen to a story)? An African saying goes, "Stories would not flow from a wise elder's mouth if the pot were not cooking." The mothers' cry, "*Bana bange, bana bawe*," was in itself a form of active thinking about how to maneuver the inevitable while searching for solutions.

The adjustments mothers have to make may not seem significant to agencies' protocols and policies regarding need-assessment and resource allocations. According to Zin Mar Oo and Kyoko Kusakabe, conventional refugee analyses of the legal, social, and political dimensions of the crisis tend to see displaced people as passive victims. In their article, "Motherhood and Social Network: Response Strategies of Internally Displaced Karen Women in Taungoo District," Oo and Kusakabe observe that "internally displaced people are often seen as helpless victims depending on the humanitarian community" (483). Agencies working with displaced people do commendable work at different levels to alleviate poverty, improve health, eliminate violence against women, and empower displaced people to re-build their lives. However, my experience with mothers in Bundibugyo and Fort Portal reveals that internally displaced people think actively about their lives, and if their input were solicited, their situation would greatly improve right from the beginning. In my observation of internally displaced mothers and the refugee agencies I worked with, the approach tends to be a top-bottom pyramid system that largely ignores indigenous social and cultural systems on which displaced people rely to make meaning in life.

Top-Bottom Practices in Relation to Displaced People

In October 2009, the African Union, in collaboration with other international agencies such as the UNCHR, developed a tool: The Kampala Convention for the Protection and Assistance of the Internally Displaced People in Africa. This tool, centrally focused on internally displaced people, was the first binding international agreement on internally displaced people, drafted and promoted by UNCHR. The UNCHR has worked in many countries to adopt the policies on internally displaced people. Kenya, Somalia, and the State of Chiapas in Mexico have adopted these policies on internally displaced people. As a result, a number of countries have seen displaced people return home due to peace talks, such as those between the Philippines and Colombia, and the National Dialogue in Yemen. At the same time, despite notable improvements, agencies continue to work without input from refugees and internally displaced people, and hierarchical language often ignores their voices even when the humanitarian focus is on them.

The structure and the language of the policies as well as their implementation reveal a great deal about the hierarchies that govern them and about whose voices are left out or included.

An example can be located in Article 1 of the Preamble of the African Union Convention for the Protection and Assistance of Internally Displaced People in Africa. In this article, persons are represented in general terms as human beings, which include all sexes, genders, age groups, religions, and classes. However, two other classifications—"child" and "women"— are separately identified. Categories of gender "man" or the sex "male" do not appear in the articles of the preamble of the Kampala Convention. In article 1, Clause *h* identifies the category "child" and defines it as "every human being below the age of 18 years" while Clause *k* identifies and defines the category "women" as "persons of the female gender, including girls." All articles and clauses mention persons in general terms with specific mention of women and girls in relation to prevention of sex trafficking in Article 7, and female heads of households, expectant mothers, and mothers with young children in Clause 2c of Article 9. The category of "men" and/ or "males" is left out, which subtly but unmistakably reinforces the idea that man is a universal category of human beings. To be fair though, the UNCHR specifically mentions men on its website:

> Adult men and boys are often neglected in discussions of forced displacement, and yet they have particular needs and are confronted with specific threats to their life and liberty. They are at risk of forced recruitment into armies and militia groups and often experience a serious loss of self-esteem as a result of the way that gender roles change when households and communities go into exile and become recipients of international assistance.

The gender roles upon which the UNCHR policies are based assume that all communities are constructed in the colonial and traditional model of gender roles, whereby a male figure is the breadwinner and protector of the family. When such ideologies guide policies and need-assessment regarding internally displaced people, mothers are doubly displaced because they rely on a collective system of mothering, which the hierarchical notions of family do not recognize. hooks's idea that the conventional family should be transformed speaks directly to agencies that work with IDPs.

This is not to claim that agencies are often unaware of the vulnerabilities of IDPs. In fact, in its definition of IDP the Kampala Convention states that:

> Displacement tends to make people vulnerable to a number of threats. Having been obliged to leave their homes and sometimes their land, IDPs are often deprived of their livelihoods. They may have no choice but to live in isolated, insecure or inhospitable areas. They may be victims or witnesses of violence such as killings, rape or forced recruitment into fighting forces. They may have been separated from their families or continue to fear for the safety of family members left behind. (6)

With this in mind, why would voices of IDP mothers be left out? In her article, "Children and War in Africa: The Crisis Continues in Northern Uganda," Margaret Angucia observes that while studies claim that African societies mistreat their children by recruiting them into military organizations, those studies brand children who are forcibly recruited in militia groups as "child soldiers," yet parents of the so-called child soldiers do not refer to them in the same way. The difference in linguistic perspective reveals how agencies think differently about motherhood in conflict zones. War and conflict may change and compromise motherhood, but motherhood remains continuous in its focus on raising, counselling, and nurturing of children's growth and development into to full human beings; a child requires a space to grow, play, and develop (Angucia). That is why maintenance of a support system of mothering must inform refugee agencies' need assessment, policies, and implementation.

Mothering as Support System in IDP

Four weeks after I survived the ADF in Bundibugyo, I returned to Fort Portal where I worked in my capacity as social worker with refugees from DRC who had come to Fort Portal with their relatives from Bundibugyo. Catholic Relief Services in Kampala, through the Bishop of Fort Portal Diocese and Sisters of the Holy Cross in Fort Portal, asked me to carry out need assessment on their behalf. There were one hundred families with young children in the range of one to six per family. Refugees and internally displaced people told me they wanted aid, but not in the form of tents, food portions of maize, beans, and cooking oil. Instead, they needed to "raise our children." What they meant was that they needed hoes and machetes, pans, plates, cups, blankets, soap, and jerry cans for fetching water. They wanted to create a home space for their children through networks of mothers—sisters and sisters-in-law, grandmothers, mothers, and mothers-in-law—among themselves and those in their families in Fort Portal. One mother insisted that I speak to all of them as a group and not as individual families or individual caretakers of a family. Together they claimed that the greatest threat was the loss of land to raise their children and not displacement. I realized I needed to listen very carefully to what they wanted, and not tell them what we (Catholic Relief Services) were going to do for them. It became clear to me that displaced mothers experienced collective mothering as a means to reduce poverty for families and to eliminate total reliance on aid.

As a social worker assessing the needs of IDPs, my experience with mothers in Bundibugyo and Fort Portal highlighted that motherhood in conflict zones must remain closely tied to a dialectic relationship between mother and child and among mothers within their own cultural sensibility. I realized how mothers continue to embody the responsibility of raising a child with the values, etiquette, and cultural expectations to the best of their ability, even improvising cultural resources under the conditions of displacement. For these mothers, mothers' networks were the cultural resources needed to facilitate the two-ness of the relationship necessary to sustain a mother's responsibility and accountability of her children. Mothers' networks were clearly important to these internally displaced mothers and it would be helpful if refugee agencies capitalize on mothers' networks to better serve them.

THE CASE OF KENYA: ROLE OF MOTHERS IN REBUILDING COMMUNITY

Between 2002 and 2008, about 700,000 Kenyans were forced into IDP status due to political and ethnic violence. The consequences of missteps in the 2002 elections manifested in the country through sporadic violence and displacement between 2002 and the violence related to the presidential elections in 2007.

The family, the basic social unit, and its reconstruction become critical where people are displaced and attempting to rebuild community. The family, expanded in definition here to spaces defined as "household," is a practical site to focus community-rebuilding efforts because it already functions in IDP camps as the unit for the distribution of services and resources. Rebuilding communities within IDP camps requires rejuvenation of functioning family units, which then serve as basic operational centers for IDPs participation in community rebuilding. While no conclusive statistics are available, mostly due to the changing composition of the space, many reports, including those cited in this text, reveal that women, mothers, head most of the single-parented families. Motherhood is a location vested with protest and social change influence (Muhonja; Oyewumi "Abiyamo"; *The Invention*), and this section of the chapter explores ways in which efforts to rebuild communities and resolve resource and service delivery issues to IDPs can capitalize on this fact.

Motherhood-related responsibilities for IDPs are heightened for a number of reasons. The loss of men in conflict leaves more women to parent alone. Many men, too, have lost partners in the conflicts discussed in this chapter, but because of the widely held notion that men are not primary caregivers, they often thrust this responsibility upon a female relative or other support person. This further expands the accountability of mothers. Wanyeki captures this loss of male support and its effects when she points out that "sexual violence among internally displaced persons was also reported—particularly for girls and women, many of whom had lost the male members of their families, in the post-elections violence" (96). Fathers also leave the camps to "bring home the bacon." Ironically, because of the lack of employment opportunities or extremely low wages, and the added strain of providing for family life in two locations (because fathers have to establish a new residence where they work away from the family who are in the IDP camp), the fathers' contribution is negligible, leaving the mother to fulfill most of the financial needs of the family.

Girls and women engaged in involuntarily parenting of children born as a result sexual assault illustrate another extreme of mothers parenting alone. During the 2008 post-election violence in Kenya, "Nairobi Women's Hospital reported an upsurge in cases of sexual violence—with such cases being three times the normal intake. The cases primarily involved girls and women from the low-income areas of Nairobi" (Wanyeki 94). According to Lucy Kiama, head of the Gender Violence Recovery Centre at the Nairobi Women's Hospital, "90 percent of the cases we are seeing since the political crisis began are gang rapes" (IRIN "Sexual Violence").

The role of mother as primary overseer of services and resources in the home is a reality of many indigenous communities in Kenya. So, this intensifying of expectations on the mother's role among IDPs is rooted as much in a historically established zone of power as it is in default modern definitions of a gendered domesticity. Because in the African conceptualization of motherhood, most women, whether they have birthed children or not, self-identify as mothers, this is a reasonable identity to engage in re-organizing and rebuilding community. I use the concept "African motherhood" deliberately, not to erase the unique experiences of mothers in many cultures on the continent, but rather to emphasize that, as Oyewumi states, "African constructions of motherhood are different in significant ways from the nuclear motherhood that has been articulated by feminist theorists" (*The Invention* 1097) and these bear significant commonalities across African cultures. The fact that there are no male spiritual and social dimension parallels to this space further enhances the sacred and privileged nature of motherhood. Understanding this increases the possibilities of looking at most women and not just bio-mothers in IDP camps as mothers. This multiplies the demography available for partnership for and in community rebuilding efforts for IDPs.

IDP MOTHERS: AGENTS FOR COMMUNITY REBUILDING

Displacement of persons denotes a breakdown of constructed multi-ethnic publics where victims had invested in communities and support networks. For many, returning to their former communities is not an option. Njoki and Ombati are examples of these. Phyllis Njoki, an elderly resident of one of the IDP camps, spoke for many when she said, "How can I go back to live with my neighbors ... you see I am old and I can't fight them, they will kill me this time round ... they will kill me...." Lydia Ombati expressed her fears thus: "I have visited my farm but my crops are uprooted while my neighbors' are intact. When I ask what happened, I get blank stares. Tell me, how do I live comfortably with these people?" (Oyaro).

For women especially, displacement compromises their grassroots organizing and sustenance. IDPs, with most of their networks destroyed, need grassroots support more than most. Requisite therefore are new channels and identities through which women IDPs can reconnect and (re)organize. In the context of living as IDPs, the one identity that in all its manifestations for most women still holds some authority is that of mother. Oyewumi explains that "although wifehood in many African societies has traditionally been regarded as functional and necessary it is at the same time seen as a transitional phase on the road to motherhood. *Mother* is the preferred and cherished self-identity of many African women" (*The Invention* 1096).

African motherhood provides the best model and designation of motherhood through which to engage the altered family structures within IDP settlements. The immediate family constituency is reconstructed during conflict and displacement. Families are separated by distance and death. New families are refabricated as separate, broken families blend. In the following section I will suggest that power, merit, and potential are encased within collective motherhood that can be used as advantage in rebuilding operative communities for IDPs.

Collective Mothering: Mother Power

Mothering in many indigenous Kenyan communities is a communal enterprise. The dependability of collective mothering offers the added benefit of cooperative authority to make demands on the larger society. Familial or societal support structures that mothers enjoy are no longer available to IDPs. Their access to collective mothering and capacity to exploit it is absent at precisely the moment and in the situation they need it the most. Collective mothering, imbued with power that is recognized, respected, and feared as a locale for cooperative action, would induce pressure on societal systems and IDPs' service agencies towards the realization of educational, health, food, and other securities. Such facilities free mothers to work outside the home and, for IDPs, would alleviate challenges related to their capacity to do motherwork.

Historically, mothers have politically, economically, and socially exploited their position as an instrument to effect change. IDPs experience a loss of mother power in two ways: loss of capacity to do motherwork and loss of clout attached to motherhood. Oyewumi defines this power ingrained in motherhood thus:

> In all African family arrangements, the most important ties within the family flow from the mother.... The ties link the mother to the child and connect all children of the same mother in bonds that are conceived as natural and unbreakable. It is not surprising, then, that the most important and enduring identity and name that African women claim for themselves is "mother." However, motherhood is not constructed in tandem with fatherhood. The idea that mothers are powerful is very much a defining characteristic of the institution and its place in society. (*The Invention* 1097)

The following story elucidates some of the ways in which IDPs encounter powerlessness to fulfill their role as mothers:

> She stares at her three tents and wipes tears before whispering how women in the camp are forced to sleep with men to earn at least Sh100 in a desperate move to get food for their children. "Women take the risk of contracting STIs by sleeping with men to fend for their families because

there is virtually no job to give us money," she says. (Kulei)

There is a lack of freedom and opportunities to perform mother work. Outlets that would support mothers to provide and nurture development in their children, including good housing, schools, and health facilities, are inadequate or completely absent. With nowhere to direct a mother's good intentions, she occurs as impotent and immobilized in numerous ways, as this coverage demonstrates: "I watched two children die of pneumonia in my arms; they needed a professional health expert who could administer strong drugs, but I was helpless," Njeri, herself an IDP who also serves as a medical officer at the Mawingo IDP camp, told IRIN ("Stuck In Camps"). IDP mothers focus on basic survival, a reality that leaves them with limited functionally as nurturers, in itself an imperative facet of parenthood. It is hard to nurture, in a traditional sense, under the conditions of an IDP camp especially when institutions that support mothering are absent. Gitonga quotes the experience of another woman, Julia Njeri, an IDP mother of four: "'We were left without food and water in the middle of wildness.' She added that there were no schools, trading centers or hospitals in the area. The absence of these basic facilities negatively affected their lives, she said."

Violence against women in IDP spaces impinges on mothers and mothering in various ways. IDP mothers lose children via separation, violence, disease, and lack of basics like food and medical care. An IRIN 2010 report quotes 23-year-old Milka Waceke as saying, "I still feel the pain of losing my child, I wish I was near a hospital or had money to pay for a taxi, then I would not have lost my baby" ("Stuck in Camps"). Trauma experienced by the mother, especially without social support, affects her ability to nurture other children who, because of their own trauma, make greater demands for psychological and emotional support than their peers. Kulei describes Milka Chepkurui's daughter at Kurupanayat IDP camp thus: "Jelang'at Abigail, 14, recalls how she used to go to school and play with other children. Her Swahili tells of an erstwhile ambitious pupil who had lots of dreams, but now she has been reduced to a babysitter." Insecurity separates mothers from resources for accomplishing motherwork. A relinking of mothers in groups towards reciprocal physical and emotional support will serve the project of rebuilding mother power and the community.

Women IDPs and mothers grapple with changed roles they occupy as unplanned mothers, single parents, community watch, educators, protectors, sole breadwinners, and widows. Chepkurui in an East African Standard article shares, "You can see for yourself, all my nine children stay here with me. They don't go to school. My husband left us two years ago.... I am now left with all these children" (Kulei). Amidst all the change, children require stability, consistency, and certainty, needs an IDP mother cannot control or guarantee.

A performing community executes development. IDPs identify with each other as a displaced and deprived class. The society recognizes the value of mothers as a fulcrum for a serviceable society and so local and international bodies that attend to IDPs need to consider mothers and motherhood an asset in formulating discourses and practices for/of community rebuilding. The identity "mother" should be foregrounded, and its power tapped, as illustrated in mothers' roles as custodians of resources, traditions, peace, and community networks.

Mothers as Custodians

Mothers in many indigenous communities, including the Kalenjin, Luhya, Luo, Kikuyu, and Kamba, were/are custodians of basic resources in the home, and controlled and supervised various spaces in the home and the labor force within them (Muhonja). These were mothers running households and managing distribution of resources where there were/are children present in the home, whether these are sons, daughters, nieces, or nephews. IDPs, because of their struggles for survival, are preoccupied with basic needs. Efforts at designing systems for distribution and delivery of basic resources should therefore be directed at mothers.

Mothers are custodians of traditions in societies across the world. Family and collective societal traditions are maintained and facilitated by women, primarily mothers who care about maintaining traditions and stability for their children. For mothers, traditions afford a sense of belonging, history, self, family, and pride for their children. Developing new or reinstituting old traditions would support the establishment of new communities in IDP camps.

As custodians of peace, mothers draw from the sacred deference attached to their location in the creation process and the fact that, by default, they are the glue that keeps families and communities together. While government, policy makers, and others debate questions of peace, mothers on the ground are often actively working on efforts to realize peace at the grassroots, primarily for the sake of their children. Mothers are also custodians of family and social networks, including interfamily relationships and organizational networks at micro and macro levels. Such networks need to be the starting point for developing and maintaining community participation while providing space for people to have a stake in their community's rebuilding, and governments and other aid agencies working with IDPs need to provide structures for such participation.

CONCLUSION

We believe that maximizing the potential of mothers in their location as socializers, custodians of resources and knowledge, economic partners, educators, culture developers, networkers, and moral compasses will enhance better services in IDP camps. Oyeronke Oyewumi explains that "because mothers symbolize familial ties, unconditional love and loyalty, motherhood is invoked even in extra-familial situations that calls upon these values" ("Abiyamo" 1). Common interests, identity, and location define a community. In constructing a community, people seek to build values, cohesion, engagement and participation, relationships, social and organizational structures, and a space for building sustainable resource access and development.

The role of women as guardians of community is mostly grounded in their collective motherhood and their power to influence society through the power and agency encompassed in collective motherhood. It is of vital importance that agencies that work with mothers position mothers as subjects during need assessment and service delivery processes, and find structural ways to affirm the contributions mothers make, realizing that such affirmation empowers mothers to remain valued resource persons.

WORKS CITED

Angucia, Margaret. "Children and War in Africa: The Crisis Continues in Northern Uganda." *International Journal on World Peace* 3.26 (2009): 77-95. Web. 15 April 2015.

hooks, bell. *Feminist Theory: From Margin to Center*. Boston: South End, 1984.Print.

Gitonga, Anthony. "IDPs Return to Naivasha Camp, Say State has Abandoned Them." *Standard Digital* 8 October 2013. Web. 20 May 2014.

Internally Displaced Monitoring Center (IMDC). "The Global Overview 2014: People Internally Displaced by Conflict and Violence." IMDC. Web. 27 May 2014.

IRIN Kenya. "Sexual Violence Continues in IDP Camps. *IRIN: Humanitarian News and Analysis, a service of the UN Office for the Coordination of Humanitarian.* IRIN News. March 8 2008. Web. 19 May 2014.

IRIN Kenya. "Stuck in Camps Three Years after Post-poll Violence." *IRIN: Humanitarian News and Analysis, A Service of the UN Office for the Coordination of Humanitarian.* IRIN News. 8 October 2010. Web. 19 May 2014.

"Kampala Convention. Two Years On: Time to Turn Theory into Practice." African Union Convention for the Protection and Assistance of the Internally Displaced Persons in Africa. IMDC. 2009. Web. 15 April, 2015.

Kulei, L. "Mothers Cry for Help: At Least 35 Babies Have Died of Pneumonia at Kurupanayat IDP Camp Since the Beginning of 2013." *Standard Digital*. December 3 2013. Web. 02 May 2014.

Muhonja, Brillian Besi. "She Loved and She Ruled That Kitchen: Space and Autonomy in Kenyan Societies." *JENdA: A Journal of Culture and African Women Studies.* 1.15 (2009): 6-25. Print.

Oo, Mar Zin and Kyoko Kusakabe. Motherhood and Social Network: Response Strategies of Internally Displaced Karen Women in Taungoo Disrict." *Women's Studies International Forum* 33 (2010): 482-491. Print

Oyewumi, Oyeronke. "Abiyamo: Theorizing African Motherhood."*ENdA: A Journal of Culture And African Women Studies* 4 (2003): 1530-5686. Web. 15 April, 2015.

Oyewumi, Oyeronke. *The Invention of Women: Making an African Sense of Western Gender Discourses*. Minneapolis: University of Minnesota Press, 1997. Print.

United Nations High Commissioner for Human Rights (UNHCR). "Engaging with Internally Displaced People." 2009. Web. 15 April, 2015.

Wanyeki, L. Muthoni. "Lessons from Kenya: Women and the Post-Election Violence." *Feminist Africa* 10 (2008). 91-98. Print.

PART III:
MOTHERS AS FIGHTERS, ACTIVISTS, RESISTERS

14.
Mothers as Soldiers

Beyond the Veil of Gendered War

LIDIYA ZUBYTSKA

CIVILIAN CASUALTIES IN THE TWENTIETH century have become a gruesome feature of modern wars, in sharp contrast to predominantly combatant death toll of wars about a century ago (Gurr). Violent modern warfare affects civilian communities and blurs conventional distinctions: home versus battlefield and civilian versus soldier. Whereas the gendering of war is still pervasive—violence is often construed in terms of a justifiable battle to defend idealized women, innocent children, and other vulnerable groups (or "beautiful souls" as Laura Sjoberg describes them)—the reality on the ground is that women currently make up thirty to forty percent of active militants in certain types of conflicts, such as guerrilla struggles, separatist movements, and ethnic hostilities (Ness). On the one hand, women continue to be specifically targeted within a larger civilian population and suffer as victims in conflicts that bring violence from the battlefield straight into their homes, yet on the other hand, they also demonstrate active agency in reshaping hostilities that rage around them.

In this paper I examine the interactions and tensions between parental and militant roles of women engaged in combat: Under what circumstances do mothers choose to become active in battles versus staying home with their young children? What parental challenges do mothers face as soldiers? In order to shed light on these questions, I undertake a case study of Ukrainian mothers who joined the Ukrainian Resistance forces to fight different Polish, German, and Soviet troops in Western Ukraine, 1942-1954. As mothers engaged in violent partisan and other subversive activities, they relied on a civilian network of Ukrainian villages to sustain their military activities and take care of family members left behind the front lines.

My evidence comes from a close investigation of archival documents on the activities of the Ukrainian Insurgent Army that have recently become electronically available. I also draw on other sources, such as publication of women-soldiers memoirs and autobiographies, their poetry to their children from prisons, and various editions of "Litopys UPA." Whereas the selection of stories to be highlighted in the case study is necessarily limited to those public and historical records that are presently available on this formerly secretive (due to its partisan nature) and historically controversial (due to its political ideology) movement, I attempt to cover the widest scope of stories from survivors.

Recent literature on this topic has explored both dimensions of victimization and active agency of women in violent conflicts. Some researchers, following the feminist approach, attempted to deconstruct the socially conceived role of women in violent conflicts as a "false dichotomy between biology and culture" arguing that there is nothing biologically intrinsic about gender to make either men or women more predisposed towards violence than the other (Goldstein 2). In other words, violent men versus non-violent women are culturally generated and sustained norms of behaviour. Women do choose to become active combatants, suicide bombers, or proponents of war. Further, women engage in gender-specific agency as bereaved widows, sisters, and mothers in attempts to prevent perpetuation of war or other forms of injustice, often through a collective action, as for instance did Mothers of La Plaza De Mayo in Argentina or Mother's Front in Sri Lanka.

Whereas much scholarly effort continues in this line of research on the gendered roles of women in violence and peacebuilding in general, not much attention has been paid to the specific roles of mothers as afflicted by violent conflicts. They are either subsumed under the wider category of victimized women in war, but laden with an additional psychological and physical strain of providing for their children in times of war strife and deprivation, or they emerge in scholars' accounts as mother activists, but again under specific assumptions that their actions stem from their gendered roles as caretakers of their children and husbands already involved in violent conflicts. Even those studies that do examine the role of women in active combat rarely devote any attention to women's parental functions and the challenges of committing to militancy while leaving young children behind (Pennington); it is often remarked that women soldiers are mostly unmarried and/or childless (Peteet). However, such mother-soldiers do exist and they do not fit easily into the gendered understanding of the role of women in conflict, since they neither comply with the "beautiful soul" image of women in war, nor do they conform to the traditionally conceived "motherly" agency: acting to alleviate the fate of their children by providing specific kinds of care.

I begin with an overview of the approaches to the role of mothers in international conflicts in International Relations (IR) as a discipline. I then analyze several stories of Ukrainian militant mothers focusing on their parental and military journeys and the resulting trajectories of their maternal experiences in wartime. With this study I hope to lift up, even if to a modest degree, the persistent veil of gendered perceptions of the role of women and mothers in war. The experience of Ukrainian insurgent mothers presented here can help reveal how motherhood has been and may continue to be combined with active militancy in most volatile times.

MOTHERS AND WAR, MOTHERS AT WAR: AN INTERNATIONAL RELATIONS PERSPECTIVE

Whereas its sociological, educational, and psychological aspects have been a subject of plentiful research in related disciplines, the political aspects of motherhood rooted in social functions has received much less attention in political science in general and international relations in particular. Motherhood is often relegated to the level of inherently personal experience, and the mainstream IR rarely deciphers politics at the level of individuals, since it predominantly deals with states, organizations, epistemic communities, and other international actors.

However, alternative theoretical approaches in international relations, such as critical theory and feminist IR in particular, have been much more attuned to the effects of international and domestic politics on everyday life experience of the underprivileged, silenced, and voiceless social groups. As a result, in IR, motherhood has been theorized most clearly from a feminist standpoint (Ahall). Far from viewing it merely a category of narrowly conceived personal experience, feminist IR regards motherhood as thoroughly political. In the words of Annelise Orleck:

> Personally, socially and politically, it is impossible to speak about motherhood without speaking of social systems of power and domination. For, while motherhood is an individual and highly personal experience, it is also a social institution, shaped by and tied to the ideology of the nuclear family. Looked at in this way, motherhood is always a politicized role, especially in its most romantic and idealized portrayals. (7)

In their early attempts to examine motherhood as political and politicized phenomenon, Orleck and her colleagues noted that mothers entered onto the visible scene of political life in diverse ways and capacities: some formerly uninterested in politics were moved to take political action out of concern for their own children. For them "the radicalizing process involved a series of crucial leaps from caring about their own children, to caring about other mothers and children, to engaging with pressing social and political issues of national and even international import" (Orleck 4). Next, some of these women "used their motherhood strategically, aware that speaking out as mothers would give them more credibility in sexist societies than they would have as individual women" (4). Others, however, "sincerely believed that motherhood conferred upon them special insights and responsibilities to solve the problems plaguing their families and communities" (4).

This latter kind of maternal experience is what is laid in the foundation of a theoretical framework within feminist IR termed *maternalism*. Maternalism traces it theoretical origin to the political thought of Sara Ruddick and Nancy Hartsock, long-time researchers into the connection between motherhood and politics. Specifically, Sara Ruddick posited that "maternal thinking" arises from the activity of raising children, since a mother engages in particular modes of thinking care, and discipline where s/he "asks certain questions rather than others; she establishes criteria for the truth, adequacy and relevance of proposed answers; and she cares about the findings she makes and can act on" (24). Or put in different terms, "Mothers are, for example, preoccupied with the limits of control, the necessity for and abuse of obedience, conflicts between hope and truth-telling, principles and techniques of non-violent fighting"—these are the transformative experiences that are all capable of being translated into politics, and which some men and women do choose to put to public use (Ruddick 373). Significantly, Ruddick does not consider caring for children as "natural" for women. Although it has been predominantly women's practice in most societies, any person committed to responding to children's needs and demands is engaged in motherwork.

What is important is that mothers in Ruddick's estimations, being predominantly concerned with preservation of fragile life, with growth and acceptability, thus become latently peaceful and averse to destructive violence when it comes to their ideological positions. Thus, Ruddick sees enormous political potential in maternal thinking for international peace and justice, since she imagines that maternalism could help forge a new, "alternative disruptive, transfamilial and transcultural *maternal* identity" that would break the divisive lines of racist, sexist, and other kinds of bigotry (379).

In a more recent strand of research, Laura Sjoberg investigated how traditional narratives and security discourses equate women with the cause of war men die for—life back home. Thus, women become idealized as "beautiful souls," as they are set up "as prizes of most wars—fragile, removed from reality and in need of the protection provided by men" (Sjoberg 255). Mothers in "beautiful souls" narratives carry out their service to the nation at home and on battle field: they "provide love and nurture, and at once serve as a support for the logistical and moral fighting for the war and as a symbol for the good and pure that requires the evil of fighting to save it" (Sjoberg 56). Sjoberg underlines that in such views of women and mothers in times of war "there is no room for women fighting wars—they are at once fought over in war and protected from it" (Sjoberg 56; see Gentry and Sjoberg).

How are we then to make sense of maternal and militant ex-periences that run parallel for mother soldiers engaged in war? Maternalism in IR posits that mothers are predominantly inclined to engage in conflicts as peacemakers, but if they do resort to violence such acts are attributed—in a "twisted" version of ma-ternalism—to women's bereaved and unfulfilled motherhood. And whereas feminist approaches in IR criticize such objectification of women in wars, and mothers in particular, the feminist perspective is still developing its conceptual apparatus (or language) as well as logical propositions that would fit into a coherent framework for understanding the complexities of parenthood and militancy for mothers who go to war.

Such theoretical underdevelopment on the topic of mothers-sol-diers in feminist IR is partly reflective of larger uneasiness with motherhood that feminist theory had to grapple with since its historical beginnings. For many feminists since the 1970s mother-hood and mothering implied a much-despised patriarchy, a social arrangement of roles and functions that presupposed women in subservient roles and locked them in disempowering relationships with their partners and/or government (Taylor). Ilene Rose Fein-man emphasized the need to understand the position of women in militant roles thorough "a dialog about women in the military that simultaneously acknowledges the horrors of militarism and the achievements, interests and longing of women soldiers" (17). I would only add that in this dialogue there has to be an acknowledgement of the specific challenges and interests of *mothers-soldiers*. And to this dialogue I intend to make a contribution with the following case study of the Ukrainian Insurgent Army mothers.

UKRAINIAN INSURGENT MOTHERS ON
THEIR MATERNAL EXPERIENCES

Iroida Wynnyckyi analyzed 70 interviews with Ukrainian women survivors of the Second World War collected by the Ukrainian Ca-nadian Research and Documentation Centre in a joint oral history project with L'viv National University. Twenty-two respondents were eighteen to thirty-five years old and married, and seventy-two percent of them gave birth during the Second World War. In her analysis, the researcher concluded that despite the difficulties of war, Ukrainian women in general continued to build a family life and to care for their children. To a degree this also applies to women women of the Ukrainian Insurgent Army (or UPA, from Ukrainian *Ukrayins'ka Povstans'ka Armiya*). For, as Chris Coulter argues, war is not somehow exempted from the social world, and it is not asocial either, but rather "it creates its own social orders; sometimes these are a rejection of past traditions, while others clearly reproduce and strengthen the former social order" (55-56). The stories of UPA mother soldiers clearly illustrate that.

In her written memoirs, Yaroslava Romanyna-Levkovych, a liaison and combatant member of UPA until her capture by KGB in 1952, recollects the unexpected discovery that her co-fighter nicknamed "Mariyka" was a mother of a young daughter to whom she had given birth and changed the infant's last name before she entrusted the infant into the care of another family "by a good lady." In Yaroslava's words, "Maryika" visited her daughter and was heart-broken to hear her daughter call her "auntie" rather than "mommy." But the girl was always happy to see her and never wanted to let "Mariyka" go, as if feeling that she was her true mother. Yaroslava's reaction is interesting in this regard; she writes:

> I reprimanded her [Mariyka] saying "How could you have let it come to a point that you gave birth to a child? You probably haven't even been wedded in the church!" She responded that she was indeed wedded by an underground priest from Zheldtsi village who was performing rites clandestinely since he refused to become Orthodox.[1] As for Stepan, she loved him and so wanted to have a child by him. So then I told her, "See, now the child's father is gone and who knows what is to become of us, whereas your child is being raised by strangers, an orphan." (201-202)

But Mariyka did not relent, apparently, and even asked Yaroslava that if she is were to outlive her, could she find the little girl about whom she feels "peace in her heart, for the lady taking care of her child had 3 sons and loves her a lot since she hadn't had a girl" (201-202). This conversation remained very vivid to Yaroslava because only a few hours later they were both trapped in their bunker and arrested by the KGB.

This episode, however, captures a complex set of interrelated expectations and personal choices of women and mothers in times of war: on the one hand, Yaroslava is appalled that Mariyka entered into relationship without a proper—socially expected— religious sanctioning. Through Yaroslava's perspective we see how pre-war traditional ways of family life are being upheld when it comes to relationships and marriage. And Mariyka agrees and confirms those expectations by citing her religious wedding. On the other hand, Yaroslava points out that having a child in these conditions is a hardship to both Mariyka as a mother, who cannot reveal her true identity to her own child, and to the little girl as well because her father (an insurgent too) already died, and her mother is most likely going to as well. Yaroslava raises concern for the child, but Mariyka insists that she made the choice to be married and have a child out of love for her husband. Thus she defies the idea that war presupposes her to abandon the "normalcy" of personal life, and by going the traditional route—dating, marriage, giving birth to a child—while all along being an UPA insurgent, she actively exercises her agency by reaffirming the social order that the war had warped and torn. Yet on the other hand, she cannot escape the consequences of living the life of a partisan: death is always imminent and has already claimed the life of a loved one. Mariyka holds on to her motherhood with warm affection and continues to provide care for her child by seeking out the best possible arrangement in a new family where her daughter is likely to be well loved. Furthermore, Mariyka does not abandon the girl psychologically, but guards her in memory and tender emotions, as well as with a longing to be somehow reconnected with her child, despite the odds.

Marriages, celebrated in secret by Catholic priests supportive of the liberation movement, as in Mariyka's story, were common at all levels and ranks of UPA, from the head commander Roman Shukhevych and UPA colonels in his entourage, to sergeants and regular rank and file soldiers. Parenthood that fitted in the traditional pre-war way of building gender and family relationships followed for the insurgents without much delay. In most stories

I examined, couples had their first child within two years and often in their first year of marriage. It provoked a combination of concerns and joys for a mother. Maria Savchyn, on learning about her first pregnancy reflected:

> I did understand as well that a difficult life was set in front of me and that I will have only myself to rely on. And yet I accepted pregnancy with joy and did not worry as much as he did. If one desires something strongly, one can always find enough positive arguments to support one's decision. For me at that point, it was enough to know that the wives of other underground insurgents were giving birth and somehow raising their kids, and not even here, but in Ukraine, where conditions were much harder. So somehow I would find a way. For instance, among my friends, Sviatoslava as well as Iryna, the latter being a wife of the regiment commander Krylach—both had had little daughters, so now it was my turn, too. (Savchyn 111)

In most stories I examined, by 1952 when the UPA movement was starting to be curtailed, the married militants had one or two very young children and often the father of the child had already perished in the fight or had been arrested. Olha Ilkiv, for instance, who served as a messenger for UPA chief commander, was one of the founders of the "women's network" while raising a one-year-old daughter. She lost her husband of five years who died in battle while she was pregnant with their second child. She continued the underground activities until 1950, relying on her mother for the care of her children, until Olha was captured, tortured, and sent for 25-year prison term by the Soviet regime. At that point, the Soviet authorities placed her four-year-old girl and a three-year-old boy in an orphanage under new fake names. She recalled how at every station during her deportation to Siberia she tried to tell her co-prisoners that:

> My kids are taken to an orphanage and have fake names and family names, and I have no way of letting my relatives know that because they are imprisoned too. On walls I

would write the same, informing of this all people of good
will whoever would happen to be from L'viv. I did it so
that my dearest children would not be lost in depth of this
"golden Moloch" [Soviet regime]. (19)

While in labour camps she wrote touching poems and children's
rhymes to her own children, holding on to her motherhood psychologically throughout that time. After twelve years in labour
camps, she was finally able to reunite with her children.

Deportation of mothers with small children for participation in the
UPA liberation movement or for being related to someone engaged
in UPA was a punishment that many mothers had to grapple with.
Burds reports that by the end of 1947 a total of 76,192 persons
from the "rebel families" were deported from the Western Ukrai-
nians to Siberia and Russian Far East, including 35,152 women
and 22,174 children. Mariya Andrushko, whose husband served
in UPA, recalls how in the middle of winter 1944 she was deported
with her two sons, a three-year-old and a three-month-old:

We were shipped in cargo carriages. At night, your hair
would freeze to the walls of the carriage, so cold it was.
Even though there was an iron stove, there was nothing
to kindle the fire with. In our carriage there were women
and children—a total of 21. We were not allowed to open
the train doors for two to three days in a row, they would
not let us out during stops. Children were crying—they
were all hungry. But we were not given anything to eat,
only after we passed Moscow, we were given one loaf of
bread per person. (qtd. in Lyalka 424)

Mariya's infant died on the third day of this arduous trip and her
own hardships continued in the labour camps.

For some UPA women soldiers, the journey of motherhood would
start in the bunker where they were hiding, side by side with their
co-militants, as was the story of Mariya Kurochka. She gave birth
to a son in a tight dark underground hideout made in the middle of
an open field where five more partisans were sheltered, including
wounded soldiers. Her newborn infant was wrapped in pieces of

torn shirts from her co-militants. Post-partum Mariya was suffering from thirst and dehydration, but was not able to get out—their bunker had been under siege for two weeks. Eventually, Mariya passed on her infant to the care of her relatives (Kis).

Similarly, Antonina Korol fought as a front line combatant, along with her husband Yaroslav, and in the underground gave birth to twins. The mother had been exhausted by battles and the newborns needed intensive care. Having disguised herself as a civilian, Antonina tried to smuggle the baby boy to her extended family in a nearby village, but the boy was too weak and died in transition. She later successfully transferred her infant girl to a local family. A year later, in 1946, Antonia died alongside her husband while fighting off a week-long siege by Soviet troops—they shot themselves in order to avoid getting into enemies' hands (Hinda).

Whereas these tragic and tragically triumphant stories may be continued in this chapter, they all illustrate that motherhood was chosen by most women as a continuation of a traditionally accepted path from dating to marriage to parenthood that was customary and "normal" in the Ukrainian society of the day, despite the vagaries of war. For some, such a path was a way of reclaiming a lifestyle that the international conflict destroyed by claiming the lives of loved ones. However, the very journey of mothering because of war and military involvement presented these women with parenting options that were devoid of any "normalcy": a rebel woman often had to give birth to her child in secrecy, often in places unfit for the child's survival and her own well-being, such as in bunkers, hideouts, or prisons. In order to take care of a new human being who is completely dependent on others, in these conditions the mother had two options. One was to come out from underground with fake documents and continue hiding as a civilian, risking being pursued by Polish, German, or Soviet secret services for her own or her husband's involvement with the liberation movement. The other was to arrange for the child's care with her own family, in which case the secret services would often identify and target the child and use her/him as a bargaining chip against rebels. Alternatively, a mother could arrange care for her child in an unrelated family, but even then the child could be identified by authorities.

In all of these "best" options, the physical separation of mother and a child was imminent. In case of Mariya Savchyn, such separation was even most drastic: when Polish agents crashed in on her safe house in 1947, she decided to leave her five-month-old child in enemies' hands and escape:

> I was overtaken by the idea of escape—even if I were to die but not to get into their hands alive. "They will torture me to get to my husband, torment me to give him up. And what about the child? How can I ever leave him? But even now they are tearing me away from him, they will take him and I will never see him again. Or even, they might bring him to me during my tortures and will show him to me to break my will, so that through him they could get to their father. And even without my husband, they have enough to convict me or even torture me to death. I will never be able to go back to my child." In these critical moments, a terrible battle was raging in my soul, where with every conclusion my mind came up with, my heart was blasted to pieces. Only a firm conviction that they have already separated me from my child for many years of jail to come or even until death won over my doubts and I was ready to rather die escaping them than be arrested. (Savchyn 129)

But the physical separation did not preclude mothers from considering themselves parents of the children they had given birth to, nor did they lose a psychological connection and concern for the fate of their progeny for years, even decades after the separation. Whether by writing poems to her children as did Olha Ilkiv, arranging occasional secret meeting with her child as did "Mariyka" in Yaroslava's story, through long grieving over the loss of the child (Halyna Skaskiv and Mariya Savchyn), or even through developing an elaborate decade-long correspondence with her children from prison as did Kateryna Zarytska (a co-founder of UPA women's network undertook), in all of these stories, mothers display profound psychological connections to their children, a connection that bespeaks a form of togetherness and care. In this way, motherhood for UPA insurgents, under the grave pressures of war that left no better option except being physically separated from their young children and other loved ones, on a psychological level compelled them to expand their agency to a new kind of human relationships: UPA mothers cared not only for the fate of their country, Ukrainian independence, and for similarly minded co-militants, but also for the fate of their children, whose life has not been marked by any conscious affiliation with the militant cause at that point.

Did the challenges of being a mother and an insurgent present a tension in the mind of UPA women? Interestingly, none of the stories I examined show evidence that UPA women regretted their militancy in the face of challenging parenting decisions they had to face. Just as the idealistic cause of their nation's statehood—although realistically deemed unattainable in those historical circumstances—was esteemed beyond questioning and doubts (such was the workings of the Organization of the Ukrainian Nationalists (OUN) official propaganda instilled in many UPA members), so was the status of a mother and her exercise of parental functions: it was considered necessary, unquestionable, and psychologically valuable. These two experiences—militancy and motherhood—even though placing conflicting demands on UPA rebels did not erase each other from a woman's life. Children were arranged in the best possible care; women retained emotional and often spiritual attachment to their offspring (prayers for their children are mentioned in many testimonies) and continued the insurgent struggle. Thus, 37-year-old Hanna Svystun, a mother of five and an active combatant and messenger for UPA, left her children in her own mother's care and continued in the liberation movement until her capture, torture, and 25-year long imprisonment by the Soviet authorities. Kateryna Podolska left her two young children with her older parents and continued the guerrilla struggle along with her husband (Kis). And Olha Tverdokhib placed her little son with her sister, who was not able, however, to spare him from being uncovered by Soviet MVD forces and placed in an orphanage. When Olha continued her insurgency in the underground, the Soviet agents would circulate through intermediaries the pictures of her son and offered her to trade in her insurgency for "normal" and secure life with her child. Olha, although emotionally torn, never took up any such offers and ended her life with a gunshot when being encircled in a bunker by Soviet forces (Hrytskiv).

CONCLUSION

Seeking analytical ways to approach motherhood and militancy, I investigate the experience of Ukrainian Insurgent Army women from the feminist IR perspective of maternalism. Originally, maternalism attempted to posit that the uniqueness of mothering would lead women to prefer peace to war in effort to save fragile life. Maternalism, however, was not the motivating factor to militant mothers in UPA. Rather, UPA women most often entered the army ranks out of political and ideological considerations—the cause of Ukrainian statehood in the precarious conditions of Second World War—as did their men co-fighters. Whereas the women fulfilled a variety of gendered functions at war to start with—from cooking meals to secretarial tasks—in the mid-1940s precisely because of their gender they were able to engage in highly risky military operations and espionage while remaining inconspicuous to their enemies. But after the discovery of their prominent role in the underground movement by the Soviet authorities, women became special targets of the communist secret police and fell into high suspicion along with their UPA co-insurgents.

In these historic conditions, motherhood followed a traditional social path: most often insurgent women first dated, then clandestinely got married to co-militants and gave birth to their children in hiding. Such re-enforcement of the pattern characteristic to "normal" life in circumstances of raging war for some was a way to reclaim "normalcy" in their lives as well as to make a strong political statement. Even though motherhood presented additional challenges to militant women who gambled their own life on a daily basis, to which the caring for a newborn child was added, the political and militant commitments of these women were not altered. To a degree, their militancy predetermined their liability in the eyes of multiple adversaries thereby making rebel women into targets wherever they found themselves after the birth of their children—either briefly as civilians in hiding or as returned active combatants. In these circumstances, in the larger context of Second World War, the personal choice of engaging in militancy presented for a mother no better option than eventually leaving her child behind the frontlines.

Examining the stories of UPA women, I find myself in agreement with Gentry who emphasized that women have political reasons to engage in militancy that are not necessarily fuelled by their motherhood identity, and so when "women's own political rationale is ignored, this subordinates women's agency and objectifies her politicization" (247). While maternalism in IR refuses to separate cognition and emotion, its framework is problematic when used to present a women's political decision as being not about strategy or politics but about emotions and relationship (Gentry). The experiences of UPA women contradict such position and showcase that political considerations—commitment to insurgency—most often were and remained primary motivators for engaging in militancy both prior to and after becoming mothers for UPA women.

However, motherhood cannot and should not be easily dismissed as subordinate to militancy in major life choices of militant UPA-women. Women were specifically pressured by the Soviet repressive regime through their connections to spouses, parents, siblings—and importantly, to their young children—to cooperate with the regime and some yielded and switched sides out of concern for their loved ones (e.g., Lyudmyla Foya etc.) (Burds). Even when they were forced to become turnovers for the regime, or when they were physically and socially reduced to prisons and labour camps, UPA women retained the capacity to hold on to their nationalist convictions despite the efforts of the regime that sought to destroy them and their families. This part of individual agency—the ability to hold on to your political ideals—was not superseded by larger structural forces for Ukrainian insurgent women.

In a similar way, despite the destruction of traditional family life by the Second World War, when the "best" scenario meant being separated from their children, such physical separation did not eliminate in UPA mothers a strong psychological connection to their progeny they carried for many decades after the war. This is another aspect of personal agency that could not be eradicated by larger structural forces of a brutal international conflict storming into a life of an individual. Or, put differently, war can take away your loved ones, but it cannot take away your love for them.

In the extreme conditions of war, Ukrainian women would become guerilla soldiers defying the existing social expectations and using their gendered identity to confuse the enemy at the frontlines. By contrast, in their personal lives they became mothers choosing the socially accepted norms of progression in developing a family: engagement-marriage-motherhood. For young UPA women, the combination of militancy and motherhood presented challenging life choices devoid of any "normalcy." Nevertheless, the case of the UPA women reveals that insurgent mothers, despite the destructiveness of war, were able to exercise their agency in staying committed to their military cause while at the same time holding on to their motherhood psychologically. These two commitments—militancy and motherhood—often placed irreconcilable demands on the physical abilities of UPA women, but they did not combine in such ways so as to push each other out from the psyche of an insurgent mother.

[1]In 1946, the Soviet government required all Ukrainian Catholic religious and laity to abandon the Catholic Church and enter Moscow Patriarchate Orthodox church controlled by the communist government. Thousands of religious and laity resisted, including the head of the Ukrainian Catholic Church, Cardinal Josyf Slipyi, and were sent to Siberian labor camps and gulags. Other faithful continued to practice clandestinely, a phenomenon to which "Mariyka" is making reference.

WORKS CITED

Ahall, Linda. "Motherhood, Myth and Gendered Agency in Political Violence." *International Feminist Journal of Politics* 14.1 (2012): 103-120. Print.

Burds, Jeffrey. "Gender and Policing in Soviet West Ukraine, 1944-1948." *Cahiers du Monde Russe* 42.2-4 (2001): 279-320. Print.

Coulter, Chris. "Female Fighters in the Sierra Leone War: Challenging the Assumptions?" *Feminist Review* 88 (2008): 54-73. Print.

Feinman, Rose. *Citizenship Rites: Feminist Soldiers and Feminist*

Anti-Militarists. New York: New York University Press, 2000. Print.

Gentry, Caron. "Twisted Maternalism." *International Feminist Journal of Politics* 11.2 (2009): 235-252. Print.

Gentry, Caron and Laura Sjoberg, *Mothers, Monsters and Whores: Women's Violence in Global Politics.* London: Zed Books, Ltd, 2007. Print.

Goldstein, Joshua. *War and Gender.* Cambridge: Cambridge University Press, 2001. Print.

Gurr, Tedd. *People Versus States: Minorities at Risk in the New Century.* Washington, DC: United State Institute of Peace Press, 2000. Print.

Hinda, Volodymyr. "The Specifics of Clandestine Marriage: How Married Life Unfolded for OUN and UPA Militants." *Korrespondent* 36, 2013. Web. 27 May 2015.

Hrytskiv, Roman. *"Hrim" – UPA Colonel Mykola Tverdokhlib: Memoirs and Documents.* Toronto: Litopys UPA, 2008. Print.

Ilkiv, Olha. *In the Chains of Two Prisons: Poetry.* Lviv: Kamenyar, 2011. Print.

Kis, Oksana. "Women's Experience of Participation in Liberation Movement in Western Ukrainian Lands in 1940-1950s." *Skhid-Zakhid: Istoryko-kultorolohichnyi zbirnyk* 13-14 (2009): 101-125. Print.

Lyalka, Yaroslav. *The Chronicles of Unbroken Ukraine.* Lviv: Prosvita, 1993. Print.

Ness, Cindy D. "The Rise in Female Violence" *Daedalus* 136.1 (2007): 84-93. Print.

Orleck, Annelise. "Tradition Unbound: Radical Mothers in International Perspective." *The Politics of Motherhood: Activist Voices from Left to Right.* Eds. Alexis Jetter, Annelise Orleck and Diana Taylor. London: University Press of New England, 1997. 3-20. Print.

Pennington, Reina. "Offensive Women: Women in Combat in the Red Army in the Second World War." *Journal of the Military History* 74 (2010): 775-820. Print.

Peteet, Julie. "Icons and Militants: Mothering in Danger Zone." *Signs* 23.1 (1997): 103-129. Print.

Promanyna-Levkovych, Yaroslava. "The Life of the Underground

Woman." *Memoirs of the* UPA *Soldiers and Members of the Armed Underground in L'viv and Liubachiv Regions.* Toronto: Litopys UPA, 2003. 143-240. Print.

Ruddick, Sara. "Maternal Thinking" *Feminist Studies* 6.2 (1980): 342-367. Print.

Ruddick, Sara. "Rethinking 'Maternal' Politics." *The Politics of Motherhood: Activist Voices from Left to Right.* Eds. Alexis Jetter, Annelise Orleck and Diana Taylor. London: University Press of New England, 1997. 367-381. Print.

Skaskiv, Halyna. "Living History of Berezhany and the Surrounding Areas in 1930-1945: Interview." *Ivan Franko National University of Lviv.* 23 Aug, 1997. Web. 27 May 2015..

Savchyn, Mariya. *Thousands of Roads: Memoirs.* Toronto: Liptopys UPA, 1995. Print.

Sjoberg, Laura. "Women Fighters and the 'Beautiful Soul' Narrative." *International Review of the Red Cross* 92.877 (2010): 53-68. Print

Taylor, Diana. "The Uneasy Relationship between Motherhood and Feminism." *The Politics of Motherhood: Activist Voices from Left to Right.* Eds. Alexis Jetter, Annelise Orleck and Diana Taylor. London: University Press of New England, 1997. 349-351. Print.

Wynnyckyj, Iroida. "How World War II Affected the Lives of Ukrainian Women: An Oral History." World War II and the (Re)Creation of Historical Memory in Contemporary Ukraine: Conference. 23-26 Sept 2009, Kyiv, Ukraine. Web. 27 May 2015.

15.
"The Change Was Very Strong"

Rural Mayan Motherhood and Activism during the Guatemalan Civil War

RACHEL O'DONNELL

What was the real reason? How can it be best understood?
—Ricardo Falla

FOR MAYAN WOMEN IN THE highlands of Guatemala, guerilla activity during the civil war was not a necessity, but an obvious extension of their role in the community. As mothers and community members, women in Maya villages in the Quiché developed their agency through specific guerilla activity: leadership and fighting, gathering supplies, and helping other women preserve their community role. This activism reveals how the tendency among academics to cast women who lived through the war as "war-widows" is limited, often inaccurate, and ultimately politically dangerous.

The government of Guatemala and its military have been condemned for committing genocide during the thirty-six-year civil war (1960-1996) and for widespread human rights violations they initiated against civilians, especially the indigenous Maya, who make up most of Guatemala's highland population and rural poor. Up to 200,000 people died or went missing during the war, including many who "disappeared." Human rights sources have estimated that 5,000 Guatemalans were killed by the military for "political reasons" in 1980 alone (Guatemala), making it the worst human rights violator in the hemisphere. In a report titled "Guatemala: A Government Program of Political Murder," Amnesty International stated, "Between January and November of 1980, some 3,000 people described by government representatives as 'subversives' and 'criminals' were either shot on the spot in political assassinations or seized and murdered later; at least 364 others seized in this period have not yet been accounted for." In the remote Guatemalan highlands, the military identified many villages and communities as targeted for annihilation, and indeed, entire communities were destroyed during the "scorched earth" campaign. This was especially true in El Quiché, where the army held the belief that the entire indigenous population was on the side of the guerillas.

Repression in the countryside began in the early days of the war and escalated in the early 1980s with a counterinsurgency offensive in El Quiché. El Quiché is mountainous and rural, and remains the region with Guatemala's highest indigenous population. Also during the 1980s, civilian paramilitary bands that had worked in the rural highlands were renamed "civilian self-defense patrols" (PACs), and the army began conscripting large portions of the rural civilian population into these militias. This often left families in the Quiché struggling to support themselves without critical members. For women in the highlands, it meant they were often parenting alone, fleeing military assaults, attempting to farm small plots of land to feed large families, and maintaining their community under the army's campaign.

In *Massacres in the Jungle,* published in 1992, Ricardo Falla proposes that the collective memory of the rural Guatemalan Maya reveals a clearer historical truth when it is merged with what is presently most important to these communities. As a result, he says, such memories can continue to reveal what political action and what steps should be taken next. Falla names some individuals directly responsible for the massacres: military leaders, state officials, the Guatemalan elite, wealthy landholders, coffee plantation landlords, and owners of foreign and transnational corporations. In contrast, Maya community members remain innocent victims of the army's campaign, but often with a purposeful political project: to resist the army's campaign, reclaim community land, and maintain community autonomy.

Women's testimonies have provided crucial evidence for challenging normative views of history and have been vital to more nuanced understandings of women in popular struggle, especially in Latin America. Social scientists who write about Guatemala's state violence surrounding the Civil War at its height in the early 1980s, often claim that Maya who suffered the majority of the aggression were either the innocent victims without agency or the naive constituency of the guerillas. Recent history has also been marked by women's increasing participation in political struggle. Although historical interpretations are always in flux, Guatemalan literature categorizes many of the women involved in Guatemala's struggle against the state's counterinsurgent campaign as the innocent victims of state violence and labels them primarily as war-widows. Guatemalan women's *testimonios* of the war occupy a particularly controversial place in the literature because of the book by Rigoberta Menchú that changed the paradigm of research on oral history surrounding Guatemalan violence, and became the focus of a charged debate among intellectuals of different disciplinary and ideological backgrounds.

Although Menchú's testimony is not the focus of those I will discuss here, such testimonies marked an important move in feminist literature, as women's stories previously presented as apolitical autobiographies became personal accounts connected to literary narrative and radical social action: "The *testimonio* has emerged as one of the most important literary sites for the generation of women's collective and oppositional consciousness in Latin America and India in the last three decades" (Panjabi 151). Eye-witness accounts and collective memory are particularly important in light of new interpretations of Central American civil wars and violence, and because anthropological, political, and sociological texts are often guilty of directly or indirectly claiming a history of Maya disinterest in Maya future. As academics, we are too often responsible for making claims similar to those who perpetuated the violence against the Maya: in attempting to support the victims of armed conflict, we reproduce the army's ideology that such people are only guiltless if they refute their role in political action and claim a lack of political agency, lack of consciousness, as well as lack of understanding of the issues surrounding the civil war and the racial and class conflicts in Guatemala altogether.

Maya communities depend on women to support and maintain the community. Maya villages are small, but most people live in large households of extended family, and women wash clothes, cook, and gather water in large groups. Mothering is part of this community work as well, as children are carried by their mother until they are two and then expected to be independent enough to assist with daily chores. Outsiders often comment that it is difficult to find the "real mother" in a Maya community because parenting is a community activity (McAllister). For Maya women, guerilla activism during the civil war became an extension of their community role: many cooked in groups for the guerillas, obtained and delivered supplies in groups, and even joined the fighting to be with other community members. For many women, mothering and activism were interdependent, and they were successful organizers and activists precisely because they were able to see their guerilla activity as part of their community role as women and mothers.

Ajpu, the Maya women's group in Chiché's rural communities, is named for the day of the Maya calendar on which the group was formed. Ajpu currently has 693 members who represent eighteen rural communities of the municipality of Chiché, in the lower part of the highlands of El Quiché, the area of Guatemala most affected by the civil war. Many of these members openly discuss their active roles in the insurgency throughout the 1970s and 1980s, and they also articulate a connection between the current group and the women's specific role in the guerilla front that operated in the mountains between the neighbouring municipalities of Joyabaj and Zacualpa. This connection to the insurgency underlies the current identity and political focus of their organization.

In 2004 and again in 2006, I interviewed a number of the Ajpu women who play an important role as activists in their community. More than eighteen of these women acknowledge their involvement with the guerillas twenty years earlier. This "involvement" varied from those who were responsible for preparing meals only once or twice during the year, to those who left their homes and families to join groups fighting the military in the mountains. I interviewed these 18 women in small groups of three or five, except for the two women who were most vocal about the extent of their activity during the war, Angela and Justina, who were interviewed separately. I asked all of the groups of women only two questions to begin each interview: "How did you first become involved with the movement during the war?" and "What kinds of things did you do to support the movement?" Follow-up questions varied accordingly.

Angela and Justina are both 44 years old, and not many questions were required, especially since Justina said "Let me tell you about my work in the clandestine forces," when I asked about the development of Ajpu. Now she is on the mayor's committee at the municipality, but she is proud of the ten years she spent fighting in the mountains against the army and delighted to be part of an all-female household. When the war ended and she returned to Chiché, she formed the women's group to support development in the community.

Ajpu originally broke from CONAVIGUA (Coordinadora Nacional de las Viudas de Guatemala or National Coordination of Guatemalan Widows) in order to reclaim Maya women's identities in Chiché "beyond widowhood" and also to engage in the "community development work" they undertake now.[1]

CONAVIGUA, with whom Ajpu broke in 2002, is a national Maya widows' organization whose political project involves the ongoing search for disappeared family members and seeks reparation for widows and families. In one of my first meetings with Ajpu, I asked why the group had broken from CONAVIGUA ten years earlier. One Ajpu woman answered, "We're not widows," and many others nodded their heads in agreement. When I asked for clarification, one woman spoke up: "The war made me a widow, for example, but it's not that we're only interested in finding out why that happened. We know why. They shot our husbands" (Justina 2003). Ajpu differed with CONAVIGUA, she added, because Ajpu women did not wish to be portrayed primarily as widows, and many were unhappy with the group's leadership style and resulting decisions about political activity. Ajpu was more interested in development work and community restructuring than they were in continuing to look for disappeared family members. One Ajpu member spoke to that directly: "We wanted to help ourselves, especially the women who are older and do not have adequate housing."

The legacy of the displacement that resulted from the civil war is noticeable in Chiché's rural communities. Many Maya have a particular distaste for any kind of political organizing, as they had previously had their lives severely disrupted and watched as the state reorganized their lives along military lines: "It is now known that between 1.3 and 1.5 million people, up to eighty percent of the population in the most indigenous areas of Guatemala, were at least temporarily displaced in the course of the scorched earth campaign" (North 157). This makes the work of the Ajpu women even more extraordinary at a time when many rural Guatemalans are becoming increasingly dependent on the state and its modest hand-outs, with little infrastructure or fertile land to enable high-land communities to maintain their previously esteemed autonomy. In addition, Maya communities in the Southern part of the Quiché, where Chiché is located, still rely much more heavily on local and community organization, as municipalities operate with fewer NGOs and cooperative structures than do communities in the Northern Quiché (the Ixil Triangle and the Ixcán/Playa Grande region), which are more often the recipients of financial support from international organizations. Local leaders often blame such lack of attention from the state on the ongoing power of the URNG (the combined guerilla party after 1982) in the region and the lack of support to the URNG from the international community.

The Guatemalan army, or *la institución*, continues to strike fear in rural populations, since the military campaign was carried out

> not by killing guerillas, but by killing their supporters and potential supporters within the civilian population, and by doing so in such an arbitrary and vicious fashion that people in the region came to feel an intense and overwhelming fear, not merely of supporting the guerillas, but of doing anything that might suggest they sympathized with the guerillas' cause. (Wilkinson 351)

Chichelense women in particular continued to maintain a certain level of autonomy from the state and formed the majority of those who placed a Maya identity above a Guatemalan one. Women in Chiché's rural communities, for example, are less likely to go to state-sponsored educational institutions, more likely to maintain Mayan language as their primary language, and less likely to enter the formal labour force. Many Ajpu members make connections between their revolutionary past and members' present actions, in terms of their relationship with the state. They note that women who were leaders among the insurgents were later forced to retreat to traditional roles. Indeed, community mothering during the war allowed for work in the insurgency; when the fronts rejoined the communities, women were once again expected to retreat to traditional roles and remain at home. These more traditional roles include day-to-day activities for large families, such as gathering water, cooking, and building fires. Yet some Ajpu members have taken on more traditionally male roles outside of the home, including going to the mountains to find wood to build fires for cooking or selling at the weekly market in the center of town. Three Ajpu women in a group interview noted that their involvement with the guerillas began only after their husbands, who were supporters, had been taken or killed by the military. One of these women was first approached by another when both women were at the funeral of the third. I asked her what inspired her to begin to cook and obtain supplies for the guerilla forces and she answered:

> I don't know, there was nothing else to do. My husband had already been taken and my sister's husband too. While we were at the [funeral] procession, she [holding the arm of another woman in the interview] said, "It is too much, they have taken all the men" and that the guerilla was trying to make sure the army did not kill all the men in our community. So we started to cook [for them]. They always wanted meat, but we only gave them tortillas and beans and sometimes an egg if we could get it. They could come for food every Sunday and then another day they would go to another village. (Juana 2006)

When I ask her how she cared and cooked for her seven children at the same time, she said, "I cooked for everyone, and also my sister came with her children, and we just cooked and made tortillas on the fire."

For this woman, the guerilla activity of obtaining and providing supplies was no different from cooking for her family and fulfilling her community role. She did it alongside other women, in much the same way she performed many of her other community roles. Like many of the women who became involved with the guerillas, the violence had affected her family and community personally, and the work she began to do became an extension of the community role she already had, or as she says, "There was nothing else to do."

Ajpu women talk openly and freely of their guerilla activity and direct all who will listen to take their stories to other places where they might be retold. When I asked Angela, the woman who is now acting *coordinadora* of Ajpu, and who was also a leader in the guerilla front between Zacualpa and Joyabaj for 15 years, how she became a fighter and what changed the day she walked into the mountains from her daily school bus, she answered that nothing had changed but "only the violence had come." She paused a moment and added, "No, we were different then, before the violence," referring to the group of women she works with now. She makes immediate connection to the group: "We cannot have a more revolutionary strategy now, but we hope to sometime soon. We don't like the [state] programs, but at the same time we need them to make sure the women have houses and food." Their role as mothers and guerillas combined in the mountains, as many women left children behind with other family members and many were responsible for caring for children there. Many women in Ajpu, for example, spoke of leaving children they had given birth to in their villages or caring for children that had been born in the mountains temporarily until it was safe to deliver them to other family members. In this way, mothering was a community responsibility and rarely an individual task. Angela gave birth to two children in the mountains with assistance from community midwives (*comadronas*) who risked their lives to attend women in the mountains. Now, many of the Ajpu women live in households of women only, as they say they became used to this during the war when there were no men around.

Ajpu women impart stories of the army's violence and their organized response during the civil war with the same rich description with which they tell ancient stories of creation and the significance of planting the fields. As Maya narratives are passed down from generation to generation, the stories of experienced violence during the war have become part of Maya history as well. But should we not record such political history in the social sciences? As many scholars, from anthropologist Carol Smith to historian Jim Handy, have written that *la violencia* was part of the state's tightening of the army's hold on the Maya countryside. The Ajpu women were not only widows and victims of such violence, but a collective group of active opponents to the army's campaign. While Falla asks the real reason for the violence, and proposes that collective memory be used in retellings of the violence, he reveals his own tendencies to hope for a certain kind of political project and future for Guatemala.

MOTHERS BUT NOT WAR WIDOWS:
IDENTITY CHANGES DURING THE CONFLICT

Much of the academic literature that comes out of that post-war period categorizes the Maya who suffered the majority of the aggression as either the helpless victims of the army or the naive constituency of the guerillas. Such work, in that context, classifies many women involved in political resistance against the army's violence as "war-widows." Gender is an important component in these oral histories, but not only in women's roles of wives and widows. Many analyses reinforce the victimhood of Maya women, play up their vulnerability, and remain indicative of the Guatemalan army's ideological claims that the only victims of the war were those who can claim complete ignorance of the guerilla movement. Lack of understanding of women's experiences of the war denies the development of women as politically conscious subjects, as though Maya women were disempowered and suffered at all points in the past, were later widowed, and then became conscious of their larger situation only as a result. Such assumptions present Maya women as reclaimers of their previously denied human rights who are now fully able to do and act as they wish, and ignore ongoing state repression and militarization in Maya communities as well as the many socio-political constraints such women face when attempting to organize.

The individual experiences of the Ajpu women certainly contrast these assumptions. Many Ajpu women were energized during the time of the fighting, and though they lived with constant fear during the war, their roles as women expanded to community caretakers as they directed the front. Angela became an important leader during fifteen years of fighting, and later an organizer among Maya women. Her birth experiences in the mountains remain particularly important to her identity as a mother and a fighter and to her ongoing development work. At the same time, while only a small number of Ajpu women were able to formally join guerilla movements, participation did not lessen among women in other non-direct-combatant roles, such as preparing food and obtaining supplies. Others were responsible for caring for the children of combatants.

Angela became a leader in an important combat unit in the guerilla front between Zacualpa and Joyabaj. She speaks of other concrete events in her development: her cousin's rape by soldiers, her father's death on a coffee plantation where there wasn't enough water, her family's struggle to remain on ancestral land, and her own decision to leave home for a one year at a private Catholic school. *Testimonios* of widows that both Green and Zur provide, in contrast, make it easy to highlight the guerillas' loss of the war and widows' consciousness development as things that happened as a result of the ending of the war and ongoing peace process, without providing a clear understanding of a political project that was incredibly hopeful and powerful at the time in which rural Guatemalans were heavily involved.

Women in Ajpu cite their involvement in the women's group as a result of earlier understandings of the Maya situation during the war and later beliefs in the importance of involvement in the community of women. The group has successfully solicited grants from international organizations for housing for rural women and has prioritized politically active Ajpu members in development projects. Ajpu also began agricultural cooperatives and solicited funding from the municipality to support a full-time women's coordinator for the group. One of the goals of Ajpu is to now work toward development locally. The members do this on local terms with local URNG leadership, an attempt to maintain autonomy from Guatemalan state structures by seeking recognition of the group from local cooperatives and local government.

Angela nicely connects the importance of the group's development work to their direct revolutionary work in the guerilla. Her telling of the events that led to her mothering in the conflict zone of the mountains deserves to be quoted here at length:

I was very busy working in the mountains when I had my first son. I had a lot of responsibilities: moving when necessary, keeping the arms together and enough, making sure we had enough food and clothing for everyone. We mostly had tortillas, sometimes beans, sometimes eggs. There were a lot of plants to eat in broth. We lost a few in the clandestine so my role was always changing. I mean the army killed them when they went to get food or something else. I was the first one who had a child in our group and I talked to the others about keeping him there with us, which I did for a little while, until I was able to take him to my parents when it was safe. Others had children, but he was born in the mountains. He was still small but maybe over a year then. They had not seen me in a long time, so this was a surprise for them, but they had him for years and then my daughter too. She did not stay in the mountains with me. When my son was born, it was a surprise, I think it was earlier than I thought and one other mother there knew a comadrona [traditional midwife] who lived nearby and could get to where we were in the mountains. I did not want to go to the community because I would not be able to get back to the mountains and what if we had moved by then? I would be lost. We did not have to move much in those days, the army did not always know we were there, near the communities. It made it easier for us to get food too, along the footpaths.

After the baby came, the change was very strong. I had to be a mother and a fighter and still lead us if the army came. Everyone helped care for him, of course, and he never cried. I had to make sure everyone else could collect food and maintain their arms and keep them dry also our clothes so no one got cold. It was difficult to keep warm in the mountains. My son stayed on my back while I worked,

the same way at home washing in the pila or collecting
wood, so he was warm and he was with me.

Here, Angela notes how she reconciled her mothering with her
community activism, and how she continues to do so. Like others who responded that they had cooked for their families and
then moved to cook for the guerillas, they were able to reconcile
guerilla activity with mothering and looked at it as one and the
same: providing and helping the community, which is central
to a woman's role in Chiché. This is the art of mothering in the
mountains during dangerous missions, as Angela describes it. In
a daily life of fighting, running, and fear, Angela was able to do
her political work and her work as a mother because of support
from the community, both in the guerilla front and from her
family who helped raise her children while she worked in the
mountains. (In a later interview, in December of 2006, Angela
shared that she still wakes every morning afraid that the army is
after her.) Interestingly, Angela does not separate her mothering
from her community role. When I asked her specifically what
types of activities she performed in the mountains, she does not
mention her children, as though they were part of her and her
communal work. Instead of becoming a "war-widow" during the
war, Angela became a community leader, a role that influences
her life and community role to this day.

Scholars such as Judith Zur are especially adept at placing the
identity of widowhood among Maya women above all others. In
her book *Violent Memories: Mayan War Widows in Guatemala*,
Zur writes as though women lived completely apolitical, disempowered, and unaware lives in their pre-widowed past:

> Many [Maya] women had not known what a guerilla was
> until the army accused them of being one and even then,
> most of them failed to understand the concept—beyond
> realizing that the label was (and remains) dangerous. Their
> monolingualism, together with the gender barrier which
> separates male and female activities, prevents all but the
> most determined women from participating in the popular
> movements. (84)

Zur primarily offers a description of widows developing political consciousness only at the exhumations of clandestine graves, years after the conflict had ended: "These monolingual Q'eqchi' women had successfully stood up to those who threatened them, to those who killed their husbands, sons, fathers, and brothers" (68). Zur effectively replaces Maya women's earlier political consciousness during the violence with what was a direct result of losing male family members, and offers an analysis of their later widowhood when she describes her interviewees:

> Their experiences of repetitive violence are representa-tive of the experiences of a large segment of Guatemala's female, Indian population. For almost every man killed or kidnapped, a dependent woman—wife, sister, mother or daughter—was left without male protection, a crucial concept in K'iche' social relations. (8)

Male protection of the female Maya population may be import-ant in maintaining highland social relations, but this relationship was severely disrupted in earlier periods of Guatemalan violence when women were attacked or tortured by soldiers, or raped by members of civil patrol units from their own communities. Again, such acts are represented by Zur as happening first to male political actors and secondarily to their wives, reinforcing the construction of Maya women as passive victims during the war as if they were only politically conscious after. The stories Zur writes, for ex-ample, are detailed retellings of female lives only in light of male experience without actual analysis of the term "war-widows" or mention of whether or not the women claim it themselves, and assumes Maya women were *only* affected by the violence when some lost their husbands.

The sense of helplessness that dominates much of the writing on Maya women is an attempt to deny the many ways in which they were actors in the struggle and remain agents in the reshap-ing of Guatemalan politics. Such writing also ignores the ways in which researchers are often the actors and not mere retellers of testimonies by assuming such oral histories necessitate scholarly mediation. Not only do we not understand why these widows' husbands were killed or why the researchers find this central to understanding politics in Guatemala, we have no sense of why widows' political agency now takes the form it does: why these particular widows are joining particular political organizations, seeking justice understood in a particular form, and provoking particular controversies (McAllister).

By placing marriage at the center of her research in *Fear as a Way of Life: Mayan Widows in Rural Guatemala*, Linda Green allows a Western concept to take hold in Mayan community. Marriage is relatively new in Mayan communities, and there is considerable variation in what can be considered traditional marriage practice. What signifies a married couple or that a marriage has taken place varies—from a couple beginning to live together to spending a day apart from their families. While Green refers to marriage as consisting of a "complementary division of labor" (95), what she does not consider is that women's labour necessitates their being at home, while men work in the fields where they are able to have social interaction, learn additional languages, and have community responsibility that extends outside the household.

What I found among the women of Ajpu was different. Choosing to join the guerillas varied by age in Chiché; many young women joined and cited lack of family responsibility as allowing them the freedom to do so. Many in Ajpu admitted they had older sisters to care for parents or children they had left behind. Angela had attended a private Catholic school in Chichicastenango (another town) at one point, which allowed her autonomy from her family, the experience of resisting authority with the school's administration when she continued wearing the *traje* of her community and not that of Chichicastenango, as well as an opportunity to meet other politically active young people.

Angela's direct experience as a mother certainly speaks to the importance of her community role. Angela contacted her midwife and translated for her from K'iche' though the midwife asked not to be named. At first, they discuss how the "scorched earth" policies carried out by the government against the Mayan people during the war destroyed many of the medicinal plants they used, and contributed to a breakdown in the oral transmission of knowledge of these herbs. The *comadrona* has been attending births for more than thirty years, and learned from her mother, who assisted births in the community with her until her death. When I told the *comadrona* I was surprised to hear that she had attended women in the mountains, she said:

> *It was the same as seeing women in the community. Sometimes it was easier to find plants in the mountains, though one time I went to a birth to attend it and I got lost on the way back because there was no foot path. Later I found the community but I was walking in the mountains for some time.*

Angela and her *comadrona* allow us to see how necessary it is to think about the political implications of conducting research in these communities and the assumed similar experiences of women during the civil war. Again, the woman acting as midwife to the guerillas in the mountains was just doing her community work and said "it was the same," meaning that for her the guerillas became an extension of the community.

Most tellingly, Angela does not mention the children's father as part of her story; rather, the midwife who attended her and the other people working in the mountains became her mothering supports. These *testimonios* push us to think about category construction and how our assumptions may reflect on the lives we are attempting to (re)present. This is not to say that the category of widowhood is not necessarily relevant or important to study. Rather, the category of the Guatemalan war-widow was constructed in a variety of contexts that overlapped and helped to erase women's own experiences. Angela's story encourages us to look at the resulting specific assumptions of the category of "war-widow" and what this term may conjure for us: a suffering woman alone, victimized because her husband died, perhaps innocently and tragically in battle. As a result, the state violence is assumed to be correct and removes the idea of state repression and social structure that may serve in the subordination of women. This perception places blame somewhere else and implies women's certain victimhood; he dies, she suffers afterward—and since he died, he was the only political actor there. Angela's story demonstrates how central her role was to the guerillas, how she was able to mother in the mountains, and how important her community was to her maintaining her leadership role in this important front in the Quiché.

A special thank you to the women of AJPU who volunteered their stories and interpretations of events for this research. Financial support for this work was provided by the York Centre for International and Security Studies (YCISS) and the Martin Cohnstaedt Research Award for Studies in Non-Violence, which supported fieldwork in Central America. This research was subject to review and has met research ethics guidelines maintained by York University's Human Participants Review Committee (HPRC), responsible for ensuring that research involving human participants is consistent with the guidelines set by the University.

[1]From brochure prepared for the Swiss Embassy, 2004, titled "*Ajpu: Organización de las mujeres Chichélenses*" (Ajpu: Organization of Chichélense Women). Above is the author's translation for *fuera de las viudas* and *desarrollo de la comunidad*.

WORKS CITED

"*Ajpu: Organización de las mujeres Chichélenses*" (Ajpu: Organization of Chichélense Women). Brochure prepared by Ajpu for presentation to Swiss Embassy, 2004.

Amnesty International. "Guatemala: A Government Program of Political Murder." *Amnesty International Publications*. 19 March 1981. Web. 14 April 2015.

Angela, oral interviews by Rachel O'Donnell, May 2003, December 2006, in Municipal Building of Chiché, El Quiche. Original in Maya K'iche' and Spanish, translated and transcribed by Rachel O'Donnell.

Arias, Arturo, ed. *The Rigoberta Menchú Controversy*. Minneapolis, University of Minnesota Press, 2001. Print.

Bunster, Ximena. "Surviving Beyond Fear: Women and Torture in Latin America." *Surviving Beyond Fear: Women, Children & Human Rights in Latin America*. Ed. Marjorie Agosin. New

York: White Pine Press, 1993. Print.

Burt, Jo-Marie and Fred Rosen. "Truth-telling and Memory in Postwar Guatemala: An Interview with Rigoberta Menchú." *NACLAReport on the Americas* 32.5 (1999): 6-10. Print.

Carey, David, Jr. *Engendering Mayan History: Kaqchikel Women as gents and Conduits of the Past, 1875-1970*. New York: Routledge, 2005. Print.

Crosby, Alison Diana. *A Moment of Truth? Towards Transformative Participation in Postwar Guatemala*. Dissertation. York University, 2002. Print.

D'Amico, Francine. "Feminist Perspectives on Women Warriors." *The Women and War Reader*. Eds. Lois Ann Lorentzen and Jennifer Turpin. New York: New York University, 1998. Print.

Falla, Ricardo. *Massacres in the Jungle: Ixcan, Guatemala, 1975-1982*. Chicago: Westwood Press, 1994. Print.

Grandin, Greg. "A More Onerous Citizenship: Illness, Race and Nation in Republican Guatemala." *Reclaiming the Political in Latin American History: Essays from the North*. Ed. Gilbert M. Joseph Durham: Duke University, 2001. Print.

Green, Linda. *Fear as a Way of Life: Mayan Widows in Rural Guatemala*. New York: Columbia University Press, 1999. Print.

"Guatemala and El Salvador: Latin America's Worst Human Rights Violators in 1980." The Council on Hemispheric Affairs. Princeton University Library. Department of Rare Books and Special Collections.

Enloe, Cynthia. "All the Men are in the Militias, All the Women are Victims: The Politics of Masculinity and Femininity in Nationalist Wars." *The Women and War Reader*. Eds. Lois Ann Lorentzen and Jennifer Turpin. New York: New York University, 1998. Print.

Hale, Charles R., et al. "Consciousness, Violence, and the Politics of Memory in Guatemala." *Current Anthropology* 38.5 (December 1997): 817-39. Print.

Juana, oral interview by Rachel O'Donnell, December 2006, in Municipal Building of Chiché, El Quiche. Original in Maya K'iche' and Spanish, translated and transcribed by Rachel O'Donnell.

Justina, oral interview by Rachel O'Donnell, May 2003, in Municipal Building of Chiché, El Quiche. Original in Spanish, translated and transcribed by Rachel O'Donnell.

Kampwirth, Karen. *Feminism and the Legacy of Revolution: Nicaragua, El Salvador, Chiapas.* Athens: Ohio University, 2004. Print.

Kampwirth, Karen. *Women and Guerilla Movements: Nicaragua, El Salvador, Chipas, Cuba.* University Park: Pennsylvania State University, 2002. Print.

Matthews, Irene. "Torture as Text." *The Women and War Reader.* Eds. Lois Ann Lorentzen and Jennifer Turpin. New York: New York University, 1998. Print.

McAllister, Carlota. *Good People: Revolution, Community, and Consciencia in a Maya-K'iche' Village in Guatemala.* Dissertation. Baltimore, Johns Hopkins University, 2003. Print.

Menchu, Rigoberta and Elisabeth Burgos-Debray, Editor. *I, Rigoberta Menchu: An Indian Woman in Guatemala.* London: Verso, 2010. Print.

Milliken, Jennifer. "The Study of Discourse in International Relations: A Critique of Research and Methods." *European Journal of International Relations* 5 (2) 1999: 225-254. Print.

Mohanty, Chandra Talpade. "Under Western Eyes: Feminist Scholarship and Colonial Discourses." *Third World Women and the Politics of Feminism.* Eds. Chandra Talpade Mohanty et al. Bloomington: Indiana University Press, 1988. Print.

Morrison, Andrew R. and Rachel A. May. "Escape from Terror: Violence and Migration in Post-Revolutionary Guatemala." *Latin American Research Review* 29.2 (1994): 111-33. Print.

North, Liisa L. "Reflections on Democratization and Demilitarization in Central America." *Studies in Political Economy* 55 (Spring 1998): 155-170. Print.

Panjabi, Kavita. "Probing 'Morality" and State Violence: Feminist Values and Communicative Interaction in Prison Testimonios in India and Argentina." *Feminist Genealogies, Colonial Legacies, Democratic Futures.* Ed. M. Jacqui Alexander and Chandra Talpade Mohanty. New York: Routledge, 1997. Print.

Sanford, Victoria. *Buried Secrets: Truth and Human Rights in Guatemala.* New York: Palgrave, 2003. Print.

Smith, Carol, ed. *Guatemalan Indians and the State: 1540 to 1988.* Austin: University of Texas, 1992. Print.

Wilkinson, Daniel. *Silence on the Mountain: Stories of Terror,*

Betrayal, and Forgetting in Guatemala. Durham: Duke University, 2004. Print.

Zur, Judith N. *Violent Memories: Mayan War Widows in Guatemala.* Boulder: Westview, 1998. Print.

16.
Challenging the Official Story

Alicia Kozameh, Alicia Partnoy, and Mother Activism during Argentina's Dirty Waters (1976-1983)

BENAY BLEND

THIS CHAPTER EXPLORES HOW Alicia Kozameh and Alicia Partnoy, both writers imprisoned during Argentina's Dirty Wars (1976-1983), used political motherhood to challenge the official story. It illustrates the ways that motherhood has been politicized, both to silence women by state-sponsored torture, and as a way that women embraced maternal politics as a strategy. Like the Mothers of the Plaza de Mayo, some of whom wrote texts, both Kozameh and Partnoy use literature to fight injustice and build a discourse of solidarity around the disappeared. Defined by Partnoy as the "practice of motherhood as a communal experience" ("Textual Strategies" 8), the concept of socialized motherhood informs their texts. Both authors chronicle their experiences in *testimonios*, repositories of communal memory as well as a tool for activism. Both Kozameh and Partnoy re-define literary conventions by writing collective truths to inform a wider audience. Based mostly on experiences in prison, their writing blurs boundaries between personal and collective memory, fiction and reality.

In Latin America during these years, as Ana Luiza Libânio Dantas notes, an increasing number of women began writing *testimonios* as a way to fight injustice. In the months after the military coup of March 1976, thousands of Argentines, especially young people like Kozameh and Partnoy, were disappeared, tortured, and murdered. Like many others, both authors engaged in politics at their respective universities. For their efforts both spent several years as prisoners of conscience in various detention centers. While in prison, Kozameh wrote down experiences that would later inform her books (Díaz). In her introduction to *The Little School,* Julia Alvarez states that Partnoy, too, sought revenge by "seeing" through her blindfold while in prison (7). From those glimpses she recorded accounts that she hoped would indict her prison guards. Upon their release both went into exile in America. Representative of women who gave voice to the repressed, both empowered themselves and others through the written word.

Among scholars of this period, there is general consensus that Kozameh and Partnoy write collective truths in the form of fiction. For example, Gwendolyn Díaz writes that Kozameh's *Steps under Water* "goes beyond a mere testimonial" by comprising a work of fiction based on real events (310). Moreover, she adds, the work fluctuates between first and third person, Kozameh's voice and those of others, to convey a personal as well as communal story. In the foreword to Kozameh's book, Saúl Sosnowski states that its "legacy" remains the reconstruction of a world that few will want to know (xiv). In the preface, Kozameh asserts that "every episode is real; it happened" (xv), whether to herself or her *compañeras* who also lived it. It was written, she concludes, "so that events could be known" (xvi).

For Partnoy, too, her "drive to tell," she says, "makes her translate her experiences into testimony, essay, song, theater, short story" (*Revenge* 13). Scholars of her work, such as Diana Taylor, agree that it represents autobiographical and testimonial literature (*Disappearing*). In her statements before human rights groups, in the introductions to her books, and in the appendices to *The Little School,* Partnoy presents facts that could indict her oppressors. Her literary work, however, as Taylor notes, brings the disappeared back to life as she also struggles to heal from her ordeal (*Disappearing*). Alike in their experiences, the memoirs of Partnoy and Kozameh, as M. Edurne Portela states, represent collective truths that offer an alternative version of history.

POLITICAL DEVELOPMENT

For Kozameh and Partnoy, radicalization came long before conception. Already primed by personal circumstances, both joined a larger body of women's writing intended to challenge the official story. Argentina's seven years of military rule, known as the *Processo*, was a period of state-sponsored repression and violence that resulted in approximately 30,000 deaths and disappearances. Coming of age during this time, both Partnoy and Kozameh joined resistance movements. Born in 1955, the year of the coup that overthrew Juan Perón, Partnoy later joined the Peronist movement at her university in Bahía Blanca (Taylor, "Portrait"). As military presence at the college increased, Partnoy stopped attending classes. In January 1977, she joined thousands of Argentines who were abducted from their homes (Taylor, "Portrait").

Alicia Kozameh also began her life-long quest for social justice as a student. At Nuestra Señora de la Misericordia School (Our Lady of Mercy) in Rosario, she participated in *Rosariarzo*, a large-scale demonstration against socioeconomic injustice (Díaz). Inspired by potential revolutionary changes in Cuba, Kozameh went on to the National University of Rosario. Like Partnoy, she became so immersed in political activism that she quit attending classes in order to avoid arrest. Apprehended by a paramilitary enforcement group in 1975, she was charged with being a member of the PRT (Worker's Revolutionary Party) (Díaz).

DIVERSITY WITHIN THE MOVEMENT

Neither a mother herself during incarceration nor a self-proclaimed feminist, Kozameh illustrates diversity within motherhood politics in Argentina. In her study of the relationship between motherhood and political action in Argentina, Jewel Perkins found that not all women viewed motherhood as positive. Some women saw creating a better world for their children as justification for political involvement, but others viewed motherhood as a burden. Alicia Partnoy, for example, asserted that she was risking her own life for the sake of her child's future. But, as Perkins notes, other women feared becoming their own mothers. Kozameh seems to fit somewhere in-between. She had seen her mother catering to her *machista* (male chauvinist) husband who abused the entire family. She also resented that at a very young age she was responsible for taking care her disabled older sister (Díaz). For these reasons, she might have feared perpetuating what patriarchal culture defined as motherhood. Nevertheless, she later planned the conception of her child to coincide with the inception of her first novel. Like some of the *Madres* who, as Partnoy notes, referred to their disappeared children as sources of positive transformation ("Textual Strategies"), Kozameh also conflates childbirth with creativity.

Moreover, Kozameh gives voice to approximately four hundred children who were taken away by authorities, often placed in homes of those responsible for their torture. In *Steps under Water*, Alicia Kozameh writes a first-hand account about a cell in which women kept their children with them for only three months at a time before giving them over to their families. Even worse, guards often murdered women after childbirth, and then gave away their offspring to be raised by military families.

CRITIQUES OF MATERNAL POLITICS: TRAPPED IN A "BAD SCRIPT"

As Annelise Orleck notes, adherents of maternal politics often overlook those women who support violent movements in the name of patriotism as well as to protect their own children. Indeed, even though women constituted one-third of the disappeared, others chose to deny the atrocities they saw before them. In *Steps under Water*, Kozameh also documents female guards who participated in the abuse of inmates. While these women disrupt the notion that mothers are innately more nurturing than men, Taylor focuses on the Mothers of the Plaza de Mayo to critique the whole notion of maternal politics as a viable liberation strategy. In *Disappearing Acts*, she discusses these elderly women who marched weekly with placards of their missing children, eventually becoming a model for women's human rights organizations in Latin America. Although not willing to dismiss them for reiterating the stereotype of motherhood that they attempted to subvert, Taylor asserts that they were "framed" (203), trapped in a "bad script" (202), in which they unwittingly played a part.

In particular, her reading faults the *Madres* for falling short of being feminists in the Western sense of the word. Although they left the confines of their homes, by continuing to care for their own families as well as young people who sought them out, Taylor asserts that they failed to challenge women's subordinate status in Argentina. Despite these limitations, she concludes that the *Madres* moved from biological, essentialist notions of motherhood to the politicized, collective role of Mothers of all the Disappeared. In this way they negotiated a new disruptive space in which they became women with more options. Moreover, by parading with photographs of their children, they gave voice to what was hidden, a process that Partnoy and Kozameh aim for in their writing.

OSTRICH LEGS:
QUESTIONING THE ROLE OF "GOOD MOTHER"

The *Madres*' use of public spectacle raises several questions about maternal politics addressed in this chapter: How is it possible for Partnoy to transform particular loyalty for her child into concern for all affected families? How do women claim the political strength that comes from maternal politics, yet avoid what Taylor says are "essentialist, natural and immutable qualities" ("Overview" 142)? In the writings of Kozameh and Partnoy, generalizations about "natural" abilities of individual mothers fall away. For example, in her autobiographical novel *Ostrich Legs*, Kozameh documents problems in real families like her own. Moreover, both writers go beyond maternal politics to challenge economic inequality, social norms, and exploitation of developing countries.

As Ana Luiza Libânio Dantas claims, the *junta* was a patriarchal system that used state-sponsored torture to create docile bodies. It also sought to make women obedient by appealing to their role as mothers (Taylor *Disappearing*). The abduction of Alicia Partnoy while her daughter watched, the abuse of loved ones in front of others, and the raids on homes of suspected "subversives" reveal how a small group of powerful officials controlled a population blinded to its abuse (Taylor *Disappearing*).

As opposed to "good" mothers, politically active women allegedly posed a threat to social harmony. In *Ostrich Legs*, Kozameh illustrates how the dynamics of power and subjugation are transformed from politics to the social realm. Ostensibly about the relationship between two sisters, one severely handicapped, the other gifted yet overlooked, Kozameh's text goes farther. In an interview with Gabriel San Román, Kozameh says that *Ostrich Legs* "reflects abuse of power in the environment of a South American family," but it is also "a metaphor for impunity in a country under a brutal dictatorship" (4). Indeed, her interest in social justice stems from childhood experiences. In her novel, she describes the abuse of power from a political perspective, but her work also stems from unequal relations at home. For example, her parents' lack of respect for the women who worked in their home, women from whom Alicia often found affection, led to her joining the *Partido* (Party) (Díaz).

In *Ostrich Legs*, Kozameh draws from her own experience as a young girl whose spirit was broken by uncaring parents. Written under psychoanalysis, a technique popular among writers who came of age during the repression (Díaz), but in this case also an effort to deal with issues that emerged after her daughter's birth (San Román), this novel depicts a father's absolute control within his family. As for the daughter Alicia/Alcira, there is a clear distrust of patriarchy, religious dogma, and the established political regime. Underlying the text is a critique of repression, particularly of a young girl's creativity but also a commentary on the state of affairs in Argentina.

In real life, Kozameh's mother was a housewife who benefited from her husband's status as a banker, yet suffered like the rest of the family from his chauvinistic behaviour. In life, as in the novel, her older sister's difficult birth marks the family's slide into chaos. Mentally and physically handicapped, Liliana absorbs the family's attention while her younger sister draws the brunt of her parents' anger (Díaz). The principles of power and domination dominate not just Argentine society; they also surface in such patriarchal family relations that structure Kozameh's family.

Ostrich Legs portrays the overwhelming power that parents have over children, particularly when the children are abused or ignored. Alcira is a young girl who has been neglected and betrayed by her parents. Like military men, who defined masculinity as domination over the feminized population, Alcira's father mirrored the Nationalist's quest for purity and domination. A metaphor for military generals who, like a strict father, took the welfare of their people into their own hands, he used force to control his daughter's behaviour. Alcira understood this chain of command: fathers had to act as military proxies required to police their children; mothers had to perform domestic duties; and children had to respect and obey their parents.

As a couple, her parents duplicate roles played by the military. On an outing to the movies, Alcira's "father [is] in the lead with [her] sister in his arms and [her] mother following him," (Kozameh, *Ostrich* 45), while their daughter brings up the rear. As usual, Alcira is the only one who has clear vision; as she watches "the three of them walking," it seems as if they are marching in military file, "going as if they had to go, fulfilling their duty" (*Ostrich* 45). As Taylor notes, in the militarized home, families mirror armies, "reorganized and hierarchical" (*Disappearing* 104) to the extreme.

Alcira/Alicia makes the invisible visible, the unreal real. Emblematic of a society manipulated into not seeing what is really going on, Alcira's mother is "sick in the eyes," (Kozameh, *Ostrich* 40) according to her daughter. She does not see what Alcira sees because it is not in her self-interest. Privilege accrues to those who perform their roles as "good mothers" (Kozameh, *Ostrich* 5). Alcira's mother "cooks all day and sweeps," (Kozameh, *Ostrich* 42) though not as much as Tini, the domestic who defines the family's station. Benefitting indirectly from her husband's rise in status, Alcira's mother always wears high heels. Although she plays her role according to Argentine tradition, her mother is not all that she should be. In this story, power shifts back and forth between mother and daughter; refusing to take Alcira's side against her father, she also tries to force her daughter into submission. Fighting for the right to live another life, Alcira fuelled her mother's anger over her own submission to authority.

Alcira's body becomes a site of conflict between her parents differing motives to control her, as well as the sexual politics played out by her neighbour Jorge. All are played against the backdrop of what Taylor calls "a theater of operations," a scenario that expressed "the theatricality, the medicalization, and the violence of the operation exercised simultaneously on social space and human bodies" (*Disappearing* 96). Just as the *junta* promised to cleanse the public sphere by attacking "feminine spaces and bod-ies" (Taylor, *Disappearing* 96), so Jorge vowed to use his mother's kitchen knife to gain supremacy over Alcira's body. "I was the one who selected the type of surgery," Jorge brags, "since I was, as in just about every case, the doctor and you the patient" (Kozameh, *Ostrich* 18). Jorge follows behind Alcira "wielding [his] scalpel and surgical instruments" (*Ostrich* 18). By seeking to rid Alcira of what fascinated/repulsed him, "something so utterly vile and showy" (*Ostrich* 18), Jorge mirrors the *junta*'s goals to purify the environment by eradicating radical contaminates.

"Mixing a kind of objectivity with [his] plans to nail [her] once and for all with that knife" (*Ostrich* 18), Jorge planned to put Alcira's offending body literally under the scalpel. In this context power intrudes into sexual relations between men and women as well as the social and political world in which they live. Jorge mirrors what Taylor calls the nationalist narrative, that of man creating himself through the annihilation of the feminine, and his own conception of the sexual encounter as an act of domination (*Disappearing*). At Liliana's funeral, the female body plays a starring role. When Jorge replaces the red carnation that Alcira placed between the fingers of her sister with a white one, Alcira challenges his notions of sexual purity. Refusing to erase her sister, Alcira transgresses her assigned role in the family/national drama. "There's no passion to be associated with her" (Kozameh, *Ostrich* 163), claims Jorge, thereby denying the sexuality of all women in the Christian State. "But Jorge," replies Alcira, "what the hell do you mean by 'purity.' Not to make love isn't natural" (*Ostrich* 167), thus turning what the *junta* claims is the "natural" role for women upside down. Not to be undone, Jorge appropri-ates the role of father by offering to take Alcira for a walk. "I'll tell your daughter what to do, I'll do what you do, I can replace you" (*Ostrich* 174), he tells her father. "I'm carrying out your objectives" (*Ostrich* 174), he continues, and thus moves up a peg in the patriarchal chain of command.

As power shifts from father to potential husband, Alcira struggles against social expectations of women in Latin American culture; at all times she acts outside of accepted social roles of virgin, mother, housewife, or matriarch. From the political, "I never thought the president [of Argentina] has to tell each person what to do. ... And if the guy comes over to my house to tell me stuff, I'm not going to listen to him at all" (*Ostrich* 98), to the personal, "but that's the way I am" (*Ostrich* 119), she gives voice to women's struggle against the power structures that determine social interaction. To transgress social responsibility, to "do what [she] likes" (*Ostrich* 98) with no regard for consequences, meant challenging not only familial values but also the State which defined nonconformity as subversion.

Knowing that there are risks involved, Alcira/Alicia takes possession of her own story by becoming a writer. Told by her parents that she is crazy because she acts outside of accepted social roles, Alcira agrees. Flaunting her difference, Alcira claims, "I really like it when people can tell I'm doing something different from what everybody else was doing" (*Ostrich* 119), thus separating herself from all the Argentines who played roles dictated by the *junta*. Betrayed by the world in which she lives, particularly the world of her parents, what Alcira wants is the beauty that she finds in words.

Kozameh's experience illustrates the danger of rallying women behind notions of "good mother," a role that she rejected after realizing that her own mother was not all that she claimed to be. Instead, she steps out of accepted social roles to become a writer who literally conflates biological conception with the birth of her second novel. Moreover, the participation of women such as Kozameh and Partnoy in the resistance movements encouraged more opportunities to move out of accepted roles as good mothers to formulate positions on the Dirty War. In this way, other women, too, have come to realize that what they once considered "women's issues" are not isolated problems. According to Orleck, women often moved beyond their roles as "individual mothers" by organizing as collective caretakers of all children (9).

TORTURED THROUGH MOTHERHOOD:
THE IMPACT ON THREE GENERATIONS OF WOMEN'S FAMILIES

Partnoy's prison memoir illustrates how certain conceptions of what constitutes good motherhood varies according to political belief. In this way, as Taylor [which reference?] states, armed forces conflated the image of Patria even as they sought to undo familial and social bonds. According to Dantas, military regimes are by de facto patriarchal systems. In Argentina, Danta continues, the *junta* wanted to break specific groups' identities, particularly women who were assaulted through their motherhood. Indeed, women who played active roles as students and/or community workers made up one third of the disappeared (Taylor, *Disappearing*). This gendering of the enemy resulted in an assault on captive women's reproductive organs, familial bonds, and finally on their lives (Taylor, *Disappearing*). As Partnoy states, "The military attacked us as mothers, in our motherhood" (Taylor, "Portrait" 199 [Partnoy or Taylor; qtd in Taylor?]). In this way, as Taylor claims, armed forces conflated the image of motherhood with the Patria even as they sought to undo familial and social bonds ("Portrait"). These experiences are reflected in the lives and literary works of both authors.

Kidnapped in front of her small daughter, Partnoy had no knowledge of Ruth's fate for several months (*Little*). In one of her most painful memories, she relates hearing her husband being tortured in a nearby room, then told that she would be turned into soap for being Jewish (*Little*). When asked if women were tortured more than men, she replied: "It's not even ethical to ask that question. Torture is torture is torture" (qtd in? Taylor, "Portrait" 199). While guards beat men like her husband, they tailored torture in other ways specifically for women. In fact, the military's strategy, as her stories show, destroyed generational as well as communal bonds. As Partnoy writes, parents went through agony not knowing what path might best set free their children. While Partnoy was transferred to a women's prison where she could receive family visitations, her daughter could not touch her through the glass shield. On the other hand, male prisoners had no such glass, no such microphones, separating them from their families (Taylor, "Portrait").

By breaking the links between mother and child, the military attacked women through their motherhood. Partnoy and her husband reappeared, but their marriage did not survive. Despite associating motherhood with activism, Partnoy knew that she would still face painful contradictions. Like others, she was conflicted. "When we get into activism," she admits, "we're depriving them [children] for the sake of the future of the present in which we should be building a relationship with them" (qtd in? Taylor, "Portrait" 197). Devastated during her parents' disappearance, her oldest daughter felt destroyed again after the birth of Partnoy's second child. Because she did not want to witness a childhood that she never had, Partnoy's eldest went to live with her father. Though Partnoy relates that their relationship has been repaired, her family still lives with generational trauma inflicted by the *junta* (Taylor, "Portrait").

Even worse, some parents never reappeared. In Partnoy's concentration camp, Graciela Romero suffered electric shocks to her abdomen several months before giving birth. Like other children born to imprisoned mothers, her infant was most likely given to a military family to be brought up as their own (Partnoy, *Little*). More than a decade after the end of the *junta* the *Madres* continue to search for four hundred disappeared children who were taken from their parents. Graciela remains on Amnesty International's list of disappeared people. Her son, according to prison officials, was given to one of the guards (*Little*).

THE SOCIALIZATION OF MOTHERHOOD:
RECLAIMING MATERNAL POLITICS THROUGH A
COLLECTIVE VOICE

Just as the government used notions of motherhood to justify its actions, women manipulated those concepts that had previously controlled them. Confined to the domestic sphere, the *Madres*, for example, redefined conventions—providing nourishment and protection—by becoming moral guardians of the nation. Partnoy also views reclaiming motherhood as a form of revolutionary activism: "One of the things that women have to do when they're in the hands of the military is not *redefine* but *reclaim* their motherhood" (qtd. in Taylor, "Portrait" 202). Here she draws attention to the fact that motherhood is a social, not necessarily natural, construct.

According to Taylor, the *Madres* not only claimed public space as home, they also created new families based on political rather than biological connections (*Disappearing*). Kozameh, too, recreated a family among her peers. As a child, she learned to seek refuge from her parents by creating a "different reality" (Díaz 312) through writing. Later, Kozameh found with her activist friends "a camaraderie and closeness [she] had not experienced" with her family (Díaz 312). Her new home is a negotiated space reshaped by her situation.

In the context of struggle, Partnoy also expanded the notion of community. Not estranged from her own family, as was Kozameh, she nevertheless appreciated how the *Madres* redefined motherhood as a collective performance. In prison, Partnoy transforms poetry written for Ruth to fit any prisoner's child. Writing for specific occasions, something she had "always shied away from," not only helps her survive, she finds it also "helps her lift the spirit of her friends" (*Revenge* 14). In this way she takes on the suffering of all the captive mothers.

Partnoy responds to grief, as did the *Madres*, by becoming a mother to all the prisoners' children. In "Textual Strategies to Resist Disappearance and the Mothers of the *Plaza de Mayo*," Partnoy discusses how certain women became spokespeople for all the disappeared. What Partnoy calls *socialización* (socialization) of motherhood leads to a discourse of resistance. According to Taylor, the *Madres* also threatened the military machine because they invoked the "birthing capabilities" ("Portrait" 198) that the *junta* claimed for itself. As Partnoy claims: "I didn't save myself / What saved me / were the feet of my parents / walking" (*Little* 31) in front of government buildings. "It was very important to me," she recalls, "they brought me back to life, which is why I always say that the Mothers gave birth to me" (qtd. in Taylor, "Portrait" 99). By attracting international attention to the plight of the disappeared, the *Madres* enabled Partnoy's survival.

In her collection of short stories, *The Little School*, and in bilingual poetry, *Revenge of the Apple* and *Little Flying Low*, Partnoy rescripts history as *testimonio*, a powerful mode of writing as resistance. In testimonial texts such as *The Little School*, Partnoy furnishes facts about the concentration camps that could convict her attackers, but there are also fictive sections. In "Textual Strategies," Partnoy describes how the *Madres* used literature as a form of protest by "transform[ing] ... absence into presence through the written word" (3). Writing in this mode, Partnoy, too, claims to have written *The Little School* not only to heal herself, but also to bring back all the disappeared (*Little*). In her poem "Testimonial," an homage to the "many [who] do not return," Partnoy "open[s] [her] mouth / and their voice speaks, a survivor" (*Revenge* 72) who speaks for those who do not have a voice.

By sharing their stories, Partnoy accomplishes what she calls a "discourse of solidarity," testimonials that come together as a collective story of the disappeared. Although not a *Madre* herself, she employs their literary strategies to challenge the *junta*'s discourse based on power. By highlighting community over individuality, Partnoy, like the *Madres*, creates a "community of allies" ("Textual Strategies" 5) among readers, publishers, and characters in her stories. Non-hierarchical in structure, this mode fits Partnoy's refusal to claim hero status for herself. Here Partnoy challenges patriarchal, individualist ideologies that devalue the maternal, communal values upheld by the *Madres*.

As Taylor observes, the military regime in Argentina produced a masculine, hierarchical structure that filtered into every area of life (*Disappearing*). By taking over public space, notes Partnoy, the *Madres* challenged this military standard by politicizing the connotations of traditional motherhood. As mothers of all the disappeared, they transformed biological notions of motherhood into a collective that emphasizes community over individual mothers ("Textual Strategies"). In this way, Partnoy, too, breaks down barriers between author/publisher/reader as well as hierarchical relationships within academia ("Textual Strategies"). As both activist and scholar, mother of her own child and a voice for all the disappeared, Partnoy privileges values associated with collective motherhood. Like the *Madres*, she also equates motherhood with creativity in the lives of women ("Textual Strategies"). Despite struggling with the after effects of prison, "life," for Partnoy, still brings to mind "the power of childbirth" (*Little* 118), a process much akin to birthing of the word. Both signify new life as bodies bear the next generation as well as collective memory.

In 1980 Kozameh, like Partnoy, fled Argentina. Since 1988 she has lived permanently in California. Like Partnoy, she began to write long before imprisonment. According to Dantas, Kozameh's texts "construct a horizontal relationship" by reflecting her own experience in dialogue with her *compañeras* (18). As Kozameh asserts, what she writes represents "a form of fictionalizing" not only her own reality but also a collective voice (qtd. in Dantas 60: fn. 18). As she switches from first person "I" to third person "we" Kozameh creates a discourse of solidarity between personal and collective voices. In this way, as Díaz notes, Kozameh moves beyond testimonial to write fiction based on personal experience (78). While in Villa Devoto she wrote two notebooks full of memories that would become the basis for *Steps under Water* (Díaz). Written in a circular mode, the last chapter connecting to the first, *Steps under Water* very much resembles the *Madres'* circular movements around the Plaza. As Taylor notes, the *Madres'* performance also reflected family and communal values (*Disappearing*). By filling empty streets they resurrected the oppressed. In this way, too, Kozameh translates disappearance into presence through the written word.

Kozameh's work joins other Latin American women writers who wrote *testimonios* that resist the authoritarian regime. Her third novel, *259 Saltos, uno immortal* (*259 Leaps, the Last Immortal*), published in 2001, focuses on her life in exile, particularly as it relates to issues of identity, alienation and perpetual travel. It takes place in California and Mexico, the latter of which she resided for a short time. In this work Kozameh employs a "discourse of solidarity" that speaks for those who do not have a voice. "What I write is a form of fictionalizing," she asserts, "not only my reality but a collective reality" (qtd. in Dantas 61; fn. 18) of the voices that travel with her. Along with this multiplicity of voices, Kozameh credits her daughter for being a source of creativity and transformation in her life. Kozameh began writing *Steps under Water* in 1983 at the same time that she became pregnant with Sara Julia, named after Sara in her novel. "Going through the manuscript," she remembers, "I got stuck on a group of 4 letters" that eventually became Sara. "And that group... [that] represented me throughout the book ... [also] represented the women contained in my existence" (Kozameh, *Leaps* 125). Alicia, Sara, and all the prison *compañeras* are conflated here, and all give birth to each other in the novel. Eventually, *259 Leaps* evolved from fragmentary paragraphs to chapters, a process that Kozameh likens to "the various odd forms" (Kozameh, *Leaps* 126) that the fetus takes during pregnancy. So child and book become "parallel events," both efforts (though neither would be quite sufficient, she admits) to bring back the voices of the dead (*Leaps* 125). "Exile is the rebirth of the word, what was conceived one day" (*Leaps* 116), she concludes, and in so doing, just as Partnoy credits the *Madres* with her birthing, Kozameh births herself.

CONCLUSION: THERE IS NO OVER THE ORDEAL

Partnoy and Kozameh belong to a group of Argentine women writers who came of age during the 1960s. Both turned to left-wing social movements because they wanted to leave a better world for future generations. In her poem "To My Daughter," Partnoy writes to Ruth from prison: "...to walk by your side / through a better world... / For those tasks / I know what is needed" (*Revenge* 15). Dedicated to the struggle, she brings to it her writing, her strength, her lyricism, and, if need be, her life; "It is for these tasks/ I am preparing / my word, my life, my fist and my / song" (*Revenge* 15).

Despite vowing "never [to] give ourselves up for defeated / while one person ... needs our shade" (*Revenge* 51), Partnoy increasingly lost hope after decrees from 1989-1990 declared wide-spread pardons for state terrorists. For Kozameh, too, there has been no closure. She revisited Argentina briefly with Sara, but returning home from celebrating publication of *Steps under Water* two men threatened to murder her and her daughter if she "did not stop publishing garbage and leave the country" (Díaz 316). For both women the struggle is not over. Their writing continues to reflect deliberate political strategies designed to mobilize broad resistance to the military regime. Cracking open the myth of biological and emotional essentialism that hide the reality of motherhood, Partnoy and Kozameh are reclaiming and reshaping the role that the *junta* used to control activist women. Like the *Madres*, who gradually came to consider themselves mothers of all the disappeared, both writers produced personal yet collective accounts that make visible their disappeared *compañeras*. In her analysis of the *Madres'* literary work, Partnoy goes beyond what she terms the "truth value" ("Textual Strategies" 2) of their texts to highlight discourses of solidarity that privilege a community of reader/author/subject/publisher over individual writer of the work. Following in this mode, both Kozameh and Partnoy feature multiple voices interacting on an equal basis.

Understanding that activism comes with risks, both found a political strength that comes with claiming maternal politics. Nevertheless, they claim motherhood in different ways. Partnoy attributed her activism to wanting a better future for her daughter. At the time of abduction she was already the mother of a young child. Kozameh did not give birth to Sara Julia until years after she fled Argentina. While she might have delayed pregnancy because she did not want to become her mother, she eventually equated the birth of her own child with literary creativity. Partnoy, too, referred to the simultaneous recovery of her child and her poetry as a positive transformation in her life. As with other mother activists within the movement in Argentina, concerns for children proved a powerful inspiration in their lives.

WORKS CITED

Alvarez, Julia. *The Little School*. By Partnoy. San Francisco: Cleis Press, 1998. Print.

Dantas, Ana Luiza Libânio. "The Autonomous Sex: Female Body and Voice in Alicia Kozameh's Writing of Resistance." Diss. Ohio University, 2008. Web. Accessed April 2014.

Díaz, Gwendolyn. *Women and Power in Argentina Literature: Stories, Interviews, and Critical Essays*. Austin: University of Texas Press, 2007. Print.

Kozameh, Alicia. *259 Leaps, The Last Immortal*. Trans. Claire Sullivan. San Antonio: Wings Press, 2007. Print.

Kozameh, Alicia. *Ostrich Legs*. Trans. David Davis. San Antonio: Wings Press, 2013. Print.

Kozameh, Alicia. *Steps Under Water*. Trans. David Davis. Berkeley: University of California Press, 2001. Print.

Orleck, Annelise. "Tradition Unbound: Radical Mothers in International Perspective." *The Politics of Motherhood: Activist Voices from Left to Right*. Eds. Alexis

Jetter, Annelise Orleck, and Diana Taylor. Hanover: University Press of New England, 1997. 3-23. Print.

Partnoy, Alicia. *The Little School*. San Francisco: Cleis Press, 1998. Print.

Partnoy, Alicia. *Revenge of the Apple / Venganza de la Manzana*. San Francisco: Cleis Press, 1992. Print.

Partnoy, Alicia. "Textual Strategies to Resist Disappearance and the Mothers of the *Plaza de Mayo*." *Florida Atlantic Comparative Studies Journal* 12 (2010-2011): 21-27. Web. 5 April 2014.

Partnoy, Alicia. *Volando Bajito / Little Flying Low*. Trans. Gail Wronsky. Los Angeles: Red Hen Press, 2005. Print.

Perkins, Jewel. "Motherhood and Political Action during Argentina's Dirty War: An Analysis of Argentinean Feminine Literature." *Chrestomathy: Annual Review of Undergraduate Research, School of Humanities, Social Sciences, College of Charleston* 4 (2005): 178-194. Web. 5 April 2014.

Portela, M. Edurne. *Displaced Memories: The Poetics of Trauma and Argentine Women's Writing*. Lewisburg: Bucknell University Press, 2011. Print.

San Román, Gabriel. "Alicia Kozameh, The Hypnotic Novelist." *OCC Weekly*. 7 March 2013. Web. 5 April 2014.

Sosnowski, Saúl. *The Little School*. Trans. David Davis. Berkeley: University of California Press, 2001. Print.

Smith, Kathryn. "Female Voice and Feminist Text: *Testimonio* as a Form of Resistance In Latin America." *Florida Atlantic Comparative Studies Journal* 12 (2010-2011): 21-37. Web. 5 April 2014.

Taylor, Diana. "Alicia Partnoy: A Self Portrait." *The Politics of Motherhood: Activist Voices from Left to Right*. Eds. Alexis Jetter, Annelise Orleck, Diana Taylor. Hanover: University Press of New England, 1997. 198-204. Print.

Taylor, Diana. *Disappearing Acts: Spectacles of Gender and Nationalism in Argentina's "Dirty War."* Durham: Duke University Press, 1997. Print.

Taylor, Diana. "Overview: Environmental Justice." *The Politics of Motherhood: Activist Voices from Left to Right.* Eds. Alexis Jetter, Annelise Orleck, Diana Taylor. Hanover: University Press of New England, 1997: 23-28. Print.

17.
Lamentation in Classical Antiquity

Telling the Truth About Women, Children and War

KRISTINA PASSMAN NIELSON

IN *DOMINATION AND THE ARTS of Resistance: Hidden Tran-scripts*, James C. Scott documents the ways in which the most powerless members of cultures perform the public script of deference and submission as a survival strategy and the hidden resistances that offer affirmation of humanity, solidarity, and comfort. The places where public and hidden transcripts can come together are those occasions of public commemoration or ritual, where in the presence of the power elites "subordinates may gather outside the intimidating gaze of power," and where "a sharply dissonant political culture is possible" (18). This paper develops the ancient origins of this form of resistance by investigating the words of the most powerless—women taken captive in war, and, where we have the evidence, mothers taken captive in war. Scott further argues:

> This is a politics of disguise and anonymity that takes place in public view but is designed to have a double meaning or to shield the identity of the actors.... A partly sanitized, ambiguous, and coded version of the hidden transcript is always present in the public discourse of subordinate groups. (19)

In conflict regions today, mothers tell their truth of grief and loss, their words and bodies serving as witnesses. Calling these words (and silence) "lament," Nancy Lee makes a clear connection be-tween resistance, witness, social justice, and embodiment:

A modern-day women's protest movement against war, death, and violence, Women in Black started in Jerusalem in 1988 when Jewish and Palestinian women stood together silently in public, wearing black, a sign of mourning. Such women's protest movements inspire one another across cultures, including the Black Sash in South Africa and the Madres de la Plaza de Mayo in Argentina. Today these women, often mothers who have lost children, are living witnesses and symbols of women survivors over the millennia that have bourne grievous losses and lamented across cultures. They have ... decided to protest silently what they have endlessly been called upon to lament.[1] (*Lyrics of Lament* 34-5)

Until quite recently, written words inscribed the truth of an event from the standpoint of the victor. Written words can be lost through destruction, and identities erased (on forced forgetting; see Connerton). Oral transmission, incorporated in the body of the one telling, lasts as long as one person remembers and tells another. The powerless, literate or not, tend to believe the information gleaned orally from their peers; those in power rely upon peer information and written documents that maintain and further their ideology, status, and vested interests (Connerton; Scott; McClure). Whether the confrontation is silent, as in many contemporary acts of witness on the part of women, or memorialized in a written document, as in our ancient past, women use their bodies as their instruments of challenge to "the official story." "While all lament prayers, poems or songs are 'embodied' when spoken or performed, these women (i.e. contemporary women bearing silent witness) embody lament silently" (Lee, *Lyrics of Lament* 35).

In this paper, I suggest a conceptual affinity between ancient lamentation and contemporary lamentation, or "bearing witness," as embodied by culturally permitted forms of grief and loss on the part of women. Taking as my premise that for archaic Mediterranean culture lamentation texts reflected women's ritual and influenced the development of later Greek lamentation, I suggest that the War at Troy, because of its ubiquity in classical antiquity and throughout Europe up to the present day, has become emblematic of the experience of many mothers in wartime. At the same time, Sumerian, and later Biblical lamentation is a continuation of the lamentation tradition of the Ancient Near East, forms that are replicated in ancient and contemporary Islamic and Jewish poetry and prayers (Lee; Mandolfo; O'Connor; Suter). As a permitted and public ritual form, lamentation allowed women to publically tell their truth about war and its consequences for them and their children, creating a public script that affirmed the superiority of the victors, as well as a private script that questioned the maintenance of the ideological status quo of war, conquest, murder, and enslavement.

LAMENTATION: A BRIEF INTRODUCTION

Lamentation is an ancient formalized poetry of pain and loss; lamentation may be the lament for a lost loved one, or a communal lament after a great disaster (Alexiou). Our oldest written examples come from Sumer, and involve communal lamentation of the type called the "Lament for the Destruction of the City." Scholars have long believed that ritual lamentation was exclusively the province of women in the sex-segregated societies of the ancient western Mediterranean world.[2]

Cities were gendered as female and thought of as mothers; the imagery of violation and rape, used throughout the "Lament for the Destruction of the City," conflated the experience of captive women with the fate of the city. In ancient laments for the loss of the city, violation is often indicated symbolically through the ritual tearing of clothing and veils, and the uncovering and loosening of hair (Lee, "The Singers of Lamentations"; Alexiou). The conquered city was abandoned by the gods meant to protect her, leading to her destruction. This abandonment and death of the men left the women without protection, leading to the destruction of self and identity through rape, erasure of motherhood through the murder of children or eternal separation, slavery and exile. (Dué; Langdon).

This fragment illustrates the god Enki abandoning the city of Eridu, and the priestess, like Cassandra at Troy, becoming a captive woman:

Enki took an unfamiliar path away from Eridug. Damgal-nuna, the mother of the E-maḫ, wept bitter tears. "Alas the destroyed city, my destroyed house," she cried bitterly. Its sacred Ĝipar of en priesthood was defiled. Its en priestess was snatched from the Ĝipar and carried off to enemy territory.[3]

ANCIENT GREECE: *APORIA* AND ABJECTION

When we look at classical Athenian drama, the idea of *aporia* is an essential element. *Aporia* means that there is no way out of a catastrophic situation, no hope or recourse for mercy or rescue, and indicates the moment that the protagonist realizes this. In dramas about the Trojan War when the protagonist is female, *aporia* does not function in the same way it does for other dramas. There is no actual error of *Ate*, the cognitive blindness leading to *Hubris*, there is no agency powered by arrogance to bring about the willful refusal to face the truth, bringing about disaster. Male protagonists are members of the power elite, and are privileged as such in a strict patriarchal society. Their interest is in maintaining the ideological status quo at any cost, and their agency is unlimited. In this way, their hubris leads to loss of status and social death unless a god intervenes to assure the fated ideological continuity is upheld (Foley).

When the protagonists are elite women, their agency is already exceptionally circumscribed; their sphere of action limited to their households, and any decision subject to approval by male relatives, one of whom will be a legal guardian. This guardian, be he father, husband, uncle, brother, or son, has the authority to make all decisions pertaining to the woman or girl regarding her life and social status (Pomeroy; Tyrell).[4]

The public appearance of women and girls was limited by law to ritual occasions, such as festivals, and important transition periods—weddings (the transfer of a girl from one household to another) and funerals (Loraux; Pomeroy; Stears). A woman or girl member of the elite class lived a life of *aporia*, with no way out and no voice except through the carefully controlled public arena of ritual, including lamentation.

WAR AND MEMORY: HOMER'S TROY

Myth-history was known and transmitted in the oral culture of the Greek archaic period (800-480 BCE). The memory of the Trojan War and its consequences marked the transition from the Age of Heroes (Bronze Age) to the Age of Men (Iron Age) (Hesiod). Because the narrative of the Trojan War was memorized, sung, and thus performed, the Singer (known as the Rhapsode) *became* the tale; it was incorporated into his body and his performance was a ritual in and of itself (Connerton; Lord).[5]

The *Iliad* ends before the destruction of Troy. Women's lamentations in the *Iliad*, especially at the funeral obsequies for Hector, close the epic, announcing and preparing the audience for the destruction of the city to come. The women of Troy perform the ritual lamentation utilizing the themes found in the "Destruction of the City."[6] At a time probably much earlier than Homer, the lamentations were adapted into Greek oral narrative traditions.

Here, then, is the description and part of the dirge for Hector from the end of the *Iliad*:

> ...and the women made lament.
> Among them white-armed Andromachê
> led the dirge for Hector, the killer of men, holding his head
> in her hands: 'O my husband, you have perished at a
>   young age,
> and left me a widow in our halls. Our child is still an infant,
> whom we bore, you and I, doomed to a wretched fate.
>   But I don't think
> he will arrive at manhood—before that this city shall be
>   utterly
> destroyed. For you who watched over the city have
>   perished—
> you, who guarded it and kept safe its noble wives and little
> children. Soon they will be carried away in the hollow ships,
> and I among them. You, my child, will follow along with me
> to a place where you will perform degrading tasks, working
> for some ungentle master—or one of the Achaeans in his
>   anger

will take you by the arm and throw you from the walls
to a savage death—
(24.703-716)

Dirges, laments for heroes, celebrate their heroism while
mourning their loss. Heroes strive for glory (*kleos*), which is
their immortality—they will be remembered through stories of
their bravery. But something is happening here, at the end of
this terrible war. In the three extended dirges for Hector that
close the *Iliad*, Andromache and the other women do not glorify
Hector's prowess in battle. They grieve over his loss, and they
mourn the consequences to them, to their children, and to Troy.
There is nothing to celebrate. This defeat is a disruption of the
ideology of the Heroic Code, spoken *in extremis*, erupting from
unbearable loss (Scott). Having lost everything as they watched
their loved ones die in pursuit of *kleos*, the women know that
there is worse to come, and they cannot (or will not) celebrate the
heroic deeds that have led to destruction. Foley notes, "Women
historically played the role not only of physically lamenting the
dead but of expressing and even acting on views that from Homer on challenged public ideology about death and glory" (14).
By speaking their truth they openly interrogate the prevailing
ideology of heroism (Perkell).

EURIPIDES' TROY: FROM INCORPORATION TO INSCRIPTION

The *Iliad* and *Odyssey* were written down under Pericles (495-
429 BCE), who feared the works would be lost as fewer devoted
themselves to memorizing and performing the epics. This reflected the larger movement, primarily urban and elite, from oral
transmission (physical and performative) to the development of
a written literature. The inscription of words "sets" them in an
unchanging form unless they are destroyed. They create a form
of memory—the memory of those who have access to the written
word. At the same time, a great deal of communal memory remains in oral form, available to those without literacy or access.
The written word remained under control of the elite males of
Athens, and for the non-elite information and knowledge was

exchanged orally (Connerton; McClure; Scott).

Euripides is recognized for his insight into the lives of women under Athenian patriarchy. Writing in the midst of the Peloponnesian War, he used the tales surrounding the Trojan War as a means of commenting upon the experience and consequences of this war of attrition and the fates of those involved. The Peloponnesian War lasted 30 years (431-404 BCE), and the ethics of conduct degraded as the war went forward. Many atrocities were committed, and perhaps the most horrifying was the slaughter of men and boys on the neutral island of Melos in 416 BCE, immortalized in Thucydides.[7] Foley points to the connections between this event and the enslavement of women and murder of elite male children as an example of moral degradation and the justification of expediency, major themes in *The Trojan Women*.

Dué argues convincingly that the Athenians were well aware of the suffering of the defeated in myth and history; victims were publically and sympathetically memorialized throughout Athens. In what follows, I discuss two of the most poignant plays of Euripides about the Trojan War, one at the beginning of the war, and the other at the end.

IPHIGENIA AT AULIS:
"WE ARE A FREE PEOPLE, THEY ARE SLAVES"

Prior to the Hellenes' arrival on the shore of Troy, the moral action begins with the sacrifice of Agamemnon's virgin daughter, Iphigenia (Loraux).[8] It is perhaps the most cynical and effective depiction of the fate of mothers and daughters in conflict situations of the time, and in the play Euripides goes against the prevailing vilification of Clytemnestra by drawing on the mythological "back story" for her later murder of her husband.

Iphigenia, "child of sorrow," was the product of Clytemnestra's rape and coerced marriage to Agamemnon. Stung by Helen's rejection, and her choice of his brother, Menelaus, Agamemnon settled on possessing Helen's mortal twin, Clytemnestra, through the murder of her husband and newborn son. A survivor, Clytemnestra adapted to her new life as queen in Mycenae, and bore three other children, Chrysothemis, Elektra, and Orestes.

When the Achaean fleet was becalmed on the island of Aulis, the priest-seer Calchas, aided by Odysseus, convinced Agamemnon that it was because the goddess Artemis was angry, and demanded a human sacrifice, a pure virgin, his daughter Iphigenia. Agamemnon sought to trick his wife and his daughter into thinking Iphigenia was to wed Achilles, and ordered Clytemnestra not to travel with her daughter to the wedding. Custom and women's ritual roles favoured Clytemnestra and she accompanied her daughter, bringing along suitable noble young virgins for the ritual of the wedding ceremony.

Inevitably, Iphigenia and Clytemnestra learn the truth and face the *aporia*. Adding further to the horror, as a sacrifice Iphigenia had to go willingly to the altar, for unless the sacrificial animal went to the altar without hesitation, the sacrifice itself was considered ill omened (Loraux).

Through the dialogue of the play, the audience comes to know what Iphigenia knew: that the sacrifice of her life would most likely save the lives of her family, that the army was a monster that could not be swayed, and that her death would destroy her mother. Her public speech, then, is highly coded. She says the right words to protect her family, and her words allow her to die with dignity. Iphigenia begs her mother to be brave; she is dying for a great cause. What she is actually doing is pleading with her mother to comply, to give the appearance of agreement with her daughter's noble declaration that she has chosen to die for the sake of Greek glory. In a speech that is a masterful example of a coded transcript articulated publically, she presents her death as an event to be celebrated, and equivalent to a marriage—a glorious sacrifice to the gods. Reversing the expected lamentation for the unnatural sacrifice of a human girl, she forbids Clytemnestra to mourn her, but to think of her sacrifice as *kleos*, heroic glory:[9]

> The future of our Greek women rests upon my actions.
> The barbarians will no longer abduct them and carry them
> off from our wealthy shores, once Helen's abduction by
> Paris has been avenged.
> My death will bring about all this liberation and my good
> name will live into eternity. People will talk about how

I've saved Greece.

And then ... there's also this: what right do I have to love my life so much?

You haven't given birth to me simply for your own sake! No, you've brought me to life so that the whole of Greece may rejoice!

How can I insult all those countless brave warriors and their shields, all those myriads of men, clasping hard at the oars –men with courage enough to attack our enemy and die for our country, to clear her name?

How can I insult them all—insult their efforts, by trying to save myself—I, one, single life?

Would that be just?

What would my excuse be, mother?

And then there's yet this:

...For a mere woman? No, mother!

No, I'd rather see the death of a thousand women than that of a single man!

A goddess, mother, the goddess Artemis has called for my body.

How could I, a mortal, go against that? I could not. I shall give it to her for the sake of Greece.

Come! All of you! Prepare my sacrifice. Soldiers go and tear down Troy!

Let that act be what I'll be remembered by. Let that stand for me in place of the children and the marriage I could have had.

Let that be my fame!

Let the Greeks win, mother, not the barbarians.

We are a free people, whereas they are slaves.

(1380-1402)[10]

The chorus of young virgins, taking their cue from Iphigenia, sings not a lamentation or a dirge, but a victory song:

O look at the girl who walks
To the goddess' altar
That Troy may be brought low

And the Phrygian die.
Behold, she walks
With her hair in garlands of honor,
And flung upon her body the lustral waters.
(1510-16)

Iphigenia is depicted, and embodies, the willing sacrifice—hair garlanded, lustral water sprinkled, making no physical resistance as she mounts to the altar. The subversive text she speaks to her mother and to the girls who could suffer a similar fate, are of survival beyond the horror. The virgins' ambiguous public tribute to the murder of a young girl with no way out (*aporia*), who still has the moral agency of saving her family and choosing a brave death, well-illustrates a public script of the powerless adopted by those who have learned the postures and words for survival.

THE TROJAN WOMEN: "TROY NO LONGER EXISTS"

The Trojan Women is a play of lamentation. Performed in 415 BCE shortly after the massacre at Melos in 416, it is viewed by many as a direct response to the horrors of war. Euripides was careful to put into the mouths of the now enslaved chorus of Trojan women the hope that Athens might be their destination, both good politics on the playwright's part and reflective of the distancing Athens practiced from the impious practices at the end of the Trojan War on the part of the Achaeans (Dué; Foley).[11]

The play opens with Hecuba, the queen mother of Troy. She has lost all her children (Polyxena, her youngest daughter, unbeknownst to her, has been sacrificed) save her mad daughter, the priestess Cassandra. Her small grandson, Astyanax, still lives at the opening of the play, but he, too, will be killed, hurled from the battlements of Troy, to preclude any future vengeance against the Greeks on the part of the Trojans.

She is an old woman, the embodiment of grief and survival. She spends much time silent, prostrate in the dust before the partly destroyed city. When she does speak, she speaks of the loss of her children, and of her terrible future as slave to Odysseus, who has brought so much horror into Troy with the Trojan Horse. She plays a maternal role with the other Trojan women and girls about to become slaves and concubines in the homes of the enemy Greeks. She counsels them on choosing to live, to make what future they can for themselves. Her care and strength are apparent when, in the hearing of the other women immediately after learning of her daughter Polyxena's death, she speaks to Hector's widow Andromache:

> ...beloved child, you must forget
> what happened with Hector. Tears will never save you now.
> Give your obedience to your new master; let your ways
> Entice his heart to make him love you. If you do
> It will be better for all who are close to you.
> (Euripides, *The Trojan Women* 697-701)

When Hecuba speaks to Menelaus, endeavouring to convince him that Helen, who is among the captives, should be killed, she uses the rhetoric of the wise older woman, the woman who knows what is proper for a captive woman to do, to persuade him. When she agonizes over the murder of her grandson, she calls, too, on the idea of *nomoi*, of the ancient laws that prevent impiety and hold society together. Foley asks rhetorically, "What kind of political statement is Euripides making ... in pointedly assigning women (specifically mothers) to defend these ancestral laws to men?" (276).

As portended in the *Iliad*, Astyanax is killed. In the absence of Andromache, who has been taken away before she can tend to her murdered child, Hecuba must quickly gather the remaining Trojan women to properly perform the funeral rites. In the dirge for Astyanax, there is no glorification of war. She prepares the child's body for burial, and mourns:

> ...In vain
> we sacrificed.
> ...
> You may go now, and hide the dead in his poor tomb;
> He has those flowers that are the right of the underworld.
> I think it makes small difference to the dead, if they

Are buried in the tokens of luxury. All this
Is empty glorification for those who live.
(Euripides, *The Trojan Women* 1241-1250)

Hecuba embodies the mothers and grandmothers who have lost all—their city, their culture, their freedom, their children, their grandchildren: the future. Her witness is silent and she also speaks—of loss, of survival, of the uselessness of the war.

CONCLUSION

In times of defeat in war, all over the Mediterranean world and well past the Roman Empire, elite women, as well as women and girls of all other classes, became captive women—enslaved prizes of the victors, allotted to them according to status, and destined to leave the ruins of their city, separated from all that was familiar and customary (Dué; Foley; Lee; Langdon). All surviving elite boy-children would be killed to avoid the threat of future vengeance.[12]

The characterizations, words, and performances I have discussed draw upon the historical experiences of war and conflict in the ancient Mediterranean world and the written or oral memory of these events. Women and girls were not educated, and there was doubtless the oral private transcript and possibly communal memory of the experience of mothers, children, and families during and after war, a pattern reinforced by the patriarchal hegemony of these ancient cultures, sex segregation of elite (and possible not elite women), and analyses of power, resistance, and social memory that I have suggested (Pomeroy, Foley, Connerton, Scott).

Grounded in myth-history, representations of women's words and postures offer a challenge to the hegemonic and patriarchal discourse of war, violent conflict, and heroic glory. They serve to put an individual human face and an implacable reminder of the truth of what defeat in war actually means for those who have little or no social agency.

At the same time, women in these ancient cultures were not completely powerless: they have been represented as having a voice and agency through coded speech and lamentation. When captive elite women were subordinated, enslaved, stripped of status, religion, and identity, and bereft of family, they were permitted the articulation of their fear and pain through ritual lamentation.[13] Combining music, wailing, poetry, and ritual gestures, the corporate community of captive women, about to go into exile, spoke the truth of their condition in the presence of each other and their captors (Euripides, *The Trojan Women*; Dué; McClure). To lament is to resist. It is to speak truth to power through formal language and subversive words. In some cases, males will show empathy for the terrible losses women have suffered in the plays we have discussed; in one instance, Achilles even seeks to intervene (Euripides, *Iphigenia in Aulis*). In most cases, however, there is no empathy, there is no compassion.[14]

The denial of truth and the refusal of empathy to mothers who have lost all is a great outrage: the outrage of erasure of entire lives and traditions seen in collective phrases, such as the Disappeared, the Lost Generation, the Holocaust, ethnic cleansing, and genocide. Yet, these dead will not be erased, and have not been erased as long as there are those who put their bodies and lives on the line and speak their truth—overtly or covertly, supporting each other to survival and memory. These bodies loved husbands, cherished siblings, and bore children. These bodies must now bear witness.

Primarily the province of women and mothers in antiquity and today, mourning and lament continue to be embodied by those who stand in witness, providing testimony to suffering and loss as violent conflict continues. The Madres make statements silently, with their presence. The communal nature of mourning and insistence for justice is present, for example, in the worldwide response to the girls abducted by Boka Haram: "These are our daughters. It's like it's my daughter missing. Every single one of those girls is my daughter," Okonjo-Iweala (quoted in Abubakar and Levs) said. Since that day, a worldwide movement, "Bring Back our Girls," has arisen and gains strength (Litoff). The unsuccessful attempts of mainland China to obstruct all references to Tianamen Square on June 4, 2014, is another example of those in power seeking to erase the memory of a horrific incident that brings into question official ideology. The Tianamen Mothers Group, like other such groups, works to keep alive the memory of the massacre and to find answers to the deaths of their children. These actions, made in resistance to those in power, provide a counter-narrative of truth and reality to the mediated filters of ideological rhetoric.

Lamentation's concern is communal mourning and the cry for truth and justice, which might, if empathy is awakened, contain the seeds of healing (Lee; O'Connor; Segall). When, in cultures where women cannot speak, and a Euripides articulates the truth of war and loss, presented by boys and men dressed as women and using women's speech to the brokers of power, is it not possible that empathy may be born then, or, if not then, when we, who live with conflict on a daily basis, hear these words?

AFTERWORD

In January 2014, the UN Refugee Agency featured a story of Syrian refugees giving a performance in Arabic of *The Trojan Women*. In the story it was pointed out that "the play's anti-war theme clearly resonated with its cast of twenty-four Syrian refugee women, who wove their personal stories of the Syrian conflict into the production. Euripides focused his play of 415 BCE on the horrific aftermath of the Trojan War from the perspective of the women of Troy, the ruins of which lie in modern Turkey" (Habteslasie).

[1]The responses to the abduction of Nigerian schoolgirls by Boka Haram, offer a contemporary, cross-cultural example (Abubakar and Levs). The history of the Madres shows similar sentiments ("Speaking Truth to Power Madres of the Plaza de Mayo"). For more on lamentation and contemporary social justice and witness movements see essays edited by Lee and Mandolfo.
[2]Recently Bachvarova has argued that Sumerian *Gala* priests—transvestite eunuchs in service to the state and the gods—may have performed ritual laments dressed as women and representing them in a society where women's public appearances were limited. If this can be more fully established, it may be a link establishing cross-cultural continuity to the practice of ephebic males playing the roles of women in ancient Greek drama (Bachvarova; Zeitlin).

[3]A more complete fragment, dating from around 2000 BCE: "Damgalnuna, the mother of the E-maḫ, wept bitter tears. 'Alas the destroyed city, my destroyed house,' she cried bitterly. Its sacred Ĝipar of en priesthood was defiled. Its en priestess was snatched from the Ĝipar and carried off to enemy territory.... She loudly sang out a lament over those untravelled mountains: 'I am queen, but I shall have to ride away from my possessions, and now I shall be a slave in those parts.... Alas, the destroyed city, my destroyed house,' she cried bitterly. My queen, though not the enemy, went to enemy land" ("Lament for Urim and Sumer," lines 243-250, 271-280). The major themes are evident: Enki, the god of wisdom (and mischief), abandons the city (section not quoted); the queen is weeping, the sacred rites are defiled and the priestess carried off. The change in status, from elite to slave, and the total destruction of the city and the bloodline ("house") completes the essence of the lament.

[4]Historical accuracy, as we know it, did not exist in Greek drama. Social practices and status were based upon what the playwright knew, in these cases, Classical Athens. When Athenian authors interpreted the Trojan War, it was interpreted through their contemporary lens.

[5]Much as Westerners can tell from the opening bars of music whether a piece is jazz, classical, Gospel, etc., the ancients experienced genre through rhythm, performance, and presentation. See note 4. The Rhapsode was presenting sacred history, inspired by the Muses, using formalized gestures and meters that indicated what we call genre today.

[6]The term *Western Semitic* was first used in 1781 by Ludwig Slozer, to refer to a collection of languages in southwestern Asia that were related to Hebrew. As cultural studies developed and people understood the connection between culture and language, it has come to refer to the ancient languages and ethnicities (ancient and modern) of the area. The geography of the area at the time of Troy (second millennium BCE) was full of trade and cultural exchange, and covered the Middle East to the Sinai Peninsula and Malta, as well as Anatolia. Troy, located in ancient Anatolia, was part of the continuity of the Western Semitic cultural region (Bachvarova).

[7]Thucydides, Melian dialogue 5.84-116. In the sixteenth year of the war, the Melians, who tried to remain neutral, were told they had the choice of dying or living as slaves. The Melians refused to submit, the Athenians besieged them, and finally the Melians surrendered and put themselves in the hands of the Athenians. The Athenians killed all the men of military age, made slaves of the women and children, and colonized the place with five hundred men.

[8]The Trojan War ends with a similar virgin sacrifice, that of Polyxena, Clytemnestra's youngest daughter.

[9]This sets up the play *Agamemnon*, where the repressed fury of Clytemnestra can no longer be contained upon her husband's return ten years later.

[10]Translated by George Theodoridis.

[11]Dué shows the Athenian attitude that Troy was sacked unjustly and suggests that Euripides is challenging imperialist ideology. Foley, throughout, intertwines moral agency and *nomos* (law) in her discussion of the interplay of Athenian politics and tragedy.

[12]Foley discusses vengeance and vendetta in Greek tragedy throughout; so does Alexiou. For the Hebrew Book of Lamentations, see Mandolfo.

[13]I use the term "represented," because, as we have seen, there is evidence that feminized men may have performed these ritual lamentations in Sumeria (Bachvarova), and that women were not permitted to act in Greek drama (Foley; Zeitlin). This does not preclude women's public lamentation within the confines of ritual mourning, well attested in antiquity and up through the present day (Alexiou; O'Connor; Bailey; Segall).

[14]One exception is that of Talthybius, the Herald, who laments the killing of a child and shows himself in other ways sympathetic to the lot of the Trojan Women.

WORKS CITED

Abubakar, Aminu and Josh Levs. "'I Will Sell Them,' Boko Haram Leader Says of Kidnapped Nigerian Girls." CNN.com. n.p., 6 May 2014. Web. 26 May 2014.

Alexiou, Margaret. *The Ritual Lament in Greek Tradition*. Revised Dimitrios Yatromanolakis and Panagiotis Roilos. Lanham:

Rowman and Littlefield, 2002. Print.

Bachvarova, Mary R. "Sumerian Gala Priests and Eastern Mediterranean Returning Gods: Lamentation in Cross-Cultural Perspective." *Lament: Studies in the Ancient Mediterranean and Beyond.* Ed. Ann Suter. New York: Oxford University Press, 2008. 18-52. Print.

Bailey, Wilma Ann. "The Lament Traditions of Enslaved African American Women and the Lament Traditions of the Hebrew Bible." *Lamentations in Ancient and Contemporary Cultural Contexts.* Ed. Nancy C. Lee and Carleen Mandolfo. Atlanta: Society of Biblical Literature, 2008. 151-162. Print.

Chavalas, Mark W., ed. *Women in the Ancient Near East: A Sourcebook.* New York: Routledge, 2014. Print.

Connerton, Paul. *How Societies Remember.* New York: Cambridge University Press, 1989.

Dué, Casey. *The Captive Woman's Lament in Greek Tragedy.* Austin: University of Texas Press, 2006. Print.

Euripides. *Iphigeneia in Aulis.* Ed. David Grene and Richmond Lattimore. Trans. Charles R. Walker. Vol. 4. Chicago: University of Chicago Press, 1958. Print.

Euripides. *Iphigeneia in Aulis.* Trans. George Theodoridis. 2007. Poetry in Translation. Web. 10 October 2014.

Euripides. *The Trojan Women.* Ed. David Grene and Richmond Lattimore. Trans. Richmond Lattimore. Vol. 2. Chicago: University of Chicago Press, 1960.

Foley, Helene P. *Female Acts in Greek Tragedy.* Princeton: Princeton University Press, 2001. Print.

Habteslasie, Haben. *Life Imitates Art: Syrian Refugees Stage Greek Tragedy in Jordan.* UNHCR: The UN Refugee Agency 6 January 2014. Web. 26 May 2014.

Hesiod. "Works and Days." *Theogony, Works and Days, Testimonia.* Trans. Glenn R. Most. Vol. 1. Cambridge: Loeb Classical Library, 2006. Print.

Homer. *The Iliad.* Trans. Barry Powell. New York: Oxford University Press, 2014. Print.

"Lament for Urim and Sumer." *Electronic Text Corpus of Sumerian Literature.* Oriental Institute. Oxford University. Web. 1 June 2014.

Langdon, Stephen. *Sumerian Psalms and Liturgies* (Facsimile Edition). San Bernardino: Filaquarian Publ/Qontro, 1919/2014. Print.

Lee, Nancy C. "The Singers of Lamentations: (A)Scribing (De) Claiming Poets and Prophets." *Lamentations in Ancient and Contemporary Cultural Contexts.* Ed. Nancy C. Lee and Carleen Mandolfo. Atlanta: Society of Biblical Literature, 2008. 33-46. Print.

Lee, Nancy. *Lyrics of Lament.* Minneapolis: Fortress, 2010. Print.

Lee, Nancy C. and Carleen Mandolfo, eds. *Lamentations in Ancient and Contemporary Cultural Contexts.* 1st Edition. Vol. 43. Atlanta: Society of Biblical Literature, 2008. Print.

Litoff, Alyssa. "Bring Back Our Girls' Becomes Rallying Cry for Kidnapped Nigerian Schoolgirls." *ABC News.* May 6, 2014. Web. December 15, 2014.

Loraux, Nicole. *Tragic Ways of Killing a Woman.* Trans. Anthony Forster. Cambridge: Harvard University Press, 1987. Print.

Lord, A. B. *The Singer of Tales.* Cambridge: Harvard University Press, 2000. Print.

Mandolfo, Carleen. *Daughter of Zion Talks Back to the Prophets: A Dialogic Theology of the Book of Lamentations.* Atlanta: Society of Biblical Literature, 2007. Print.

McClure, Laura. *Spoken Like A Woman: Speech and Gender in Athenian Drama.* Princeton: Princeton University Press, 1999. Print.

O'Connor, Kathleen M. *Lamentations and the Tears of the World.* Maryknoll: Orbis Books, 2002. Print.

Perkell, Christine. "Reading the Laments of Iliad 24." *Lament: Studies in the Ancient Mediterranean and Beyond.* Ed. Ann Suter. New York: Oxford University Press, 2008. 93-117. Print.

Pomeroy, Sarah B. *Goddesses, Whores, Wives, and Slaves: Women in Classical Antiquity.* New York: Schocken Books, 1975. Print.

Scott, James C. *Domination and the Arts of Resistance: Hidden Transcripts.* New Haven: Yale University Press, 1990. Print.

Segall, Kimberly Wedeven. "Lamenting the Dead in Iraq and South Africa: Transitioning from Individual Trauma to Collective Mourning Performances." *Lamentations in Ancient and Contemporary Cultural Contexts.* Ed. Nancy C. Lee and

Carleen Mandolfo. Atlanta: Society of Biblical Literature, 2008. 177-194. Print.

"Speaking Truth to Power Madres of the Plaza de Mayo." Women in World History Curriculum. Lyn Reece, n.d. Web. 1 June 2014.

Stears, Karen. "Death Becomes Her: Gender and Athenian Death Ritual." *Lament: Studies in the Ancient Mediterranean and Beyond*. Ed. Ann Suter. New York: Oxford University Press, 2008. 139-155. Print.

Suter, Ann. "Male Lament in Greek Tragedy." *Lament: Studies in the Ancient Mediterranean and Beyond*. Ed. Ann Suter. New York: Oxford University Press, 2008. 156-180. Print.

Tyrell, William Blake. *Amazons: A Study in Athenian Mythmaking*. Baltimore: Johns Hopkins University Press, 1984. Print.

Zeitlin, Froma I. *Playing the Other: Gender and Society in Classical Greek Literature*. Chicago: University of Chcago Press, 1996. Print.

18.
Blaming the Mother

The Politics of Gender in Cindy Sheehan's Protest of the Iraq War

LINDA PERSHING

IN THIS ESSAY I OFFER a critical analysis of the representations of motherhood surrounding Cindy Sheehan and her peace activism from 2003-2007, during her awakening as a peace activist and the start of her leadership role in the U.S. peace movement. This analysis is based on research and participant observation in peace actions organized by Sheehan from 2005 through 2007, including encampments in Crawford, Texas, the cross-country Journey for Humanity (in the summer of 2007), and political actions and protests in Washington, DC, New York City, San Diego, and San Francisco.

I investigate the ways in which Sheehan's identity as a mother became a focal point for extensive and often derogatory cultural commentary about her. Sexist characterizations of Sheehan, coupled with stereotypes about mothering—particularly in times of war and military conflict—provided detractors with an easy way to dismiss her critique of the U.S. military invasion and occupation of Iraq. From the perspective of a feminist scholar of folklore and popular culture, I examine negative reactions to Cindy Sheehan as a mother, deciphering and interpreting significant aspects of sexism that shaped folk expression and public discourse about her. In the following exploration I examine two interrelated stereotypes that were pervasive in characterizations of Sheehan: denigrating her as a "loud-mouthed bitch" and a "bad mother."

CINDY SHEEHAN'S AWAKENING AS A PEACE ACTIVIST

Before the U.S. military invasion of Iraq in 2003, Cindy Sheehan spent much of her adult life living in middle-class neighbourhoods in California and raising four children. Her twenty-four-year-old son Casey enlisted in the army and served as a mechanic and army specialist with the First Cavalry Division. In March 2004, his battalion was deployed to Iraq. On April 4, Casey was killed in an ambush in Sadr City, shot in the head with such force that the round slammed through his Kevlar helmet and ricocheted several times through his skull (Raddatz, Sanchez; see Figure 1).

Figure 1: Banner of Casey Sheehan, killed in the Iraq War on April 4, 2004. The banner was displayed at the peace encampment Sheehan founded near George W. Bush's ranch in Crawford, Texas. Photo: Linda Pershing

Sheehan was devastated by the death of her eldest child. As was the custom, the Sheehan family met with President George W. Bush for a ten-minute consolation session. According to Cindy, Bush had not bothered to learn their names on prior to the meeting on June 18, 2004, referring to Casey generically as "the loved one." Sheehan recalled: "His entire tone was one of being at a tea party, and the first thing he uttered was, 'So, who are we honorin' here?' We all looked at one another in disbelief" (Sheehan, *Peace Mom* 82). She noted that Bush had no interest in viewing photos of

Casey or hearing about his life. In response, she called on him to consider Casey's death from the vantage point of a parent:

> "Mr. President ... Casey was my son. I think you can imagine it—you have two daughters—try to imagine one of them being killed." I saw a brief flicker of humanity in his eyes, then it was gone. I said, "Trust me, Mr. President, you don't want to go there."
> And he said, "You're right. I don't." (Sheehan, *Peace Mom* 83)

In the months following Casey's death, Cindy began to question the rationale the Bush Administration offered for going to war with Iraq. She did some research and reading about the events leading up to the war, which shifted her perceptions of the "war with Iraq" to the U.S. invasion and illegal occupation of Iraq. She soon concluded that Bush's claims about "weapons of mass destruction" and arguments about the connections between the September 11th attacks and Iraq were fabrications. In the summer of 2004, she joined an organization called Military Families Speak Out, meeting with others who advocated withdrawing U.S. troops from Iraq. As she processed her grief and became more knowledgeable about the occupation, Sheehan began writing about the war and speaking at peace events.

During the November 2004 Bush/Kerry presidential race, staff members of the Internet political action committee RealVoices.org asked Sheehan to share her story in a commercial they were making to oppose the war ("A Mother's Tears" [television commercial]). The national advocacy organization MoveOn.org bought the commercial and aired it in swing states, hoping that growing concern about the war would help unseat Bush in the upcoming election (Sheehan, *Peace Mom* 93-94). In less than a year Sheehan's life changed completely. She dedicated her time to peace activism, collaborating with others whose family members had been killed in Iraq. In January 2005, they tried to arrange a meeting with Secretary of Defense Donald Rumsfeld. When he refused, they organized one of their first political actions: a protest of the war, staged at the Pentagon. As a result of the media attention created by this small event, television journalist Diane Sawyer invited Sheehan to do an interview on *Good Morning America*, scheduled for the day of Bush's second inauguration (Sheehan, *Peace Mom*). Soon Sheehan was giving speeches across the United States. She grounded her commentary in her experience as a mother whose son was killed in an increasingly unpopular war (see Pershing, "Cindy Sheehan"). In March 2005, she appeared on the cover of *The Nation* magazine, featured in an article entitled "The New Face of Protest?" (Houppert, "Cindy Sheehan"). Artist Robert Shetterly, who has created several hundred portraits for his series entitled "Americans Who Tell the Truth," offered the following observations about Sheehan when he designed a painting of her: "I ... painted her sharp, blue eyes to the point that they were looking back at me from the canvas, talking to me about the fierceness of her quest, the eyelids red from weeping, grey-blue and ochre circles underneath from exhaustion, and an inchoate knowledge taking shape....The eyes had no fear. They had a clarity of purpose that was at once sad, defiant, and calm" (Shetterly).

In August 2005, Sheehan was invited to serve as a keynote speaker at the annual Veterans for Peace convention in Dallas, while George W. Bush was enjoying a five-week vacation at his Prairie Chapel Ranch in nearby Crawford, Texas. On August 3, she was watching the news and learned that fourteen marines had been killed in one attack. Commenting on the rising death toll, George Bush explained at a press conference, "The families of the fallen can rest assured that their loved ones died for a noble cause" (qtd. in? Nichols, "The President's Vacation"). In response, she typed the following email message and sent it out to her address list of about three hundred people: "I am going to Dallas this weekend to speak at the Veterans for Peace convention. After I am finished, I am going down to Crawford, and ... I am going to demand to meet with the m.f.'er and I am going to ask him for what noble cause did he kill Casey and to demand that he stop using Casey's sacrifice to justify more killing" (Sheehan, *Peace Mom* 136).[1]

The next time she checked her email, she found six hundred responses from people across the country. The word spread quickly about Sheehan's plans to request a meeting with the president. On August 6, Sheehan and twelve members of Veterans for Peace, along with members of the feminist peace organization CodePink and a few other individuals, travelled to Crawford in a caravan of a bus and approximately twenty cars. As they approached the ranch, county sheriffs blocked their path (Figure 2). Sheehan sat down in bug-infested ditch on the side of the road and declared that she was not leaving until the president came out to meet with her (see Figures 3, 4, 5). As luck would have it, she was in the right place at the right time. Approximately 75 reporters—already hanging around Crawford to cover Bush's activities—descended upon this grieving mother who had the audacity to mourn so publicly on the president's doorstep. Within twenty-four hours her face flashed across television and computer screens, into homes across the U.S. and around the world. This middle-aged woman who called the president into question emerged as the new symbol of the floundering peace movement, drawing crowds of supporters, as well as counter-protesters and a slew of journalists (see Figure 6). She rocketed from the obscurity of a suburban homemaker to coverage on every national news source. Soon nicknamed the "Peace Mom," Sheehan was credited with galvanizing a nation and injecting life into a sluggish peace movement at a time when approval ratings for Bush's war policy dropped to forty percent ("Approval Ratings").

Public response to Cindy Sheehan was instantaneous and emotional, with comments ranging from "Cindy Sheehan is the modern day Joan of Arc and she is confronting an ominous and soulless [sic] military machine," to "Cindy Sheehan is a traitor to her own son's voluntary service and ultimate sacrifice" ("Cindy Sheehan Is"; see Figure 7). By the end of August 2005, over 15,000 people from across the U.S. and several other countries had travelled to this remote Texas location to support her makeshift peace encampment, which stretched for miles along the sides of the country road in Crawford. Celebrities and activists (including Joan Baez, Dennis Banks, Eve Ensler, Jesse Jackson, Russell Means, Al Sharpton, and Martin Sheen) joined the encampment and resulting media circus. The Bush Administration tried hard to ignore her, while critics lambasted Sheehan as emotional, misguided, a lunatic, a "media whore," and even as satanic (see Rich; Rothschild). Arch-conservative pundit David Horowitz declared Sheehan a

Figure 2: Sheehan (on right of the banner) and supporters leading a march down the country road to Bush's Prairie Chapel Ranch. After August 2006, Sheehan returned to Crawford repeatedly, when George W. Bush was at the ranch. This photo was taken during Sheehan's March 2006 vigil in Crawford. Photo: Linda Pershing

Figure 3: Supporters at the Crawford vigils stand with Sheehan near the roadside entrance to Bush's ranch. They hold a banner created by members of the feminist peace group CodePink, who joined Sheehan in Crawford. Photo: Linda Pershing

traitor, describing her as "the most prominent symbol and chief mouthpiece of a psychological warfare campaign against her own country in time of war that can only benefit its enemies on the field of battle" (Horowitz). An Internet tracking source reported that on August 18, 2005—roughly the mid-point of Sheehan's month-long vigil outside Bush's ranch—a full fifty percent of all online blogs included discussions about Cindy Sheehan (*Blog Pulse*). By June 28, 2007, a Google search for the key words "Cindy Sheehan" resulted in approximately 1,580,000 web entries.

From left to right: Figure 4: Sheehan staging a vigil at the roadside entrance to Bush's ranch. The intense heat of central Texas made actions of this kind especially grueling.
Figure 5: After police banned them from setting up an encampment on the side of the road near Bush's ranch in Crawford, Sheehan and supporters were arrested for camping in roadside ditches. Here Sheehan is at the nearby Waco, Texas, courthouse protesting the arrest and attempt to curtail her civil rights. Photos: Linda Pershing.

ANALYASIS OF FOLK AND POPULAR RESPONSES TO CINDY SHEEHAN

The mass media coverage of Sheehan was extensive, and thousands of other expressive forms—including jokes and cartoons, websites,

From left to right: Figure 6: Sheehan was besieged by dozens of reporters who were eager to cover the story of a mourning mother who wanted to meet with the President. Here she wears a T-shirt quoting one of Bush's famous misstatements when talking about U.S. military "strategery," rather than "strategy."
Figure 7: Supporters and peace activists from across the country joined Sheehan at the encampment and at peace vigils to express their solidarity. Photos: Linda Pershing.

online blogs, and urban legends—sprang up to characterize her as a "loud-mouthed bitch" and, consequently, as a "bad mother." These provide rich terrain for feminist analysis and reflection. Sheehan's fundamental question to President Bush—for what "noble cause" did my son die?— made her a target for both admiration and scorn. Thinking back about the reactions to her efforts in Crawford, Sheehan later reflected:

> August '05 was the happiest, yet the 2nd most stressful time of my life. The people who saw my sunburned face, wild hair and chapped lips every time they turned on their TV never saw me tossing and turning in my tent or trailer on a nightly basis, totally stressed out about the [Karl] Rovian smear campaign and worrying about what lies were going to be told about me, or what attack was coming next. (Sheehan, "Turn, Turn")

Sexist stereotypes about women came to the fore almost immediately when Sheehan's Crawford vigil hit the news. Extensive critical commentary about Sheehan's failure as a mother also demonstrates what still occurs in the U.S. when women move beyond traditional roles as caregivers to offer public critique of government policies during times of war. Concurrently, well-known female entertainers who spoke out against the war were also targeted, not because they were "bad mothers," but because they were women. For example, there was a massive outcry over political commentary by Natalie Maines, a member of the Dixie Chicks musical group, and actor/television talk show host Rosie O'Donnell, when they criticized Bush's war policies ("Rosie O'Donnell Attacks Bush"). Disparagement of these women who spoke out against the U.S. invasion of Iraq often centered on gender issues. In his essay entitled "The Resignation of Cindy Sheehan and American, No World, Misogyny," Frank L. Solomon identifies sexism and misogyny as the primary reasons for personal attacks on Sheehan. Similarly, community activist Victoria Mares-Hershey commented that "politicians, journalists and political analysts have vilified Sheehan as everything close to a mad housewife, hysterical feminist, naïve peacenik and political opportunist, disgracing her country and the memory of her son." She countered these characterizations with her own assessment:

> Cindy Sheehan looks like democracy. Brash, starkly direct, given to emotional outbursts, rabble-rousing and doing it in the street, she disturbs the people's comfort zone and rationalizations, keeping democracy alive.
> Brutally honest, irritatingly persistent, "sugary icing on a cake of steel" ... she camps at the commander in chief's front door and asks him to be accountable. (Mares-Hershey; Figure 8)

THE ANTITHESIS TO A "GOOD MILITARY MOM": PORTRAYALS OF CINDY SHEEHAN AS A "LOUD MOUTHED BITCH"

People called Cindy a bitch because she was speaking truth to power. She was speaking it to Bush's face. She wasn't

Figure 8: After the August 2005 encampment in Crawford, Sheehan was invited to lead peace marches and actions across the country. Here she speaks at a January 2006 peace rally organized by students at University of California San Diego. Photo: Linda Pershing

[using] mamby pamby diplomatic double-speak. About Bush, she said: "You lied to us." She used the word "lie." And that really appealed to me. That's what I liked. She was direct, but she was also soft spoken and eloquent. — Barbara Cummings, peace activist (see Figure 9)

The first theme that quickly emerged during Sheehan's August

2005 Crawford vigil was an attempt to denigrate and discount her because she adopted a confrontational style that many people consider unbecoming to, and inappropriate for, mothers of soldiers during times of war. In contemporary American politics, mothers who speak out against national policies *as mothers* often become targets for public criticism. Rather than focusing on

Figure 9: Sheehan (second from the right holding the banner) organized and led peace actions focusing on the experiences of mothers whose children had been killed in the Iraq War. Sheehan named this event "Mother of A March," scheduled on Mother's Day 2007 in Washington, DC. Photo: Linda Pershing

nurturing activities within the domestic realm, American mothers who protest U.S. wars are dismissed and ridiculed. Stereotyping her as a "loud mouthed bitch" through countless jokes, blogs, and cartoons, pundits argued that Sheehan, because her son was in the U.S. military, had no business speaking out about the war. Some complained that as a military mother, she "didn't know her place," needed to "get over" the death of her son, and learn to grieve privately and silently, like a dutiful and patriotic military mother. Commentary of this type was especially vicious, signaling the misogyny that emerges when a woman whose primary identity has been as a mother and wife refocuses her energy on political activism. Incessant use of the term "bitch" to describe Sheehan signaled that she had transgressed socially acceptable roles for mothers. An online commentator using the name "DANCALL" objected:

> I thought it was understandable for this woman to im-
> plode, especially after her son, a true American Hero, was
> violently killed in a war. But this bitch has stepped over
> the line. All kindness and understanding are now gone.
> Ms. Sheehan, you are one stupid bitch. You have not only
> dishonored your son, your family and your country, you
> have shown yourself for the stupid bitch you are. (Online
> comment on Nichols, "Cindy Sheehan's Farewell")

The number of nasty invectives that detractors used to denounce Sheehan was breathtaking, and they exacted a considerable toll on her. In addition to calling her a "bitch," critics described her as an "ignorant cow," "whore," "slut," "dyke," "cunt," and countless other derogatory terms, many of which specifically reference women's sexuality (see, for example, Hendrie).

One stunning series of hateful expletives, written on February 28, 2006, on the personal website of a blogger identified as "Beth," exemplifies the incredible anger and hatred that some people expressed about Sheehan's decision to speak out against the war. "Beth" suggests in the following rant that a suitable punishment for Sheehan's transgressive behaviour would be to rape and eviscerate her. The term "motherfucking" emphasizes Sheehan's maternal identity and the author's desire to see her sexually violated:

> That stupid fucking cunt.... Fuck her, with a motherfuck-
> ing rusty chainsaw. ...She's every bit as bad as Hanoi Jane
> [Fonda], and I wouldn't be the least bit surprised to see
> that cunt sitting around with a bunch of terrorists, hold-
> ing one of their blood-stained knives, in solidarity with
> the "insurgency." CINDY ... you gutless piece of hellfuck.
> (Emphasis in original, Bamapachyderm)

Two minutes later, she added: "And I'm not apologizing for the expletive-laden rant, either. Since I can't punch the bitch in the face, verbal abuse will have to substitute." The next day, another blogger by the name of "RepublicanWitch" responded on the same website: "Beth, couldn't have said it better myself. Hate that woman. Hate. Hate. Have I mentioned that I hate her?" (see Bamapachyderm).

Detractors highlighted Sheehan's identity as a mother by referring to her as "Momma Moonbat," another common term used on websites and in blogs to describe Sheehan. "Moonbat" has become an all-purpose insult for liberals, peace protestors, and other ideological opponents, one that enjoyed considerable currency in libertarian and conservative online discourse. Describing Sheehan as a selfish mother who couldn't let go of her son, in April 2006 a blogger identifying himself as Max Power ranted:

> In my opinion Cindy Sheehan i[s] a hate filled whore who couldn't keep her son's umbilical on and so, is running his name through the mud and bitching as loud as she can to try to make the world feel sorry for her. ... It is also of my opinion that she has some far leftist speechwriters who are trying their best to get her elected to Congress so she can bitch at us some more and infest the world with her feminist, shortsighted, snaggle toothed, diatribes. ... Finally, it is my opinion that she fucks goats. (Power)

Denunciations such as this one often included sexual slurs. Mother-based insults about Sheehan were rampant on the Internet, where public discourse and debate often occur without personal accountability or consequences. Accusations about opportunism, insanity, immorality, and symbolic necrophilia characterize the following online tirade about Sheehan, emphasizing those characteristics as oppositional to being "a good mother." Those who attacked Sheehan's abilities as a mother sometimes made extreme statements to bolster their claims. The hatred and perverse portrayal of Sheehan's mothering, ageism, and violent sexism expressed by the anonymous author of the following comments are particularly disturbing:

> Cindy Sheehan is a opportunistic vulture, preying on the corpse of her own son to get her face on the camera. ... Sheehan is a craven, immoral old hag, who is exploiting the sacrifice of her son to feed her own ego. I am convinced she is mentally ill, raping her own progeny's corpse for political gain. Nice one, Sheehan, you fucking douche bag. (August 15, 2005 response cited in Rothschild)

The sexist thinking embedded in these epithets is striking. In my research I found no equivalents—in terms of a sexist or sexual reference—about fathers who became outspoken critics of the war after their sons or daughters were killed in Iraq (including Andrew Bacevich, Carlos Arredondo, Bill Mitchell, and Fernando Suarez del Solar; see Goodman; Houppert; Pershing, "From Sorrow to Activism" and "Do Not Go Gentle"; Rockwell). In response to the expletives used to describe Sheehan, commentator Janet Contursi observed:

> What is interesting about those horrible comments about Cindy Sheehan is the sexual/gender language used to condemn her. This says more about the speakers and our society than it does about the issue. I wonder if the outrage would be so strong if the dead soldier's father, rather than his mother, was out there protesting. And, by the way, where the hell is he??? (August 15, 2005 response to Rothschild).

Within this genre, threats of violence were common when Sheehan refused to silence her message. One unnamed critic announced: "Cindy is a communist whore and should therefore shut the hell up.... In short, I think she is a shameless bitch who needs to either a) shut up or b) be shot" (response to Rothschild). The possibility of violence against Sheehan was real. In the summer of 2005, Sheehan reported numerous threats and, as a result, had a bodyguard when she travelled with the cross-country Bring Them Home Now Tour, calling for an end to the war. An Iraq War veteran who objected to Sheehan's message told one of his professors at a community college in Ventura, California, that maybe he should bring a "Molotov Cocktail" to her upcoming speaking event on campus, "so that he could take care of the problem himself." The day before Sheehan's presentation, he was arrested for accidentally exploding a pipe bomb at his house. Police found an AK-47 assault rifle and several pipe bombs during the arrest (Sheehan, Email message).

While some bloggers described Sheehan as a "bitch," numerous journalists and writers characterized her as a loose cannon. Sheehan's public speaking style is disarming. She is direct, outspoken, and speaks from the heart, rather than choosing her words carefully for the sake of diplomacy or social conformity—an approach that drew many people to rally around her but also one that is particularly deadly for women in public life. Reflecting on her direct and confrontational public speaking style, Sheehan reflected:

> The people who supported me did so because they know that I uncompromisingly tell the truth about this war. I have stood up and said: "My son died for NOTHING, and George Bush and his evil cabal and their reckless policies killed him. My son was sent to fight in a war that had no basis in reality and was killed for it." I have never said "pretty please" or "thank you." I have never said anything wishy-washy like he uses "Patriotic Rhetoric." I say my son died for LIES. George Bush LIED to us and he knew he was LYING. The Downing Street Memos dated July 23, 2002, prove that he knew that Saddam didn't have WMD's or any ties to Al Qaeda. I believe that George lied and he knew he was lying. He didn't use patriotic rhetoric. He lied and made us afraid of ghosts that weren't there. Now he is using patriotic rhetoric to keep the U.S. military presence in Iraq: Patriotic rhetoric that is based on greed and nothing else. (Sheehan "Hypocrites and Liars"; see Figure 10)

Sheehan calls it like she sees it—raw, blunt, and accusatory—and has been roundly criticized for doing so. Those critiques often focused on her identity as a woman and a mother, who was expected to soften her language and speaking style. In August 2005, while staging her first vigil at Crawford, she responded to criticism about her speaking style: "I have been known for sometime as a person who speaks the truth and speaks it strongly. I have always called a

Figure 10: Sheehan spoke out publicly and often, criticizing U.S. war policy and the lies and ineptitude of the president and Congress. Here she speaks at a July 2007 peace rally in New York City. Photo: Linda Pershing

liar a liar and a hypocrite a hypocrite. Now I am urged to use softer language to appeal to a wider audience" (Sheehan "Hypocrites and Liars"). She frequently used pejorative terms like "neo-con" (neo-conservative), "BushCo," the "Bush cabal," and the "Bush regime" to refer to the George W. Bush and his administration. Reflecting on Sheehan's direct style, Victoria Mares-Hershey commented that "Cindy is a woman holding up a mirror to America and saying, as difficult as it may be, it's time to 'tell the truth.'"

Critics often complained that Sheehan's expletives and profanity were inappropriate for the mother of a soldier who died in the war, and that she could have communicated her message in less offensive, more "feminine" ways. Her communicative strategies alienated detractors, who said it was unacceptable for women, particularly grieving mothers, to use profanity in public life. In contrast, supporters noted that her use of language was refreshing and honest:

They would attempt to tame her by shearing away her language, not just the profanity for which she was known, but the very fierceness of her words. She had no hesitation about calling the President "an evil maniac," "a lying bastard," or the administration "those lying bastards," "chickenhawks," "warmongers," "shameful cowards," and "war criminals." She called for the President's "impeachment," for the jailing of the whole top layer of the administration (no pardons). She called for American troops to be pulled out of Iraq now. And most of this largely disappeared from a much-softened media portrait of a grieving antiwar mother.

In a world where horrors are referred to euphemistically, or limned in politely, or artfully ignored, she does something quite rare—she calls things by their names as she sees them. She is as blunt and impolite in her mission as the media is circumspect and polite in its job, as most of the opposition to George Bush is in its "opposition." And it was her very bluntness, her ability to shock by calling things by their actual names, by acting as she saw fit, that let her break through and that may help turn a set of unhappy public opinion polls into a full-scale antiwar movement. (Englehardt)

Publicly calling George W. Bush "a lying bastard," as Sheehan often did, certainly made her a target for criticism. Sheehan avoids euphemisms and cuts right to the point. There is a clear intentionality in her speech, a straightforward quality that is disarming in the arena of public discourse. And, after years of being in the limelight, she has become impressively articulate about public policy issues and assessment of our political leaders. Artist Linda Eddy captured in her political cartoon what many of Sheehan's critics have expressed: a desire to silence her. Eddy drew a caricature of Sheehan with a large bandage—decorated like a U.S. flag—affixed across her mouth, along with the slogan, "Cindy Sheehan doesn't speak for me," marketed on an array of consumer products from coffee mugs to baby bibs to T-shirts (Eddy). A female David to Bush's Goliath, Sheehan was cast in the role of the classic "bitch": an angry mother who wouldn't shut up and wouldn't go away.

CHALLENGING THE TRADITION OF GOLD STAR MOTHERS: SHEEHAN DENIGRATED AS A "BAD MOM"

Regardless of her point of view, Cindy Sheehan is a disgrace of a mother for allowing her pain to taint the memory of her son and for allowing herself, and him, to be used as she has by all of the political cronies around her. —Internet posting by "Ryan N." (Response to "Sheehan Not Coming to Utah")

From the moment Sheehan was in the public spotlight, commentators complained that she did not conform to patriarchal and conventional notions of motherhood, especially not to the idealized version of the patriotic mother who honours her son's sacrifice when he is killed in a war. Challenging the euphemisms that render the carnage of war invisible, Sheehan often comments that Casey was not "lost" or "fallen," but rather was murdered by a shot to the head. Her actions contrasted sharply to those of Grace Darling Seibold, who founded the American Gold Star Mothers during World War I. When George Seibold was killed in action in 1918, his mother created an organization for grieving mothers who suffered with pride for the "supreme sacrifice" their soldier sons made in fighting for their country. The nationalistic and xenophobic organization got its name from the gold star medal that families received and often proudly displayed in the front windows of their homes when their loved ones died in the war.[2] In 2007, the charter of the American Gold Star Mothers proclaimed that the organization was designed to "maintain true allegiance to the United States of America, ...inculcate lessons of patriotism and love of country in the communities in which we live, ...[and] inspire respect for the Stars and Stripes in the youth of America" ("Gold Star Moms/Who Are We").

Rather than conform to this pattern, Sheehan challenged the tradition of mourning mothers who support the war in which their sons (and some daughters) were killed. In the months after Casey died, Sheehan moved through various stages: experiencing intense grief, expressing anger, raising difficult questions, calling for accountability from public officials, asking others to join her in this effort, and developing a more complex political analysis of the Iraq War. Rather than mourning her son's death in private, Sheehan made her grief public, verbalizing her pain and subsequently using her experience to formulate criticism of U.S. foreign policy, nationalism, corporate greed, militarism, and a host of other political issues. In an essay she wrote in August 2005, Sheehan commented about the Bush Administration: "I think they seriously 'misunderestimated' [making fun of a term George W. Bush used] all mothers. I wonder if any of them had authentic mother-child relationships and if they are surprised that there are so many mothers in this country who are bear-like when it comes to wanting the truth?" (Sheehan, "Hypocrites and Liars"). In response, opponents attacked her moral character, family loyalty, and abilities as a mother. Patriotic mothers are expected to hold true the cherished memory of their children by making the ultimate sacrifice: the lives of their children—usually sons—for a nationalistic cause or campaign. Critics lambasted Sheehan when she refused to play the role accordingly. The following Internet blog entry, entitled "cindy sheehan doesn't love her son," exemplifies this dynamic:

> I have never in my entire life seen as woman as disrespectful to her son as cindy sheehan is. what a bitch. her son knew the risks of joining the american military, and knew what the job he was taking on meant. when he got his orders to deploy, he chose to obey them. he went willingly. he chose his destiny. then, after he gives his life in the service of not only his country, but of all of humanity, his own mother turns her back on his choice and heroism and starts whining like a selfish little bitch about a war which she obviously doesn't understand. ("Cindy Sheehan Doesn't Love Her Son")

Cynthia Enloe, a leading scholar in the study of the historical and political relationships between women and militarization, comments on the complex dynamics surrounding mothers' responses to nationalism and patriotism. Reflecting on mothers' civic engagement, she astutely identifies the friction that emerges when the pressure for women to conform to the ideal of the patriotic mother—stoically grieving after her son (rarely is the death of a daughter/soldier mentioned) dies in war while continuing to support the government that sent him to fight—coexist with the unpopular notion of a mother as a patriotic *citizen*, whose active concern for her country also entails, and even necessitates, critique of government practices and wartime policies. Enloe reflects:

> Oh! Patriotism! Many women have a very ambivalent re-
> lationship to patriotism precisely because the conventional
> prescriptions for being recognized as woman-and-patriot
> are grounded in notions of feminine "respectability." In
> exposing this ambivalence and its causes, feminists have
> made the very model of the patriot less tenable. Most
> militarizing states need women to seek to be patriots, yet
> need them to do so without stepping over the bounds of
> "proper" femininity, since that would then dispirit a lot
> of men, who would feel that their own masculine turf was
> being challenged. In a patriarchal state a woman can aspire
> to be a "patriotic mother" but not a "patriotic citizen." On
> the other hand, we now have increasing historical docu-
> mentation of women who have challenged this orthodox,
> gendered idea of patriotism. (*The Curious Feminist* 171-72)

Detractors criticized Sheehan because she spoke out not only about her grief as a "Gold Star Mother," but also about larger political and social dimensions of the war. As Enloe observes, speaking from the vantage point of motherhood is a double-edged sword, because crossing the line between grief and political commentary often puts mother-activists at risk for public criticism. Reflecting on Sheehan's evolution from being the "darling of the press," when she was portrayed as a grief-stricken mom who wanted to talk to the president, to a spokesperson for the peace and justice movement, Enloe notes:

> Women as mothers can claim a kind of legitimacy that
> government officials never have.... Their feelings—and they
> are often reduced to people who are important because of
> their feelings—are so much more authentic than anything

expressed by government officials.... Maternalism can be
a trap, too, ... since we often tend to trap women in that
narrow space, motherhood. ...We want to make her the
naïve mother, and if we hear that she is really politically
conscious, we start to doubt the authenticity of her maternal
message. (qtd. in Houppert, "Cindy Sheehan")

When Sheehan became a top news story, commentary about
her "abandonment" of her children and husband surfaced almost
immediately, despite the fact that most of Sheehan's adult life had
been devoted to caring for her family. Rumours about Sheehan
as a bad mother and wife ignited in August 2005, while she led
the vigil outside Bush's Crawford ranch and Patrick Sheehan,
her spouse of 28 years, filed for divorce. According to Cindy
Sheehan, their estrangement was fuelled by the stress of Casey's
death and her decision to take up full-time activism against the
war (Sheehan *Peace Mom*). People who had no personal knowledge of Sheehan's life circulated rumours and lies in an attempt
to discredit her.[3] These signaled more about the pervasive nature
of sexism in contemporary U.S. society and patriarchal asser-
tions about mothers in wartime than about Sheehan's actual
experiences. The double standard about parental responsibility
prevailed: fathers who are activists and social critics are rarely
scrutinized for spending time away from home or "abandoning" their families. An urban legend got started and circulated
via the Internet, claiming that Cindy filed for divorce years ago
and left her son to be raised by her former husband when she
became a political activist for the Democratic Party. According
to this fictional account, Patrick Sheehan remarried, and he and
his second wife raised Casey from the time that he was a young
child because Cindy was no longer interested in caring for him
(see "The 'Real' Cindy Sheehan"). Soon after Sheehan started
her Crawford protest, pundits reported that she had *always*
been a neglectful or selfish mother. Narratives of this type were
complete fabrications, casting Sheehan as an unfit mother who
valued her political ambitions over the care of loved ones, while
simultaneously asserting this was *never* an acceptable choice for
mothers. Stories about Sheehan abandoning her family were de-

signed to support the notion that no matter what a woman does or accomplishes in her life, claiming that she is a "bad mother" is a very effective way to discredit her.

Jeers arose from Bush supporters and public criticism sprang from Sheehan's in-laws, who accused her of promoting her own personal agenda at the expense of Casey's good name. Skeptics circulated erroneous and speculative tales via the Internet, such as this comment: "Didnt she give up custody of her son that died overseas ... and hadnt talked to him in years? and didnt she gave up custody of another minor son so she could travel around the USA spouting her BS?" ("Cindy Sheehan's a Bad Mom"). Commentators went so far as to argue that Sheehan's "failure" as a mother relegated her to subhuman status. A blogger by the name of "ransr" made the following accusation:

> We can agree that motherhood is good and that the loss of a child is awful. Something that is not meant to be. HOWEVER, this woman is not [a] mother. She abandoned her son as a child. She did nothing for him except to use his death as an opportunity for her 15 minutes of fame. I can think of nothing good to say of a woman who abandons her young. Even animals don't do that. (Comcast Community Forums)

Others contended that her "ineptitude" as a mother and wife had become Sheehan's defining characteristic. An Internet commentator named "Bindarra" complained: "The real futility of Cindy Sheehan was this: as she grieved the loss of her son, she abandoned her husband and other children, who needed her more than ever" (Pareene).

For some people Sheehan's most egregious crime was daring to leave the domestic realm and move into civic space to become a public figure. In a blog entry entitled "Cindy needs to go home," a writer using the name "gsyvrud" called for Sheehan to return to an imagined, private home life in which women are rendered invisible:

> I think of other parents who lost children in wars such as

Iraq, Vietnam, Korea, or WW2 ... parents who accepted their loss and grief and went on to remain solid citizens of the USA without having to blame and bad-mouth a President or others—public or military officials ... for their children's deaths. At Memorial Day ceremonies all across our nation yesterday, those parents ...or their descendants ... visited the graves of their loved ones and honored them along with their communities in which they live. Their quiet devotion to their childrens' memories and their support of our nation—no matter who is the President ... is a far greater and a far better testimony than Cindy Sheehan could ever hope to make with her foul-mouthed protests and constant publicity seeking. *She needs to go home, and hopefully, disappear from the public arena for the remainder of her life.* (Syvrud; emphasis added)

The notion that women's value, first and foremost, is defined by their caretaking role as mothers was deeply ingrained in this popular commentary. In times of war, mothers are expected to support American militarism and grieve the deaths of their soldier sons with piety and patriotic fervor. Sheehan's refusal to do so caused critics to dismiss her as a bad, neglectful, and selfish mother.

CONCLUSION

Cindy Sheehan became a lightning rod for heated debates about U.S. foreign and public policies, war and peace, civic rights, free speech, and a host of other important issues. Contentious disputes about mothering were central to this discourse. Journalist Stephanie Salter offered an insightful analysis of the many attempts to discredit Sheehan by claiming she was "exploiting" her son's death in the Iraq War to further her own agenda: "As for exploiting her son's death, what does that look like? If Casey Sheehan had not been killed in a war in Iraq, his mother likely would not be out stumping against that war. To acknowledge that fact is no more exploitive than when parents whose children have been kidnapped or molested react by lobbying for tougher laws and longer sentences" (Salter).

Some supporters saw Sheehan as a significant prophetic voice, one who unexpectedly arose from the life of a white, Catholic, middle-class mother to become an outspoken critic of Bush's war in Iraq and a siren to the nation. While opponents tried to dismiss her by dredging up sexist stereotypes, portrait artist Robert Shetterly developed a very different perception:

> Cindy Sheehan has painted a very accurate portrait of herself, her anger, her frustration, her determination to give meaning to Casey's death. ...Many people would now edit and censor her words, pull her teeth, make of her a grief-struck pawn of the left. The degree to which they attack her is the degree to which the power of her truth terrifies them." (Shetterly)

One journalist noted that the "trouble" with Cindy Sheehan— the real basis of the complaints and efforts to discredit her—was that she was a mother of a dead soldier who spoke out and took action to protest the war, refusing to conform to the stereotype of the patriotic, silently suffering, war-supporting mother:

> The problem with Cindy Sheehan was that she wouldn't let herself be put in a box. She wouldn't sit on a porch and grieve the way mothers are supposed to, with a wisp of a star in the window, just behind the curtains, letting the world know, if it cared, that she'd lost a son.
>
> She wouldn't be quiet and she wouldn't stay home and she wouldn't quit shouting out that the war in Iraq that took her son's life was and remains an atrocious mistake.
>
> She wouldn't stop calling President Bush and Vice President Cheney to account for their villainy in starting the war, lying as they went, keeping it going and watching sons [and daughters] like her Casey die by the thousands. (van Doorn)

Because Sheehan refused to be silenced, she became a target for many of the types of character assassination that commonly befall mothers in public life. Through political cartoons and jokes, bloggers' rants and urban legends, critics branded her as a loud-mouthed bitch and a bad mother in an attempt to discredit her critique of the war.

Special thanks to Kathie Alvizo, Nishelle Bellinger, Lindsay Riedel, and Lori Walkington, who assisted with the research and interview transcription.

[1]At the time, the misogynist connotations of the term "mother fucker" did not seem to concern Sheehan. Her understanding of sexism in language and culture developed noticeably as she became a public speaker and leader. For example, she began using inclusive language to refer to deity (Sheehan *Peace Mom*) and articulated her support for "matriotism" as an alternative to patriotism (see Sheehan "Matriotism").

[2]For many years only mothers who were born in United States were admitted to the American Gold Star Mothers, even if they had legally immigrated to the U.S. and their children had died in service to the U.S. military ("'Gold Star' Moms to Admit Non Citizens"). See Shields concerning Ligaya Lagman, a Filipina who has been a legal resident and taxpayer of the U.S. since 1982. Her son, Army Staff Sergeant Anthony Lagman, died fighting in Afghanistan, but she was barred from entrance to the American Gold Star Mothers because she was not a U.S. citizen. With pressure, the American Gold Star Mothers changed their policies and admitted her in 2005.

[3]See, for example, this Internet commentary entitled "Bad Mom," assailing Sheehan. An author named Marie wrote:

I really don't like her and I think her issues run really deep and have to do with the way she treated her son and maybe that is why she is so rabid and willing to ignore his death and go on, and on, and on, and on, and on, and on ... 'bout the war.

I do agree with Al, she needs counseling. But, not 'cause her son died. I think, maybe, perhaps, could be, that she was a REAL bad mom.

And MAYBE she is trying to justify her being a bad mom by doing the things she is doing.

...Here is what I think about Cindy Sheehan:
She is a HORRID mother and I have ZERO respect for her.
I also think she is aTERRIBLE WOMAN.
I think she is a BAD person with questionable motives.
(Renew America)

WORKS CITED

"Approval Ratings for President and Congressional Leaders Continue to Drop, According to Latest Harris Poll." *PRNewswire*, 24 Aug. 2005. Web. 11 Dec. 2007.

Bamapachyderm. Commentary on personal website. 28 Feb. 2006. Web. 6 Mar. 2006.

Blog Pulse. 13 Dec. 2007. Web. 19 Dec. 2007.

"Cindy Sheehan Doesn't Love Her Son." Blog entry. *A Rhetorical Box* 2 July 2006 (2:53 pm). Web. 7 June 2014.

"Cindy Sheehan Is." *United for Peace of Pierce County.* 18 Aug. 2005. Web. 19 June 2007.

"Cindy Sheehan's a Bad Mom." *Blogs for Bush.* 28 June 2006. Web. 6 July 2006.

Comcast Community Forums. "Cindy Sheehan." 29 May 2007. Web. 17 June 2007.

Cummings, Barbara. Interview with Linda Pershing. Crawford, Texas. 9 March 2006.

Eddy, Linda. "Cindy Sheehan Doesn't Speak for Me" Merchandise. *Rightwingstuff.* n.d. Web. 5 June 2014.

Englehardt, Tom. "Cindy, Don, and George: On Being in a Ditch at the Side of the Road." *Sign of the Times* 2005. Web. 17 June 2007.

Enloe, Cynthia. *The Curious Feminist: Searching for Women in a New Age of Empire.* Berkeley: University of California Press, 2004. Print.

"Gold Star Moms/Who We Are/History." *Gold Star Moms.* 2007. Web. 20 June 2001.

"Gold Star' Moms to Admit Non Citizens: Group Came under Fire for Barring Filipina Mother of Slain GI." *U.S. Times* 28 June 2005. Web. 25 June 2007.

Goodman, Amy. "The Endless War Memorial: Father of Slain

Soldier Joins Times Square Protest to Read Names of Iraq War Dead" (Interview). *Democracy Now* 13 Mar. 2007. Web. 26 Dec. 2007.

Hendrie, Phil. "Anti-war Mom: Another Ignorant Cow." *Free Republic* 11 Aug. 2005. Web 5 June 2014.

Horowitz, David. "Cindy Sheehan 'Doesn't Respect Her Own Son's Life.'" *Media Matters* 17 Aug. 2005. Web. 19 June 2007.

Houppert, Karen. "Cindy Sheehan: Mother of a Movement?" *The Nation* 25 May 2006. Web. 29 June 2007.

Houppert, Karen. "The New Face of Protest?" *The Nation* 28 Mar. 2005. Web. 29 June 2007.

Mares-Hershey, Victoria. "Portrait of Cindy Sheehan also a Picture of Democracy." 30 Aug. 2005. Reprinted from *Portland Press Herald* 30 Aug. 2005. Web. 21 June 2007.

"A Mother's Tears" (television commercial). *YouTube*. Prod. by RealVoices.org, 2004. Web. 13 Dec. 2007.

Moy, Catherine, and Melanie Morgan. *American Mourning: The Intimate Story of Two Families Joined by War, Torn by Beliefs.* Nashville: WND Books, 2006.

Nichols, John. "The President's Vacation from Reality." *The Nation* 15 Aug. 2005. Web. 27 June 2007.

Nichols, John. Comment in response to "Cindy Sheehan's Farewell." *The Nation* 31 May 2007. Web. 20 June 2007.

Pareene, Alex. "The Surge Worked: Cindy Sheehan Gives Up and Goes Back to Russia." *Wonkette* 3 June 2007. Web. 5 June 2014.

Pershing, Linda. "Cindy Sheehan: A Call to Maternal Thinking in the Contemporary Peace Movement." *The Legacy of Sara Ruddick's Maternal Thinking*. Ed. Andrea O'Reilly. Toronto: Demeter Press, 2009. 144-172. Print.

Pershing, Linda. "Do Not Go Gentle into That Good Night: The Tragic Death of Brian Arredondo." *Journal of American Folklore* 127.503 (2014): 82-90. Print.

Pershing, Linda, with Nishelle Y. Bellinger. "From Sorrow to Activism: A Father's Memorial to His Son Alexander Arredondo, Killed in the U.S. Occupation of Iraq." *Journal of American Folklore* 123.488 (2010): 179-217. Print.

Power, Max. "Cindy Sheehan the Movie: Cindy and the Dragon." *Blue Damage* 20 Apr. 2006. Web. 5 June 2014.

Radditz, Martha. *The Long Road Home: A Story of War and Family*. New York: Penguin, 2007.

"The 'Real' Cindy Sheehan." Urban Legends. *About.com*. 6 Sept. 2005. Web. 4 June 2014.

Renew America. Forum. 17 Mar. 2006. Web. 28 Mar. 2006.

Rich, Frank. "The Swift Boating of Cindy Sheehan." *New York Times* 21 Aug. 2005. Web. 26 June 2007.

Rockwell, Paul. "From Grief To Protest: How Peace Loving Fathers Honor Their Fallen Sons." *In Motion Magazine*. 11 June 2004. Web. June 29, 2007.

"Rosie O'Donnell Attacks Bush and Screams for His Impeachment." YouTube. 2007. Web. 13 Dec. 2007.

Rothschild, Matthew. "The Savaging of Cindy Sheehan." *The Progressive* 11 Aug. 2005. Web. 29 June 2007.

Salter, Stephanie. "Cindy Sheehan an Ordinary Woman on a Path That's Extraordinary." *The Tribune-Star* 14 Apr. 2007. Web. 22 June 2007.

Sanchez, Maria. "Sheehan's Father Finds Meaning Amid Grief." *Sydney Herald* 28 June 2007. Web. 7 July 2007.

Sheehan, Cindy. Email Message to Linda Pershing. 23 June 2007. E-mail.

Sheehan, Cindy. "Hypocrites and Liars." *Common Dreams*. 20 Aug. 2005. Web. 22 June 2007.

Sheehan, Cindy. "Matriotism." *Common Dreams* 26 Jan. 2006. Web. 9 June 2007.

Sheehan, Cindy. *Peace Mom: A Mother's Journey through Heartache to Activism*. New York: Atria Books, 2006.

Sheehan, Cindy. "Turn, Turn, Turn." *Common Dreams* 19 June 2007. Web. 22 June 2007.

"Sheehan Not Coming to Utah." News story. *KSL TV*. 29 Aug. 2006. Web. 9 Dec. 2007.

Shetterly, Robert. "Painting Cindy." *Lew Rockwell* 20 Aug. 2005. Web. 22 June 2007.

Shields, Mark. "Grief of a Gold Star Mother." *CN* 18 June 2005. Web. 12 June 2007.

Solomon, Frank L. "The Resignation of Cindy Sheehan and American, No World, Misogyny." *Frost Illustrated* 6 June 2007. Web. 10 Dec. 2007.

Syvrud, Kay. "Give Me Strength! Nancy Pelosi and Cindy Sheehan." *Buffalo Gal* 29 May 2007. Web. 3 June 2014.

van Doorn, John. "Cindy Sheehan Steps Away." *North County
Times* 2 June 2007. Web. 1 July 2007.

Conclusions and the Way Forward

ARLENE SGOUTAS AND TATJANA TAKŠEVA

THE 15TH ANNIVERSARY OF THE United Nations' "Women, Peace and Security" (WPS) agenda will be celebrated in October 2015, with a high-level review of progress towards implementation of UNSCR 1325 at the global, regional, and national levels. The WPS agenda, in particular UNSCR 1325, has called for the increasing gender mainstreaming of all aspects of the peacebuilding process—from the negotiation table to the formation of action plans and the involvement of regional and international actors like NATO. Yet, despite this effort to take gender seriously, what does the continued absence of maternal considerations signify in such contexts, and how does such absence impact an understanding of the solutions and remedies to political violence?

This collection explores the situation of mothers—mothers as victims, mothers as peacekeepers, mothers as advocates and activists—during and after they have experienced various forms of conflict. In these contexts, the collection assesses the range of barriers and challenges that mothers face. The examples provided define and respond to conflict in different ways, with varying degrees of intervention and assistance from the international community. The recommendations proposed in many chapters in this collection take mothering to be a first principle of response, advocating that planning, integrating, and placing the experience of mothers is at the heart of the response to conflict. Taken together, the chapters in this book bring to the forefront some of these mothering experiences through the themes of maternal voice, maternal resilience, and post-conflict policy.

VOICE AND RESILIENCE

One theme presented throughout this collection is the notion of voice and mothers' visibility—and invisibility—within and after conflict. Voice, or the act of speaking out, is often identified in feminist literature as one of the key conditions demonstrating empowerment and agency. Indeed, for many feminists concerned with issues of security and conflict, women's ability to make choices and speak their mind has been seen as proof of agency and empowerment. While keenly aware that speaking out and naming oppressions and oppressors is critical for challenging injustices, the link between voice and agency presumes the ability to speak out safely against tyranny and injustice. Yet, such an assumption is difficult to sustain in a world where conflicts have led to widespread gender based violence and, often, violent opposition to open dissent. There are several pieces in this collection that approach voice and agency in (in)secure circumstances to provide the basis for developing discursive strategies, reassessing possibilities and limitations for actions, and even organizing for change.

The notion of voice is used to reconstruct the narrative of women as victims of conflict. In particular, O'Donnell's piece challenges the category construction of war-widows through the use of *testimonies*. The story of Angela in her chapter encourages us to look at the resulting specific assumptions of the category of "war-widow" and what this term may conjure for us; perhaps a suffering woman alone, victimized because her husband died, perhaps innocently and tragically in battle, a battle assumed to be correct, removes the idea of state repression and social structure which may serve in the subordination of women, places blame somewhere else, and develops her certain victimhood; he dies, she suffers afterward—and since he died, he was the only political actor there.

Blend also uses *testimonios* to challenge the official story in Argentina, showing how "it illustrates the ways that motherhood has been politicized, both to silence women by state-sponsored torture, and as a way that women embraced maternal politics as a strategy" (304). Thus, voice is used to subvert categories and the tendency to label women as the victim.

Maternal pedagogies (Chaudhry) lend a different type of voice in the context of the armed conflict and reconstruction Pakistan. Here, being attuned to particular mothers' voices means to "read mother's pedagogies and perspectives from within the specificity of their epistemologies as Muslim women located in particular temporal and spatial backgrounds as well as participants in a conflict where their contribution cannot be cast as exceptional or marginal" (100). In her chapter, Passman Nielson uses lamentation as a form of resistance by investigating the words of the most powerless, women taken captive in war, showing even female/maternal acts of mourning convey a sense of agency in their critique of masculinist militant codes. She points out that "to lament is to resist. It is to speak truth to power through formal language and subversive words" (334). This argument has implications for how we interpret grieving maternal voices from contemporary conflict areas: not only as expressions of personal grief, but as public voices that undercut and delegitimize national and international discourses seeking to justify armed conflict. The example of Cindy Sheehan (Pershing) illustrates the explicit conjunction between personal grief and public critique of corrupt military policy.

In Rossman's concept of mother'hood, gang-involved mothers can envision a future beyond the gang by appropriating a new voice through which they can claim their identity as mothers:

> This new mother'hood story helps young women forsake gang warfare because it entails a re-storying of her own identity vis-à-vis the gang. It includes a challenging and sometimes alienating—yet helpful—maturing process, in which she acknowledges the consequences of her choices; a reevaluation of relationships (with the father of her child or children, their families, and their friends); and a struggle to avail herself of linguistic resources to facilitate her new life story. (132-133)

Voice is key to making mothers' stories visible to practitioners and policymakers to design methods to support mothers. What can the perspectives of those who mother offer societies emerging from extreme, systematic, and institutional violence? The transition from short-term reconstruction to longer term development is not always smooth and has been subject to criticism, primarily due to the overlapping mandates of organizations engaged in humanitarian work and the lack of expertise held by aid organizations that begin engaging in reconstruction and even longer term development work. For example, Mann's chapter highlights the challenges that arise from the lack of coordinated aid on the part of humanitarian organizations on the ground in Afghanistan, and the ensuing challenges in delivering effective programs and services to birthing women and girls. Disarmament, Demobilization and Reintegration (DDR) programming the benefit of peer support groups would be essential to "help break the social isolation that accompanies post-demobilization life" (Jones and Denov 94). In the U.S.-Mexican border (Stevens and Andrade), voice is key to the examination of policies and practices affecting immigrant mothers who are living in the U.S. and in the assistance of shaping policies and practices that diminish the lived experiences of fractured mothering.

Resilience is seen in Jones and Denov's chapter on former girl soldiers in Columbia. Their chapter argues that the characteristics that come from the girls' resilience, "ambition, courage, motherly devotion, and an ability to make the best of their situation" (94) is what makes them strong. It is from this position of strength, rather than of vulnerability, that mothers should be viewed and policies informed to bring out their full potential. In situations of armed conflict, many mothers have been displaced from their homes and communities. More typically, health clinics, schools, roads, businesses, and markets have deteriorated substantially. Political violence creates insecurity and uncertainty. As Akesson states, "when mothers' minds are preoccupied with the loss and trauma related to political violence, there is little energy left to devote to their children" (51). In her chapter, communal support from the *hamula* gave mothers some of the support needed to assume their maternal role even while adding some stress. Thus, one recommendation for policymakers is to build communal support that generates maternal competence and gives a positive self-understanding of motherhood.

As an essential trait of survival, resilience is also implied in cases the world media typically portrays as narratives of victimhood. As

Shaheen and Khan reveal in their intersectional account of mothering in conditions of displacement in the PATA and FATA regions in Pakistan, the very conditions of displacement, as difficult and tragic as they are in many aspects, can propel some potentially positive changes in the way in which women conceive of their maternal role and the extent of their agency and autonomy within the family unit.

Resilience is also found through the political agency involved in pursuing motherhood in Zubytska's chapter. She shows that:

> The case of the UPA women reveals that insurgent mothers, despite the destructiveness of war, were able to exercise their agency in staying committed to their military cause while at the same time holding on to their motherhood psychologically. These two commitments—militancy and motherhood—often placed irreconcilable demands on the physical abilities of UPA women, but they did not combine in such a way as to push each other out from the psyche of an insurgent mother. (282)

Walker illustrates in the conflict in Eastern Sri Lanka how mothers organize during conflict as survival of everyday violence: "Alarmed by the escalating violence the Valkai group brought mainly local citizens (mostly women but also a number of men) together to find ways in which they could try and reach out to those affected by the protracted conflict" (24). Voice is thus utilized as a strategy to build networks of support.

A particular kind of resilience is also demonstrated in the cases of mothers raising children born of war. In the Bosnian as well as the Rwandan context, mothers and children continue to struggle with forms of communal ostracism, discrimination, and outright rejection while trying to rebuild their lives (Umulisa; Takševa). While in the Bosnian case the post-conflict state has provided some alternatives for women who chose not to keep children conceived of war time rape, in Rwanda there exist no such alternatives and both mothers and children cope in their daily lives with experiences of physical and emotional challenges within family, community, and society in general. In Rwanda in particular, but also in Bosnia, there is an urgent need to establish and develop comprehensive networks of support for mothers and children; these networks would help them in their efforts to regain autonomy and agency, while somewhat diminishing the perpetuation of cultural and ethnic biases. It is imperative that the governments and governmental agencies of both states develop and disseminate widely different national and cultural frameworks for understanding sexual violence in war and its extensive consequences on the lives of those most directly affected by that violence, but also to provide frameworks of understanding those affected as victims as well as survivors who can regain their sense of cultural identity, national dignity, and personal agency.

POST-CONFLICT POLICY

The chapters in this collection document the experiences of mothering during conflict in different parts of the world, as well as during rebuilding. Thus, this collection also offers some thinking to address and remedy these complex issues. For example, there are suggestions for structural interventions in humanitarian aid in the midst of and during the immediate aftermath of conflict. A number of chapters offer concrete policy and service-delivery program recommendations aimed at improving the post-conflict conditions of women and mothers:

In the case of Syrian refugees, aid agencies need to be more attentive to the unique difficulties mothers face to alleviate much of the suffering of refugee families. For example, the provision of hygiene products, counselling, cash assistance, and the creation of safe spaces for discussion were all identified as responses to help refugee families (Eichert).

All humanitarian services delivered in refugee camps should be formulated in terms that counter traditional systemic forces discriminating against women and mothers, and gender-balanced distribution systems must be created and constantly monitored to prevent corruption or exploitation. A small initial step toward this goal is the employment of equal numbers of female staff, and ensuring that aid reaches women as well as men (Eichert).

Greater effort is required by governmental and non-governmental agencies working with refugees to allocate and implement education resources for school-age refugees. This will help children deal with psychological trauma and free up time for mothers, often the sole caregivers, to generate income or address personal health needs (Eichert).

Host countries must be required by the international community to remove legal barriers to refugees working, in acknowledgment of the valuable, marketable skills many refugees bring, which would improve the Syrians' abilities to create safe and secure lives for their families (Eichert).

Further, some financial problems faced by female refugees could be alleviated by allowing women equal access to charitable donations, as well as giving small investment grants to women interested in home-based income-generating activities to support their families (Eichert).

Governments should create a system of housing vouchers or cash assistance to help refugee mothers find adequate housing. This system of rent subsidy must give special attention to the needs of disadvantaged Syrian mothers and female-headed households (Eichert).

Reports of sexual violence in the refugee camps must be thoroughly investigated and impunity for sexual assault must be eradicated (Eichert).

Internally Displaced People (IDP) camps must be organized according to a culturally sensitive model with special emphasis on gender equity, and the culturally unique roles mothers play in their own communities (Tushabe and Muhonja).

Prior to setting up camps, agencies must solicit the input of IDPs on how best to offer aid, in order to avoid a top-bottom pyramid system that largely ignores indigenous social and cultural systems on which displaced people rely to make meaning in life (Tushable and Muhonja).

Integrating extensive knowledge of local cultural customs and beliefs more systematically into the delivery of humanitarian programs and services would go a long way toward improving the delivery of those programs and services to women as they become mothers in post-conflict societies, such as Afghanistan (Mann).

In host countries, culturally responsive mental health counselling must be established and maintained based on the following considerations: respect of the mothers' own culture and customs, seeking to understand the cultural implications of motherhood for a particular cultural group, and willingness to incorporate native healing practices in mental health treatment, administered by a native healer (Ciccio Parsons, Pender and Parsons).

Increasing culturally responsive resources and staff allocations in centers across Canada and the U.S. to offer free mental health counselling to immigrant and refugee populations will have beneficial results for the process of non-threatening acculturation of mothers and the enabling of effective mothering in a new culture (Ciccio Parsons, Pender and Parsons).

The issue of demobilized motherhood must receive a thoughtful consideration within the context of disarmament, demobilization and reintegration (DDR) programming and support. DDR policies and programs need to evolve with a clearer understanding of the scope of post-demobilization life and its challenges. Programs and services need to be implemented to respond to the multifaceted unique needs of ex-combatant mothers, such as having access to additional funding to help provide for their children and gaining assistance with childcare (Jones and Denov).

There is urgent need to examine policies and practices affecting immigrant mothers who are living in the U.S., especially as these policies are currently structured and delivered in such a way as to create a hostile environment and a de facto police state, targeting individuals on the basis of race, political beliefs, gender, sexual orientation, and/or religion. The U.S. Department of Health and Human Services defines health equity as "attainment of the highest level of health for all people," and declares as its aim the elimination of health disparities. However, until immigrant mothers are able to and are not fearful about seeking services for themselves and their non-U.S. citizen as well as their U.S. citizen children, achieving the highest level of health for all people is not possible. Policies and practices must change so mothers can access care without fear or threat of being separated from their children through detainment, incarceration, and/or deportation (Stevens and Andrade).

The collection offers no single mothering perspective, but one revealing that motherwork is always informed by the intersections of culture, race, class, and nation. If the safety and wellbeing of women and children in areas experiencing conflict and the threat of conflict are indeed priorities for international governmental agencies and NGOs, then considering the particular roles and responsibilities of those who do the work of mothering is of crucial importance. Therefore, we situate mother's concerns at the forefront as a means to make more effective the policy and practice of post-conflict transitional processes. Our specific intention is to probe how mothers fare and to articulate views on how various legal and political processes might work better for those who mother under fire.

Contributor Notes

Bree Akesson is Assistant Professor of Social Work at Wilfrid Laurier University, where she researches children and families affected by political violence. Her current research aims to understand how political violence affects pregnant women and their families. Dr. Akesson is also a clinical social worker for the Child Psychiatric Epidemiology Group, a research associate for the Columbia Group for Children in Adversity, and a faculty affiliate for the Child Protection in Crisis (CPC) Learning Network.

Rosi Andrade, Ph.D., is Associate Research Professor with the Southwest Institute for Research on Women (SIROW) at the University of Arizona. Her work is largely participatory action research-based in collaboration with women in the U.S./Mexico border region.

Benay Blend received her doctorate in American Studies from the University of New Mexico. She is a retired professor living in Albuquerque, New Mexico. She has published widely in such fields as Ecofeminist and Postcolonial Studies. Her current research interest focuses on the role of place for Palestinian women writers.

Lubna N. Chaudhry has researched women in contexts of conflict since 1999. She especially focuses on the intersection of structural violence with physical violence. She has co-edited a book entitled *Contesting Nation: Gendered Violence in South Asia* that was published by Zubaan Press in 2012.

Myriam Denov is a Full Professor at McGill University and holds the Tier 1 Canada Research Chair in Youth, Gender and Armed Conflict. Her research and teaching interests lie in the areas of children and youth in adversity, and international child protection, with an emphasis on war and political violence, children in armed conflict, and gender-based violence.

David Eichert recently graduated from Brigham Young University with University Honors. In Fall 2015 he will be working towards an LL.M. in international public law and human rights at the Riga Graduate School of Law in Latvia, and one day hopes to earn a Ph.D. in human rights law.

Lindsay Jones holds an MSW and is currently completing her Ph.D. at McGill University on the prevention of child soldier recruitment in Northern Uganda. Ms. Jones also works as an international Psychosocial Support delegate with the Canadian Red Cross, Emergency Response Unit (ERU).

Nazish Khan, MA (Karachi), is lecturer in Pakistan Studies, and has interest in gender, conflict and development. She has also worked on the editorial team of a magazine on culture, published by the government of Sindh. Reach her at: nazishkhanpak@gmail.com

Carol Mann, a historian and sociologist based in Paris, is the author of numerous studies and articles. She runs two NGOs linked to women in conflict zones: FemAid (www.femaid.org), a humanitarian association working with women's grassroots groups, and "Women in War" (www.womeninwar.org), a think tank dedicated to the study of gender and armed conflict.

Besi Brillian Muhonja is Associate Professor of Africana Studies and Women's and Gender Studies at James Madison University. Her areas of scholarship include Africana feminisms, motherhood studies, decolonial knowledges, and women in Indigenous and contemporary Kenyan cultures.

Kristina Nielson, Associate Professor Emerita at the University of Maine, is a Classicist. Her interests include women's studies, ancient religion and mythology, and the lives of women in the ancient world. A pacifist from an early age, she has worked for peace her entire life, and directed Peace and Reconciliation Studies.

Rachel O'Donnell is a research associate and fellow at the Centre for Research on Latin America and the Caribbean (CERLAC), York University, Toronto. She researches contemporary bioprospecting in the Americas, and has written on plant-based contraceptives in Central America. She can be reached at rachelo@yorku.ca

Jacqueline Ciccio Parsons, Ph.D., LPC (Texas), is Lead Faculty for Walden University in Field Experience - Mental Health Counseling, and a graduate school counselor and educator, as well as a mental health provider in the United States. She has published articles, encyclopedia entries and a book chapter on mothers, as well as presented on motherhood and the relational brain at the Mother-hood Initiative for Research and Community Involvement (MIRCI) Mega Motherhood Conference in Summer 2013 in Toronto.

Larry V. Parsons (MA) is the Director of the Behavioral Health at the University Health System in the U.S. He has 19 years of healthcare administration and analysis experience at the clinic, hospital, city, region, and worldwide levels, with broad expertise in data extraction, analysis and reporting, business planning, group practice management, prospective payment and reimbursement, and coding.

Rebekah Pender, Ph.D., LPC (Texas), is Assistant Professor at Kean University, graduate school counselor and educator, as well as President of the New Jersey Association of Counselor Educa-tion and Supervision. As a mental health provider in the U.S., she has experience working with refugee families and dealing with the mental health challenges associated with the experiences of refugees in a new land.

Linda Pershing is a mother, folklore scholar, and the founding faculty member of the Women's Studies Program at California

State University San Marcos. She spent several years joining Cindy Sheehan at peace actions during George W. Bush's presidency and conducting field research about grassroots peace movements in the U.S.

Liliana Castañeda Rossmann is Professor of Communication at California State University, San Marcos. She earned an MA in International Peace Studies at the University of Notre Dame and a Ph.D. in Communication from the University of Massachusetts, Amherst. She is the author of *Transcending Gangs: Latinas Story Their Experience* (Hampton Press).

Gerakina (Arlene) Sgoutas is an associate professor of women's studies and Director of the Institute for Women's Studies and Services at Metropolitan State University of Denver. Her educational background includes a Ph.D. in International Politics from the Korbel School of International Studies at the University of Denver and an MA in European Studies from Katholieke Universiteit, Belgium. She received her BA in Political Science from Emory University. Her research and teaching interests include transnational feminist movements and motherhood studies.

Anwar Shaheen, MPhil, Ph.D. (Karachi), MA (IDS, Sussex), Associate Professor, Pakistan Study Centre, University of Karachi; has also worked with national and international research and development organizations. She has authored three books, many research articles/reports, and five chapters in refereed books, regarding gender, culture, civil society, and social change. She can be reached at: shaheenhello@gmail.com

Sally Stevens, Ph.D., is the Executive Director of the Southwest Institute for Research on Women and a Distinguished Outreach Professor in the Department of Gender and Women's Studies at The University of Arizona. She conducts collaborative research on gender and race/ethnic disparities with a focus on the U.S./Mexico border region.

Tushabe wa Tushabe is Associate Professor of Women's Studies at

Kansas State University. Tushabe works on women in rural areas, women in politics, African epistemologies, and African sexualities.

Claudine Umulisa is a Ph.D. student in Peace and Development Studies at Gothenburg University in Sweden. She is also a lecturer at University of Rwanda. Her research and teaching interests are focused on sexual violence, gender, children and development, with an emphasis on African context. Her email address is: claudine.umulisa@gu.se

Rebecca Walker is a graduate of the University of Edinburgh where she completed her doctoral thesis, now a published monologue *Enduring Violence: Everyday Life and Conflict in Eastern Sri Lanka* (Manchester University Press, 2013). Rebecca currently holds a postdoctoral fellow at the African Centre for Migration and Society (ACMS) at the University of Witwatersrand, Johannesburg.

Tatjana Takševa is Associate Professor of English and Women and Gender Studies at Saint Mary's University, Canada. She holds a doctorate from the University of Toronto, and is the author of many studies in the area of motherhood studies, nationalism and the Balkans. She is a mother of three, and a passionate advocate for the rights of women and children worldwide.

Lidiya Zubytska is pursuing her doctorate in political science at the University of Kansas and focuses her research on Ukrainian foreign policymaking. Having graduated from the University of Notre Dame, Lidiya worked at the Ukrainian Catholic University in Lviv and Woodrow Wilson Center for International Scholars, in Washington, DC.